A History of the Western World

Second Edition

Volume 1

Bryce Lyon, Brown University
Herbert H. Rowen, Rutgers University
Theodore S. Hamerow, University of Wisconsin

A History of the Western World
Second Edition

Volume 1: Prehistory through the Renaissance

Rand McNally College Publishing Company Chicago

RAND McNALLY HISTORY SERIES

Fred Harvey Harrington, *Advisory Editor*

All maps in color and the black and white maps entitled "Ancient Egypt," "Ancient Athens," and "Industrial Revolution in England, 1750–1850" are from R. R. Palmer, *Atlas of World History* (Chicago: Rand McNally & Company, 1965). The maps entitled "Railways of Europe in 1850" and "Railways of Europe in 1940" are adapted from *Economic History of Europe,* Third edition, by S. B. Clough & C. B. Cole: D. C. Heath and Company: Boston, 1952. The map entitled "Economic Resources, 1914" is adapted from Harry Elmer Barnes, *The History of Western Civilization* (New York: Harcourt, Brace & World, Inc., 1935), II, 348, by permission of the author. The maps entitled "Density of Population in 1700" and "Density of Population in 1935" are adapted from Witt Bowden, Michael Karpovich, and Abbot Payson Usher, *An Economic History of Europe since 1750* (New York: 1937; New York: Howard Fertig, Inc., 1969); reprinted by permission. Cartography for all other maps in black and white is by Willis R. Heath.

Credits for illustrations are given with their listings in the Contents.

Current printing   (last digit)
15   14   13   12   11   10   9   8   7   6   5   4   3   2   1

Preface to the
Second Edition

History, wrote the Dutch historian Johan Huizinga, is man taking
account of his own past. But which past, it may be asked, is "his own"? It can be
that of a tiny community or a huge nation, a vigorous living community or one
long extinct. We are all members of many communities, formed by ties of
language, race, kinship, occupation, religion, ideology, nation, and by shared
memories and experiences, not to speak of the vastest community of all, the human
race. Our curiosity and our sympathy—not the lowest of man's qualities—carry
our interest to all peoples and all times. The three historians who have written
this book share this feeling and yet chose to write an account of the history of
western civilization , not of one fraction of it nor the whole world. Some may
question their decision but they believe it is a wise one.

Practical considerations make it difficult, perhaps impossible, to write a
"history of the world" in a single volume. Detail, without which all accounts of
the past fall into the gray gloom of unsubstantiated generalization, becomes
utterly lost. It is hard enough to gain a sense of the unity and continuity of a
single civilization; to attempt to do it for the many civilizations which comprise
mankind seems to us to be possible only after an adequate understanding has been
achieved at least of the major civilizations. There is no "world civilization" and
never has been one: whatever the future may be, its description is not the task of

history. "World history" therefore can come only after a long journey on many roads; it is not a point of departure.

Western civilization—by which we mean the civilization of Europe together with its sources in the Near East and its influence everywhere since the fifteenth century— is a manageable unit of study. There exists an overall unity of character that sets western civilization apart and gives it an identity. This makes it possible to study the history of the western world as a whole and to see the history of individual nations or particular institutions within its general framework. Furthermore, western civilization has been of primary importance in the history of the world in the last five centuries. For good or bad, however one defines good or bad, the impact of European civilization upon other peoples and places during that period has been a fact of the very first order. European power, European ideas, the European way of life, became the overwhelming challenge which all other civilizations had to face at one time or another; the history of the western world has become part of their history. Their history can no longer be understood without some grasp of the history of western civilization, just as its history is no longer comprehensible in isolation from theirs.

We have endeavored to write our account of the history of the western world in an effective way for students new to the subject or returning to it, and for teachers engaged in helping them to comprehend this vast field of knowledge. We accept the necessity of chronological sequence in our presentation without complaint; it is possible to compare events taken from various epochs without removing them from their contexts and the inescapable fact that they were shaped by their own past and not by the future which they helped to bring into being. (We see institutions and ideas as "events" no less than political happenings; it is only the time span characteristic of each which differs.) Within this chronological framework we follow a number of principal themes: the modes of man's livelihood, the arrangement of his life in society, the way he has sought to find or create a pattern of meaning for the universe and for his own existence, the varying systems of government and forms of political struggle.

We use no tricks of pedagogical or typographical presentation but rely upon the well-tried instrument of good prose, supplemented by illustrative material— maps, photographs, tables and plans—appropriately placed in the text. To make it easier for the interested student to do further reading, at the end of each chapter there are critical bibliographies that emphasize the most valuable books. Paperbacks are noted by an asterisk.

Recognizing that there are those whose interest will be centered on one or another segment of the history of western civilization, we have chosen logical points of "new beginning" for the separate volumes of the second edition.

This second edition of our work differs from the first primarily by expansion of the early chapters devoted to the ancient world, by addition of another chapter at the end to bring our account up to date, and by inclusion in the suggestions for further reading at the end of each chapter of works published since the preparation of the first edition. In the preparation of both editions, the authors have critically read each other's contributions and have used the opportunity of the second edition to clarify and sharpen the whole text. In spite of occasional disagreement on interpretations and conclusions, which they have not smoothed over in these pages, the authors have found that in general they share similar views on the history of the western world. Each is responsible for a different section of the work. Bryce Lyon has written the chapters on ancient and medieval history; Herbert H. Rowen on the period from the Renaissance to 1815; and Theodore S. Hamerow carries the account to the present. It is their hope that the student will learn as much from the reading of this volume as the authors have from its writing.

Bryce Lyon
BROWN UNIVERSITY

Herbert H. Rowen
RUTGERS UNIVERSITY

Theodore S. Hamerow
UNIVERSITY OF WISCONSIN

Contents

Maps and Charts

MAPS IN COLOR

OTHER MAPS

CHARTS

Illustrations

ILLUSTRATIONS IN COLOR

OTHER ILLUSTRATIONS

A History of the Western World

Second Edition

Volume 1

CHAPTER 1

The Emergence
of
Civilization

1. Problems of the Historian

History, as the French historian Marc Bloch has said, is a fluid in constant motion. It lends itself, therefore, to different interpretations, observations, and emphasis. But whatever the historian's approach—be it political, economic, social, cultural, or some sort of combination of these—perhaps his most difficult task is to decide where to begin his story and how broadly to cast his net. The historian writing on the United States must decide how far back to begin his account and how much European background to provide, for without some knowledge of English history, the Reformation, and the expansion of Europe into the New World, much American history would be unintelligible. Nor can the historian writing about Europe since 1815 begin with the Battle of Waterloo, because European history in the nineteenth century was moved by forces set in motion by Napoleon, the French Revolution, and the Enlightenment. And so the thread of our western history may be unwound back through the Middle Ages, the Classical World, the ancient Middle East, and the Stone Ages to that point where man did not yet exist.

While historical background is essential for understanding subsequent historical development, the historian must be realistic when deciding how much background to give. In a history of the western world, such as this, historians have solved the problem of background in various ways. Some have begun their story with the search for the origin of man, others have situated the development of western civilization in the broader context of the history of the world, and still others have limited western history to Europe and to the lands in which European civilization took root. These approaches, although valid within limits, have come to be questioned as contemporary history moves into new phases and forces historical perspectives to shift.

Increasingly historians of western civilization face a dilemma. To believe that western civilization can be studied without consistently relating it to historical development throughout the world is unhistorical and parochial. Yet to include the recent advances made in the history of Southeast Asia, India, China, Japan, Africa, and the Middle East would result in a study too bulky and complicated to be distilled into one or two volumes. The anthropologist has joined the archaeologist, geologist, and geographer to pull back further the veil surrounding the origin of man, and rightfully many pages of history should discuss this field of investigation. Periods and areas of history once discussed in a few paragraphs or pages now require a chapter or more. Until the Second World War, for example, the British Commonwealth of Nations was an area of history to which numerous books and courses were devoted. This is no longer true; instead, there are books and courses in the history of India, the Middle East, and the developing new African nations. The historian of western civilization must include these developing areas of history, but their contributions to the increase of historical knowledge makes his task of selection greater. And yet select he must, if his history is to escape being encyclopedic.

If the history of the western world has centered in and evolved from Europe, then it makes sense to concentrate upon Europe. If western civilization has its foundations in the Europe that took shape in the Middle Ages, it seems reasonable to concentrate on western history from the Middle Ages to the present. This is what the present volume has done. Obviously, however, if the Middle Ages was that period when Graeco-Roman, Christian, and Germanic elements were blended into a new western civilization, one must know something of the history that preceded the Middle Ages. To serve this purpose this book begins with a summary of the history of the ancient Middle East, the Greeks, and the Romans; this introduction is primarily a synthesis of those achievements of the ancient world that were eventually assimilated by medieval Europe and passed on to modern Europe to be transformed into a brilliant new civilization.

The historian must also choose what kind of history he is to write and what aspects he is to emphasize. During most of the Christian era writers of history limited their accounts to the political and military achievements of man while largely ignoring other dimensions of human endeavor. Since the late nineteenth century, however, historians have been steadily widening their perspectives, and it can now be said that history is concerned with all that man has done and thought. Thus understood, history is much the way it was understood by the Greeks, to whom ἱστορία meant knowledge obtained by inquiry. History today is interested not alone in politics and war, but in economics and social organization, in intellectual and artistic accomplishment, in all that man does. Today's historian welcomes the knowledge made available by economics, sociology, anthropology, psychology, geography, philology, geology, paleontology, archaeology, and the various physical and natural sciences. Obviously the more recent the historical period investigated, the more the historian can use the knowledge of these disciplines and the more complete is his understanding of human achievement. The farther back in time the historian pushes his quest, the less useful most of these disciplines become. When he arrives at that point where no written records exist, he must rely primarily upon what the paleontologist, geologist, and archaeologist tell him from their study of the rocks, fossils, and artifacts. And when that point is reached where there is no evidence of human existence, there is no longer any history in the proper sense.

The probable time of the emergence of primitive man is no longer as certain as it had seemed as recently as a decade ago. Then most scholars agreed that what could be called man had appeared about 600,000 years ago; now the date is in dispute. From discoveries made in 1959 in Tanzania some investigators have concluded that a form of man may have existed even 1,750,000 years ago. Others who have studied the site, including the soil and the artifacts, still adhere to the traditional opinion. Although such a divergence might suggest that these disciplines are imprecise and at best conjectural—depending as they do upon such skimpy evidence as a few bones, sticks, and soil samples—they can be amazingly accurate, due to improvement in their research techniques.

How the specialists of these disciplines work is a fascinating story. Until the twentieth century archaeological expeditions and the work associated with them were almost exclusively in the hands of enthusiastic amateurs who excavated well-defined sites around the Mediterranean basin. They made some amazing discoveries, but their chronology was imprecise and often more was destroyed than was discovered and saved. Today the trained archaeologist employs quite different methods. Except when a bulldozer or steam shovel accidentally uncovers a rich and unknown site, archaeologists prospect for sites by methods similar to those of geologists prospecting for oil and minerals. Contours of land, caves, burial grounds, and rock formations are systematically studied and analyzed, often with the aid of aerial photography. Studies are also made of sites said by legend or myth to have been inhabited thousands of years ago. If such study reveals a need for concentrated probing, the work begins, cautiously and slowly. Picks, shovels, and rakes are used, but more often such smaller implements as spoons and forks are employed so as not to damage or overlook any artifact or bit of evidence.

As the digging progresses the archaeologist must determine the age of the strata of soil and distinguish those with evidence of human life from those that are sterile. To establish a reasonably accurate chronology, he must date the artifacts found as, for example, crude implements of stone, bones, pottery, and vases. When working with a large site, perhaps a town, he must know how ancient peoples built and planned their towns so as to identify and date them. When certain objects discovered at one site are found at another, he must ascertain whether both sites were of the same culture or whether these objects are the result of exchange and trade. The fewer the artifacts found, the more complicated it becomes to date a find. When, for example, an interesting human skull is uncovered without the presence of a single other artifact, what can be done to establish the age of the find? Anthropologists will certainly be consulted, because cranial capacity is extremely important for dating primitive man, and some anthropologists are convinced that true man had to have a cranial capacity of at least 700 centimeters. If the cranial capacity is the same or close to that of a modern man, the find is unimportant. But if the capacity is considerably smaller, the find can be important.

Further work must be done, however, before any conclusions can be drawn. The skull could be that of a baby. Therefore the age of the skull, that is, its stage of development, must be determined. It must be compared to other skulls of primitive men or of other primates. The geologist must analyze any remains of former organic material so as to date the stratum in which the skull was found. Rocks will be analyzed in the laboratory. When dealing with extremely ancient finds, the anthropologist must depend mostly upon the knowledge of the geologist. For discoveries from more recent ages laboratories are able to analyze metal objects, pottery, glass, wood, and fibers of cloths so as to determine age. Perhaps one of the most valuable advances in the dating of primitive finds came in 1949 when scientist Willard Frank Libby discovered that he could calculate the proportion of radioactive carbon (C14) contained in archaeological and geological remains. He showed how C14, which is found in the atmosphere along with C12 (normal carbon), is constantly being incorporated by vegetables, animals, and men at the same time as normal carbon. After the death of these living things C14 disintegrates and gradually disappears. By measuring the radiation of the remains of dead objects, Libby demonstrated that he can precisely date their age as far back as 65,000 years.

Although some scholars are still dubious about the results obtained from this method, most concur that it enables them to establish an accurate chronology for the past sixty-five thousand years, taking the historian back into the period of the so-called Neanderthal man who lived during the Middle Paleolithic Age. It would be absurd to argue that even with the advances in technique made by anthropologists, geologists, and archaeologists during the twentieth century their research can produce the exact knowledge obtained by historians working with ample written evidence from more recent times, but the results of their investigations have greatly aided the historian and have increased man's knowledge.

2. *Before Civilization*

ANTHROPOLOGISTS SEARCHING FOR EVIDENCE of earliest man cannot confine their search to any area of the world. They have uncovered evidence in regions as widely scattered as Southeast Asia, south-central Africa, Europe, and the Middle East. Only in this last region, however, around the valleys of the Tigris, Euphrates, and Nile rivers, is there substantial evidence of a real civilization more than seven thousand years ago. It is in this area that the history of the western world begins.

What was the world like before true civilization appeared? Until the climate and the land of the earth made conditions possible for life, there can be no talk of man. This may have happened over a million years ago, but certainly no later than six hundred thousand years. Most of the next six hundred thousand years have been designated by archaeologists as the Pleistocene or Paleolithic Age (Old Stone Age), which they have divided into the Lower Paleolithic (400,000 years in duration), Middle Paleolithic (150,000 years), and Upper Paleolithic (about 30,000 years). During the Lower and Middle Paleolithic periods man changed from his early apelike appearance to his present form. His material progress during this period was extremely slow. His implements were crudely fashioned from stone and bone; he lived in caves and rough homes of rocks; he survived by hunting animals such as bison, reindeer, and mammoth. During the Upper Paleolithic period came technological and cultural progress, more than in all the previous hundreds of thousands of years. Tools of stone and bone and ivory were skillfully fashioned, making hunting and fishing more efficient. With the invention of the thread and needle man could wear skin clothing. He began to light and warm his caves with lamps and fires. When he could see the walls of the cave, he was inspired to cover them with paintings and drawings. Evidence of this remarkable period of Upper Paleolithic cave art may be seen in the caves of Altamira in northern Spain and of Lascaux in southwestern France. These pictures provide our first reliable information on man's material and cultural condition and on his magical and religious beliefs.

Archaeologists have named the next period, from about 8000 B.C. into the fifth millennium B.C., the Holocene or Neolithic Age (New Stone Age). In these three thousand years man greatly improved his condition. He perfected his stone and bone weapons and implements, developed spinning and weaving, fashioned pottery, and shifted from a nomadic life of hunting to a sedentary life of agriculture. He still gathered much of his food, but he now began to grow some, and his diet consequently improved. His habitation also changed; he moved from caves into primitive huts made of timber stakes, grass, and mud, which came to be clustered in small agrarian villages. Man began living in a community that gave him a social consciousness and made necessary primitive regulations and controls.

The Neolithic Age constitutes an essential stage in the development of human history. During this period occurred the transition from a plundering economy, one where man destroyed and consumed such natural resources as animals and vegetables without replacing them, to an economy of production where he began to raise those plants and animals that were useful to him. He began to adapt his environment to his basic needs. Rather than merely killing and eating what grew naturally around him and then moving on to another area where he could repeat the process, he settled down, planted and harvested cereals and vegetables, captured rather than killed animals, and permitted them to reproduce. This was the economy and society of the little Neolithic village of Jarmo in the valley of the Zagros in Iraq discovered and excavated between 1948 and 1951. Such villages had as many as five hundred inhabitants and a few, like Jericho in Palestine excavated between 1952 and 1957, embraced an area of seven acres where approximately two thousand people lived, protected by a massive stone wall. These complexes were headed by chiefs or councils of elderly men and possessed a strong sentiment of solidarity fostered by the essential agrarian tasks done in common. Though there was a common economic effort and periodic redistribution of the fields, men lived in their own small houses and possessed their own private property. To say that this village economy was a primitive communism would be inaccurate.

As he became sedentary and dependent upon the production of his crops and animals, Neolithic man began to feel a need for understanding and protecting his possessions. At this point he developed primitive religious beliefs and practices. Extremely sensitive to the natural elements and to the cyclical return of the seasons, he became obsessed by the fecundity of the nourishing earth and associated it with his own fecundity and that of his animals. He began to reason by analogy. Comparing his hatchet to lightning because both had points and sharpness, he made a hatchet which evoked the idea of lightning and which he therefore believed could cause a rain storm. In evoking human sexual relations, he believed it possible to increase the fecundity of the soil. He developed magic believing that a symbolic action automatically produced a desired end. Such important phenomena of his world as the sun, moon, and land were made into divinities; around them arose myths that were recitals of their deeds as well as explanations of fertility, human reproduction, storms, and catastrophes. These myths eventually came to be recounted according to a strict ritual by special men respected for their supernatural

WILD BOAR AND BISON. This example of Upper Paleolithic art is from a series of paintings spanning about 45 feet on a cave ceiling at Altamira, Spain (ca. 13,000 B.C.).

powers, men of magic or priests held in high esteem by the village community. This led finally to the creation of religious ceremonies and the construction of a small sanctuary for their performance. From what has survived of the art of this age we see that it was strongly influenced by magical and religious belief. The stone and ceramic statuettes depict the divinities of nature or of female figures symbolic of fertility. Generally, however, this art, less natural and exalted than that from the preceding nomadic age of the hunter seen in the paintings on the walls of such caves as Altamira and Lascaux, reflects the modest and routine existence of sedentary agrarian life.

Although the development of village communities came in various parts of the world during the sixth millennium B.C., it came most easily and developed most quickly in the first-known civilizations at the eastern end of the Mediterranean in the valleys of the Tigris, Euphrates, and Nile rivers where the climate was warm and where rich soil, carried down the rivers during periods of annual flooding, was deposited over the flat land along the rivers and at their mouths, enabling the land to be cultivated indefinitely. Climate and terrain explain the origin of civilization in the Fertile Crescent of Mesopotamia (modern Iraq) and Egypt.

3. *The Origins of Civilization*

THE PERIOD FROM 15,000 B.C. TO 3000 B.C. saw the peoples of Mesopotamia and Egypt pass from the last stages of the Neolithic Age to one in which copper and then bronze were smelted and forged into implements and art objects. Agrarian villages turned into cities, some with as many as twenty thousand people. As the valleys came to be irrigated more extensively, social and economic organization and technological knowledge increased. Embryonic political units also appeared, and by 3000 B.C. man developed the art of writing. From this point on written records are available and become numerous. For the first time the historian has enough evidence to evaluate the level and progress of civilization.

In both Mesopotamia and Egypt civilization arose in geographical settings essentially alike. Rivers provided the water necessary for life in arid regions and replenished the fertility of the land with deposits of soil from distant uplands and mountains. Because the richest lands were at the deltas of the rivers, civilization began and developed most rapidly there. The geography of the two regions differed, however, in two respects, and this difference accounts for some of the distinctive qualities of civilization in each region. In Mesopotamia, because the lands away from the rivers were slightly more fertile and better supplied with water, man could live farther from the rivers. Consequently, early civilization there spread over a wide area. This diffusion was possible in Egypt only along the last one hundred miles of the Nile near its delta. The rest of the Nile (for some six hundred miles to the first cataract) flowed through a very narrow valley of ten to twenty miles, situated in an extremely arid plateau. Here civilization was limited to a long thread of land. Since the plains of Mesopotamia were so located as to form a crossroads for peoples from the Arabian peninsula, the plateau of Asia Minor, the steppes to the north, and the vast Asian mainland to the east, they were occupied and conquered by many different peoples, with the result that Mesopotamian culture spread to other cultures and borrowed from them. Egypt, on the contrary, was relatively isolated. To the south was Equatorial Africa, on both sides of the Nile were vast deserts; and by being on the underbelly of the Mediterranean, Egypt was seldom crossed or occupied by other peoples. Egyptian civilization, therefore, developed in relative isolation with unique features.

In contrast to the geography, little is known about the people who inhabited Mesopotamia or Egypt. Some time before 3000 B.C. Lower Mesopotamia, where the Tigris and Euphrates rivers flow into the Persian Gulf, was settled by the Sumerians who probably came from the highlands of what is today Turkey and Iran. Their linguistic and social group is not known. Moving in later from the Arabian peninsula were Semitic peoples, who were followed in the second millennium B.C. by Indo-Europeans from the area north of the Black and Caspian seas. All that can be said about the inhabitants of Egypt is that they were part of the Mediterranean group of the Caucasoid (white) race.

4. Civilization in Mesopotamia

EARLY BABYLONIA AND ASSYRIA

Politically Mesopotamia was characterized first by the rise of small city-states near the Persian Gulf. Here in Sumeria during the first half of the third millennium B.C. small states arose around such cities as Ur, Larsa, and Lagash, which fought for the political hegemony of Lower Mesopotamia. For over five hundred years these little city-states, like the later Greek city-states and the city-states of Renaissance Italy, warred against each other until they were conquered by a vigorous power from the north. Like Philip of Macedon who ended the independence of the particularistic Greek city-states in the fourth century B.C., the mighty Sargon of the Semitic Akkadians conquered all of Sumeria about 2350 B.C. and incorporated it in a state extending from the area east of the Tigris River to Asia Minor. About

CITY PLAN OF NIPPUR. This fragment of a clay tablet shows the plan of the wall that surrounded ancient Nippur in lower Mesopotamia (modern Iraq).

four hundred years later Akkadian power was toppled by another group of Semites, the Amorites, who moved in from the southwest across the Euphrates River. Political power now gravitated to the city of Babylon which became the capital and cultural center of Mesopotamia. By 1800 B.C. when this new state was at its acme under the famous Hammurabi, one may justly speak of a Babylonian culture common to all Mesopotamia extending from just north of Babylon to the Persian Gulf.

This new power centered in Babylon was short lived; between 1700 and 1500 B.C. it succumbed to a new wave of invaders that upset the entire Middle East, plunging it into an era of political upheaval and cultural darkness lasting almost to the first millennium B.C. This time the invaders were Indo-Europeans: the Kassites occupied Mesopotamia; the Hyksos, Egypt; and the Hittites, the eastern half of Asia Minor. For the historian this long period remains obscure, which means perhaps that uncertain political conditions hindered cultural advance. About 1000 B.C. the darkness was lifted by a new invasion of Semitic peoples known as Assyrians who came from land along the Tigris River northwest of Babylon. Brutal, tough, and effective fighters, the Assyrians soon hammered out the first great empire of the ancient Middle East which, at its summit under the ruler Esarhaddon (681–669 B.C.), encompassed a vast area stretching east to west from the Taurus Mountains in eastern Asia Minor almost to the Zagrus Mountains, and south to include all Mesopotamia, the coastal region along the Mediterranean, and, as a dependency, even Egypt. The center of political power again moved north, this time to Nineveh. Peoples who resisted Assyrian domination were rooted up en masse and relocated in distant parts of the empire. This was the fate of the Ten Tribes of Israel, told so dramatically in the Old Testament Book of Chronicles, an episode that inspired Lord Byron to write, in "The Destruction of Sennacherib," "The Assyrians came down like the wolf on the fold." The importance of the Assyrian Empire for the history of the ancient Middle East was its introduction of the concept of control of a huge land area by one ruler assisted by efficient administrators. Like the Roman Empire, the Assyrian Empire excelled in military and political organization but was content to appropriate the superior culture of its conquered subjects and then to transmit that culture over a wide area.

During the seventh century B.C. Assyrian power began to crack and revolts erupted throughout the empire. The end came in 612 B.C. when the capital Nineveh fell before the combined attack of the Babylonians under Nebuchadnezzar of biblical fame and his allies, the Medes, from northeast of the Tigris River. During the reign of Nebuchadnezzar (605–562) Babylon was again a political power and the center of a flourishing culture. This renaissance, however, was brief; Babylon soon fell to the Persians, who were to establish the greatest and most permanent of all the empires of the ancient Middle East.

PHOENICIANS AND HEBREWS

While political and military power in the ancient Middle East was concentrated for approximately twenty-five hundred years between the Tigris and Euphrates rivers, there were other areas which, although never centers of political power, made basic cultural contributions to the western world. The most important was a thin band of land lying along the eastern coast of the Mediterranean west of Mesopotamia and north of the Arabian Peninsula; it was inhabited by the Phoenicians and the Hebrews, both of Semitic origin. During the troubled period between 1700 and 1000 B.C. the Phoenicians settled along the coast and built up the important ports of Tyre and Sidon. They never tried to extend their political power inland but concentrated instead upon building up their naval power and, at least until the sixth century B.C., possessed the most powerful fleet on the Mediterranean, dominated the trade, and set up colonies as far away as Cadiz and Carthage. The role of the Phoenicians was primarily the dissemination of the culture of the Middle East throughout the Mediterranean world.

To the east and south of the Phoenicians were the Hebrews, a nomadic people who seem to have come to this region as early as the eighteenth century B.C. Leaving few archaeological vestiges behind them, these remarkable people recorded their thoughts, beliefs, and deeds in a magnificent sacred book, the Old Testament. The dominant theme of the various books of the Old Testament is the frequent and regular intrusion of a supreme god in the events of the world, even correcting the course of the natural world. For centuries biblical experts have argued over the authenticity of the Old Testament, but as a result of recent archaeological discoveries confirming various of its statements there is now general consensus that it is a reliable historical record. Composed gradually between the tenth and fourth centuries B.C. by various authors who utilized such oral traditions as family genealogies, religious poems, laws, judicial decisions, and such written texts as chronicles and official acts, the Old Testament constitutes not only a theological and ethical guide of the Hebrews but also a precious description of the daily life and spiritual values of both the Hebrews and their neighbors.

Genesis, the first book of the Old Testament, explains how God created the world and then traces the history of the great Patriarchs of the Hebrews—Abraham, Isaac, and Jacob. The twelve sons of Jacob were the forebears of the twelve tribes of Israel. Some time after the death of Jacob, perhaps because of a severe famine, the Hebrews migrated to Egypt where they were oppressed until escaping under their leader Moses during the thirteenth century B.C. After years of nomadic wandering they finally returned to Palestine, their original homeland, which they had to retake from such hostile peoples as the Canaanites. This task appears to have occupied the twelfth and eleventh centuries B.C. Despite military successes under a series of religious leaders known as Judges, the Hebrews eventually felt the need for a permanent war leader and king to defend them against such warlike neighbors as the Philistines. A little before 1000 B.C., the last Judge, Samuel, anointed Saul as the first king. Under his successors, David (1000–970 B.C.) and Solomon (970–930 B.C.), the Hebrew kingdom achieved its greatest pre-eminence. David, composer of some of the Psalms, unified the twelve tribes under his efficient rule, conquered more Canaanite territory, and occupied Jerusalem. He made Jerusalem the capital and holy city of Judaism, the name by which the Hebrew faith came to be known. Under Solomon the famous temple was constructed. An efficient administrator and an intelligent man, he initiated more active and regular commercial relations with such neighbors as the Phoenicians, renowned around the Mediterranean for their trading prowess, and he encouraged the reception of other cultures of the Middle East. Solomon gained a reputation for the magnificence of his court, even receiving the Queen of Sheba (Saba) from her land bordering the Red Sea. After his death came a civil war that divided the kingdom into the northern state of Israel and the southern one of Judea. Fighting each other as well as their neighbors, these two kingdoms inevitably declined during the eighth century B.C.

To the east, meanwhile, was evolving the great Assyrian power that was to overrun the northern Hebrew kingdom of Israel in the late eighth century B.C., capture its capital, Samaria, and scatter all its inhabitants. When the Assyrian Empire declined in the late seventh century B.C., its place was taken by Babylonia, which captured Jerusalem and destroyed the temple in 587 B.C. Those Jews who did not flee to Egypt were deported to Babylonia and remained captive there until the Persian king Cyrus conquered the country and permitted them to return to their own land, now incorporated into the Persian Empire. Thus began the long history of the so-called *Diaspora* (dispersion, in Greek) that spread the Jews across the known world. With the creation of the independent state of Israel after World War II, finally, after more than twenty-five hundred years, there was again a Jewish state to which flowed Jews from all over the world, many of them participants in more recent *Diaspora,* most notably those who fled Nazi Germany during the 1930's.

JUDAISM

Hebrew history, politically insignificant, was culturally and spiritually of immense influence. The unique contribution of the Hebrews, and perhaps the most important made by the ancient Middle East to the western world, was their concept of religion. As told in the Old Testament, the Hebrew religion of Judaism evolved as strict monotheism. All were taught to believe in and obey one omnipotent God, Yahweh, known as Jehovah in English. From all people Jehovah demanded strict adherence to that highest standard of moral and ethical behavior expressed in the Ten Commandments given by Jehovah to Moses and in other books of the Old Testament where the prophets repeatedly proclaim Jehovah's word and warn people not to trangress against the moral and ethical precepts found in it. All Hebrew history is interpreted by the Old Testament as reward or punishment meted out by Jehovah. When the Hebrew peoples obeyed Jehovah, they flourished; when they did not, Jehovah punished them and evil times befell them. For the first time a religion of high ethical principles was closely bound to society, so that religion became an inspiring and deterring force in human conduct. From the vital concepts of this religion later arose the two most widespread modern religions—Christianity, with its domination over the West, and Islam, with its sway over the Middle East.

THE PERSIAN EMPIRE

The Persian Empire was the work of those Indo-Europeans who had come from north of the Caspian Sea and had filtered south into the area east of Mesopotamia in the seventeenth century B.C. After their migration little is known about these people until the early sixth century B.C. when they were living in what is now southwestern Iran under the domination of the Medes, another Indo-European people. At that time Cyrus the Great (559–530), the ruler of one tribe, emerged as a vigorous leader; he united all the Persian tribes and led a revolt against the Medes, whom he totally defeated by 550 B.C. and incorporated into his kingdom. After this victory Cyrus swiftly moved to dominate most of the Middle East. At his death he had conquered Babylonia, all the land west to the Mediterranean, and Asia Minor. His son Cambyses (530–522) conquered Egypt, and then a usurping noble named Darius (522–486) pushed the borders outward toward the northwest, across the Dardanelles into southeastern Europe, and consolidated the conquests. This Persian Empire, the greatest of middle eastern empires, embraced all the land from the Indus River to Europe and from the Caucasus Mountains and Aral Sea down to the Persian Gulf and Indian Ocean. This ancient empire, surpassed only by that of the Romans, remained intact for one hundred and fifty years until its conquest by Alexander the Great.

The Persians, like the Assyrians, excelled in war and political organization and absorbed the civilization of Mesopotamia which became the center of their empire, an empire that for its time was amazingly well organized. In his *History of the Persian Wars* the Greek historian Herodotus has described Persian government under Darius. An autocratic king ruling by divine right, Darius held absolute power. Assisted by a few powerful officials who composed a council of state, he divided his time among his three capitals—Persepolis, Susa, and Ecbatana. The empire was divided into some twenty provinces known as *satrapies* administered by *satraps* who levied taxes, kept order, and defended the frontiers. Out from the

royal court went inspectors who traveled all over the empire checking on the
satraps. To hold together their sprawling lands, the Persian kings constructed a
marvelous system of roads and posthouses. A uniform system of coinage was established and was followed by enlightened economic policies. As long as the tributary
peoples paid their taxes and did not revolt, they were treated most leniently, free
even to follow their own religious precepts. It is no wonder, then, that the Persian
Empire knew a peace longer than any the ancient world was to experience except
under the Roman Empire.

To understand the political developments in Mesopotamia and the areas adjoining it between 3000 and 500 B.C. is essential, but to learn about the culture is
far more important because much of it eventually passed into the western world.
The West received little from the Middle East politically and institutionally until
Alexander the Great conquered it in the fourth century B.C. Then the westerner
discovered oriental despotism, and Hellenistic monarchs subsequently modeled
their powers upon those of the Persian rulers; in this way, the Greeks were introduced to Persian political organization, some of which they applied to the Hellenistic realms in the eastern Mediterranean. Oriental influence was limited, however,
to the eastern Mediterranean, never finding its way westward.

ECONOMY AND SOCIETY

The economy of ancient Mesopotamia was basically agrarian. The peasants
who tilled the soil and lived in small villages sometimes owned their land but more
often held it from the priests of the temples, the king, or great lords. The fields
were laid out geometrically and so arranged as to benefit from the water diverted
by canals and irrigation ditches from the Tigris and Euphrates rivers. To insure
proper and equitable use of the water, there developed communal cooperation and
strict regulation that imbued the inhabitants of the villages with a sense of cor-
porateness and responsibility. Despite annual flooding which deposited rich soil
over the fields, peasants also fertilized their fields with manure, eventually producing a surplus of vegetables and such grains as wheat and barley that were market-
able in the cities.

The cities of Mesopotamia, generally fortified by brick walls and canals, had
narrow, crooked streets lined with flat-roofed brick houses. At the center was
usually the temple placed on an elevation and built in typical ziggurat fashion.
Besides the priests and functionaries the cities harbored merchants who operated
first on a barter economy and, later, on one based on precious metals. Extant legal
records and laws show that the merchants were organized into guilds and that
they fabricated goods, traded them, and engaged in money lending. The principal
exports were woolen cloth, silver, and vegetable oils; the imports were copper,
pearls, wood, and sheep. At the frequent and well-regulated markets, products of
the city were exchanged for those brought in from the agrarian villages.

WINGED LION DRAGON. Sun-dried bricks covered with reliefs were used by Darius the Great to construct his administrative capital at Susa in the fifth century B.C. All the bricks are glazed and enameled in blue and gold, highlighting the mythical figure.

In society those in power were the kings or their royal families, the great land-lords, and the priests. The rest, except for the merchants in the cities, were peasants or slaves. The rights of each class and protection under the laws were closely related to social and economic status. "Rights," however, refers only to social and economic rights; all political power resided in the king who delegated some of it to his most powerful advisers and officers.

As society became more complex and organized, there was need for codes of laws to insure some degree of order and justice. Of these codes, some of which appeared as early as the third millennium B.C., the most famous is that of Hammurabi in the eighteenth century B.C. Hammurabi's code of laws incorporated numerous previous laws and added others. Beginning with a statement that the laws had been handed down by Hammurabi who had been selected by the sun-god, the god of justice, to dispense justice, it provided for both civil and criminal cases and well illustrated ancient man's concept of justice, a strict concept that demanded an eye for an eye and a tooth for a tooth. This legal spirit resembles that of the Old Testament and that of the Germanic law codes of the early Middle Ages. Besides providing penalties for crimes, the code regulated marriage, divorce, inheritance, wills, slavery, and business transactions, and guaranteed a surprising degree of freedom to women. Most of our knowledge of early Mesopotamian society comes from this remarkable code.

CULTURE AND RELIGION

Religion was a vital force in Mesopotamia as in all primitive societies. It underlay and stimulated the development of architecture, sculpture, literature, astronomy, and cosmology. There were numerous gods who were associated with natural phenomena and were arranged according to power and function as were those of the Greeks and Romans. Some deities were only local; others were universal. For the Babylonians the father and ruler of all Gods was An, deity of the sky, who was sometimes represented by the perfect basic numeral sixty. Below An was a hierarchy of gods and each god had priests responsible for the sacrifices thought necessary to propitiate him. Like the Greek and Roman deities, those of Mesopotamia were regarded as having human qualities. To explain the earth, natural phenomena, and catastrophes, myths arose and became parts of fascinating epics. One poem explains the origin of heaven and earth from the sea. Another incorporates a legend about a certain Ziusudra who constructed an ark and floated about for seven days and nights. The most beautiful of all describes the adventures of the great hero Gilgamesh who was two-thirds divine. His fantastic feats and adventures resemble those of Homer's heroes in the *Iliad* and *Odyssey* and, interestingly, Gilgamesh strangling a lion became a motif on the capitals of medieval cathedrals. Much of the material in the Old Testament was taken from Mesopotamian legend and remolded to fit the religious concepts of the Hebrews.

From ancient Sumeria came the first writing. Originally pictographs scratched on clay, it evolved into characters comprised of wedges and crescents made in damp clay tablets with a square-tipped stylus. This writing, known as cuneiform, became the characteristic style of writing for Mesopotamia. The development of writing, which made expression easier and provided a permanent record, stimulated speculation in all fields of thought, enabled poetry to be created, and initiated business records such as contracts. Double-entry bookkeeping began, events were set down year by year, and men started to measure time by dividing the year into twelve months, each beginning with the appearance of the new moon. This was the origin of the lunar calendar.

Men were obviously interested in astronomical observation. They constructed sky charts upon which they recorded the major constellations from which came the twelve signs of the zodiac. They were intrigued by the course of the sun and moon. To help them in their calculations they devised a sophisticated mathematics based on the sexagesimal system, in which the number sixty rather than ten is the

ALABASTER CYLINDER SEAL. The small cylinder seal, carved in the Akkadian style of the twenty-second century B.C., was rolled on wet clay to imprint this design of a goddess and two attendants offering incense before an altar.

base unit, with thirty as one-half, twenty as one-third, fifteen as one-fourth, and so on. Our hour of sixty minutes and our circle of 360 degrees derive from this system of sixty as a base unit. Mathematics so progressed that primitive algebra and geometry began to develop. With a knowledge of reasonably advanced mathematical principles, it was possible to engineer more advanced irrigation systems and to construct the brick temples, the ziggurats, that spiraled up toward heaven. A sense of proportion developed and is manifested in the stone reliefs and frescoes that decorated temples and palaces.

Whether the people were Hittites, Assyrians, Persians, Phoenicians, or Hebrews, much of their culture was that which had developed in Mesopotamia between the fourth and first millennia B.C. They mainly borrowed and adapted, even the Assyrians and Persians who had a flair for organization, and only occasionally made unique contributions of their own. From Persia during the sixth century B.C. came the new religion of Zoroastrianism named after the prophet Zoroaster. The beliefs of this religion are significant because they parallel many of those in the Old Testament. Zoroastrianism forbade the worship of idols, taught an admirable system of ethics, emphasized monotheism, and, like the Hebrew religion, saw a conflict between the forces of good and evil.

Because of their location the Phoenicians became the most accomplished sailors of the ancient Middle East and excelled in shipbuilding. They ranked first as disseminators of Middle Eastern culture. Besides the development of the most advanced business techniques of the age, their cardinal role in the creation of a new alphabet during the second millennium B.C. must be noted. Some peoples who had developed the art of writing somewhat later than the cuneiform in Mesopotamia and the hieroglyphic in Egypt benefited from these systems and invented syllabic forms of writing using between forty-five and ninety phonetic signs. These syllabic signs were then broken down into consonants and vowels represented by letters. At this point it may be said that the alphabet came into being. Improvement of the alphabetic system of writing continued until the eleventh century B.C., when there appeared a linear alphabet whose simple and geometric letters were designed for writing by a type of pen on papyrus. This kind of alphabet, first used in the Phoenician town of Byblos, is the ancestor of all modern alphabetic writing. Spread around the Mediterranean by the Phoenicians, it was later adopted and modified by the Greeks and became the basis of our alphabet.

5. Civilization in Egypt

THE PATTERN OF CIVILIZATION that developed in Egypt, though unique, had some aspects of the civilization of the Fertile Crescent, a civilization that probably instituted the first basic developments—agriculture and essential inventions. Toward the end of the fourth millennium B.C. Egypt had become civilized and, seldom involved in the political developments in the lands to the northeast, lived in relative isolation except when occupied by the Hyksos during the troubled times in the eighteenth century B.C. and until it was conquered by the Persians in the sixth century B.C. Egyptian history, therefore, is essentially internal.

POLITICAL DEVELOPMENT

Just prior to 3000 B.C. the rulers of the so-called First Dynasty united Lower and Upper Egypt into a unified state extending from the first cataract to the mouth of the Nile. The subsequent period to 2200 B.C. is known as the Old Kingdom. With the weakening of central authority came civil war and revolt in the provinces which continued for about two hundred years. Order was restored around 2000 B.C. and lasted down to 1700 B.C.; this three-hundred-year period is known as the Middle Kingdom. The Hyksos then occupied Lower Egypt and during this period little is known except that no advance was made in civilization. When the Hyksos were expelled about 1600 B.C. the New Kingdom was established. It survived until almost 1100 B.C. when Egypt then lapsed into decline and apparently could not be revived. Like her neighbors to the northeast, Egypt was paralyzed for almost three

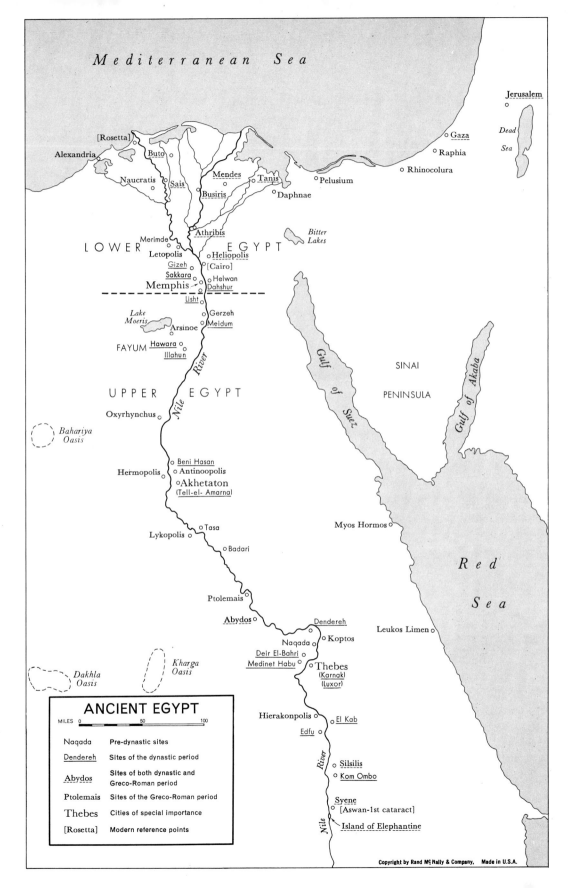

Mediterranean Sea

Jerusalem ○

[Rosetta]

Alexandria ○   ○ Gaza   *Dead*
                       Buto ○   ○ Raphia   *Sea*
       Naucratis ○   Mendes   Tanis   ○ Rhinocolura
              Sais ○   ○   ○   ○   ○ Pelusium
                       Busiris ○   ○ Daphnae

L O W E R   Merimde   Athribis   E G Y P T   *Bitter*
              ○   *Lakes*
         Letopolis ○ ○ Heliopolis
           Gizeh ○   ○ [Cairo]
           Sakkara ○ ○ Helwan
  Memphis ○   Dahshur
                   Lisht ○
                          ○ Gerzeh
     Lake   ○ Meidum
     Moeris ○   Arsinoe ○
  FAYUM   Hawara ○
          Illahun ○

U P P E R   E G Y P T   SINAI
                                   PENINSULA
  Oxyrhynchus ○

Bahariya
Oasis

              ○ Beni Hasan
  Hermopolis ○ ○ Antinoopolis
              ○ Akhetaton
              (Tell-el- Amarna)

                   ○ Tasa   Myos Hormos ○
  Lykopolis ○
              ○ Badari   *R e d*

                                                S e a
       Ptolemais ○
                        Dendereh   Leukos Limen ○
   Abydos ○   ○
                   Naqada ○ Koptos
              Deir El-Bahri ○
              Medinet Habu ○ ○ Thebes
                              (Karnak)
                              (Luxor)

       Hierakonpolis ○   ○ El Kab
              Edfu ○

                              ○ Silsilis
                              ○ Kom Ombo
                        Syene
                        ○ [Aswan-1st cataract]
                        Island of Elephantine

Gulf of Suez   *Gulf of Akaba*

Nile River

Dakhla Oasis   *Kharga Oasis*

ANCIENT EGYPT

MILES 0   50   100

Naqada	Pre-dynastic sites
Dendereh	Sites of the dynastic period
Abydos	Sites of both dynastic and Greco-Roman period
Ptolemais	Sites of the Greco-Roman period
Thebes	Cities of special importance
[Rosetta]	Modern reference points

Copyright by Rand McNally & Company,   Made in U.S.A.

STELA OF PRINCE WEPEMNOFRET. Uncovered at Giza in 1905, this painted relief is from the Old Kingdom of Egypt, twenty-seventh century B.C. Various panels of this relief extol Prince Wepemnofret (a high-ranking member of the family of Cheops), and list offerings in his tomb.

centuries by renewed invasions from the north. In about 800 B.C. she became a tributary state of the Assyrian Empire and she was conquered in the sixth century B.C. by the Persian Cambyses.

Egyptian history is not remembered for its political achievements but for those in other fields of human accomplishment. Indeed the Egyptians contributed nothing to political organization except the concept of kingship. From the outset the king or pharaoh of Egypt had absolute power which he wielded autocratically over a united realm. He was regarded as a real god and this divinity justified his absolute political power and control of religion. Politically he headed a highly centralized bureaucracy that concerned itself with the most minute problems of government, society, or economics. All officials, from the officers who administered the district known as *nomes* to the functionaries who regulated the flow of water for irrigation, were appointed by the pharaoh and under his tight and personal control. Owner of all the land, he strictly supervised the royal estates and the peasants. As a kind of high priest he regulated every facet of religion. As a god, he guarded the land, influenced the growth of crops, and protected his property from the flooding Nile. From top to bottom, then, Egypt was strictly regulated by the pharaoh in all aspects of life, and this tradition was taken over later by the

Hellenistic rulers who came to control Egypt and the Middle East and who derived their ideas on royal monopolies and land taxes from the pharaohs. Egypt, contrary to Mesopotamia, had no codes of law; the pharaoh was the law.

RELIGION AND CULTURE

The one feature of Egyptian life that profoundly influenced the western world and underlay most Egyptian architecture and artistic expression was the belief in life after death. Although at first only the pharaohs and those in their entourage were considered eligible for achieving immortality, by the second millennium B.C. it was believed that everyone could look forward to life after death. Why the Egyptians developed this belief in immortality is not known, but some scholars relate it to the annual flooding of the Nile and the renewal of the soil and its fertility. Whether or not this explanation is true, we know that the Egyptians believed their souls would live on as long as their bodies were preserved. This is why their bodies were mummified, why food and all other necessities of life were buried with them, and why burial was in tombs of stone. Obviously preservation of the mummies was facilitated by the dry climate.

With their great resources and command over labor, the pharaohs were able to construct for themselves monumental tombs known as pyramids. The great pyramids were built during the first half of the third millennium B.C. and, according

PYRAMID OF KHUFU. Known as the Great Pyramid, this tomb constructed by Khufu, the second pharaoh of the Fourth Dynasty, is a monument to the power of the pharaohs and the engineering skill of the Egyptians.

EGYPTIAN WRITING TOOLS. This reed pen, small pot for water, and palette are typical of the implements used by Egyptian scribes. The palette was designed to hold two inks, red and black.

BOOK OF THE DEAD (*below*). A religious text dating from the second half of the fourth century B.C., this hieroglyphic papyrus is in the form of a roll approximately forty feet in length. On the side are scenes illustrating typical Egyptian activities.

to the Greek historian Herodotus, the great pyramid of Khufu required the labor of one hundred thousand men for twenty years. This estimate is plausible in view of the construction devices available because the huge pyramid, 755 feet square at the base and 481 feet high, was constructed of some two million massive blocks of stone, each weighing two and one-half tons. The walls of the rooms inside the tomb were painted with scenes of the departed's life and the rooms were filled with many finely executed art objects. Most buildings constructed by the Egyptians were, like the pyramids, monumental. Typical are their temples to various deities, that of Luxor being the most famous. The style of these temples with their huge columns is reflected later in Greek architecture. These architectural feats obviously required skill in mathematical engineering. With the application of mathematics to engineering the Egyptians invented the true arch and experimented with other building materials such as adobe and plywood. The Egyptians were also well advanced in mathematical notation and arithmetic calculation and passed on their knowledge to the Greeks. Our division of the day into twenty-four hours is due to the Egyptians. From excellent astronomical observations the Egyptians computed a solar year of 365 days.

In Egypt, as in Mesopotamia, when civilization achieved a degree of complexity, when records were desired for administration and business and for preserving religious precepts and thoughts of men, writing began. In Egypt writing dated back to the fourth millennium b.c. and took the form of hieroglyphics which are essentially pictographs, ideographs, and phonetic characters. Words were represented by an ideograph or pictograph or put together phonetically. Eventually there came improvements and modification such as the development of cursive writing. Unlike the Mesopotamians, the Egyptians never used clay tablets but inscribed their figures on stone or wood and eventually on papyrus, a material much like paper made from the pulp of the papyrus plant. More abundant and practical than stone or wood, papyrus became the standard writing material of the ancient world and remained so until the early Middle Ages when parchment replaced it. Thanks to the dry climate numerous papyri texts have survived, giving us rich insights into the life, thought, and aspirations of the Egyptians.

What should be emphasized about the phenomenal progress of civilization in Mesopotamia and Egypt is that a rich culture had developed in both regions by the first millennium b.c., when the Greeks began their rapid climb to cultural dominance of the eastern Mediterranean world. Those intrepid merchants and travelers, the Phoenicians, had so familiarized the Greeks with the culture of Mesopotamia and Egypt that as the Greeks increasingly came into control in the Middle East they became the debtors of much that we have talked about. While the Greeks fused both the culture of Mesopotamia and Egypt to their own, they retained a culture and outlook that were unique, quite unlike the middle eastern, especially in regard to the high value placed on the individual. The Greek way of life was western and that is why the conflict between Persia and Greece has always been dramatized as the struggle between two great civilizations and as the victory of the western way of life.

Further Reading

As noted in the Preface, books available in paperback editions are indicated by an asterisk.

The finest short survey of early history is that of *G. Childe, *What Happened in History,* rev. ed. (Harmondsworth, 1954). Also excellent is *G. Clark, *World Prehistory: A New Outline,* 2nd ed. (London and New York, 1969). More specialized studies are provided by *M. Wheeler, *Archaeology from the Earth* (Harmondsworth, 1956); G. H. R. von Koenigswald, *Meeting Prehistoric Man* (New York, 1957); M. C. Burkitt, *The Old Stone Age,* 3rd ed. (New York, 1956); *K. P. Oakley, *Man the Tool-Maker,* 2nd ed. (Chicago, 1957); *S. Lloyd, *Foundations in the Dust* (Harmondsworth, 1955); and *G. Childe, *New Light on the Most Ancient East,* 4th ed. (New York, 1957).

On the emergence of human civilization there are excellent studies based upon meticulous archaeological scholarship. Two fine introductions are those of *H. Frankfort, *The Birth of Civilization in the Near East* (New York, 1956) and *Before Philosophy* (Harmondsworth, 1949). For other stimulating studies see *A. Montagu, *Man: His First Million Years* (New York, 1958); D. Diringer, *The Alphabet: A Key to the History of Mankind* (New York, 1948); and P. V. D. Stern, *Prehistoric Europe: From Stone Age Man to the Early Greeks* (New York, 1969).

Ancient civilization in Mesopotamia is well covered in *S. Moscati, *Ancient Semitic Civilizations* (New York, 1960). For more detailed studies see *S. N. Kramer, *The Sumerians: Their History, Culture and Character,* 2nd ed. (Chicago, 1971); T. B. Jones, *The Sumerian Problem* (New York and London, 1969); *O. R. Gurney, *The Hittites* (Harmondsworth, 1961); H. T. Olmstead, *History of Assyria* (Chicago, 1960); *History of the Persian Empire* (Chicago, 1948); and S. Moscati, *The World of the Phoenicians* (New York and London, 1968). Artistic achievements are best surveyed in *H. Frankfort, *Art and Architecture of the Ancient Orient* (Harmondsworth, 1955); J. B. Pritchard, *The Ancient Near East in Pictures* (Princeton, 1955); and S. Lloyd, *The Art of the Ancient Near East* (London, 1961). For those interested in the sources the best collection is that of J. B. Pritchard, *Ancient Near Eastern Texts Relating to the Old Testament* (Princeton, 1955).

The most useful survey of ancient Egyptian history is by *J. A. Wilson, *The Culture of Ancient Egypt* (Chicago, 1951). Another clear exposition is that of G. Steindorff and K. Steele, *When Egypt Ruled the East* (Chicago, 1957). The best study in English on artistic developments is by W. S. Smith, *Art and Architecture of Ancient Egypt* (Harmondsworth, 1958). Various aspects of Egyptian culture are treated by experts in S. R. K. Glanville, *The Legacy of Egypt* (Oxford, 1942).

CHAPTER 2

The Greeks

Although the first significant steps in civilization were made in the ancient Middle East and ultimately found their way into what is regarded as the western tradition, they must be placed in proper perspective and compared with the cultural advance made slightly to the west in an area embracing western Asia Minor, the shores of the Black Sea, and the Greek peninsula with its ring of adjacent islands in the Mediterranean and Aegean seas. It was in this area that the Greeks created another civilization, one that was truly western. And it is to the Greeks, more than to the peoples of the ancient Middle East, that the western world is indebted for its underlying ethical, esthetic, literary, social, and political outlooks.

1. Early Greek History

FOR CENTURIES historians had known that in the third and second millenia B.C. there was a thriving civilization on the island of Crete, on the neighboring islands of the Aegean, and on the southern part of the Greek peninsula around Mycenae.

25

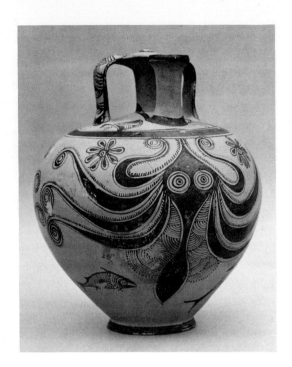

OCTOPUS JAR. Known as a stir-rup jar, this terra cotta vase has designs representing octopi and other fish. It is Mycenaean and dates from between 1200–1125 B.C.

This knowledge was based, however, mostly on myths such as that of a great hero Theseus who had killed a horrible monster known as a Minotaur which the rich king Minos kept in a labyrinth at Cnossus on the island of Crete. In the last quarter of the nineteenth century and the early part of the twentieth, however, much myth became reality as the shovels of archaeologists uncovered an amazing civilization. Determined to discover the site of Troy and other places renowned in Homer's *Iliad* and *Odyssey,* German amateur archaeologist Heinrich Schliemann worked in Asia Minor first and then later uncovered the civilization of Mycenae. Shortly afterward the British archaeologist Arthur Evans located at Cnossus on Crete a kindred civilization which he called Minoan after King Minos. Since these two great discoveries archaeologists have continued to work and to piece together the parts of this early civilization, and in 1953 scholars finally deciphered the written materials.

MINOAN AND MYCENAEAN CULTURE

The people of Crete seem to have come from Asia Minor whereas the people at Mycenae came down from northern Europe and probably got to southern Greece a little after 1800 B.C. Since much of the Mycenaean culture was borrowed from that of Crete, both have been called Minoan. Culture began to develop in Crete around 3000 B.C. during the Bronze Age and reached its culmination from about 2000 B.C. to 1500 B.C. The civilization of Crete was apparently built upon sea power; this kingdom has, in fact, been called a thalassocracy from the Greek word *thalassa,* the sea. As with modern England, a fleet protected the shores of Crete, and the fact that its inhabitants traded all around the eastern Mediterranean facilitated cultural development because the Minoans exported and imported their culture. The quality of civilization is seen in the great palace at Cnossus with its colorful, frescoed walls; built about 1600 B.C. by King Minos, it was a huge structure that only a well developed economy and extensive technological knowledge could have produced. Minoan bronze and pottery work also illustrates sensitive and creative esthetic qualities, resembling in some respects those of the later Greeks.

After 1500 B.C. the island of Crete was invaded by the Mycenaeans who, though destroying much of what the Minoans had created, preserved part of the culture of Crete, which they had previously embraced, and maintained it until some time before 1000 B.C. when they were conquered by a new wave of Greeks. The Mycenaeans are best remembered for their palaces constructed around central courts, some with as many as sixty rooms, and their *tholos* or beehive-shaped

NESTOR'S PALACE. This view of the central courtyard of the palace at Pylos in the southwestern Peloponnesus, dated about 1200 B.C., shows the massive structure which was characteristic of all Mycenaean architecture.

tombs. The stones used to construct these buildings and burial chambers were so huge that the later Greeks called the masonry Cyclopean, convinced that only the Cyclopes—giants—could have moved such massive stone blocks. A good example of Mycenaean architecture is the famous Lion Gate of Mycenae, so named because of two huge sculptured lions above the square portal.

As the culture of Crete had been partially destroyed and appropriated by the Mycenaeans, so the Mycenaean fell before a new wave of Greek people that began rolling down from the Balkans about 1200 B.C. and by 1000 B.C. had swept over the whole peninsula of Greece and moved on to Crete, Rhodes, and the coast of Asia Minor. Known as Dorians, these Greeks plunged Greece into a period of darkness which lasted for almost four hundred years, during which time geography dictated the future political configuration of Greece. Forced to settle in valleys and plains separated by mountains, the Greeks isolated themselves from each other and developed their political and social life around small units. Thus was born that spirit of particularism that was to be both the nemesis and glory of the Greeks, that ultimately destroyed Greek political life but also nourished the individualism responsible for the supreme creations of classical civilization. Though there is little direct information on the Greeks prior to the eighth century B.C., archaeological study shows that they borrowed features of the Mycenaean civilization and that they also appropriated the Phoenician alphabet and improved it by the addition of vowels.

EARLY GREEK POLITICAL AND ECONOMIC ORGANIZATION

That early Greek political organization resembled that of most primitive societies is substantiated by the immortal epic poems of Homer, the *Iliad* and the *Odyssey,* which express and embody the ideals and aspirations of the early Greeks in the so-called Heroic Age. Composed some time during the ninth or eighth century B.C., they reflect both contemporary Greek life and that of at least two or three centuries earlier. Greek life was at first tribal, aristocratic, and patriarchal, with the most successful warrior becoming the military leader and the most powerful figure in the tribe, and eventually making himself king (*basileus*). Normally the king would claim descent from a god such as Zeus and assume primary responsibility for war, justice, and religion. He was assisted in his tasks by the other aristocrats with whom he consulted when necessary. The common people, the farmers and artisans, had no voice in affairs. This was the typical organization of the Greeks when they occupied and divided up the Greek peninsula. Once settled, the Greeks began to fortify a high point, such as the Acropolis at Athens, and the people would cluster around the fortress and spread out from it into the rural areas. So arose in the seventh century B.C. the Greek city-states such as Athens, Sparta, Thebes,

Corinth, Argos, and others that dotted the mainland and the Aegean islands, city-states that were combinations of people living in town and country and owing their loyalties to a common political authority.

Until the seventh century B.C. life in the city-states depended mostly on a simple agrarian regime. The aristocratic families possessed the largest amount of land which was cultivated by peasants. Even the aristocrats, however, went into the fields to work and closely supervised their estates. Most men of the city-states were small farmers who, besides cultivating barley, grapes, and the olive, had their vegetable gardens and orchards of apples, pears, and figs. Generally each farmer also had beehives and herds of sheep and goats. Only the aristocrats owned horses and hunting dogs. This picture of Greek life is derived from the eighth-century poet Hesiod who in his *Works and Days* describes agrarian routine throughout the year, portraying the drudgery, yet praising the simple and bucolic virtues of farming. In the towns proper there were some craftsmen, while on the coast men naturally turned to the sea for their livelihood. The poems of Homer and Hesiod depict the Greeks as intrepid sailors, as Ulysses in his famous wanderings or the naval expedition from Greece to Troy so vividly illustrates. Many men engaged first in piracy before turning to honest trading and to exploring the shores of Asia Minor and northern Africa. By the seventh century B.C. the Greeks were experienced and shrewd traders contributing to the economic development and cultural advance of Greece. Chalcis and Corinth were already prominent trading centers, noted for their contacts across the sea.

THE CITY-STATE

Despite a lack of figures on population for this period, developments in the eighth century B.C. clearly suggest that Greece proper was beginning to suffer from overpopulation. Confined to narrow valleys and plains, the Greeks were finding it ever more difficult to make a living from the soil, often stony and unfertile, and many were sinking into slavery. It was natural, therefore, that, surrounded by water and observing their fellow Greeks along the coast making a decent living, men from the interior should seek homes overseas where there were better economic opportunities. The eighth to the end of the sixth century B.C. was the great era of Greek expansion and colonization. Out from the established city-states poured colonists headed for Asia Minor, Thrace, the lands ringing the Black Sea, and southern Italy and Sicily. Greeks, taking their way of life with them, were soon dwelling all over the eastern Mediterranean, particularly in Ionia in Asia Minor which became the center of a brilliant civilization. They founded city-states, introduced their culture abroad, and stimulated the economy of Greece. This development was an essential step in the cultural exchange between Greece and the Middle

East. Inevitably, close political, social, and religious ties were established between the mother city-state and her colonies which generally modeled their governments on that at home.

While Greece was expanding, the city-states were undergoing political trans-formations that were to result in the forms of government that characterized Greek political life in later centuries and subsequently became typical in the western world. Although kings continued to rule over the city-states for quite some time, their power was never absolute. Confronted with serious problems, they consulted with the aristocrats, the powerful men of the state who excelled in war and possessed the most land. Political privileges were early restricted to men holding much land and occupying high social position. That such men should covet more power and grasp any opportunity to seize it was natural. When a king was weak, unsuccessful in war, or an advocate of policies unfavorable to this elite, they used such an occasion as a pretext to overthrow the king and establish themselves as the ruling power. When this occurred, the city-state became an oligarchy, a government ruled by a few wealthy men whose power was ordinarily derived from the land. Where city-states had larger areas of land and were more agrarian and less commercial, oligarchies became the typical form of government and remained so until the Greeks lost independence in the fourth century B.C. Such was the case with the city-states in the Peloponnesus, especially Sparta. Oligarchic government was in-variably conservative because it existed to preserve the interests of the wealthy few; the masses were ignored as much as possible.

In some city-states where agriculture was less important and where trade provided a living for numerous citizens, oligarchic government was less easily preserved. Freer from routine than farmers, the sailors, merchants, and artisans chafed under a rule that benefited the wealthy few. Excluded from the govern-ment, the richer traders agitated for change, often allying themselves with the lesser citizens. Under such conditions a political opportunist with personal appeal could easily capitalize upon a grievance, exhort the people to action, and place himself at the head of a revolution that would overthrow the oligarchy and establish himself as ruler. The Greeks called such a man a tyrant because his power was illegal and be-cause he usually recognized no law but his own. A tyrant almost always maintained immediate power by surrounding himself with a select military guard, but his power ultimately depended upon how effectively he met the demands of his sup-porters. If he was simply an opportunistic demagogue, he soon lost his power; but if he had some ability and sense, he could retain power and occasionally pass it on to a successor as did the Athenian tyrant Peisistratus who seized power in 546 B.C., held it until his death in 527 B.C., and passed it on to two sons. Peisistratus in-gratiated himself by appropriating land from the aristocrats and allotting it to the poor, and by giving to the peasants legal title to the land which they held as tenants. Tyranny did not, therefore, always denote despotic government. Other successful and benevolent tyrants of the sixth century B.C. were Polycrates of Samos, Periander of Corinth, and Cleisthenes of Sicyon who developed the trade of their city-states and made them powerful political forces in Greek political life.

Sparta, which emerged as the dominant land power of Greece and controlled most of the Peloponnesus from the eighth century to the fourth century B.C., developed a regimented form of government. Since the middle of the seventh century B.C. Sparta was essentially a military state, with all aspects of life regimented in order to produce an efficient war machine. The education of every male citizen was primarily devoted to military training and physical exercise: from the age of seven to thirty men lived in barracks and were under constant training, with little time or respect for any knowledge except that of war and with complete devotion to their own narrow way of life. Few intellectuals or artists flourished in this oppressive atmosphere. Even the women were imbued with a desire to sacrifice all for the state. Theoretically two kings ruled Sparta, but actual power was wielded by five magistrates known as *ephors* elected annually by the Spartans who were landed aristocrats. In a supervisory and consultative capacity there was a council which served for life and whose members had to be sixty years of age to be eligible. Essentially a military oligarchy that favored and supported oligarchic government in other states, Sparta produced little but victories in war for years, and ultimately it was left with nothing but failure and memories of past military victories.

POLITICAL REFORMS

The city-state of Athens was the antithesis of Sparta. Deriving a large part of her income from trade, Athens developed a form of government that fulfilled the needs of an urban civilization with its merchants, artisans, and sailors. By the early sixth century B.C. the Athenians had replaced their government of limited kingship with an oligarchy in which an aristocratic council known as the Areopagus held executive power and governed under a severe code of laws formulated by Draco in the late seventh century B.C. In the first quarter of the sixth century B.C. the oligarchic regime was slightly liberalized by the chief *archon* (magistrate) Solon who, by arranging the population into classes based upon the value of property, gave to each class of citizens various political rights and obligations. Solon also extended citizenship to the poor and decreed that no man could be made a slave because of indebtedness.

Despite Solon's boast that his reforms were fair to all classes, no one seemed satisfied. The aristocrats fretted over the loss of some of their power and the poor complained that Solon's reforms were but a token improvement. The result was a period of civil war (*stasis*) from which Peisistratus, supported by the poor citizens, emerged as victor. He broke the power of the aristocrats and became a benevolent ruler, pushing economic reforms which benefited trade and industry, improving the lot of the poor citizen, and patronizing the arts. His sons were not as successful, and when the last was driven out by a revolt in 510 civil war again erupted between those desiring a return to the oligarchy and those wanting to extend political privileges to more of the citizens. Finally in 508 the latter were victorious under their leader Cleisthenes who at once initiated major political reforms which made possible the democratic government that emerged in the fifth century B.C.

Cleisthenes limited the power of the aristocratic Areopagus by restricting its authority to reviewing the constitutionality of legislation and by putting in its place a new Council of the Five Hundred known as the *boule*. Each year the citizens elected five hundred men, fifty from each of ten tribes so distributed geographically that tension was removed between those who made their living from the land and those who made it from trade. The *boule* was divided into ten committees of fifty, each wielding power for a tenth of a year. Each of these executive committees presented legislation to the Assembly for approval by all the citizens, and each, while in power, carried out administrative functions and represented Athens in her relations with other city-states. Military power was given to a band of ten generals (*strategoi*) elected annually. The ultimate organ of control was the Assembly, composed of all citizens eighteen years of age and older. In addition to passing legislation the Assembly elected some committees, distributed state funds, and tried crimes committed against the state. It also had the power to investigate any magistrate at the end of his term of office and, if it desired, it could recommend that he be *ostracized*—that is, exiled for as long as ten years. However, it was possible to ostracize a magistrate only if a majority of the citizens voted to do so. Misuse of this power often deprived Athens of some of her most gifted leaders. Almost all justice was handled by a huge jury of six thousand known as the *heliaea*. Six hundred were chosen by lot from each tribe and served as a tribunal for a portion of the year. The plaintiffs and defendants pleaded their own cases after which the tribunal decided by secret ballot whether to find for the plaintiff or the defendant. With such large juries the procedure was slow and hindered efficient and swift justice. During the late fourth and third centuries B.C. the juries were severely criticized for being inadequate and at times corrupt.

To have developed such a democratic government was a remarkable achievement in the sixth century B.C. even though it was a democracy that was limited solely to Athenian citizens, denied citizenship to new and talented people, and still operated on the principle that only a chosen few should be privileged to enjoy citizenship. Although full political rights were extended to all Athenian citizens, citizenship became very exclusive, with slaves and alien residents known as *metics* denied citizen status. Compared, however, to the numerous Greek tyrannies and to the oppressive Spartan regime, Athenian democracy was fresh and nurtured the brilliant culture associated with classical Greece.

Especially significant for Greek culture was the period between 800 and 500 B.C. when the Greek city-states were colonizing the eastern Mediterranean, entering into economic and political relations with the Middle East, and developing their peculiar political structure. With expansion and new contacts came new ideas and cognizance of different cultural patterns. That, in city-states where aristocratic and democratic government arose, the individual could participate in political life and have a voice in his political destiny, inevitably spurred individualism and created an atmosphere sympathetic to criticism, analysis, and probing of the fundamental questions of human existence.

RELIGION AND PHILOSOPHY

Greek speculation about religion and its relation to human existence is a good index of the intellectual ferment in the archaic period of Greek culture. In the *Iliad* and *Odyssey* of Homer the various Greek gods totally controlled the life and destiny of man. Woe to the individual who incurred the wrath of a god! In the sixth century B.C. this concept of man's relation to the gods began to change. While the hierarchy of gods remained and patron gods and goddesses of the city-states retained their importance, the Homeric view was challenged. Retaining their belief in divine punishment, the Greeks began to agree upon standards of moral conduct, some man-made, which the individual ignored at his own peril. Whoever disregarded accepted moral behavior and ignored the gods tempted fate; he had become too proud and was certain to suffer divine retribution. The Greeks believed that man should lead a life not of extremes but of reasonable moderation, of "nothing too much." Some denied the traditional belief in anthropomorphic gods and questioned whether there could be more than one god. Others, becoming mystical, were almost convinced that man had a divine part, or soul, that survived after death. Mystery cults arose to celebrate the mysteries of nature and the seasonal cycle, especially spring which symbolized fertility and rebirth. Such views suggest that the Greeks approached a belief in some kind of immortality.

Related to this transformation in religious beliefs was the beginning of philosophic and scientific speculation. It was only logical that certain Greeks, having questioned the nature of the gods and their relation to them, should turn to examine the world about them. For the first time men were becoming thinkers. Thales (640?–546 B.C.) of the city-state Miletus in Asia Minor concluded that the world came from the primary substance of water. Toward the end of the sixth century B.C. Heraclitus of Ephesus was speculating that all the world was in constant flux, while at about the same time Parmenides contended that essentially there was no change in the world. Some thinkers saw man as an independent natural (rational) being while others, like Pythagoras, argued that only reason could produce

PROCESSION OF GREEK GODS
AND GODDESSES. This marble
bas-relief dates probably from
the first century B.C. and was
found in southern Italy. The gods
and goddesses with their attributes are, from left to right, Perse-
phone, Hermes, Aphrodite, Ares,
Demeter, Hephaestus, Hera, Poseidon, Athena, Zeus, Artemis,
and Apollo.

ethical conduct. Although this philosophical speculation also contributed to the
enrichment of mathematical knowledge, particularly geometry, the thinking of the
Greeks was largely theoretical. As yet few were concerned with empirical knowledge, that is, the observation of phenomena and induction from facts. Slowly, a
beginning was made in the direction of medicine.

LITERATURE AND ART

The ferment in religion, philosophy, and science seems nevertheless to have
stimulated the rich expression in literature and art characterizing the archaic
period. To provide fitting homes for the gods and places of worship, the Greeks
began to erect the familiar rectangular temples with their porches and pillars. At
first pillars were placed only at the front, but later, Doric and Ionic columns were
placed on all four sides. Figures were carved in the triangular space formed by
the gabled roof and on the capitals of the columns. This was the beginning of the
architectural development that achieved supreme heights of perfection in the
fifth and fourth centuries B.C.

Painted pottery, used mainly as containers for the storage of oil and grain,
also reflected the shift in thought and style. In the late eighth century B.C. stiff and

tight geometric designs were gradually replaced by much more complicated designs depicting animals, human forms, gods, and objects such as ships, chariots, chairs, tables, and various utensils and implements. Corinthian pottery was of great excellence until the sixth century B.C. when it was superseded by Attic pottery of which the most famous was painted completely black except for figures in red. The figures were often mythical, characterized by grace and natural loveliness.

Prior to the archaic period the supreme Greek contribution to literature was in the form of epic poetry, above all, the ninth- or eighth-century epics of Homer. Whether Homer was entirely responsible for both the *Iliad* and the *Odyssey* is uncertain, but he did have a vital part in their composition. Their greatness lies not only in their appealing tales and dramatic plots but in their insights into human nature. Proud, courageous, vengeful, passionate, and individualistic, the heroes of Homer are also free and rational. In these poems we see how men react under stress and emotion, how they meet fundamental problems of human existence, and how they face death. One can recognize here many virtues, vices, and qualities regarded as typical of western man. Late in the eighth century B.C. Hesiod, the second great poet, composed his verses. Already mentioned because of its information on early Greek agrarian life, the epic hexameter poem *Works and Days* is didactic in character. Making no attempt to camouflage the difficult life of the

GREEK POTTERY. Greek pottery frequently uses the figures of athletes and scenes illustrating the games as decorative designs. The detail *above,* from a black-figured vase of ca. 525 B.C., shows a Greek charioteer racing. *Below left* is an Athenian black-figured Lekythos vase of the sixth century B.C. which shows athletes practicing; and below *right* is a detail from a red-figured Attic vase from the late sixth century B.C. which shows a victorious athlete being crowned.

farmer, Hesiod yet praises such a life because those who work the soil are industrious and generally possess the virtues of thrift and justice. In his other poem, the *Theogony,* Hesiod traces the genealogy of the gods and gives his version of the world's creation. That Hesiod was influenced by ideas from the Middle East is evident from some of the mythical and astrological lore that he included.

It is obvious that in the seventh century B.C. increased contact between the Greeks and the peoples of the Middle East, along with better organized government and more advanced economic practices, were influencing literature. Poetry became shorter and epics became rare. Experimentation in new poetic forms such as the elegy and lyric became popular. The elegy was often written to be accompanied by a flute or pipe, as, for example, the martial elegies written by Callinus of Ephesus. Early in the sixth century B.C. Sappho of Lesbos excelled in the writing of personal love lyrics. In beautiful verse she expressed her love for other young girls and praised their intermarriage. Anacreon of Teos praised wine and love. Pindar of Boeotia, who spanned the sixth and fifth centuries B.C., excelled in choral odes written to celebrate military triumphs and victories in the Olympic games. For religious celebration the lyric, sung by trained singers, became a popular form. Little prose was written until the sixth century B.C. and what has survived, such as the writings of Hecataeus of Miletus on geography and of some authors who composed genealogies, is fragmentary. By the end of the sixth century B.C. the Greeks had prepared for the great cultural achievements that were to follow in the next two centuries. The immortal poetry of Homer had already been produced. The poetry of Sappho and Pindar was the first of its kind. The architecture and pottery intimated later excellence. The skepticism encountered in religion and the critical thinking characterizing the first steps in science and philosophy show that the Greeks were infused with a great desire to systematize, to discover first causes, and to search for truth.

By the late sixth century B.C. Greek city-state civilization had developed to a critical point. The expansive economy responsible for more and more Greeks settling along the shores of Asia Minor and around the Black Sea made them increasingly sensitive to the importance of close ties with city-states across the seas. There was an ever greater need for raw materials and food, especially grain, in growing urban centers such as Athens. Wherever they lived, the Greeks derived from awareness of a common tradition, already rich in achievement, a sense of solidarity and pride in their language and culture. They regarded non-Greeks as barbarians and eventually so considered all people not of Greek culture. Although politically the Greek city-states, whose governments ranged from tyranny to aristocracy and democracy, were local and particularistic in outlook, with strife and animosity within and between them, most Greek city-states felt themselves members of a common Greek culture, a feeling that could unite them temporarily in a common cause, as it did in the early fifth century B.C.

2. *The Golden Age of the City-State*

WHEN BY 500 B.C. the Persian Empire included all Asia Minor and had thrown a
bridgehead across the Hellespont into Europe, the Greek city-states along the coast
of Asia Minor actually had little reason for complaint. Persian rule was surprisingly
lenient. Each city-state had its preferred form of government and traded quite
freely with Greece and the empire. All that was required was obedience to the Great
King and his satraps and regular payment of taxes. Conflict with the Persians arose
from the stasis endemic in most of the Greek city-states. In 499 B.C. there was civil
war in some of the city-states of Asia Minor between political factions that were
pro-Greek and pro-Persian. The pro-Greek factions prevailed and revolted against
the Great King Darius who subdued them by 494 B.C. and destroyed Miletus, the
center of the revolt. But because Athens had sent military assistance to that rebellious city-state, Darius perceived the close bond between the city-states of Asia
Minor and Greece and decided to teach the Greeks not to interfere in Persian
affairs. The stage was set for the Persian Wars, interpreted by the Greek historian
Herodotus as an epic struggle between a free western society and a despotic
oriental one.

THE PERSIAN WARS

In 490 B.C. Darius sent a fleet bearing an army across the Aegean Sea. Reducing Aegean islands as it proceeded, the army landed on the Plain of Marathon
only a few miles from Athens. The Athenian hoplites, though outnumbered, had
heavier armor and a higher esprit de corps which enabled them to defeat the
Persians who fled to their ships. While victorious in the first round, the Athenians
realized that Darius would mount a more ambitious offensive. Darius, however,
died before completing his plans, and the task fell to his son Xerxes who assembled the greatest fleet and army yet seen in the ancient world. Plans called for
the fleet to sail along the coast of Greece down to Athens while the army would
cross the Hellespont and march toward Athens. In 481 B.C. Xerxes supervised last
minute preparations in Asia Minor and in the spring of 480 B.C. the combined
operation began.

This time the Greeks realized that they must cooperate if they were to escape
subjugation. There was consultation on the strategy for defense, with the leadership
assumed by Sparta and Athens—Sparta because of her superb army and Athens
because of her previous experience and fine navy which had been greatly expanded
under the shrewd political leader Themistocles, who saw that the economic welfare
of democratic Athens with her maritime interests depended upon a strong navy. By
480 B.C. Athens possessed two hundred good galleys rowed by Athenian citizens.
Sparta's plan for defense advised falling back below the Isthmus of Corinth, con-

centrating the combined land forces, and then fighting. If it had been followed, this strategy would have sacrificed all northern Greece and Athens. Themistocles argued that the Persian fleet on which the army depended for supplies should be destroyed, while the Greeks worked to hold back the advance of the Persian army. Themistocles finally prevailed. Meanwhile, the Persian army and navy moved southward, and many Greek city-states to the north surrendered or cooperated. While a Spartan army under King Leonidas held off the huge Persian army at the Pass of Thermopylae, Themistocles twice engaged the Persian fleet in the Strait of Artesium. When neither naval engagement was successful for the Greeks and when a Greek traitor led the Persians through a pass to the rear of the Spartans, the Greeks had to retreat. Leonidas and his bodyguard held off the Persians so that the main Greek army could retreat and Themistocles withdrew the Athenian fleet to the Strait of Salamis. The Persian army then occupied and burned Athens. The decisive engagement came on September 23, 480 B.C. As Xerxes watched from a hill, his fleet moved down upon the Athenians. This time the Athenians, assisted by a small fleet from Aegina, fought brilliantly. They rammed numerous Persian vessels which the heavily armed hoplites then boarded. Most of the Persian navy was destroyed which was, as Themistocles had predicted, a disastrous blow for the Persian army. Xerxes immediately returned to Asia, but his army, which remained in Greece, was decisively defeated by the Spartans and Athenians in the spring of 479 B.C. The Persian peril would never again endanger the Greeks. It was the Greeks who were now on the offensive, and the final act was to be the conquest of the Persian Empire by Alexander the Great.

The miraculous victory of the Greeks stemmed from their high spirit and flexibility which were reflections of an extremely gifted and dynamic society. Secure and proud in their achievement, the Greeks now entered upon that phase of their history that was to produce some of the greatest achievements of western civilization. After 480 B.C. Greece was the hub of the ancient world; the center of civilization had moved from Asia to Europe.

ATHENIAN HEGEMONY

Although Sparta had contributed mightily to the Persian defeat, most of Greece recognized that Athens had borne the brunt of the fighting and had produced the leadership resulting in victory. It was also obvious that the Spartans were mentally incapable of leadership during peace; they excelled only in war and ignored the intellectual, social, economic, and political aspirations of man. From 479 to 431 B.C. Greek history is basically that of Athens which wielded a political, economic, and cultural hegemony.

To provide a navy to sweep the Persians from the Aegean, Athens immediately organized the Delian League with headquarters on the island of Delos. Each member city-state was to supply a quota of ships or an annual contribution

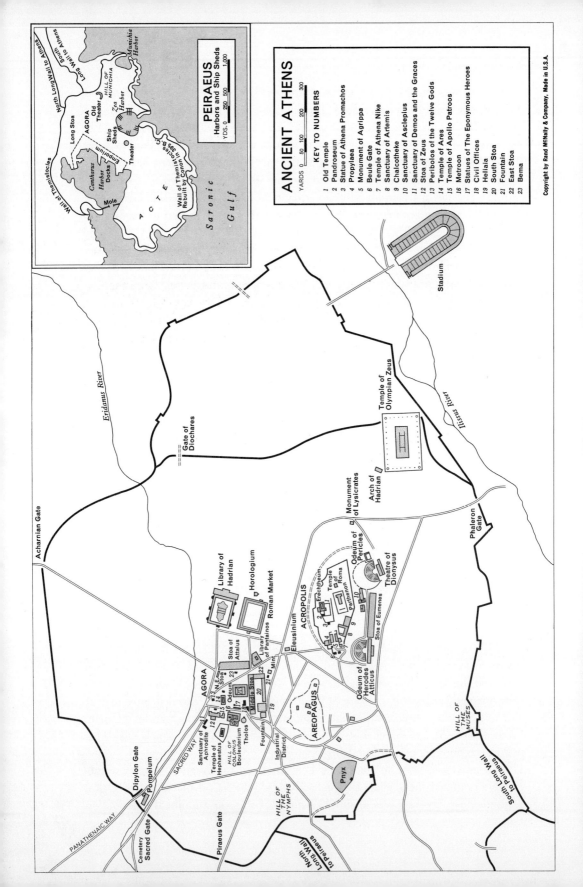

ANCIENT ATHENS

YARDS 0 50 100   200   300

KEY TO NUMBERS

1 Old Temple
2 Pandroseum
3 Statue of Athena Promachos
4 Propylaea
5 Monument of Agrippa
6 Beule Gate
7 Temple of Athena Nike
8 Sanctuary of Artemis
9 Chalcotheke
10 Sanctuary of Asclepius
11 Sanctuary of Demos and the Graces
12 Stoa of Zeus
13 Peribolos of the Twelve Gods
14 Temple of Ares
15 Temple of Apollo Patroos
16 Metroon
17 Statues of The Eponymous Heroes
18 Civil Offices
19 Heliaia
20 South Stoa
21 Fountain
22 East Stoa
23 Bema

Copyright by Rand McNally & Company, Made in U.S.A.

PEIRAEUS
Harbors and Ship Sheds
YDS. 0 250 500 1,000

Saronic Gulf

North Long Wall to Athens
South Wall to Athens
Long Wall to Athens
Wall of Themistocles
HILL OF MUNICHIA
Munichia Harbor
Zea Harbor
Old Theater
Ship Sheds
AGORA
Long Stoa
Cantharus Harbor
Emporium
Docks
Theater
Mole
Wall of Themistocles Rebuilt by Conon in 395 B.C.
ACTE

Eridanus River
Ilissus River
Gate of Diochares
Temple of Olympian Zeus
Monument of Lysicrates
Arch of Hadrian
Stadium
Phaleron Gate
Acharnian Gate
Library of Hadrian
Horologium
Roman Market
Library of Pantainos
Stoa of Attalus
Mint
Eleusinium
ACROPOLIS
Erechtheum
Temple of Roma
Parthenon
Odeum of Pericles
Theatre of Dionysus
Stoa of Eumenes
Middle Stoa
N. E. Stoa
Odeum
AGORA
Sanctuary of Aphrodite
Temple of Hephaestus
HILL OF COLONUS
Bouleuterium
Tholos
Fountain
Industrial District
AREOPAGUS
Odeum of Herodes Atticus
HILL OF THE MUSES
Pnyx
SACRED WAY
Dipylon Gate
Pompeium
Cemetery
Sacred Gate
PANATHENAIC WAY
Piraeus Gate
HILL OF THE NYMPHS
North Long Wall to Peiraeus
South Long Wall to Peiraeus

of money. For a while the arrangement worked, but with the passing of the Persian menace some city-states asked to drop out of the league. This Athens forbade. She not only forced all the city-states to remain members, but compelled others to join. Eventually Athens supplied almost all the ships, levied payments on all members, and moved the headquarters to Athens. By the middle of the fifth century B.C. the league had been transformed into the Athenian Empire. Although it should be said in her defense that Athens maintained peace in the Aegean and created favorable conditions for economic growth, her role was essentially one of naked imperialism; the league benefited Athens more than the other members, and much of the wealth responsible for Athenian architectural and artistic achievement came from the payments of the other city-states. As long as the military supremacy of Athens was unchallenged and as long as she was led by the astute Pericles, the empire survived; but when war came and Pericles died, the empire disintegrated. To the credit of Athens some Athenians spoke out against imperialism and its inconsistency with Athenian democracy.

Athenian domination was ended by the Peloponnesian War that ravaged Greece from 431 to 404 B.C. The causes and events of this conflict were recorded by the Athenian Thucydides, one of the greatest of historians. Long jealous of her dynamic neighbor, Sparta finally allied herself with Corinth, a state that resented Athenian encroachment on her economic preserve. The war that ensued drained the resources of both sides but, even worse, it compelled Sparta to ask Persia for assistance and led to political excesses in Athens that sometimes verged on ochlocracy and at other times on demagogy. The pressures of war destroyed Athenian reason and moderation. In his timeless work, *A History of the Peloponnesian War,* Thucydides portrays the disintegration of collective and individual character. Although Sparta finally emerged victorious, after a few years her place was taken by Thebes, which in turn proved incapable of constructive leadership.

THE RISE OF MACEDONIA

By the middle of the fourth century B.C. each Greek city-state was going its own way, almost oblivious of the growing military power of Macedonia to the north. Driven by their tough king Philip (382–336), the rough Macedonians were whipped into a formidable military force; their battle formation was the square phalanx which swept all before it. In an almost Machiavellian manner Philip played upon the particularism of the Greek city-states, bribing this one, bullying that one, fomenting disputes between others, and brewing civil war. One after another fell to Philip, while Athens, Thebes, and other city-states seemed unaware of the peril. The famous Athenian orator and statesman Demosthenes (384–322), alone, understood the design of Philip and tried to stir his countrymen to action. After his death Athens and Thebes united to repel the northern peril, but it was then too late; their combined forces went down before Philip's phalanx at Chaeronea in 338 B.C. Philip was master of Greece. With a vast empire as his goal he at once prepared an expedition to wrest Asia Minor away from the Persians. In the midst of preparations, however, he was murdered by one of his own Macedonians who may have been the instrument of a plot engineered by the queen Olympias, resentful of her husband's affairs with other women and desirous of ensuring the succession for her son Alexander. When this remarkable young man succeeded his father in 336 B.C., a new era began for Greece and for much of the civilized world.

With the conquest of Greece by Philip of Macedon and of most of the known world by his son Alexander the Great, the age of the small, independent city-state ended. From then until the end of the Roman Empire in the West the Mediterranean world and the Middle East were dominated by large political structures or empires in which the city-state was but a local unit. With the age of Alexander the Great the culture regarded as typical of the Greek city-state was also greatly transformed. It is necessary, therefore, to examine Greek culture during the apogee of the city-state, from 500 to 338 B.C., before turning to the age of empires.

ATHENIAN DEMOCRACY

A book known as the *Constitution of Athens,* ascribed by some scholars to Aristotle, is the best known analysis of Greek government. Concentrating upon Athens, it also describes the different governments of the city-states and compares their strong and weak points. We learn that in most city-states there was little change in government after 500 B.C. We also learn from it and other sources that the most interesting experiment in government was the democracy at Athens which modified itself in response to social and economic demands and provided an atmosphere most sympathetic to free thought, artistic expression, and experimentation.

Except for a few periods, such as during the Peloponnesian War and immediately after, Athens remained committed to democratic government and opened up participation in government to every male citizen twenty years of age. All citizens were members of the Assembly, which met twice a year or more if necessary. Theoretically the Assembly was a town meeting based on direct democracy, but in practice only a small portion of the citizenry attended, and they dealt only with business previously discussed and put on the agenda by the Council of the Five Hundred, an organ that was much more powerful because it was actually an executive and steering committee for the Assembly. Under the Council's system of rotation the committees that had direct responsibility for the government during part of the year controlled finance, foreign relations, the navy, and public property. Since the Council was elected by lot, membership was scattered across a wide spectrum of the citizens. The power of the ten generals or strategoi remained important. Originally military, these officials became primarily political in the fifth century B.C. and could be reelected, as was Pericles who literally dominated Athenian politics from 461 to his death in 429 B.C. Keen political insight, natural ability, and personal attractiveness gave Pericles ascendancy in the Council and Assembly. His position resembled that of a modern prime minister who retains power until he loses a vote of confidence.

That almost every citizen participated in some part of the government explains the vitality of Athenian democracy; each citizen felt that he had a stake in what was done. It was the jury system, however, that enabled the citizens to retain ultimate control over the government. The large juries tried both civil and criminal cases, tried officials for maladministration, and even decided whether legislation was valid. This system worked well except when a demagogue held sway or when the state was under severe strain as during the Peloponnesian War; then, unfortunately, juries often punished officials under pressure from a mob or an opportunistic demagogue.

While Athenian democracy was generally successful because it functioned in a small state with a small citizen population, it must be emphasized that a large portion of the Athenian residents had no voice in government. Neither the third of the residents who were slaves nor another large segment of the population, the resident foreigners, or metics, who handled much of the trade, had any political rights and neither acquired citizenship which was limited to individuals of Athenian birth. Citizenship was not opened up, but, in fact, became more exclusive, thereby depriving Athens of a source for recruiting new talent. Yet, although Athenian democracy was government by an elite few, we must agree with the historian Thucydides that at its best it was superior to any contemporary form of government and created an environment in which all forms of culture flourished. Thucydides expressed the values of Athenian democracy by means of a speech he attributed to Pericles. Athens was a democracy because government was in "the hands of the many and not of the few." All citizens were equally protected by the law and poverty did not bar one from public service. What Thucydides, through Pericles, praised most was the happy versatility of the Athenian citizen who mixed his public and private life, who cultivated his mind while at the same time working at a profession. The Athenian citizen was, in short, the whole man, the man who, unlike the Spartan, did nothing to excess, the man who followed the golden mean. There has been no finer definition of the humane man. This definition underlies the values associated with citizenship in modern western democracies.

GREEK SOCIETY AND ECONOMY

Throughout Greece in the fifth and fourth centuries B.C. agriculture remained the most important economic activity, rivaled by trade only in Athens, Corinth, and perhaps Megara and Aegina. Even in Athens, however, the feeling persisted

THE CALF-BEARER. This marble figure of a man bearing on his shoulders a calf as a sacrificial offering illustrates the rigidity of line as well as the full-front pose and fixed smile characteristic of archaic sculpture.

that those who derived their living from the soil were the best citizens, while those engaged in industry, trade, and banking activities were regarded as departing from the behavior expected from a good Athenian citizen. This explains why the metics, freedmen, and slaves dominated the non-agrarian enterprises.

Around most urban centers were small farms specializing in fruits and vegetables. Grain was grown in Boeotia and the Peloponnesus. The principal products of Greece, though, were wine and olive oil which could be produced more easily in the narrow valleys and on the sides of the hills, and in large enough quantities to be exported. Grazing of sheep and goats, especially in mountainous regions, was important for the by-products of wool, hides, cheese, and milk. To the north, in Thessaly, horses were raised. Most of the city-states, however, had to import a large quantity of their food. Wheat and barley came from the area around the Black Sea, Cyrene, and Sicily. Fish from the Black Sea supplemented the local catch. Dates were imported from Phoenicia.

In Athens and, it must be assumed, in most city-states, industrial enterprises were small. The typical shop consisted of a master craftsman—a metic or freedman —and ten or twelve slaves. Every part of the item was fabricated in the shop and it was sold there. In this respect the process resembled that of the medieval craft guild. For a shop to have a hundred or more workers was exceptional. The principal products were metalwork, such as armor and weapons, textiles, pottery, oil lamps, sculptured marble, and furniture. The exports and imports were transported in galleys which required numerous oarsmen in addition to sailors and the merchant personnel. Because ships were expensive, men often pooled their resources; they became partners or bought shares in the ships. Unquestionably the imperialism of Athens in the fifth century B.C. was determined primarily by economics. Deficient in land, Athens depended upon trade, and this required a large navy to dominate the Aegean and eastern Mediterranean. The navy controlled piracy and kept city-states which were members of the Delian League loyal to Athens. Although all members of the empire benefited economically, as did the subject countries of the British Empire in the nineteenth century, Athens, like England and London, was the chief beneficiary. The balance of trade favored Athens; to her flowed the money for financing her cultural achievements. Athenian imperialism is one of the first examples in western history of a structure in which political and foreign policy was determined by economic need.

By modern and even by later Roman standards few Athenians were very rich or had a high standard of living. There were some wealthy aristocrats like Cimon. The aristocratic Nicias owned a thousand slaves whom he rented out to Athens to work in state-controlled silver mines and quarries. Politicians like Pericles and the metics successful in trade and industry were well off. Also, Athenian money changers who made loans and accepted deposits obviously did well financially. But these were the exceptions. Most citizens, as the remains of houses indicate, lived in humble circumstances in small houses along narrow, dirty streets. The great buildings that glorified Athens were public buildings subsidized by state funds. Social class did not depend upon difference in wealth but upon one's civic status. Citizenship put one at the top. A poor citizen usually had a much higher status than a wealthy metic or freedman. Even those slaves who were respected for what they knew or could do were nevertheless regarded as degraded individuals. At one point during the Peloponnesian War twenty thousand artisan slaves escaped from Athens: that they should want to do so demonstrates both that those who were slaves hated their condition, and that slavery existed on a large scale. The slaves were generally maltreated only in the mines and quarries; but, however well treated, they had to do the hard work, including much of that resulting in the glorious temples and theaters.

3. Greek Culture

IN THE HISTORY OF MODERN EUROPE culture is associated with Paris, Rome, Vienna, and London, centers that set the tone and style for culture elsewhere. So, in classical

Greece, Athens was the undisputed center of culture, dominating Greece as Florence dominated Renaissance Italy, and Paris dominated Europe in the seventeenth and eighteenth centuries. The fifth and fourth centuries B.C. were a classic period with achievements equalled by few subsequent ages. That an area so small could create so much that has become a vital part of our western civilization is almost incredible. Such creative drive and spirit may be partially explained but never fully accounted for; what is evident is that the golden age of Athens is one of the high peaks in our western history.

THE SPIRIT OF GREEK CULTURE

The unerring concern of the Athenians with the fundamental problems and ideals of human existence is amazing. In seeking true and perfect beauty they plumbed the depths of human reason, experience, and insight into truth and understanding of man and life. How often they hit the mark or came close to it is evident in much of the architecture, sculpture, painting, literature, philosophy, history, science, and mathematics of today where the Athenian feeling for balance and moderation, the sense of proportion, the desire for saneness, the love of beauty, the urge to create, and the spirit of free inquiry, qualities that prevailed in Athens except during periods of abnormal pressure and crisis, are still expressed. These finer qualities of Athenian culture triumphed over cynicism, skepticism, the base opportunism of demagogues, mob excesses, and loyalty to tradition and conformity. It is a tribute to the freedom of Athens that values and policies were under constant criticism, and it is a reflection upon their way of life that the Athenians could criticize their own values and actions in an atmosphere of freedom and tolerance.

ARCHITECTURE AND SCULPTURE

Although there was less faith than formerly in the power of the gods, the Greeks still believed the gods could determine the course of human existence. Each had his special place in the life of the Greeks and each city-state regarded one god or goddess as its protector and patron. Associated with this belief was a spirit of loyalty or patriotism to the city-state symbolized by the splendid temples built for the patron gods, temples comparable to the national shrines of modern states. The temples on the Acropolis in Athens, attributable largely to Pericles who urged that the temples destroyed by the Persians be replaced, achieved the height of perfection. The ambitious program of reconstruction betokened the Athenian pride in the triumph over the Persians and kept the Athenians occupied and more content than they might have been. Pericles, a shrewd political manager, always aimed to direct the thoughts of the citizen toward Athenian grandeur.

THE ACROPOLIS. Situated on the Acropolis which dominated Athens is the beautifully proportioned Parthenon shown in the foreground.

Approaching the Acropolis, one entered by way of the Propylaea (gates), a monumental structure of Doric and Ionic columns with a gallery of paintings in one wing. Beside the Propylaea was the small and delicately proportioned Ionic temple dedicated to Athena Nike. Farther, on the other side of the Propylaea, was another Ionic temple, the Erechtheum, in honor of Athena and Erechtheum (a mythical king of Athens). The roof of the south porch of the Erechtheum was supported by a row of columns sculptured in the form of lovely maidens. At the bottom of the southeastern section of the Acropolis was the conical, wooden-roofed Odeon (music hall) of Pericles. Overshadowing and crowning all, however, was the Parthenon in majestic Doric style. Designed by the architect Ictinus, this temple was the supreme architectural triumph of the Greeks, a monument of beauty and dignity. Constructed of marble, it had seventeen columns on each side and eight on the front and rear. The sculptor Phidias (490–432 B.C.), a friend of Pericles, planned the frieze, the gold and ivory statue of Athena in the interior, and other sculptured figures. The frieze around the outside walls depicted the Panathenaic procession which was an annual parade through the city to the Acropolis where a new garment was offered to the statue of Athena. On the eastern and western pediments, respectively, were depicted two well-known legends: the birth of Athena and the struggle between Athena and Poseidon for Attica. Phidias more than any other sculptor is responsible for the majesty and dignity attributed to the Greek gods; from his representations comes our image of them.

Phidias was the first of a series of gifted sculptors. Later Polyclitus of Sicyon (fl. 452–412 B.C.) sculpted statues of athletes looking natural and very much at ease. In the fourth century B.C. statues of both gods and men became more human and lifelike, as evidenced in the work of the Athenian Praxiteles (fl. c. 350 B.C.), whose statutes of Hermes with Dionysus and of Apollo have become immortal. Lysippus of Sicyon excelled in busts of men, most notably that of Alexander the Great, and his statue of Poseidon, god of the sea, has influenced all later attempts to represent the god. Little can be said about painting because it has survived only on pottery; there it typically depicted scenes composed of mythical and human figures.

GREEK DRAMA

Prior to the fifth century B.C. the Greeks wrote down their thoughts and feelings in epic or lyrical poetry. Pindar, who, as we have seen, excelled in odes composed to celebrate the victories of athletes in the Olympic games, continued to compose in this poetic form in the early fifth century, but now dramatic poetry,

STATUE OF HERMES. This statue of Hermes carrying the infant Dionysus is one of the best known works of the Athenian sculptor Praxiteles who, during the second half of the fourth century B.C., became famous for the grace of his figures and his rendition of drapery.

which probably had its origin in Corinth or Megara, became the fashion. Drama seems to have evolved from the narrative lyrics sung by the choruses at festivals of gods such as Dionysus. A dialogue between the chorus and its leader would narrate the mythology of the gods and great heroes. The first important innovation was made by Aeschylus (525–456 B.C.) who added a second leader or actor, gave both a larger role, and developed the descriptive dialogue into a more dramatic plot. Aeschylus, who is reputed to have fought against the Persians at Marathon and in other battles, wrote a drama entitled *The Persians* in addition to such other noted dramas as *The Suppliants, Prometheus Bound,* and *Oresteia,* a trilogy considered by many the greatest of his plays. At the competition held in Athens to select the drama to be performed for the various festivals, Aeschylus took first place on seventeen occasions between 484 and 468 B.C.

A younger competitor of Aeschylus was Sophocles (496–406 B.C.) who became the most popular dramatist in the fifth century B.C. He increased the number of actors, gave each more character, and by weaving the plot around a central issue made it more subtle and complex. Under the genius of Sophocles the drama became a tragedy revolving around a single theme. In his famous *Oedipus the King,* portraying the decline and fall of the mythical hero King Oedipus of Thebes, Sophocles, using a myth well known to an Athenian audience, showed that the life of Oedipus was completely determined by destiny. Oedipus is fated to kill his father and marry his mother. Learning from the Delphic oracle that this is his fate, he strives to escape it. The audience, knowing that he cannot, witnesses his unsuccessful struggle which ends in his realization that he has not escaped his destiny, a realization that leads him in horror to gouge out his eyes. No drama better displays the Greek mind. The proud Oedipus despite his mighty accomplishments must submit to his fate. He senses this and at one point exclaims: "I must not hear of not discovering the whole truth." What better expression is there of the Greek search after truth?

Euripides (480–406 B.C.), the third great dramatist of the fifth century B.C., was the first to express some of his ideas about man through the principal actors. In so doing, he made his characters more human, made them feel and think more like men, and showed how love and passion influenced the course of men's lives. The plays of Euripides are superb psychological studies, especially into female nature. Medea, for example, has become the prototype of the woman scorned; Phaedra, of the woman driven to suicide by unhappy and impossible passion; and Alcestis, of the faithful wife who sacrificed her life for her husband. In all these dramas, contrary to modern plays, there was little action on the stage; what occurred in act, thought, and feeling was related in dialogue between chorus and actors. Knowledge of these tragedies combined with that of the Platonic dialogues and the histories of Thucydides provides the clearest insight available into the Greek mind.

An art form associated with the celebrations of the festivals became popular around the middle of the fifth century B.C.; this was another form of drama—the comedy, which was intended to be humorous and to delight the spectators. Its themes came not from the lives of gods or mythology but from contemporary life. Politicians, typical citizens, and social customs provided the material which was often handled in a bitingly satirical manner. In the hands of writers such as Aristophanes (448–388 B.C.) the comedy could be a bitter criticism of contemporary life. Even during the Peloponnesian War Aristophanes let fly his barbed shafts at the mobs he considered stupid and the politicians he distrusted. His comedies, the first contemporary evidence for social and political history, are a brilliant commentary on Athenian manners and foibles. Even Socrates was held up to ridicule. In the *Babylonians* and the *Knights* the demagogue Cleon is harshly attacked. In *The Clouds* intellectuals are ridiculed. *The Wasps* strikes at the Athenian love of litigation and jury service. In *The Birds,* perhaps the finest play of Aristophanes, two Athenians, sick of the life and bustle in Athens, found a bird commonwealth.

GREEK HISTORIANS

Prior to the sixth century B.C. there was some of what we would call history, geography, and social anthropology written, but only a few fragments have survived. Greek historians did not become seriously interested in the study of man

AESOP AND THE FOX. In this witty design from a bowl dated about 470 B.C. the artist has depicted a small but didactic fox narrating to Aesop the tales of the animals; not only in the Aesopian fables but also in the Greek comedies animals were frequently used to portray satirically the foibles of men.

until Herodotus (484–425 B.C.) wrote his *History of the Persian Wars.* Although the central theme is that great conflict, Herodotus includes generous background material on the Persians, the peoples of the empire, and the Greeks. He traveled quite widely, described all that he saw, and repeated most of what he heard. His accounts of geography, customs, religion, and human character are superb, and his history, except for some obviously incredible parts, is quite trustworthy. Remarkable for the broad views he takes of history in time and space, Herodotus certainly deserves to be known as the "father of history."

Thucydides (460–400 B.C.), the author of the *History of the Peloponnesian War,* is perhaps an even greater historian who wrote history more as it has come to be written in the nineteenth and twentieth centuries. He was not interested in just telling a good story, as was Herodotus, but searched for underlying causes or explanations based on evidence that probed deeply into human motives. Thucydides, approaching history under the influence of the new Greek science and of the rational and empirical methods followed by Hippocrates and his school of medicine, was a philosophic rationalist. His explanation of historical phenomena had to be logical; his history had to reflect the contours of reality. No one has ever expressed a deeper appreciation of the strength and weakness of democratic government than Thucydides, no one ever provided a more clinical analysis of the disintegration of a state under the pressures of a long war, nor a more sober judgment on the dangers of imperialism and of military and naval competition. The *History of the Peloponnesian War* is one of the four or five greatest histories ever written. It has been valued by men of all ages for its eternal reflections on human motives and acts and on the historical process. In contrast, the *Anabasis* of Xenophon 430–355 B.C.) with its graphic account of the retreat of ten thousand Greek mercenaries who had served Persia is exciting reading, because its author was a leading participant in the events, but hardly profound history.

GREEK SCIENCE AND PHILOSOPHY

Although Greek science and medicine advanced in the fifth and fourth centuries B.C., the work was mainly theoretical. Discontented with traditional explanations that credited the gods with creating or causing natural phenomena, Greek thinkers sought more rational explanations. In this they were hindered because they had almost no implements or instruments for making accurate measurements or observations. Consequently science and medicine were speculative rather than empirical. Most speculation dealt with the composition of the universe. Typical was that of Empedocles (490–430) whose conclusion that the universe was comprised of four elements, fire, air, earth, and water, was accepted until the Renaissance, as were also the equally erroneous speculations of Hippocrates (460–357) on the composition of the human body. Hippocrates, however, did influence the development of good health habits and better nursing care, and his high ideals of the role of a doctor are enshrined in the famous Hippocratic Oath.

Because of the speculative nature of Greek thought, the most enduring contributions were made in philosophy; almost all western philosophical systems derive something from Greek philosophy. In their relentless probing for truth, Greek thinkers developed logical and rational methods of thought that destroyed shoddy and loose thinking in favor of fundamental questions: what was the nature and purpose of man, what was the value of the state, what were the moral and ethical problems of man, and what were the relations of the individual man to society and to the state? The first to excel in such analysis was Socrates (469–399 B.C.) who never wrote anything himself but whose thought is brilliantly and sympathetically presented by his student Plato in the famous dialogues. The son of a stonemason and one himself, Socrates became associated with a new group of thinkers known as the Sophists who had become influential in Athens about the middle of the fifth century B.C. Although most of the Sophists were teachers, what distinguished them was their concentrated attention on man and his relations to his social environment. With their interest in man and his institutions they can be rightly called the founders of humanism. In this intellectual milieu Socrates developed. So highly regarded did he become that the Delphic oracle supposedly said that no man was wiser than Socrates. His school was the market place where he engaged all who would in conversation. Among his followers was a group of brilliant young aristocrats, including Alcibiades. The conversation revolved around moral and ethical problems. To dispel false notions and to arrive at truth Socrates used a dialectical method of question and answer by which he would first convince his companion that his opinions were utterly erroneous. Then, using the same technique, he would begin with questions on specific instances and proceed toward the formulation of general propositions with the aim of inducing his listener to discover for himself ethically right concepts. He deeply impressed those whom he taught not only with his skillful dialectic, high ethical precepts, and personality, but also with his life which exemplified what he taught. Accused eventually of corrupting his youthful followers with impiety, he contested the right of the state to levy such a charge against him. He skillfully defended himself but accepted a verdict of guilty to demonstrate the unreasonableness of a law and people who would support such a charge. By drinking the hemlock he became the first great martyr for the principle of freedom of thought.

Socrates' brilliant student Plato (427–347 B.C.) continued the dialectical method, preserving it forever in his beautifully written dialogues. After some travel around the Mediterranean, he settled at Athens where he organized the famous school, the Academy, so called because the place where he discoursed with his students was the gymnasium of Academus. Contrary to most of the Sophists who emphasized humanistic learning, Plato concentrated on mathematics because he considered that discipline the best method of preparation for abstract thinking. In his various dialogues such as the *Phaedrus, Banquet,* and *Phaedo,* Plato is concerned with the analysis and definition of some moral quality such as courage, friendship, and self-control. In the *Republic* he is interested in the art of government and in composing a guide for an ideal city-state. Fundamental to an understanding of most of his dialogues is his theory of forms or ideas. According to him, all objects of sense are unreal and transitory; only general forms or ideas have reality and they can be apprehended solely by the mind. Objects known by sense are only copies of the form or idea. The supreme idea is the idea of good from which all other ideas emanate. From the good, therefore, comes the idea of a man, tree, house, cat, etc. which finds expression in sensible things such as men or trees. In the Middle Ages these ideas were known as universals and exerted a profound influence on Christian theology. In the *Republic,* his most influential dialogue, Plato constructed a brilliant argument for government by the best, the aristocrats, meaning those who excelled in the mind. The *Republic* has become the chief weapon in the arsenal of those who decry democracy and prefer government by a few elite.

Plato's most distinguished student was the formidable Aristotle (384–322 B.C.), the tutor of Alexander the Great and possibly the greatest of the Greek philosophers. He taught for a while in the Academy and then founded his own school which adhered to his philosophical approach to knowledge. He repudiated Plato's theory of universal ideas and forms and denied that they had a real existence apart from the sensible or individual object that represented them, a philosophical position that also found strong support in the Middle Ages. Aristotle, less concerned with abstract thinking and beautiful prose, neglected mathematics and concentrated on factual knowledge, upon phenomena that were observable. This led him to specialize in the natural sciences from which emerged his empiric and inductive thought. His writings are encyclopedic, all expressed in a stern and economical scientific prose. He wrote not only on physics, astronomy, biology, and psychology, but also on metaphysics, logic, and ethics. He was likewise interested in esthetics and rhetorical and poetic theory. In the *Politics,* a penetrating work, he produced a remarkable analysis of the role of government and, instead of attempting to write a guide for an ideal state, made a rational argument for a form of government that was possible and workable. He conceived such a government as a moderate democracy based on a restricted number of citizens from the middle class. Although much of what Aristotle taught the world about science was proved wrong in the sixteenth and seventeenth centuries, it is incredible that, without any precise scientific instruments, he arrived at so many accurate conclusions. Ultimately he had more influence on western thought than even Plato, and in the Middle Ages it was he who was entitled "The Philosopher."

In a sense Aristotle draws down the curtain on the classic golden age of Greek culture created in the environment of the small city-state, especially Athens, where each citizen mattered and felt himself to have some value. Aristotle was the friend and tutor of Alexander the Great who ended the age of the small independent state and ushered in the age of the empire. Though aware of some of this transformation, Aristotle preferred to look back rather than at the present or future. Inevitably the demise of the city-state as a viable form of political organization had a drastic impact on the individual who eventually had to reevaluate his relation to society and the state and to seek other values to guide him. This transformation occurred during the long age of the Hellenistic monarchies and Roman domination.

Further Reading

There are numerous good surveys of Greek history, of which the following are especially valuable: G. W. Botsford and C. A. Robinson, *Hellenic History,* 4th ed. (New York, 1956); M. L. W. Laistner, *A History of the Greek World from 479 to 323 B.C.* (New York, 1939); *H. D. F. Kitto, *The Greeks* (Harmondsworth, 1951); N. G. L. Hammond, *History of Greece to 322 B.C.* (Oxford, 1959); *A. R. Burn, *Pelican History of Greece* (Harmondsworth, 1965); A. Andrewes, *The Greeks* (London, 1967); M. I. Finley, *Ancient Greeks: An Introduction to Their Life and Thought* (New York, 1968); and C. Starr, *The Ancient Greeks* (New York, 1971). Cultural history is emphasized by *V. Ehrenberg, *From Solon to Socrates: Greek History and Civilization* (New York and London, 1968). A handy collection of sources is provided by *T. S. Brown, *Ancient Greece* (New York, 1965).

For a scholarly evaluation of the Mycenaean and Homeric periods the pertinent chapters in Volumes I and II of the new edition of the *Cambridge Ancient History* are recommended. Good surveys of early Greek history are by C. G. Starr, *The Origins of Greek Civilization, 1100–650 B.C.* (New York, 1961); E. T. Vermeule, *Greece in the Bronze Age* (Chicago, 1964); V. R. d'A. Desborough, *The Last Mycenaeans and Their Successors* (Oxford, 1964); and M. I. Finley, *Early Greece: The Bronze and Archaic Ages* (New York, 1970). The works of Homer and Hesiod are available in many translations, but there are also pertinent books by C. M. Bowra, *Heroic Poetry* (London, 1952); A. Lesky, *A History of Greek Literature* (London, 1966); and *M. I. Finley, *The World of Odysseus* (Harmondsworth, 1962). For the movement of the Greeks overseas see A. G. Woodhead, *The Greeks in the West* (London, 1962); and J. M. Cook, *The Greeks in Ionia and the East* (London, 1962). The book by A. Andrewes on *The Greek Tyrants* (London, 1956) is the best on early Greek political organization.

General works on Greek government and law are by G. Glotz, *The Greek City* (London, 1929); V. Ehrenberg, *The Greek State* (Oxford, 1960); and J. W. Jones, *The Law and Legal Theory of the Greeks* (Oxford, 1956). For Athenian government see C. Hignett, *History of the Athenian Constitution* (Oxford, 1952); and A. H. M. Jones, *Athenian Democracy* (Oxford, 1957). Spartan institutions are dealt with by H. Michell, *Sparta* (Cambridge, 1952); G. L. Huxley, *Early Sparta* (London, 1962); and *W. G. Forrest, *A History of Sparta, 950–192 B.C.* (New York and London, 1969).

Of the numerous studies on economic history it suffices to cite F. W. Heichelheim, *An Economic History of the Ancient World* (Leiden, 1958–1964), Vols. I–II; and J. Hasebroek, *Trade and Politics in Ancient Greece* (London, 1933). Greek social values are treated in C. M. Bowra, *The Greek Experience* (London, 1957); and in A. W. H. Adkins, *Merit and Responsibility: A Study in Greek Values* (Oxford, 1960). Two excellent books on Greek religion are those of H. J. Rose, *Handbook of Greek Mythology,* 6th ed. (London, 1960); and W. K. C. Guthrie, *The Greeks and Their Gods* (London, 1950). The standard work on military development is F. E. Adcock's *The Greek and Macedonian Art of War* (Berkeley, 1957).

All the Greek philosophers have been translated and their works are available in paperback editions. The scholarly literature on Greek philosophy is massive. An old but still reliable study is that of J. Burnet, *Early Greek Philosophy,* 3rd ed. (London, 1920). A very comprehensive three-volume work is that of W. K. C. Guthrie, *A History of Greek Philosophy* (New York and Cambridge, 1962–1969).

A more general work is that by J. M. Warbeke, *The Searching Mind of Greece* (New York, 1930). Books on more specialized aspects of Greek philosophy are the following: J. E. Raven, *Plato's Thought in the Making* (Cambridge, 1965); D. J. Allan, *The Philosophy of Aristotle* (London, 1952); and E. R. Bevan, *Stoics and Sceptics* (Oxford, 1913). Greek science is well covered by B. Farrington, *Greek Science* (Harmondsworth, 1953); by S. Sambursky, *The Physical World of the Greeks* (London, 1956); and by *M. Clagett, *Greek Science in Antiquity* (New York and London, 1966). Every student should read the histories of Herodotus and Thucydides, both available in paperback editions. Perhaps the best discussion of the Greek historians is that of J. B. Bury, *The Ancient Greek Historians* (London, 1909).

The finest and most recent survey of Greek art is by J. Boardman, *Greek Art* (London, 1964). Other reliable works are those of C. M. Robertson, *Greek Painting* (London, 1959); and R. M. Cook, *Greek Painted Pottery* (London, 1960). Two books which explain and interpret Greek architecture are those of A. W. Lawrence, *Greek Architecture* (Harmondsworth, 1957); and of R. E. Wycherley, *How the Greeks Built Cities,* 2nd ed. (London, 1962).

Almost all the Greek poets and dramatists have been translated and made available in paperback editions. The best way to understand Greek literature is to read selectively in the corpus of Greek literature. Excellent studies are those of M. Hadas, *A History of Greek Literature* (New York, 1950); and of *H. D. F. Kitto, *Greek Tragedy* (New York, 1954). For various aspects of literature and drama see C. M. Bowra, *Early Greek Elegists* (Cambridge, Mass., 1938) and *Greek Lyric Poetry,* 2nd ed. (Oxford, 1961); J. Jones, *On Aristotle and Greek Tragedy* (London, 1962); and T. B. L. Webster, *Greek Theatre Production* (London, 1956).

CHAPTER 3

The Age of
Empires

1. Alexander the Great and His Heritage

Of all the great figures of the ancient world none, not even Caesar,
rivaled Alexander the Great. No other changed so profoundly the ideals, values,
outlook, and intellectual development of men, or the forms and size of future states.
Despite weaknesses, this remarkable man, this genius, transformed in thirteen
years all that he touched. Like few men in history, he so captured the imagination
and loyalty of men that they believed in him and unified their resources to support
his grand undertakings. Although it is difficult to distinguish the historical from
the mythical Alexander, the fact that he was the hero of the many deeds and marvels woven into the Alexander Legend in succeeding ages speaks clearly of his
deep influence upon his own age and those that followed. Who can forget the tale
of Bucephalus, the horse that he tamed, that carried him across the world, and
whose death he commemorated by founding a city in India? Who can forget how
the knot tied by King Gordius of Phrygia, that no one was believed capable of
untying except the future ruler of Asia, was easily cut by Alexander with his sword,
thus showing his capacity for solving knotty problems? Such tales were many.

CONQUESTS OF ALEXANDER

When Alexander succeeded his murdered father in 336 B.C., all of Greece could easily have lapsed back into particularism had not Alexander dramatically taught the Greeks that history would not this time repeat itself. Holding a congress with all the Greeks in the Peloponnesus, Alexander there proclaimed the political unity of Greece, then subdued an uprising in Macedonia, and finally, as an object lesson, destroyed Thebes which had the poor sense to revolt, sparing only Pindar's house as a symbol that, as Pindar had been recognized not only as a Theban but as a Greek poet, so should Alexander be recognized as the ruler of all Greece. Petty localism was to end. By 334 B.C. Alexander's hold on Greece was so firm that he crossed into Asia to conquer the Persian Empire and then the world beyond, never returning to Greece.

Brought up on Homer, Alexander loved and appreciated a symbolic act. He visited Troy because he believed or desired to believe that his ancestor was the great warrior Achilles. Master of Asia Minor by the end of 334 B.C., he initiated its Hellenization, which was so thorough that it remained Greek to the end of the Byzantine Empire in A.D. 1453. Alexander's great victory at Issus in 337 B.C. gave him Syria, Palestine, and Egypt, lands ruled for a thousand years afterwards by Greek and Roman successors. With the ports of Tyre and Gaza reduced by 332 B.C., Alexander secured naval supremacy over the eastern Mediterranean. In Egypt in 331 B.C. he performed two acts, one natural and the other mystical. At the mouth of the Nile

COIN OF ALEXANDER THE GREAT. This silver tetradrachm was struck about 320 B.C. On the *left* is the obverse side, depicting the head of Alexander, and on the *right* is the reverse.

he founded the city of Alexandria destined not only to become a great port and commercial center, but the center of a cosmopolitan Mediterranean culture. He then rode five hundred miles westward across the desert to the Oasis of Siwa to a temple of the Egyptian god Ammon, believed to have been visited by the Greek mythical heroes Perseus and Hercules to whom Alexander thought himself related. Thereafter it was commonly believed that Alexander descended from Ammon, that in his lineage were both heroes and a god. Was there a spark of the divine in him? It seemed so because that same year he defeated the Persian king at Gaugamela and ended the Persian Empire. Its ancient capital Persepolis was occupied and burned for reasons that are not known, but perhaps to avenge the burning of Athens by the Persians in 480 B.C.

For Alexander it was not enough to have subdued the Persian Empire in four years and, as he said, to have "avenged Greece." Making arrangements for the governance of the conquered lands, he pushed east through Afghanistan and into the Punjab. There he defeated an Indian army using elephants and captured King Porus. Arriving at the Indus River in 326 B.C., Alexander was forced to stop by his troops who refused to budge, exhausted after campaigning for eight years. Alexander explored the Indus and then returned with his main army, marching across the desert to Babylon, while his admiral Nearchus sailed from the mouth of the Indus along the coast to the Persian Gulf where he explored the coastal area and studied all the natural life. At Babylon in 323 B.C. Alexander, then only thirty-five years old, died from a fever.

LIFE IN THE HELLENISTIC MONARCHIES

What did Alexander accomplish? Sudden death ended his plan for a universal empire which he and his successors would rule. His wife Roxana and infant son were murdered and his conquests were fought over and divided among his generals. Three large kingdoms gradually replaced the empire. The general Ptolemy secured Egypt and Palestine over which his successors ruled until the death of Cleopatra in 31 B.C. The general Seleucus gained control of Asia which his house ruled until 65 B.C., but which was soon reduced to Asia Minor and Syria because India was lost and the Parthians established themselves in much of the Persian Empire by the middle of the third century B.C. After prolonged civil war the general Antigonus won Greece, and his descendants maintained tenuous control until 168 B.C. These three Hellenistic kingdoms were not a complete denial of Alexander's hope—peace throughout a vast empire. Large, they eradicated or reduced particularism. Although their rulers fought each other, they were so evenly matched that a balance of power was created which limited frequent and major wars. With their armies composed mostly of mercenaries who wished to win but also to live, war was a business and became less savage, with fewer city-states destroyed or whole populations sold into slavery. The conquests of Alexander, therefore, resulted in large states and more peace which contributed to the economic development and cultural advance of the Hellenistic world.

The treasure that Alexander secured from the Persian kings was fabulous. There was so much gold that its transfer west into Asia Minor and Greece altered the political and economic center of gravity and upset the economic balance. Whole Greek regions and city-states ceased being poor and became prosperous. Put into circulation, the vast wealth powerfully stimulated the economy of the Hellenistic world. While ultimately there would again be a flow of wealth eastward, for hundreds of years the spread of wealth into the West supported a new civilization both Hellenistic and Roman and created a higher standard of living.

With piracy and political instability reduced for a long period by the large kingdoms, widespread trade flourished. Alexander reportedly founded seventy new cities throughout his lands to serve as military points and as centers for the spread of Greek culture. To them came thousands of Greeks, inaugurating a new period of Greek colonization that spread Greeks throughout Asia and northern Africa. The impact on trade was tremendous. It increased by land and sea; ships, harbors, and navigational aids improved; eastern goods from as far as India and China were brought to the Mediterranean world while Greek products went East; Alexandria became a great international emporium for trade: it exported papyrus, glass, and textiles; parchment, silk, and agrarian products came from Asia Minor; grain from the Black Sea region and Sicily; tin from Britain; silver from Spain; and luxury items from the East.

Such trade spawned new business and industrial organizations. In Ptolemaic Egypt the state came to control and operate factories producing oil, wine, linen, and papyrus, and to control rigorously the land. Egypt, in fact, was regarded as the king's private property. Men began to invest money in industry and commercial ventures and even to speculate. Adventurous Greeks went out to the new cities, began enterprises, and became immensely rich. Factories expanded and banks developed all over the Hellenistic world, most not only receiving deposits but making loans, honoring checks, and issuing letters of credit. In breaking down political barriers the Hellenistic kingdoms broke down economic barriers, and the economic development, thereby stimulated, continued to support the Mediterranean world until the flow of gold eastward into Asia Minor and beyond deprived the West of adequate monetary resources. In the second and third centuries A.D. this unfavorable flow became a flood, hastening the decline of the Roman Empire in the West.

The Hellenistic age created social change. With an enlarged and quickened economy came greater urbanization and larger urban populations. The participation of more Greeks in trade and industry produced an important middle class that came to dominate urban affairs and to control the greater number of urban inhabitants who comprised what we would call the proletariat, living miserably, little better than the slaves who became ever more numerous because of Alexander's conquests. Since the Hellenistic economy rested upon the labor of slaves and of the proletariat, the social, economic, and political power of the middle class depended upon the exploitation of this labor which was so plentiful that there was no incentive to transform the scientific knowledge of Hellenistic society into labor-saving machines. In cities everywhere except in Greece, the Greeks were a minority, often hated as foreign masters and exploiters by the native population, a situation that produced social and racial tension resulting in riots. Gradually as Greeks intermarried with natives such tension lessened. Another element of Hellenistic urban life, quite different from that of the Hellenic period, was the individual's loss of identification with the city-state. It was soon evident that all the important decisions were made by a powerful and distant ruler, that what the individual did politically on the city level counted little. This sense of futility and isolation impelled people to organize craft guilds, religious societies, and other organizations which gave the individual a sense of belonging and an outlet for his social drives.

Although they had lost local political power, the Greek city-states and the other cities that sprang up in the Hellenistic monarchy became more cosmopolitan; they teemed with Greeks, Persians, Syrians, Jews, Egyptians, and others. While initially the Greeks did not marry non-Greeks, gradually they did so, following in this respect the example of Alexander, who married a Persian princess, encouraged his soldiers to marry Persians, employed natives in his administration, and even incorporated them into his army. Perhaps Alexander hoped to blend together the peoples of his empire; perhaps he was rightly portrayed by his biographer Plutarch who wrote: "He conceived that he was divinely sent to be the harmonizer and conciliator of Greeks and barbarians alike. He sought to blend as it were in the mixing-cup of good fellowship all civilizations and customs." This blending that occurred in the large Hellenistic monarchies explains the development of a feeling of universalism and of syncretic and eclectic trends in culture and religion.

RELIGION AND PHILOSOPHY

To support the autocratic power he felt must be his if he was to command respect throughout his empire, Alexander cultivated the belief that he was a god or was divinely sanctioned. He became a god-king in Egypt, a king by divine right in Persia, and a god in Greece, although neither he nor the Greeks really believed he was divine. By this device Alexander centered attention upon himself and hoped to secure the loyalty of his subjects and to promote unity. His successors in the three monarchies followed his example. The old city-state divinities retreated as the city-state lost political power and as the people realized that their security and welfare depended upon the all-powerful king. Why not pay respect to him for what he did? As man lost identification with his small political community, he came to feel alone and powerless in the vast new monarchies; he desperately needed to believe in some force that would sustain him. Many people turned to the oriental mystery religions because some of them promised eternal life and others offered participation in symbolic rituals. This longing to believe in some extra-human power partly explains the vitality of Judaism in this period. The Jews, dispersed throughout the Hellenistic world, needed to believe in a divine power that would protect and sustain them.

For numerous intellectuals and educated people, however, religion was not the answer; they required some doctrine with a more rational appeal. This they found in some of the new philosophies of the age. Whereas Plato and Aristotle had been primarily concerned with knowledge and a search after truth, the Hellenistic philosophers were concerned with more immediate human problems. How was man to achieve happiness and find value in his life in the new super states that had replaced his tiny city-state? There were various answers to this question in the fourth century b.c. The Cynics taught that man would achieve immense satisfaction only by adhering to ascetic morality and by being contemptuous of the world and its affairs. Aristippus of Cyrene was hedonistic, arguing that pleasure should be the ultimate goal of man. The Skeptics ended by denying the existence of any knowledge, a belief that could lead to nihilism.

The philosophies with the largest followings were Epicureanism and Stoicism. The former was propounded by Epicurus (342–270 b.c.) who, withdrawing from the bustle of life, devoted himself to a search for the good life. To Epicurus the good life was one without pain. To escape pain man must avoid as many of the demands of life as possible. He must live simply and not overindulge in any activity. The founder of Stoicism was Zeno of Cyprus (335–263 b.c.) who taught his philosophy at the Stoa Poikile (Painted Porch) in the Agora of Athens. He contended that the world was directed by Divine Reason of which man had only a spark. To understand Divine Reason man must use his own reason. He would then understand that he should lead a virtuous life emphasizing temperance, justice, good sense, and courage. Above all, he must carry out his objectives in the framework of society. The divine spark of reason inherent in men was the bond that united them as brothers of the world. To the Stoic, race, class, and sex had no importance because all men were brothers with a common tie and belief in a Divine Reason (a kind of god). Stoicism epitomized the universality and cosmopolitanism of the Hellenistic world; it became vital for educated men and contributed greatly to Christian doctrine and ethics. The Christian notions of God and of the brotherhood of man have much in common with Stoic precepts.

CULTURE AND ART

Reflecting the developments in religion and philosophy, much Hellenistic culture was cosmopolitan and urbane, although some was individualistic and specialized. Above all, the Hellenistic age was a time when Greek culture spread throughout much of the inhabited world. It went to Asia, northern Africa, and eventually to Italy and the West. So firmly did it take root that it prevailed in Asia until the Arabs swept all before them in the seventh and eighth centuries A.D. It retained its dominance in the Byzantine Empire and much of it was introduced by the Romans into the lands around the western Mediterranean. There was some reciprocity in the process because the Greeks learned from the people they conquered; never, however, did the eastern cultures supplant the Greek.

Hellenistic culture was a modified continuation of the Hellenic. Its chief characteristics were more individualism, a greater emphasis on man and nature, less idealism, and more realism. Knowledge became more specialized. Less often did thinkers concern themselves with all knowledge, as did Plato and Aristotle, but rather they concentrated on some area of knowledge. The most enduring contributions of Hellenistic culture were made in science, generally by scientists patronized by the Hellenistic monarchs. In mathematics Euclid (fl. 300 B.C.) developed geometry which he explained in his book the *Elements*. Hipparchus (fl. 150 B.C.) invented trigonometry for his measurements of the earth and his astronomical calculations. He supported the geocentric theory which triumphed over the heliocentric theory of Aristarchus of Samos (fl. 275 B.C.). Eratosthenes (276–196 B.C.) projected a map of the earth with lines of longitude and latitude and calculated the circumference of the world to within two hundred miles of the exact figure. The gifted Archimedes of Syracuse (287–212 B.C.) discovered specific gravity, explained the movement of heavenly bodies, and made marvelous mechanical inventions. He even did elementary calculus and solved the value of *pi*. Stimulated by the vast conquests and the new lands and peoples they saw, other thinkers did good work in geography and botany. The excellent achievements in medicine helped to relieve human suffering, to improve medical care, and to prevent disease. Studying the human anatomy, Herophilus (fl. 300 B.C.) identified the functions of the brain and nervous system and showed the role of the arteries in the circulation of blood. In this period the science of physiology began.

Scholarship flourished also in the humanities which were supported by the Hellenistic monarchies, especially the Ptolemaic at Alexandria. Since Greek was the universal language of the Hellenistic age, cultivated scholars studied its construction and wrote grammars on it. Others worked at literary criticism and rhetoric. Great libraries developed at Alexandria, Pergamum, Rhodes, and Antioch. In the museum at Alexandria scholars were subsidized by the Ptolemies just to "do scholarship."

Although Hellenistic literature did not rival the excellence achieved in the fifth and fourth centuries B.C., it retained a vitality and the ability to develop new forms and themes for expressing the feeling of men whose sensibilities and tastes had been altered by the changes in politics, economics, science, philosophy, and religion. The poet Callimachus (fl. 250 B.C.), for a time head of the library at Alexandria, popularized the short epic dealing with mythological themes not used previously by poets. He engaged in a bitter literary feud with Apollonius of Rhodes (fl. 210 B.C.) who adhered to the style of the long Homeric epic and who composed the immensely popular *Argonautica* with its tale of Jason and his quest for the Golden Fleece. Callimachus, after reading this poem, made his famous comment: "A big book, a big evil." The *Argonautica*, however, is still a favorite whereas the short epics of Callimachus have not enjoyed such success. As a protest against the more complex urban life, Theocritus of Sicily (fl. third century B.C.) wrote pastoral idylls praising the rural life with its shepherds, flocks, and natural, bucolic scenes. Unfortunately only one complete play and fragments of others by the playwright Menander (342–290 B.C.) are extant, but they show that he created a new form of comedy and was a worthy continuator of Aristophanes. Menander portrayed life and its manners rather than some general incident or theme. His insights into ordinary people and his reflections on life are indicative of the realism and cynicism that, in contrast to the Hellenic period, pervaded the Hellenistic Age. His observation, "We live not as we will, but as we can," reveals the contemporary view of life. Menander became a model for later Roman comedy and inspired the comedies of Molière in the seventeenth century.

There was no history in the Hellenistic age to equal that of Herodotus or Thucydides, but the *Histories* of Polybius (205–125 B.C.) who wrote about Rome from 266 to 146 B.C. has been acknowledged in all ages as great history. Originally a Greek politician, Polybius became a prisoner of the Romans in 168 B.C. and was taken to Rome. There he soon became a friend of cultivated Romans, among them the general Scipio Africanus. The perspective of Polybius was later widened by visits to lands overseas under Roman rule. He became an enthusiastic admirer of Rome and decided to write a history that would attempt to explain why the Romans became the masters of the Mediterranean world in fifty-three years. Like Thucydides, Polybius was not content merely to describe historical events; he wanted to know why events occurred. His analysis of why Rome was so successful in politics and military affairs is still largely accepted by historians. His theory that history moves in cycles has long influenced historians interested in the rise and decline of states and civilizations.

Hellenistic architecture and art were inspired by styles of the fifth century B.C., but there were adaptations and a decline from the supreme perfection of style, proportion, and beauty associated with such buildings as the Parthenon. Temples continued to be constructed, but less frequently, as the decline of the city-states weakened belief in the traditional Greek gods. The Hellenistic period witnessed the erection of more secular and practical buildings such as stadiums, theaters, office buildings, and elaborate residences. Generally the columns of these structures were in the ornate Corinthian style rather than the simple Ionic or Doric. To facilitate the increasing maritime trade, large docks, harbors, and lighthouses were constructed. The Pharos of the port of Alexandria was a wonder of the age. Great progress was also made in fortifications. Rather than stray into the realm of the abstract, the typical Hellenistic architect worked to achieve buildings that would meet practical requirements. For the first time there was an attempt at city planning, with thought given to the location of public buildings and market places and to rectangular blocks with straight streets.

The famous centers of sculpture at Pergamum, Alexandria, and Antioch strived for realism in sharp detail. Some of the best work came from Pergamum; the most famous examples are the Great Altar and the Dying Gaul, the latter a compelling depiction of human suffering. Lysippus (fl. late fourth century B.C.), who sculpted Alexander the Great, excelled in figures of athletes. His statue of an athlete scraping oil from his body set a standard for athletic figures. The most ambitious and dramatic sculpture was by Chares of Lindos (fl. 290 B.C.) who executed the huge Colossus of Rhodes, known as one of the Seven Wonders of the World. Located at

THEATER AT EPIDAURUS. The great amphitheater at Epidaurus, constructed about 340 B.C. by Polyclitus the Younger, is an early example of secular architecture of this type; it represents the transitional period which bridges the classical and the Hellenistic worlds.

the entrance to the harbor of Rhodes, this work was a statue of Helios the sun god and it epitomized the Hellenistic desire for grandeur, a taste that could be indulged because of greater economic resources and the support of the wealthy Hellenistic monarchs. In contrast to the monumental architecture and sculpture were the finely engraved coins of Alexander and his successors and the skillfully painted portraits that achieved unrivalled excellence in the graceful work of Apelles (fl. late fourth century B.C.).

Hellenistic culture, compared with that of the preceding age, is inferior in all respects except science, which enjoyed a brilliant period and then declined, had little influence in the Roman world, and was lost from sight during most of the Middle Ages. It may be justly said that the Hellenistic age saw a gradual withdrawal from reason and belief in man's ability, and a gradual embracing of the philosophies and religions that offered extrahuman support and hope. It is important to remember, however, that the brilliant achievements of the Greek city-states were preserved and, although transformed, introduced to much of the inhabited world. Greek culture became cosmopolitan; all people could appreciate and benefit from it. This was the heritage of the new Roman power in the West, a power that was to extract the essence of Greek culture and transplant it to western Europe where, after some perilous years in the early Middle Ages when Graeco-Roman culture was almost lost, it again bloomed forth and became a fundamental part of the new western European culture that developed in the Middle Ages and the Renaissance.

2. *The Roman Republic*

DURING THIS SURVEY of the ancient world there has seldom been occasion to look elsewhere than at the lands around the eastern Mediterranean. Civilization developed first in Egypt, Mesopotamia, and the surrounding regions. Then the center shifted westward and it was necessary to concentrate on western Asia Minor, the Aegean, and Greece. With the spread of Greek culture into the East during the Hellenistic Age, focus again shifted to Egypt and the Asian lands east of the Mediterranean. Throughout this long period there has been only brief reference to the western Mediterranean. We have noted that the Phoenicians founded a successful trading city in northern Africa at Carthage, just across from Sicily, and that during the age of colonization the Greeks established numerous city-states in southern Italy and Sicily. It is now time to consider this region of the Mediterranean where, while the Greeks were engaged in the development of their brilliant civilization, a power was slowly arising in Italy that would ultimately control the Mediterranean world and provide a long era of peace during which Greek culture was absorbed, modified, and spread into western Europe.

POLITICAL DEVELOPMENT

While the Greeks were engaged in colonization and in the development of their peculiar political institutions, one first hears of a settlement of people at Rome on the Tiber River along the west coast of Italy. The inhabitants of this small town and the surrounding region known as Latium seem to have been a mixture of hill people and Latins descended from Indo-Europeans who had come into Italy from north of the Alps during the second millenium B.C. To the end of the sixth century B.C. the history of Rome is imperfectly known because sources are few. We do know that from the seventh century B.C. Latium was ruled by the Etruscans who had come to Italy from Asia Minor or Lydia early in the ninth century B.C. This was an important period for the history of Latium because the Etruscans introduced their highly developed culture to the simple farmers, while from the Greek city-states to the south came another superior culture.

According to legend, in 509 B.C. some aristocratic Roman families led a revolt against the Etruscans and ousted the Etruscan king Tarquin the Proud. This date marks the independence of Rome and its dominance over Latium as well as the beginning of its expansion throughout Italy. There is no need to follow this expansion in detail; it suffices to note that the citizen farmers of Rome and Latium were disciplined and courageous fighters who repeatedly defeated the other peoples of Italy. To the north and to the south the Romans moved outward. Gradually the Greek city-states in southern Italy were subdued. In 272 B.C. Tarentum, the last independent Greek state, surrendered, and by 264 B.C. Rome controlled the Italian peninsula.

Although available sources are not as explicit as one would like they provide a reasonably clear picture of the structure of Roman government. It was republican in form, dominated by aristocratic families whose power and wealth derived from the land. For some time the *patricians,* as these aristocrats were called, held all the offices and formulated all policies. The mass of ordinary people, the *plebeians,* had few civic rights and were economically deprived. This inequitable situation led to class struggle which characterized Rome and its republican form of government to the latter part of the first century B.C. Through upheavals and revolts the plebeians gradually acquired some political rights and powers. By 264 B.C. they had forced the patricians to draw up a written code of laws known as the Twelve Tables, had obtained the right to elect officials known as *tribunes* to represent and protect their interests, and had won the privilege of being elected to public offices and passing laws in their assemblies without the consent of the patricians.

The form of government developed by the third century B.C. cannot be called democratic. The plebeians could meet in the assemblies and pass laws, and the tribunes could defend their rights and interests, but political and economic power still resided with the patricians who continued to hold most of the offices and thereby controlled the executive part of government. Even though the plebeians had won the right of standing for office, only those who had acquired wealth could hope to be elected. Annually the assemblies elected two officers called *consuls* who wielded the supreme executive and military power. There were also annual elections of lesser financial, legal, and administrative officers, who, after holding office for a year, normally became life members of the Roman Senate. They became part of a senatorial aristocracy. Supposedly the Senate could only advise, but because almost all the executive experience, wisdom, power, and prestige were concentrated in its members, its authority was supreme in Rome from 509 B.C. until the republic was replaced by the empire. Despite the political and military triumphs achieved under the direction of the Senate, its basic political, social, and economic philosophy was conservative and narrow. Only slowly and grudgingly did it extend partial and full citizenship to the peoples of Italy. Too often the conquered lands were awarded not to the poor plebeian legionaries, but to the aristocratic senators. Continually the laws and desires of the plebeian assemblies were ignored. What is therefore amazing is the cooperation and unity between patricians and plebeians in times of crisis. Their high concept of civic responsibility and military duty alone explains the phenomenal success of the Roman republic down to 264 B.C. and the equally remarkable performance during the next two hundred years when Rome withstood the severest challenges in her history and went on to control the civilized world around the Mediterranean.

Before 264 B.C. Rome had been concerned solely with the Italian peninsula; she was uninterested in affairs outside Italy. Agriculture sustained most of the people and what trade there was with the Greeks and Carthaginians was conducted by the Carthaginians and in their ships. The Romans as yet had no ships. This landed isolationist situation was doomed, however, after Rome had expanded to the toe of Italy just across from Sicily. Although Sicily had been controlled for centuries by various Greek city-states such as Syracuse, their constant warfare among themselves had furnished Carthage an ideal opportunity for intervention. If the Carthaginians with their excellent fleet could secure Sicily, they would be the indisputable masters of the western Mediterranean. Not until Rome got to southern Italy and saw Carthage attempt to control Messina and dominate the trade between Italy and Sicily did she become aware of the great Carthaginian sea power and its menace. The result was a succession of wars with Carthage known as the Punic Wars.

During the First Punic War (264–242 B.C.) Rome finally built a fleet and drove Carthage out of Sicily, which became the first Roman overseas possession and was organized as a province under a military governor known as a *praetor*. Soon Sardinia also fell to Rome. To compensate for these losses Carthage encouraged expansion in Spain under her general Hamilcar Barca who subjugated the Mediterranean coast of Spain. After his death the task continued under his famous son

Hannibal, one of the world's military geniuses. After building up a superb army, Hannibal suddenly struck in 218 B.C., instigating the Second Punic War which lasted until 202 B.C. Before the Romans realized what he was doing, Hannibal had brought his army with its elephants through Alpine passes into Italy where he remained for the next fourteen years, defeating every Roman army sent against him. Although his battles were masterpieces, brilliantly planned and executed, he could not take Rome or break Roman resistance. In 207 B.C. the Roman general Scipio Africanus took an army to besiege Carthage. Hannibal, recalled to defend the city, was finally defeated in 202 B.C. Again Carthage paid a price. She was reduced to the land about her, lost Spain and her fleet, and had to pay a huge indemnity. Rome's total destruction of Carthage in 146 B.C. was therefore unnecessary and but an act of cruelty that made no sense. By 202 B.C. Rome was master of the western Mediterranean world. She had withstood her most serious crisis and demonstrated, despite the social, economic, and political evils throughout Italy, her ability to hold the loyalty of most of the people. Owing to its successful direction of the Punic War, the Senate emerged more powerful and influential than ever.

Aware perhaps for the first time of Rome's immense power, the Senate took an interest in political affairs all around the Mediterranean. It soon became interested in Greek affairs, possibly, according to some scholars, because of admiration for Greek culture. Rome, previously not concerned with the Hellenistic monarchies and their wars, now changed in attitude with the result that the Hellenistic balance of power in the eastern Mediterranean was destroyed and replaced by the power of Rome. Fearful that an alliance of the Antigonids of Macedonia and the Seleucids of Syria might be unfortunate for the Greek city-states, Rome sent her legions eastward in 197 B.C. and defeated Macedonia. In 191 B.C. her legions overran a Seleucid army. Rome followed up the victories by guaranteeing the freedom of the Greek city-states and establishing a protectorate over them. Step by step Rome increased her power in the Greek peninsula until by 146 B.C. all of Macedonia and the city-states were under her rule. In 133 B.C., when the king of Pergamum died, by his will Rome acquired much of Asia Minor. In succeeding years Rome extended her hold in Asia Minor. One hundred years of severe war and expansion, however, had made an impact upon the social and economic structure of Rome that became painfully evident in the last years of the second century B.C.

PROBLEMS OF THE LATE REPUBLIC

The prime beneficiaries of Rome's military success were the aristocratic senators. Not only in Italy, but in Sicily, North Africa, Spain, Greece, and Asia Minor, they acquired immense areas of land. They obviously benefited from the huge indemnities and tributes and liberally shared in the tax receipts as the captured lands were organized into provinces. Another beneficiary of Rome's conquests was the rising class of *nouveaux riches* composed of men from the plebeian class who took advantage of expanding economic opportunities. This new class of men called *equites* (knights), while not altering the social and political status of the senators, secured tremendous wealth by contracting to build public works, to operate public facilities, to supply the army, and to work state mines and forests. Their greatest profits came from farming provincial taxes and lending money. Content to leave trade and industry in the hands of easterners such as Greeks and Syrians, the equites, having acquired wealth, aspired to political power and increased their demands for it toward the end of the second century B.C. Along with money and goods from the conquered lands came thousands of slaves. The talented secured good positions in senatorial households as tutors, teachers, and secretaries; others worked in trade and industry; and the less skilled were used in the mines and forests and on the land. This huge influx of slaves worked to the benefit of the aristocrats. For years the plebeian farmers and humble craftsmen had been fighting Rome's wars. Naturally they obtained some share of the spoils, but it was inconsequential. Absent for years from his land, the farmer lost it either by having to sell it to senators or forfeiting it for failure to pay debts on it. He then drifted to Rome or other cities. By the third century B.C., therefore, Italy had become a land of huge estates known as *latifundia* owned by the senators and worked by the plentiful supply of slaves. Diversified farming was replaced by specialized farming in such lucrative products as wool, olive oil, and wine. Even the farmers who had remained at home could not compete against the huge estates, and soon nearly all gave up the hopeless task.

After the middle of the second century B.C. there was grave social, economic, and political discontent on the part of the equites, legionary veterans, displaced farmers, and unemployed urban craftsmen. The three latter groups formed a bitter urban proletariat that became desperate and ready to do anything to improve its lot. Between 133 and 124 B.C. two brothers, Tiberius and Gaius Gracchus, attempted idealistically to improve the situation by reforms. Gaining election as tribunes, the Gracchi obtained laws that would take land from the latifundia and distribute it among veterans and landless farmers. Gaius also secured legislation that would enable the equites to obtain various public offices. The Senate was infuriated, accused the Gracchi of unconstitutional behavior, and secured their murder. The failure of the Gracchi was a prelude to the last century of the republic, an agonizing period of further expansion, civil war, social revolt, and corruption, and a period in which the Senate showed itself incapable of ruling an empire and unfit for the high public trust it had held for so long. By its corrupt and inept behavior the Senate killed itself and the republic.

That the Gracchi could secure such legislation from the assembly of the people and that they could win such support indicated what leaders could do if they had the backing of the Roman legions. Henceforth Rome lived from crisis to crisis as the Senate lost control of the state and as its former power was contended for and usurped by a succession of strong men. Reluctant to give citizenship to people who lived outside Rome and the surrounding area, the Senate eventually provoked the Social War of 90 to 88 B.C. that ravaged and divided Italy. Though victorious, Rome had to extend citizenship to the Italian people. But even this concession was hedged by the condition that one had to come to Rome to vote. The Senate seemed unaware of what had happened politically and socially to Rome in the past century and behaved as it had prior to the Punic Wars.

Even more serious than its failure to see the wisdom of social and economic reform and the strength and unity to be gained from extending full political privileges to all Italians was the Senate's incapacity to see that its members were using war and conquest only for personal gain, that this was undermining confidence in its ability to govern and leading rapidly to its loss of control over the conduct of war. The legionaries and people began to turn to the generals for leadership, for necessary action in government, and for social and economic reform. A first sign of this development came late in the second century B.C. during a war fought in northern Africa against Jugurtha, king of Numidia. Under aristocratic generals there were only defeats, and the war dragged on and on. It eventually became known that Jugurtha was bribing the corrupt aristocratic generals. He is reputed, in fact, to have described Rome as "a city for sale." Such corruption and inefficiency resulted in the election of an equestrian as consul, a man called Marius who gave the people what they wanted—a swift victory over Jugurtha whom he dragged back to Rome as a prisoner. Marius then marched north into southern France and swiftly defeated the Cimbri and Teutones, Germanic tribes who had threatened to invade Italy. A hero, Marius underscored the corruption and inefficiency of the senators. Despite the rule that no consul should succeed himself, Marius held six successive consulships. The Senate was impotent against his popularity and it should be noted that his army, rather than formed by traditional conscription, had been recruited and trained by him, and that the legions that had fought under him were loyal to him rather than to the Senate, a development that did not augur well for the Senate's future. The Senate recognized that any popular general could recruit an army of discontented and landless men and, in return for promises of booty and land, command their loyalty. In 88 B.C. the aristocratic general Sulla marched on Rome with his army and drove out Marius and his supporters. No sooner had Sulla departed for the East to fight Mithridates, king of Parthia in Asia Minor, than Marius came back with an army and slew numerous senators and supporters of Sulla. Upon his victorious return in 84 B.C., however, Sulla threw out Marius and systematically proscribed and killed thousands of men. Sulla boasted that he had done all this to restore the power of the Senate, but all could see that henceforth the destiny of the republic lay in the hands of men like Marius and Sulla.

Powerless before these new men of iron, the Senate sent them out to conquer new provinces in order to open up fresh areas for revenue and corruption. By the first century B.C. it is obvious that all Romans, regardless of class, looked upon war and more provinces as a lucrative affair; Rome was in the business of imperialism. It became a way of life to live on the spoils of war and the money extorted from provinces. The successful general Pompey added the Asiatic provinces of Bithynia, Cilicia, and Syria. The famous prosecution by Cicero against Verres, the corrupt governor of Sicily, illustrated how dishonest and parasitic was the whole Roman administration. Obviously this unfortunate trend had to be stopped, the government reorganized, efficiency introduced, social and economic reform accomplished, and civil war ended. There was need for a leader who would use his power for these ends. Such was Julius Caesar who, after a rather ordinary political career prior to 60 B.C., moved swiftly to the forefront.

After serving as consul and forming a political alliance with Pompey, Caesar turned to the conquest of Gaul, which he completed by 49 B.C. He now had enough military experience and enough knowledge of politics to know his objective—to be the sole ruler of Rome. Pompey, suspecting this, attempted to thwart Caesar by allying himself with the Senate. He proved no match for his opponent, however, and retreated before the advance of Caesar into Italy, going to Greece to recruit a larger army. In 48 B.C. the two met at Pharsalus and Caesar was victorious. Pompey fled to Egypt where he was promptly assassinated, leaving Caesar master of the Roman world. Caesar stamped out the rest of the Pompeian group and reorganized the provinces between 48 and 45 B.C. and then began to revamp the government so as to end the republic. He quickly obtained powers making him the absolute ruler of Rome, a dictator who could push through necessary laws, control the army and foreign policy, and head the state religion. With these powers he reformed municipal government, pushed colonization, reduced provincial taxation, introduced his famous calendar, and extended citizenship, a move that contributed to the romanization of the provinces. Despite his power and popularity Caesar still had enemies in the Senate. On the Ides of March, 44 B.C., he was assassinated by a group of conspirators led by Brutus and Cassius who declared that they did so for the restoration of the republic. This rash and ill-conceived act only returned Rome to the agony she had known earlier in the century.

Immediately after Caesar's death three men allied themselves in a triumvirate to oppose the senatorial party led by Brutus and Cassius. These men were Mark Antony, a political henchman of Caesar; Lepidus, another political associate; and Gaius Octavius (Octavian), the grandnephew and adopted son and heir of Caesar. In 42 B.C. the triumvirate defeated Brutus and Cassius, both of whom committed suicide. During the next six years Lepidus was pushed out of power while Antony assumed control of the eastern part of Rome's possessions and Octavius ruled over the western part. After 36 B.C. the two contended for mastery of the Roman world.

Antony steadily lost influence at Rome, especially after he courted and married Cleopatra, queen of Egypt, and oriented himself to the East. Octavius meanwhile increased his strength in the West and in 32 B.C. declared war on Cleopatra and Antony. After the naval battle of Actium in 31 B.C. where their fleet was defeated, Antony and Cleopatra took their lives while being pursued in Egypt. In 30 B.C. Octavius annexed Egypt and in 29 B.C. returned to Rome as the sole master of the Mediterranean world which he was to reorganize into the majestic Roman Empire.

CULTURE AND ART

The greatest achievements of the Roman Republic were political and military. Despite the failure of the Roman Senate to provide stable government during the last century of the republic and to meet the responsibility of rule over an empire, the Romans, it must be admitted, had a more realistic understanding of politics and war than the Greeks, but they were much less gifted in arts, letters, and contemplative areas of knowledge such as philosophy. There was little Roman culture until the third century B.C. Prior to then what evidence has survived points to some inferior Latin prose and poetry, little artistic or architectural activity, and no philosophical speculation. Religion was simple and polytheistic, much like that of the Greeks prior to the Hellenistic period. Only in the third century B.C. when the Romans conquered the Greek city-states of southern Italy and Sicily, and later when they occupied Greece, did they become aware of and begin to appreciate culture. They subsequently developed a proud culture that was, however, fundamentally an adaptation of the Greek.

As the Romans came into contact with the superior civilization of the East and as Greek slaves and captives poured into Rome, Greek customs and culture began to work a real change. The traditional public religion of the old gods and goddesses was retained as a buttress for civic spirit, but it lost ground as the lower classes embraced the oriental cults such as the mystery religions, and as the educated Romans turned to the Greek philosophies, especially Epicureanism and Stoicism. The Roman poet and philosopher Lucretius (99–55 B.C.) wrote his great poem *De Rerum Natura* to explain the ethical and scientific ideas of Epicureanism. The poem attempts to show the folly of superstition and fear of death and advances an interesting theory on creation. Most cultivated Romans, however, preferred the more practical Stoicism. The idea that all men were united by a spark of reason and governed by a natural law of reason appealed to men forging a great empire and interested in laws just and practical for Roman and non-Roman. In his philosophic works *De Republica* and *De Legibus* Cicero explained Stoic philosophy to the Romans; in other writings he illustrated the efficacy of Stoic principles for the guidance of one's life. Through the interest of the Romans, Stoic ideas found their way into Christian thought and exerted a vital influence on Roman legal principles.

There was little of value in art and architecture until the imperial period. The Romans continued to apply the interesting Etruscan techniques of portraiture and sculpture and borrowed the three styles of Greek architecture, their favorite being the ornate Corinthian which they further embellished. The Romans did not build their first theater until 55 B.C., but meanwhile they were developing the marvelous round arch, which we still call Roman, and employing concrete and stucco to good effect.

Surely one of the grand legacies of the Romans to the western world is the beautiful and expressive but sane and restrained Latin language. The Roman talent for stating ideas clearly and simply is already evident in the republican period. Excellence in Latin literature came first in drama, probably because the Romans could better understand ideas expressed orally than in written form. The models were Greek, chiefly the Hellenistic New Comedy of Menander. Plautus (254–184 B.C.) wrote very earthy and raucous comedies, in contrast to Terence (195–159 B.C.) who expressed Greek themes of comedy in a less rough and more refined manner.

As the Romans began to appreciate the shadings of the written word, drama was joined by poetry and prose. Catullus (84–54 B.C.), the most accomplished poet of the republic, excelled in lyrical love poems. Influenced by the Hellenistic poet Callimachus, Catullus polished the Latin language and expressed his thoughts with exquisite grace and style. With him began the perfection of meter and rhythm that culminated in the great poets of the early imperial period.

The greatest excellence in literature during the republic was achieved in prose which afforded the practical Romans a vehicle better adapted for the expression of their ideas and emotions. Julius Caesar in his *Commentaries on the Gallic Wars* and *Commentaries on the Civil War* demonstrated, in language terse, economical, and logical, his mastery of historical writing. Always in control of his thoughts, he constructs graphic descriptions of battles, memorably pictures the Germans and Gauls, and shrewdly evaluates character. Less objective and more propagandistic are the short histories of Sallust (86–34 B.C.) on the Jugurthine War and the conspiracy of Catiline. The acknowledged master of prose, however, was Cicero (106–43 B.C.). Living in an age when effective speeches could sway the Senate, change policy, lead to the conviction of corrupt officials, and even destroy political enemies, Cicero developed Latin rhetoric to its highest form. His famous orations against Verres, the corrupt governor of Sicily, employed every rhetorical device conceivable to expose Verres and to show the Senate what it had to lose by permitting such men to represent it. In his prosecution of Catiline, Cicero developed a case in which evidence presented in successive speeches incontestably proved Catiline's complicity in a conspiracy to overthrow the republic. So fiercely did Cicero attack Antony that at Antony's instigation he was proscribed and killed. Fortunately the survival of some eight hundred of Cicero's letters to various friends portray him more intimately as a warm and humane person, chatty and even at times gossipy. Cicero was obviously responsible for making the letter an accepted form of literature. Besides the two major philosophic works cited earlier Cicero wrote the shorter philosophical essays *On Friendship, On Duty,* and *On Old Age,* introducing Stoic and other Greek philosophical principles to the Romans. The work of no other prose writer, not even the epigrammatic Tacitus, equaled the prose style of Cicero; he was a master of the Latin language, attuned to sound, rhythm, and emphasis, sensitive to the value and function of each word. Less than successful as a statesman and sometimes less than admirable as a man, Cicero is chiefly remembered for perfecting Latin and molding it into a superb literary language.

3. The Roman Empire

THE ROMAN REPUBLIC could win wars and conquer lands, but it had failed in ruling the empire it had acquired and in establishing a form of government that provided peace and security and commanded the respect and loyalty of its citizens. This task faced Octavius in 29 B.C. He had to succeed or meet the fate of numerous predecessors who had struggled for power. Evidence of his success was the magnificent Roman Empire that enjoyed two centuries of unparalleled peace and prosperity and that maintained its political sway over the western world despite weakness and decline for almost another two hundred years.

CHANGE UNDER OCTAVIUS

Recognizing that he could not dispose immediately of all republican institutions, Octavius rapidly assumed control over all of them while creating the impression that he still relied upon and cooperated with them. Behind this diplomatic facade Octavius soon wielded a power absolute and autocratic which was implied in the title that he bestowed upon himself—Augustus. As first man in the state Octavius, now called Augustus, also had himself named *princeps,* but his most significant title was *imperator,* meaning victorious general, which under him came to mean general or commander-in-chief of the armies for life and, ultimately, emperor. With the army under his control Augustus could reorganize the government. He retained the Senate but merely as a sounding board, as a municipal council for the city of Rome, and as an order of social recognition. To introduce new laws he usurped the authority of the tribunes. To facilitate control over public religion he exercised the office of *pontifex maximus* (chief priest) and initiated a policy in which religion was used to bolster civic loyalty to the state and devotion to

THE ROMAN EMPEROR AU-
GUSTUS. This statue which is in
the Vatican Museum is the best
known of the statues of the emperor Augustus. It imparts clearly
the firm and decisive character of
Rome's first emperor.

himself as its supreme head. No aspect of power, no institution escaped his attention or control; his authority was unchallenged. When he died in A.D. 14 the concept of imperial rule was so firmly implanted and had proved so successful that it prevailed for centuries. Augustus had wrought a tremendous revolution, a necessary one if Rome was to rule the civilized world in peace and enable its subjects to reap the benefits of membership in a huge empire.

While establishing his power, Augustus was also reorganizing the military and civil administration. At Rome he instituted an imperial bodyguard known as the praetorian guard. After a few forays in the Rhine area he committed Rome to a strong defense of its existing frontiers. At small fortresses (*castella*) and large camps (*castra*), located strategically, he stationed legions and auxiliary forces. He set the military strength at thirty legions of five thousand men each. The legionary was a professional soldier who had to be a citizen and had to serve for twenty-five years. Supplementing this elite force were auxiliary units of varying size; members of the auxiliary forces did not have to be citizens and were usually rewarded with citizenship at the end of their service. Such was the military organization until the empire began to weaken in the third century. Except during the reign of Claudius (41–54) when Britain was conquered up to the border of Scotland and made into a province, and during the reign of Trajan when there was expansion in the Danube area and Mesopotamia, the frontiers of the empire remained basically as they were under Augustus. His other innovation, a permanent fleet to eradicate piracy, made the Mediterranean a peaceful highway of trade and communication and contributed to the unification of the empire. When Rome eventually lost control of the Mediterranean and it was no longer the central link, unity disappeared and the empire disintegrated.

Augustus permitted the Senate to appoint governors to the older and peaceful provinces, but to others more recently absorbed and more strategic militarily, he appointed his own men. He was, of course, the master of all the provinces with the governors responsible for defense, order, administration, taxation, and justice. They and subordinate officials came increasingly from the equestrian class rather than the senatorial because Augustus was more certain of their loyalty. He thereby created a new civil service loyal to him and efficient in the performance of its duties. To encourage honest government Augustus strived to keep in touch with his provincial officials by augmenting the already excellent network of roads and operating a post system that facilitated swift communication. In the cities (*civitates*) local municipal government remained in the hands of the urban inhabitants. Though most of the municipal constitutions resembled Rome's, government was the responsibility of local officials who came from the wealthy and socially prominent citizens. Whoever possessed a certain amount of wealth was automatically enrolled on a list of *curiales,* a situation that made him eligible for membership on the municipal council (*curia*) and for other political appointments. For two centuries the curiales gave the cities efficient government. They were generous with their time and talent, and their money helped to provide the roads, theaters, amphitheaters, baths, marketplaces, and public spectacles. As long as the curiales were prosperous and devoted public servants, the cities of the empire thrived; when, however, the curiales began to suffer economic and social reverses, the cities reflected this trouble, lost their vitality, and began to decline. No explanation of the decline of the Roman Empire can be divorced from the decline of the cities.

The more the people of the empire held in common, the stronger were the bonds holding it together. Augustus furthered the romanization of his empire in various ways. He founded new cities throughout the provinces and gradually extended citizenship. These policies were continued by most of his successors; by an imperial decree in 212 all inhabitants of the empire born free were declared citizens. An even stronger bond was the system of law that was adopted throughout the empire and ultimately became the foundation of most modern legal systems in Europe. Under the republic all citizens had been subject to the law of citizens or the civil law (*ius civile*), but as the republic expanded the law had to be adjusted to meet the legal needs of peoples who were not Roman and of situations where legal settlements had to be made between Romans and foreigners. The judges (*praetors*) responsible for adjudicating differences between Romans and non-Romans quite sensibly resorted to making decisions on the basis of what would be fair to all men regardless of their own civil law. In this way arose universal principles of law, a law of men (*ius gentium*), that expanded with the emergence of Roman power. Gradually the equitable principles of the *ius gentium* were borrowed by the *ius civile* until there was an amalgamation. The Roman jurisprudents responsible for legal decisions very intelligently adopted the view that the law to be viable should be flexible and reinterpreted. Imperial edicts continued this practice. Roman lawyers were also convinced that behind the *ius civile* and *ius gentium* were universal principles of law founded on reason. These universal reasonable principles were regarded as the natural law of the universe (*ius naturale*) binding upon all men. Such legal ideas came from the Stoic teachings that a universal, natural law of reason united all men in justice and brotherhood. After two centuries all free men of the empire were cognizant of their common citizenry and of the universality of law.

This, then, was the imperial edifice begun by Augustus and completed by his successors during the next two centuries. So well did the imperial government function that even an incompetent emperor could not upset its routine. It could even function temporarily without a head. The matter of imperial succession was, however, a problem. Augustus realized that he must designate a successor, and preferably one from his family, if the new empire was to escape civil war and a resurgence of senatorial power. He finally settled upon his stepson Tiberius who succeeded him at his death in A.D. 14. Tiberius and his successors, known as the Julio-Claudian emperors, were unfortunate in not having close or suitable heirs, a situation that contributed to senatorial interference and even to pressures from the praetorian guard. In A.D. 68 Nero, the last of the Julio-Claudians, proved so unbearable that revolt flaring up at Rome forced him to take his life. Immediately numerous generals competed for the purple and, with anarchy imminent, the general Vespasian gained control and inaugurated the Flavian dynasty that ruled until 96. From 96 to 180 was the age of the Good Emperors when the empire was in the hands of the exceptionably able emperors Nerva, Trajan, Hadrian, Antoninus Pius, and Marcus Aurelius. These men solved the problem of succession by adopting the ablest man in the imperial government and designating him successor.

SOCIAL AND ECONOMIC LIFE

While war and conquest may temporarily benefit certain sectors of an economy and bring fortunes to a few men, an economy must have peace and security to flourish. The *Pax Romanum* of the empire provided this condition. The Mediterranean, centered in the empire, symbolized the new era of peace and unity. It was the central boulevard for the interchange of goods and ideas from the Strait of Gibraltar to the Middle East. All around its shores were men of the same citizenship, obedient to the same law, enjoying similar privileges, using a uniform coinage, and bound together by a common language and culture. Stimulated by such favorable conditions, the economy prospered; provincial, interprovincial, and foreign trade increased; the standard of living improved. Even in the outermost limits of the empire, such as the province of Britain, the new peace had an influence and introduced the culture of the Mediterranean world. It must be emphasized, however, that, economically, the western part of the empire never equalled the eastern with its older traditions and greater savoir faire. Greece and the Middle East remained the center of trade and industry. Here were the largest cities with the bankers, traders, and skilled artisans; here were the money centers and the producing centers of most of the finished goods. The West, though excelling in some products, remained essentially agrarian, a supplier of raw materials, a consumer. Ultimately, as we shall see, this unbalanced economy produced a severe economic strain in the West and may have been responsible for the decline of the empire in the West.

As previously, the rare items came from outside. From the East came spices, gems, and silk goods; from Africa came ivory, gold, and rare woods; from northern Europe and Russia came furs, amber, and slaves. Trade within the empire was based mostly on necessities. Typical items were grain, olive oil, wine, lumber, metals, cloth, and paper. From Syria came exquisite glass and purple dyes. Italy developed a fine glazed pottery superseded eventually by that of Gaul. All these goods were free from tariffs and subject only to local and minimal excise taxes.

An important element of the imperial economy is that as many goods as possible were produced locally and that few goods were brought in from other regions. This meant that, despite the favorable conditions for trade, the economy remained local and in a sense self-sufficient, a circumstance that limited the volume of trade and restricted industry to small-scale operations. Mines and quarries used large numbers of men, mostly slaves, but other industries were generally small. Here and there an entrepreneur would organize a small factory by concentrating some potters or weavers in one building. Generally an artisan fabricated a particular product in his shop, where he also lived, and sold it there. Technologically there was little advance over previous centuries. Labor was so plentiful and cheap that there was no incentive to apply other forms of power or to develop machines to lighten burdens and produce goods more rapidly. Such advance came only later in the Middle Ages.

While trade and much of the manufacturing was controlled by men from the eastern part of the empire, less productive but highly remunerative economic activities centered in Rome. Aristocrats and equestrians derived much wealth from lending money and contracting for the collection of taxes and the construction of public works. Such activity was of course parasitical and did not really produce goods or more money. Since there was a prevailing tradition in the West that aristocrats and other men who aspired to social and political status must own land, the West remained primarily agrarian with most of its inhabitants sustained by the soil. The large estate continued to prevail, and rich men regarded land as giving status and guaranteeing a safe and easy income. Overseers assumed complete responsibility for the management. They supervised the slaves, rented out plots of land to free farmers in return for rents, marketed the agrarian products such as grain, olive oil, and wool, and rendered the accounts to the absentee landlord who used his estate only as a place to vacation. Specializing in single crops or in sheep, the estate employed reasonably progressive farming techniques. Rotation of crops and the planting of crops good for the soil became customary. The large estates eventually absorbed all small farms. The small farmers sold their land to the great landowners and either rented plots from them or joined the proletariat of the cities. Those remaining on the land barely subsisted, while a few great landlords reaped the economic benefits. The great landed estate so typical of the Middle Ages was already well developed.

Society remained much as it was during the late republic except for the old senatorial families. Those who opposed the imperial regime were gradually liquidated; others died out. Their place was taken by a new senatorial aristocracy loyal to the emperors. Generally the new senators were appointed by the emperors from the equestrian class which ranked just below the senatorial and provided most of the officials in the imperial administration. Another tendency clearly marked by the second century was the recruitment of senators from the provinces. No longer did Rome monopolize the senatorial aristocracy; it now came from the curiales who already formed a local municipal aristocracy. To attain the exalted rank of imperial senator became the goal of the curiales. Aware that their local accomplishments could result in such promotion, they zealously governed their cities, and those who attracted the attention of the emperor were rewarded. This broader recruitment of members of the senatorial class worked to the imperial profit because it provided the emperor with a new, loyal aristocracy and established closer contacts with local government.

Below the senatorial and equestrian aristocracy were men who had made fortunes from banking, trade, and industry. Often they had worked their way up from slave to freedman and were sometimes successful enough to achieve equestrian rank. Below them were the small merchants, professionals such as teachers and scribes, artisans, and laborers who formed a poor middle class, a step above that part of the urban population composed of unemployed laborers and the growing number of unsuccessful farmers. At the bottom were the slaves. If educated,

MOSAIC DECORATION FROM POMPEII. In the wealthy society which flourished at Pompeii mosaic designs such as this one, which shows parrots drinking at a fountain while a cat lashes his tail angrily but ineffectively below them, were used to decorate the luxurious private villas.

skilled, and talented, a slave could aspire to freedom and subsequent social mobility; if unskilled, he could look forward only to hard labor under wretched conditions and to early death.

Most urban residents lived miserably. Their abodes were humble wooden shacks, poorly ventilated and heated, without sanitary facilities and generally overcrowded. Whole quarters of these squalid huts commonly burned out as, for example, during the great fire of Rome in A.D. 64. Yet from archaeological evidence in such cities as Pompeii and Herculaneum it is obvious that a fortunate few had a high standard of living. Their spacious houses of stone, brick, and plaster with tiled roofs surrounded open courtyards decorated with pools, fountains, and plantings. Sculptured figures were tastefully arranged throughout the houses, and frescoes and mosaics decorated the walls and floors. In the imperial period when the Romans began to appreciate the value of city planning, much of Rome was rebuilt, especially quarters with public buildings and imperial residences such as the Forum and Golden Palace of Nero. New cities were laid out in square and rectangular blocks. Squares, marketplaces, forums, and public buildings were so located as to be within easy range of the inhabitants. Most of the streets were paved and a good water supply was insured by bringing the water from mountains via beautiful aqueducts like the Pont du Gard near Nîmes in France. Roman cities were designed to be lived in; here the classes of wealth could enjoy a stimulating life, withdrawing to the country only during hot weather or for a change of scenery.

CULTURE AND ART

While the last two centuries before Christ saw the perfection of Latin as a literary language, the apogee of literary achievement came during the reign of Augustus. The superb compositions in prose and poetry were in a sense expressive of the new imperial era, and some of them glorified the new age of peace. Augustus realized that literature could buttress his strength, that it could express and extol the ideas and values he desired to engender. Epic and history could paint the glorious past of Rome and draw elevating lessons. The value of civic duty, of devotion to the man responsible for peace and stability, could find expression in a variety of literary forms. So celebrated a patron of the arts was Maecenas, the trusted friend and advisor of Augustus, that his name has become synonymous with literary patronage. He requested Virgil to write the *Eclogues,* a collection of pastorals, and gave Horace the Sabine farm celebrated in that poet's verse.

The most accomplished poet was Virgil (70–19 B.C.). His long poem the *Aeneid,* modeled upon the Homeric epics, praised the Roman virtues of duty, courage, and patriotism while presenting an historical theme that associated the beginning of Rome with Troy. Like Horace, Virgil also sought to inculcate an appreciation of the value of rural life. In his *Georgics* the farmer is the hero who combines his simple life on the soil with fighting and makes Rome the master of the world. Under the brilliant touch of Horace (65–8 B.C.) the short lyrical Latin poem and the more formal ode attained their highest form. His love lyrics praising Lydia are models; no other compositions quite achieve their clarity and balance. Ovid (43 B.C.–A.D. 18) fashioned his love poetry after the Greek elegy. His *Ars Amatoria,* a collection of satirical and practical poetry explaining the art of love, became a great favorite with medieval poets writing in Latin and the vernacular. Another great poem, the *Metamorphoses,* which was a collection of two hundred and fifty stories taken from classical mythology introduced later generations to the mythological love themes of the classical world.

The finest prose of the Augustan period was the *History of Rome* by Livy (59 B.C.–A.D. 17), of which there is extant not quite a fourth of the original one hundred and forty-two books recounting Rome's history from Romulus and Remus, the semi-historical founders of Rome, down to 9 B.C. Livy, like Virgil, hoped to rekindle patriotism and a sense of duty by telling the Romans about the glorious achievements of their ancestors. Because it fluctuates between sober, verifiable facts and legend, the history of Livy, though beautifully written, does not rank with those of Thucydides or Polybius. Yet it is certainly the finest history of Rome in the Latin language and its view of Roman history underlies modern interpretations.

Besides these notable writers of the Augustan Age were others of great talent such as the poets Tibullus (54?–18 B.C.) and Propertius (fl. 25 B.C.), and the essayist and rhetorician Pliny the Elder (A.D. 23–79). In the period from Augustus to A.D. 180, the so-called Silver Age of Latin literature, there were fewer accomplished writers and the quality of writing declined. While the language retained its excellence, what was expressed was less original, repetitious, and shallow. This was the age of the epigram, a form very appropriate to the taut and terse Latin language. In satirizing aristocratic society Juvenal (50–130) and Martial (40–104) excelled in epigrammatic poetry. The epigram achieved grandeur, however, with the historian Tacitus (55–117) who could create in a few epigrammatic sentences an atmosphere, an effect, or a feeling which other authors could not achieve in pages. In one sentence, for example, Tacitus creates an adverse feeling against the emperor Tiberius: "It was a policy peculiar to Tiberius to shelter under venerable names the villainies of modern invention." In spite of bias and lack of perspective the *Annals* and *Histories* of Tacitus dealing with the period from 14 to 96 are the best sources for early imperial history; without them we could not understand the Julio-Claudian emperors, their court, their officials, and the senatorial aristocracy. Tacitus, who detested the Julio-Claudians, concentrated upon them and Rome with only occasional references to the empire. In the *Agricola* (name of a Roman general) Tacitus gives a reasonably balanced account of the conquest of Britain, and in the *Germania,* still our most valuable source for early Germanic customs and institutions, he presents a very interesting and detailed description of the Germans living on the other side of the Rhine and Danube. Roman erudition is best displayed in Pliny the Elder who wrote a compendium of knowledge known as the *Natural History.*

In the eastern provinces, meanwhile, much writing continued in Greek. Generally inferior to that of the Hellenic and Hellenistic ages, some, like that of Plutarch (46–120), was well phrased and interesting in its approach. Plutarch's famous *Parallel Lives,* which provide some of the best information available on distinguished figures of classical antiquity, is a collection of biographies of great Greeks and Romans arranged to facilitate comparison between the two cultures by pairing off a Greek and a Roman general, or a Greek and a Roman statesman.

With few exceptions Roman imperial art and architecture were adaptations of the Greek, especially the Hellenistic, forms. Seldom did a Roman art form equal any of the Greek. Occasionally the Romans excelled in sculpture. Imperial sculpture, like the later republican, had pleasing qualities of realism and naturalism; the sculptured figures and the portraits on coins exude individualism. Later, as the emperors sought to glorify themselves, to build up their imperial grandeur, and to promote themselves as divine, realism disappears and idealized forms predominate. The triumphal arches of the emperors Vespasian and Trajan, typical of the huge monumental sculpture of the imperial period, provided ample space for

PORTION OF COLUMN OF TRAJAN. Completed in 114 A.D., this 125-foot column is embellished with reliefs representing events of Trajan's two Dacian campaigns. Twenty-three spiral bands of carved marble cover the column shaft; the Emperor Trajan is buried within the base.

memorializing in stone the deeds and triumphs of the emperors. The vast palaces, altars, and columns presented further opportunity for sculpture, mosaics, and frescoes.

Roman architecture was chiefly noteworthy for its gargantuan proportions and its frequently pretentious and florid ornamentation. The Romans found the ornate Hellenistic style more appealing than the simple Hellenic of the fifth century B.C. The complicated Corinthian column was very popular. Too often there was a mélange of styles, as on the huge Colosseum constructed late in the first century A.D.; its three levels of arches were decorated by Doric, Ionic, and Corinthian columns. Other buildings were overlaid with superficial entablatures. The Romans, too imbued with the desire to achieve grandeur, forgot about proportion and simplicity except in the more practical construction of camps, aqueducts, bridges, amphitheaters, and basilicas. Here, using their famous arches which they regarded only as essential supporting elements of masonry and therefore made no attempt to ornament, they achieved a simple but powerful effect. Such arches support the celebrated Pont du Gard at Nîmes and are evident in numerous public buildings. From these arches eventually developed the Romanesque and Gothic styles of the Middle Ages. In some public buildings the Romans also experimented with the dome, which became a typical feature of Byzantine architecture.

Vitruvius (fl. late first century B.C.), who served Augustus as an engineer and architect, wrote a most useful work on architectural principles, describing the materials and techniques of construction, the essential knowledge required by the architect, and the style employed in public and private edifices. This work indicates that Roman scientific, mathematical, and technological knowledge rested almost solely upon Greek achievements. Except for Roman innovation in brick and concrete construction the machinery used and the building techniques and materials employed came from the Greeks. Human labor continued to provide the power.

Ptolemy (fl. A.D. 150), astronomer, mathematician, and geographer of the second century, wrote in Greek the last important book on mathematics produced in the ancient world. In the *Almagest* he digested the mathematical knowledge of his Greek predecessors and added to it a masterly section on trigonometry. What he wrote became the basis for mathematical knowledge for the next thousand years. In his *Geography* he made a map of the earth which he broke down into circles noting latitude and longitude. His contemporary, Galen of Pergamum (130–200), composed a medical encyclopedia making available all existing medical knowledge. For the next fifteen centuries medicine was essentially Galenic. The work of

THE COLOSSEUM AT ROME. This huge amphitheater, traditionally the symbol of the greatness of Rome, was built by the emperor Vespasian in A.D. 79. It had space for 45,000 spectators.

Ptolemy and Galen, though useful, indicates how rarely one finds originality with the Romans. What original work was done was by Greeks; the gift of the Romans was the ability to assimilate knowledge and to use it.

RELIGION AND PHILOSOPHY

Although Augustus did what he could to revive interest in the traditional religion of the Romans, even building temples to the gods and lavishly supporting festivals and processions dedicated to various gods, he realized that these ancient and local beliefs were passé and must be replaced by more meaningful ones that would symbolize imperial unity and devotion to the person responsible. He borrowed, therefore, the practices of the Hellenistic monarchs who had cultivated emperor-worship. He pushed himself so skillfully as a god in the eastern provinces where tradition for such belief was strong that before his death all the East regarded him not only as a divine being but as a god. In the West where there was no such tradition he did not press the belief but did what he could to inculcate the idea that in him there was a spark of the divine. Toward the end of the first century, even in the West, the emperors were accepted as gods and emperor-worship subsequently became a state religion.

Emperor-worship, however valuable in engendering devotion to the head of state, did not satisfy the deeper longings of men for spiritual comfort and support. Like their republican predecessors, most intellectuals embraced the Stoic philosophy. Members now of an empire united by common bonds of language, institutions, and culture, these men were intrigued by a philosophy which taught that all men were bound together by participation in the reason of a universal and supreme natural law. Building upon the precepts of the Greek Stoics as explained by Cicero and Seneca the Younger (4 B.C.–A.D. 65), Roman intellectuals regarded Stoicism as a guide to a reasonable and dignified life of achievement. It assisted them in controlling their emotions, it justified devotion to work and loyalty to the empire, and it tied together all men of reason no matter what their social position. Epictetus (fl. A.D. 75), a crippled slave at the court of Nero, expressed his understanding of Stoicism in reflections and precepts collected in the *Discourses*. He counseled men not to complain and fret about conditions over which they had no control or to aspire to power that could not be theirs. The free and happy man valued only that which he could control; all else must be endured with good courage. Similar were the reflections of the emperor Marcus Aurelius (A.D. 121–180) in his *Meditations*. Although he had power, he had with it almost overburdening and ceaseless duties. But such was his lot; his duty was to fulfil the obligations of his position.

Stoicism was a noble creed for men with tough, educated minds. But what of the masses who needed help from beyond themselves? These people increasingly embraced the oriental mystery religions with their hope of suprahuman assistance and reward of eternal life. Demeter, goddess of the harvest, symbolizing fertility and rebirth of life, appealed to men. A Phrygian goddess known as Magna Mater drew unto her others because, through her powerful love, she had restored to life the slain Attis. From Egypt came the goddess Isis who had given life to Osiris. From Persia came the cult of Mithraism with its ritual of the *taurobolium* whereby devotees—all men—were purified through baptism with the blood of a bull. These were typical of the many mystery religions winning the devotion of the masses whose miserable lot and life on earth were unlikely to improve.

The empire, while bettering the lives of its subjects through peace and security, had deprived most of them of any faith in their own ability and worth. As the emperor and his huge empire became all powerful and important, the individual felt himself to be a minute object tossed about on a vast ocean by distant forces over which he had no control; he could no longer believe in local institutions or identify himself with them, and yet he desperately needed to believe in something and to be reassured that somebody cared about him. The traditional mystery religions, despite their appeal, often failed to satisfy his spiritual needs and aspirations. Another religion, also from the East, was to proclaim a faith and message of hope so sympathetic that ultimately it became the church triumphant in the empire. This new faith was Christianity. At the moment what is more significant than the triumph of the Christian faith in the empire is its origin and growth during the first two centuries of the empire. Much of the spiritual heritage of Christianity came from Judaism. Jesus, called by his followers Christ, was born around 4 B.C. in Bethlehem of Judaea and died there around A.D. 33. This humble man who spent his life in Judaea and was nurtured upon the precepts of Judaism came to believe, as did some other sects, that one day God would give the Jews a saviour or Messiah to deliver them from their oppressors. He believed also in the brotherly love preached by still other sects. Although relatively little is known about the short life of Christ, it is certain that His words and actions distinguished Him as a remarkable man. Around Him gathered a group of followers, disciples, who believed that He was the Messiah, the Son of God, that after His crucifixion God had briefly restored Him to life and that He had then ascended to heaven but would some day appear again as a saviour on the earth. They and others told stories of His love for men and of His promise to bring all men to His Father in heaven, until soon it was thought that whoever believed in Christ would be saved and gain eternal life.

At first limited to Jews, Christianity, through the preaching and missionary work of its disciples, particularly Paul who proclaimed that Christ's teachings were for all men, Jew and Gentile, became a faith for all people, men and women, rich and poor, powerful and weak. By the end of the first century it had swept around the Mediterranean and had taken root in all the cities. Churches were

THE ROMAN EMPEROR MAR-
CUS AURELIUS. Shown here is
the head from a bronze equestrian statue of the last of the
Good Emperors. The sculptor
captured the serious and pur-
poseful personality of the famous
Stoic emperor.

organized by the believers, a doctrine and a ritual developed, and even a hierarchy of clergy began to take form. An embryonic form of government already existed. The unity of the empire and the ease of communication made it simple for Christians to travel about, talk about the faith, and develop common beliefs. Because of their special beliefs and ritual the Christians attracted attention as a group different and clannish. This was not unique, but the fact that Christians would only worship God was unusual, a circumstance that marked them as a people who would not worship the emperor and who might, therefore, be subversive. After all, did they not proclaim Christ as their saviour and leader? Despite this suspicion the Christians suffered less than subsequent legend alleges. There was a brief persecution of Christians in Rome by Nero in A.D. 64, but the reasons are not clear; they may have served the emperor as scapegoats. More surprising was a persecution during the reign of Marcus Aurelius who seemed persuaded that the growing numbers of Christians might be a disruptive element to imperial unity and the reasonable sovereignty of the natural law.

Christianity, whatever its early vicissitudes, had attained by the third century a sway over the people greater than any other philosophy or faith. Like the Latin language, Roman law, imperial institutions, and Graeco-Roman culture, Christianity had become a significant, vital aspect of imperial life. When the empire disintegrated in the following centuries, Christianity was the only force and institution to survive and to pass on the accomplishment of classical antiquity to the succeeding centuries known as the Middle Ages.

Further Reading

Two excellent surveys of the Hellenistic period are by *W. W. Tarn and C. T. Griffith, *Hellenistic Civilization,* 3rd ed. (London, 1952); and M. Cary, *The Legacy of Alexander: A History of the Greek World from 323 to 146 B.C.* (London, 1932). The Greek penetration into the East is studied by W. W. Tarn, *The Greeks in Bactria and India* (Cambridge, 1951). Hellenistic social and economic developments are treated in the massive study of M. I. Rostovtzeff, *Social and Economic History of the Hellenistic World* (Oxford, 1941), Vols. I–III. On the achievements of Alexander see *W. W. Tarn, *Alexander the Great* (Cambridge, 1948); and *U. Wilcken, *Alexander the Great* (New York, 1932). All students should read Plutarch's life of Alexander.

Hellenistic philosophy is well explained in the following books: E. Bevan, *Stoics and Sceptics* (Oxford, 1913); C. Bailey, *Epicurus* (Oxford, 1926); and D. R. Dudley, *A History of Cynicism* (London, 1937). On science see the translations of sources assembled by M. R. Cohen and I. E. Drabkin, *A Source Book in Greek Science* (New York, 1948); C. Singer, *Greek Biology and Greek Medicine* (Oxford, 1922) and *A History of Ancient Technology* (Oxford, 1956), Vol. II. Other aspects of Hellenistic culture are discussed in H. I. Marrou, *A History of Education in Antiquity* (New York, 1956); and M. Bieber, *The Sculpture of the Hellenistic Age* (New York, 1955).

Of the many histories of the Roman Republic the two best are by H. H. Scullard, *A History of the Roman World from 753 to 146 B.C.* (London, 1935); and F. B. Marsh, *A History of the Roman World from 146 to 30 B.C.* (London, 1935). More specialized studies on republican politics are provided by R. Syme, *The Roman Revolution* (Oxford, 1939); *L. R. Taylor, *Party Politics in the Age of Caesar* (Berkeley, 1949); H. H. Scullard, *Roman Politics, 220–150 B.C.* (Oxford, 1951); and *F. R. Cowell, *Cicero and the Roman Republic* (Harmondsworth, 1956). The expansion of Rome throughout the Mediterranean is covered by T. Frank, *Roman Imperialism* (New York, 1914); *E. Badian, *Roman Imperialism in the Late Republic,* rev. ed. (Ithaca, 1968); H. H. Scullard, *Scipio Africanus: Soldier and Statesman* (Ithaca, 1970); and G. R. Watson, *The Roman Soldier* (Ithaca, 1969). Caesar, Cicero, Sulla, and Pompey are best studied by reading their writings and their lives by Plutarch.

Social and economic developments in republican Rome are dealt with by W. W. Fowler, *Social Life at Rome in the Age of Cicero* (New York, 1909); and J. Carcopino, *Daily Life in Ancient Rome* (New Haven, 1940). For literature in the republican period see M. Hadas, *History of Latin Literature* (New York, 1952). Historians such as Livy and Sallust have been translated and their works are available in good editions. Of special relevance is *M. L. W. Laistner, *The Greater Roman Historians* (Berkeley, 1947). Artistic achievement is studied by H. B. Walters, *The Art of the Romans,* 2nd ed. (London, 1928); R. J. Charleston, *Roman Pottery* (New York, 1955); and S. B. Platner and T. Ashley, *A Topographical Dictionary of Ancient Rome* (Oxford, 1929).

Two standard histories of the imperial period are those of E. T. Salmon, *A History of the Roman World 30 B.C.–138 A.D.,* 2nd rev. ed. (London, 1950); and H. M. D. Parker, *A History of the Roman World from A.D. 138 to 337* (London, 1935). Short studies are provided by M. P. Charlesworth, *The Roman Empire* (Oxford, 1951); *H. Mattingly, *Roman Imperial Civilization* (London, 1957). On the expansion of the Roman Empire see *M. Wheeler, *Rome Beyond the Imperial Frontiers* (Harmondsworth, 1955); and F. Millar, *The Roman Empire and Its Neighbours* (New York and London, 1967). The writings of Tacitus and Suetonius should be read by anyone who hopes to understand politics in the Julio–Claudian period. But see particularly D. R. Dudley, *The World of Tacitus* (Boston, 1968); and S. Usher, *The Historians of Greece and Rome* (New York, 1970).

The most comprehensive study of social and economic history is by M. I. Rostovtzeff, *Social and Economic History of the Roman Empire* (Oxford, 1926). Another good source book on imperial economic history is that of M. P. Charlesworth, *Trade Routes and Commerce of the Roman Empire* (Cambridge, Mass., 1926). Social history is best discussed by *S. Dill in *Roman Society from Nero to Marcus Aurelius* (New York, 1956) and in *Roman Society in the Last Century of the Western Empire,* 2nd rev. ed. (New York, 1958). See also J. A. Crook, *Law and Life of Rome* (Ithaca, 1970); and J. P. V. D. Balsdon, *Life and Leisure in Ancient Rome* (New York, 1969). For a stimulating study of imperial culture see *C. G. Starr, *Civilization and the Caesars* (Ithaca, 1954). Latin literature is very well covered by J. W. Duff, *A Literary History of Rome from the Origins to the Close of the Golden Age,* 3rd ed. (New York, 1953); and H. E. Butler, *Post-Augustan Poetry from Seneca to Juvenal* (Oxford, 1909). Imperial art and architecture are very well explained and illustrated in G. Hanfmann, *Roman Art* (Greenwich, Conn., 1964); and in M. Wheeler, *Roman Art and Architecture* (New York, 1964). On pagan and oriental religions one should consult W. R. Halliday, *The Pagan Background of Early Christianity* (Liverpool, 1925); and *F. Cumont, *Oriental Religions in Roman Paganism* (New York, 1957). The rise of Christianity is intelligently discussed in A. D. Nock, *Conversion: The Old and New in Religion* (Oxford, 1933) and *St. Paul* (London, 1955); and E. R. Goodenough, *The Church in the Roman Empire* (New York, 1931). Pertinent sources in translation dealing with various aspects of imperial civilization are found in *W. G. Sinnigen, *Rome* (New York, 1965).

CHAPTER 4

The New Europe

The years from A.D. *96 to the death of Marcus Aurelius in 180*
Edward Gibbon, in his monumental work *The Decline and Fall of the Roman
Empire,* has termed "the period in the history of the human world, during which
the condition of the human race was most happy and prosperous." Most historians
have agreed with this appraisal, but what they and Gibbon have found tantalizing
to explain is why, immediately after a long period of such well-being, the empire
should begin to disintegrate and ultimately cease to exist. Because the fall of the
Roman Empire in the West is one of the great catastrophes in western history, it has
always been a topical problem for historians of every generation and has tested
the talents of some of the most accomplished ancient and medieval historians. All
that we can do here is describe what happened and make some observations on why
the empire disintegrated.

1. From Ancient to Medieval

WHEN MARCUS AURELIUS DIED, he was succeeded by his incompetent son Com-
modus who was assassinated in 192. This violent death triggered civil war among
the legions who were supporting various commanders for the emperorship. The

victor, Septimius Severus, ruled until 211 and bluntly recognized that his power came solely from the army. Shedding those traditional practices that cloaked imperial power, Septimius openly embraced military autocracy and advised his successor to be good to the legions from whence came his power. Members of his family ruled until 235 when the assassination of one of them threw the empire into total confusion and led to fifty years of anarchy during which there were twenty-six emperors, only one of whom died peacefully in bed. During this period central and local government disintegrated; distant provinces temporarily were lost; and the Persians in Mesopotamia and the German tribes in Europe breached the imperial borders. Occasionally an exceptional emperor like Aurelian (270–275) was able to restore order for a brief time, but confusion generally prevailed until Diocletian, a general from Illyria, became emperor in 284. During his reign (284–305) and that of Constantine (310–337) imperial disintegration was stemmed and the empire temporarily rejuvenated.

POLITICAL AND ECONOMIC DISINTEGRATION

Realistic, cynical, and extremely capable, Diocletian knew that he must take drastic action to save the foundering empire. He ruled much like an oriental despot, concentrating all power in his person and basing it upon control of the army. He proclaimed himself a god, introduced court ceremonial, wore clothes that reminded all of his superhuman position, and surrounded himself with a court bureaucracy radiating out into the provinces. All important officials received grandiloquent titles such as *clarissimi* and *nobilissimi*. Administration central and local was revamped. To provide for orderly imperial succession Diocletian associated with himself another man to whom he gave the title Augustus and added two more subassociates with the title of Caesar. Diocletian retained the supreme authority but the rule of the empire was divided among the four. His plan was that he and the other Augustus should retire and be succeeded by the two Caesars, who would then appoint two men to succeed them.

To facilitate administration Diocletian reduced the size of the provinces and increased their number. All local government, even that of the cities, was closely supervised, and members of the local aristocracy who governed the cities were worked into the general imperial administration. Diocletian ceased living at Rome and centered the government in Nicomedia so as to be closer to the eastern provinces. Perhaps this move indicates that he realized the East was economically more viable than the West and that he should base his power in the eastern provinces, a policy that Constantine later embraced. Stationary defenses along the frontiers were replaced by mobile defenses. Placed strategically within the empire were mobile armies that could be swiftly dispatched to threatened points.

Retiring in 305, Diocletian attempted to implement his plan for orderly succession but without success. Out of the civil war that followed, Constantine emerged in 310 as the sole ruler of the empire. He scrapped the scheme for associate emperors but continued all the other innovations of Diocletian. In 330 when he moved his capital from Rome to the city of Byzantium on the Bosphorus, renaming it Constantinople, he was only completing the eastern move already initiated by Diocletian and admitting that his power could be more easily supported from an eastern base. Though subsequently used as a capital, Rome lost its exclusive position and had to share first place with Constantinople. By moving his capital to the Bosphorus, Constantine hastened the split between East and West. In the fourth and fifth centuries it was customary to have two emperors, one ruling the East from Constantinople, another ruling the West from Rome. Events were to cause the western part of the empire to fall while the eastern part was to survive in the form of the Byzantine Empire until 1453.

While Diocletian and Constantine managed to shore up the empire politically and militarily, they had less success with other problems that developed in the third and fourth centuries. Even before the anarchy of the third century, which inevitably hobbled the economy, the empire was in trouble, especially in the western part. Already in the second century many cities could not meet their financial obligations because of declining economic activity and required imperial assistance and supervision. Not as productive or as rich as the East, the West continued losing money to the East until the flow became a hemorrhage. By the third and fourth centuries economic activities such as industry and trade which sustained urban life were in decline. In the West particularly cities grew smaller and lost their populations. The economy was ceasing to be city-oriented and was becoming land-oriented; it was shifting from a money to an agrarian economy. The aristo- crats left the cities to live on their large estates which they now sought to increase in area. No longer able to obtain slaves to work on their estates, the landlords turned to small free farmers, who had either owned their own small plots and had turned them over to great landlords in return for security and the right to live on the land, or who were landless and promised labor in return for some land and security. During the third and fourth centuries, therefore, Europe became a land of large estates controlled by powerful lords and worked by small tenant farmers called *coloni* who, at first economically and legally free, gradually lost their economic freedom and, by 332, their legal rights. Henceforth they were bound to the soil and under the political, economic, and legal control of the great lords who constantly acquired power as central and local authority crumbled. The social, economic, and legal condition of the coloni became hereditary. As Europe became a land of large self-sufficient estates producing almost all that they needed, the economy consequently became localized and regionalized. The middle-class merchants and artisans of the cities disappeared, and with this decline of the middle class came the decline of the cities, some becoming deserted and others barely surviving. Socially Europe was divided into two classes—the aristocratic lords and the economically and legally dependent peasants. Europe had already become what it was to be for almost the next one thousand years; in this period seignorialism (manorialism) took root.

Although Diocletian and Constantine seemed unable to stem or reverse this economic development, they did attempt to regulate the economy and society so as to prevent total disintegration. Aware that the economy was becoming agrarian, they reorganized taxation so that more revenue came from the land, with much of it paid in kind. Each province became liable for a certain annual amount in kind based upon the assessed value of the landed estates. Supposedly this new tax, known as the *annona*, was to be periodically reassessed, but in practice it often remained too high and became impossible to pay. As it became more difficult to collect the tax, the local municipal senators, the curiales, who were responsible for collection and for making up any deficiency from their own resources, had to pay more and more of it themselves until eventually they were ruined. Only those who fled from the cities and from their obligations to estates in the countryside escaped ruin.

To keep men at their posts all those in essential work were, like the coloni, bound to their jobs, and their professions made hereditary. Men, and their sons after them, were thus bound to their occupations in the building crafts, transportation, mining, and the production of food. The same was true for curiales and even

ARCH OF CONSTANTINE. This triumphal arch was erected in Rome by Constantine in 315 to commemorate his liberation of Rome from his rival Maxentius.

administrators and generals. From top to bottom almost all society was arranged into castes, each with its duties. To insure essential goods and services Diocletian even initiated control of wages and prices. This grim regime over which Diocletian and Constantine ruled with dictatorial authority depended upon forced labor for even sluggish functioning; it preserved the political fabric of the empire but at the price of destroying vital esprit, individual freedom, and initiative.

CULTURAL DECLINE

Inevitably the political, economic, and social malaise of the empire adversely affected culture. In the centuries after Marcus Aurelius, writers, artists, and thinkers stopped being creative or even productive. An atmosphere conducive to cultural achievement no longer existed. The cities, economic resources, and skills essential for cultural activity were disappearing. No longer was there a dynamic empire or great rulers to inspire creative talent or initiative. What continued to be done simply mimicked previous style and form and summarized or commented upon previous work. Cultural vitality was lacking. Though yet supported by the emperors who still commissioned grandiose buildings, art and architecture had little beauty or value. Craftsmen lost their skills. To see the abysmal decline one has only to compare the arches of Septimius Severus and Constantine with those of the first century. Crude designs decorate the arch of Septimius and sculptured sections taken from previous arches decorate that of Constantine. Talent in portraiture and carving disappeared. Even mosaics were hard to find. No historian equaled Livy or Tacitus. Poets wrote merely pedestrian verse. Study of grammar and rhetoric continued, but only for its own sake; essays and other compositions, while written in flawless Latin, said nothing. Latin became ornate and elaborate. As West drifted away from East, intellectuals in the West became ignorant of Greek and were thus deprived of the stimulus of Greek thought. Philosophical speculation became arid with less and less attention directed to rational modes of thought. Philosophy gave way to oriental religion and to mystic systems of pseudo-philosophy such as Neoplatonism formulated by Plotinus (203–262). Although borrowing some of Platonic thought, Plotinus repudiated reason as an avenue to truth, teaching that revelation of truth came through ecstatic vision. This so-called philosophy was more of a religion. Truly the centuries after Marcus Aurelius saw the death of many fundamental values of Graeco-Roman culture, some of which were forever lost to western culture.

TRIUMPH OF CHRISTIANITY

The only spiritual force and institution that showed vitality and growth in this period was the Christian faith with its embryonic church organization. During the third century Christianity outpaced the oriental mystery religions, withstood a last great persecution by Diocletian in 303, and proceeded in the fourth century to become the faith triumphant. Increasingly winning converts, not only from the underprivileged but from the rich and powerful, during the reign of Constantine it gained legal recognition. Constantine, a follower of Mithraism, became interested in Christianity, seemingly associating it with his triumph over his rivals for the emperorship. According to a story which may be legend, in 312 Constantine, having defeated lesser contenders, was about to engage in the Battle of Milvian Bridge against his chief rival Maxentius when he saw the words *In hoc Vince* (In this I have conquered) emblazoned on a fiery cross in the sky. Interpreting this as an omen of victory from the Christian God, he had the name of Christ inscribed on the shield of his soldiers, and he carried the day. To express his gratitude to a faith which he perhaps regarded as instrumental in giving him victory, Constantine had the Greek letters *Chi Rho* (*Christos*) put on military and civil emblems and coins, granted freedom of worship to Christians in 313, permitted the church legally to hold property, and, in addition, took a personal interest in the Christian faith. He had his children reared in the faith, gave preference to Christians for imperial offices, concerned himself with problems of doctrine, and finally was baptized. Historians dispute as to why Constantine became a Christian, some arguing that he had a genuine religious experience, others that he underwent a profound psychological drama, and still others that he embraced Christianity because it was emerging as the dominant faith and would contribute to imperial unity. What is indisputable, however, is that Christianity became the favored and predominant religion of the empire; it won its final victory in 392 when the emperor Theodosius proclaimed it the sole legal religion and ordered all Roman subjects except Jews to become Christian. To be a Christian was henceforth a matter of law, not of religious conviction. It is important to note that, while the empire in the West declined, the Christian church continued to grow and to remain dynamic. Having grown up under the empire, it had absorbed and borrowed much of the Graeco-Roman heritage which it was to preserve and pass on to the new civilization that would arise in the West. Christianity provided the spiritual and intellectual foundation for the Middle Ages, and in so doing gave to the West new ideas and a new view of the world.

THEORIES ON THE DECLINE OF THE EMPIRE

It is evident that the period from the death of Marcus Aurelius to the fifth century was one of decline for the empire in all respects, political, military, economic, social, and cultural. Although imperial disintegration was more severe in the western part of the empire than in the eastern, the decline was general, involving the whole civilization of the ancient world and leading to a new historical period known as the Middle Ages. The end of the ancient world and the beginning of the Middle Ages was a development so critical that historians have long pondered it and have attempted to state specifically when the West was no longer ancient but medieval. Dating the fall of the Roman Empire has become a classic problem in historiography.

Into the nineteenth century the end of the ancient world was regarded by most historians as a great catastrophe that came rapidly as a result of the conquest of the western empire by uncivilized German tribes during the fourth and fifth centuries. With the German occupation of the West, they believed, came ignorance and that long gloomy night of Gothic barbarism known as the Middle Ages. This was the view developed by Renaissance scholars and adorned by historians of the eighteenth century, notably Voltaire and Gibbon, the latter blaming also the Christian church because it undermined Roman civic duty and military courage. Historians in the nineteenth and twentieth centuries, examining the evidence more closely, became convinced that the German conquest of the West was not alone responsible for the end of the ancient world, that the Germans could not have conquered the western empire unless it had been previously weakened by internal disintegration.

But what caused this internal decline? Political historians have argued that failure to provide for orderly imperial succession caused anarchy and governmental collapse, that control of the emperors by the legions led to civil war and imperial impotence, and that imperial reliance on the military brought despotism which destroyed initiative and freedom. According to military historians, decline in the size of the army enabled the Germans to pour across the frontier defenses, and the infusion of non-Roman soldiers into the legions attenuated their military effectiveness. Economic historians, while recognizing that economic decline in the empire was related to political and cultural decline, could not agree on the reasons for economic decline. Some stated that the unfavorable economic balance between East and West caused the latter to collapse. Others thought that the West remained too underdeveloped economically, especially in trade and industry, and that economic regionalism and self-sufficiency based on an agrarian economy led to decline. Still others were convinced that an economy based on slave labor was doomed to disintegration.

It is true, as some historians have noted, that much depended upon the vitality of the cities, that with their decay all else also rotted away. But why should the cities decay? Their dependence upon trade and industry is obvious, but was their vitality also generated from the middle class with its political, economic, and cultural know-how? Certainly when the middle class declined and disappeared so too did the cities. But what causes a class to decline? Some historians believe that the Roman middle class was overwhelmed by the illiterate proletariat, peasants, and soldiers. Historians who ascribe peculiar abilities to certain races contend that all went well when only Romans did the governing and fighting but that political and military superiority was lost when intermarriage began and the pure Roman stock disappeared. Rabid racists have even written that the Romans were absorbed by inferior oriental peoples who, despite cultural achievement, were deficient in political and military ability. Some historians have seen what they call race suicide on the part of the old aristocratic families which practiced strict birth control or failed to reproduce. Others have seen a deterioration in the aristocracy and middle class whose members lost ambition and drive and became weak and effete, corrupted by money, leisure, and vice.

Some scholars have tried to relate the decline to physical phenomena. Soil erosion around the Mediterranean has been suggested as a major cause for the drop in agricultural production. Improper rotation of crops and insufficient fertilization are alleged to have impoverished the soil. There are geographers who believe that during the third and fourth centuries the Mediterranean basin underwent a period of abnormally hot and dry weather which had a devastating effect upon vegetation and human life. Plague and disease are also causes suggested for the decline of population.

Cultural historians have noted the general decline in culture. Summarizing, commenting, and copying supplanted creative and individual endeavor. Men seemed unable to press forward and appeared content to use what they had in literature, history, philosophy, science, medicine, and other fields. Artistic ability seemed almost to have disappeared. Skills necessary for the crafts were scarce or non-existent. What was constructed was without taste, for men no longer seemed to know what was beautiful. Having said all this, however, the cultural historian cannot account for this bankruptcy. Writers, thinkers, and artists may well have lost their drive and spirit to create, but why? Certainly cultural decline and loss of spirit must be linked with the unsettled politics and the sinking economy; a thriving culture must have stability and support.

Obviously historians, influenced by their own fields of interest, methods, and approaches, project different reasons for the end of the ancient world. Each age and generation has supplied its answers. The reasons advanced are numerous and complex. Because the troubles which assailed the empire occurred over a long period of time, it is clearly unhistorical to state that the Roman Empire in the West was destroyed by the Germanic invasions in the fourth and fifth centuries, that it ended when the Visigothic chief, Alaric, sacked Rome in 410, or when the Vandals pillaged Rome in 455, or when the German chief Odoacer deposed the last Roman emperor of the West in 476. Nor can one set dates for the decline on the basis of political events or economic, social, and cultural change. Historians attempting to assign the end of the ancient world to a year, decade, age, or century do not see their history in proper perspective.

So complex and diverse in time and place were the forces eroding the empire that the decline of the ancient world took a long time, longer than the third, fourth, and fifth centuries. If one agrees with the historical interpretation that the life and unity of the ancient world depended upon control of the Mediterranean, then the ancient world did not end until that unity was broken by the Arabs as they swept around three sides of the Mediterranean during the seventh and eighth centuries. While politically the empire in the West may have ceased to exist in the fourth or fifth century, the ancient world may well have continued to survive until the Mediterranean was no longer a Roman but an Arab lake in the eighth century. The end of the ancient world and the beginning of the Middle Ages took centuries, possibly from the third to the eighth. In this long process of transition an old world gradually ended, a new one began.

2. *The Germanic Kingdoms*

HOWEVER HISTORIANS MARK THE END of the Roman Empire in the West, by which they mean the end of the ancient world with its Graeco-Roman civilization, they agree that in the last years of the second century the empire began a long period of internal decay that led to German infiltration and, by the end of the fifth century, to conquest. For almost the next thousand years the inhabitants of Europe were learning about and preserving the remnants of Graeco-Roman civilization that had survived the chaos of disintegration. By adapting this weak heritage to their needs, fusing it to their primitive ambition and high spirit, they eventually forged a culture in which new ideas and institutions were blended with the classical civilization that had been rediscovered by the fourteenth and fifteenth centuries. These years of transition in Europe, from the end of the Roman Empire to the modern European epoch beginning in the sixteenth century, comprise what historians label the Middle Ages. Fundamentally it was a long period of assimilation, creation, and rediscovery that was to draw Europe back up to the level of the classical world and to furnish the conditions for further advance.

The beginning of the Middle Ages is associated with the end of the Roman Empire in the West. Likewise, the close of the Middle Ages is foreshadowed in the fifteenth century by the rise of national monarchies, the discovery of the New World, the religious discontent inaugurating the Reformation, new techniques in trade and industry, and a dynamic new culture based upon a humanistic view of man's role in the universe. Imbued with a sense of importance and destiny, man was to take this new Europe to great and unsurpassed heights. We can better understand this transformation if we know what characterized the first five hundred years of the Middle Ages, the years so often called the Dark Ages.

Through movements and battles too detailed to concern us here the German tribes, originally located north and east of the imperial defenses along the Rhine and Danube rivers, pushed gradually into the imperial provinces until by the end of the fifth century they occupied all the territory of the Roman Empire in the West. Although the westward push of the fierce Huns from their central Asian home in the fourth and fifth centuries pressed the Germans against the Roman frontier and caused some mass dislocation, as with the Visigoths and Ostrogoths, it must be remembered that the majority of the Germans infiltrated the empire peacefully as military allies (*foederati*) or occupied Roman soil with scarcely any opposition; they took over the West almost by invitation. Why the German tribes moved into the western part of the empire in such numbers during the fourth and fifth centuries will never be known with certainty, but Roman political and military weakness, the desire of the Germans for the amenities of civilized life, land hunger, and pressure from the fearsome peoples of the East were surely primary reasons.

KINGDOMS IN THE SOUTH

After crossing into the Danubian provinces and defeating the Roman emperor Valens at the Battle of Adrianople in 378, the Visigoths remained in the Danubian area until they moved West under their chief, Alaric, into Italy and eventually into the Roman provinces of Spain and the southwestern part of Gaul where, with varying political vicissitudes, the Visigothic kingdom existed from 415 to 711. Its history was one of weakness and decline. Less numerous than some of the German tribes, the Visigoths were outnumbered and easily absorbed by the Roman population, a circumstance resulting in a weaker and less warlike people who repeatedly fell victim to greedy enemies from the north and south. They lost their conquests north of the Pyrenees to the Franks and, unfortunately, their kingdom saw little but savage civil war between factions of venal and greedy aristocrats. In the early eighth century, when the Arabs poured across the Strait of Gibraltar from northern Africa, they had only to march across Spain to the Pyrenees and occupy it.

The history of the Ostrogothic kingdom in Italy and the Balkan region bordering upon the Adriatic Sea was somewhat happier. From their location east of the Danube and north of the Visigoths, the Ostrogoths had first pushed to the head of the Adriatic, and then in 471 under their able king Theodoric had occupied the lower Danubian provinces vacated by the Visigoths.

The relations of the Ostrogoths with the emperors of the eastern empire at Constantinople were as unsatisfactory as those of the Visigoths. Though appeased for a while with empty titles, grants of Roman land, and plundering expeditions, Theodoric was such a dangerous neighbor for the emperor Zeno that the latter contrived his removal in 488 by empowering him to take Italy from the German chief Odoacer. Within a few years Theodoric had conquered Italy and murdered Odoacer. He had established *de facto* another independent German kingdom, although in theory the emperor was ruler and Theodoric governed in his name with the majestic titles of *magister militum* (master of the horse) and *patricius* (lieutenant). With Ravenna as his capital, Theodoric forgot about the eastern emperor, established a fairly well-organized state, and then expanded north, east, and west at the expense of other German tribes. But however rapid the rise of Ostrogothic power, its decline was equally precipitous. It rested upon one man—Theodoric— and when he died in 526 it practically evaporated. By the middle of the sixth century, armies from the eastern empire had reconquered Italy, but managed only to reduce it to political anarchy and brigandage and to pave the way for another German invasion. Thereafter Italy was to remain a geographical expression until its political unification in 1870. All that survives of Theodoric and his ephemeral kingdom are his tomb in Ravenna and his role as Dietrich von Bern, the hero who conquered Siegfried in the German epic, the *Nibelungenlied*.

The plummeting of the Vandal comet through the troubled western sky was even more swift. Settled in the early fifth century as military allies on Gaulish soil, the Vandals took advantage of the chaos to begin marauding campaigns that turned into conquests. After ravaging Gaul they passed into Spain, and then later, in 429, into Africa. They marched eastward, defeating the Moors, and by 439 had occupied Carthage and set up a kingdom in the territory now called Tunis. From this vantage point they molested Mediterranean shipping and even pillaged Rome

GERMANIC KINGDOMS AT DEATH OF THEODORIC (526)

in 455, an event that led to a somewhat unjust association of their name with brigandage and wanton destruction and inspired a French scholar of the eighteenth century to coin the word *vandalism*. With the death of their king Gaiseric in 477, Vandal power speedily crumbled, and their state was conquered by the forces of the eastern emperor Justinian in 532.

Other German tribes meanwhile established kingdoms all over Roman soil, only to experience equally transitory existences. The most important were the Lombards, who dropped southward into Italy to fill the political vacuum left by the Byzantine-Ostrogothic war. They reduced all the northern and central area; only the eastern shore and the region below Rome remained to the eastern empire. Their hold on northern Italy was, however, ineffective. Having first embraced Arianism, considered an unorthodox and heretical belief, they incurred the bitter enmity of a Papacy fearful of their political designs. Even their conversion to orthodox Christianity in the seventh century did not win papal amity. The Popes feared any power that threatened their political sway around Rome and their independence of action. It is not surprising, then, that the Lombards were easily subjugated by the mighty Charlemagne who came southward over the Alps in the eighth century.

KINGDOMS IN THE NORTH

The feature common to the southern German kingdoms is that none of them proved to be permanent political structures; all succumbed before Moslem, Byzantine, or other German conquests. But there were two Germanic kingdoms which, from a combination of geographical and fortuitous political factors, were destined to become permanent and to survive the early Middle Ages. One of these was the Anglo-Saxon kingdom established across the English Channel in what had been the Roman province of Britain. By 430 all vestiges of Roman power had vanished, and Britain was temporarily held by native Celtic chieftains who feuded and warred for more extensive territory. Foreign invasion soon broke this interlude. From the north, the fierce Picts and Scots poured across Hadrian's Wall, a military defense constructed by the emperor Hadrian, and from the south, across the North Sea in their long open boats, came bands of Angles, Saxons, and Jutes from the northern coasts of Germany and Denmark. Arriving in ever increasing numbers after 450, they had by 600 reduced all Britain, except for Wales, as far as the border of Scotland.

After political consolidation began in the seventh century, Britain was comprised of seven Germanic kingdoms, sometimes called the Heptarchy by historians. Hegemony over all the island was wielded by a succession of kingdoms, and then in the ninth century political leadership fell to the Wessex kings, located in southwest Britain, whose destiny it was to unify Britain into a strong English kingdom. The rise of Wessex power coincided with a new wave of Germanic invaders, this time the Danes from Denmark and the northern Scandinavian area. Appearing first as raiders along the east coast in the late eighth century, they eventually came to

winter in England and to begin its conquest. During the ninth century these fierce adventurers conquered all the region north and east of the Thames River, an area subsequently called the Danelaw because Danish custom ruled there. Meanwhile, other marauders plundered Scotland, sailed around the Orkney Islands, and established small principalities on the Isle of Man in the Irish Sea and on Ireland.

By the last quarter of the century only Wessex had escaped Danish conquest; this was due to the exceptional organizational ability of its king, Alfred the Great (870–900), who held the Danes at the Thames and forced them into concluding a settlement whereby they were to be content with the Danelaw and were to accept the Christian faith. To his able successors of the tenth century, the efficient Alfred passed on a small fleet to help parry the landing of additional Danes from across the seas and a military system geared for both defense and offense. Alfred and his successors constructed large earthen and wooden fortifications called *boroughs* (similar to the American frontier stockades) to defend their land as well as to hold and consolidate their conquests. By 950 all the Danelaw had been conquered and there had been forged under the drive of the Wessex kings the Anglo-Saxon kingdom of England that lasted down to 1066. The protection afforded by the North Sea and English Channel explain the long life of this most Germanic of kingdoms.

However remarkable the political and institutional achievements of the Wessex kings in creating their island realm, its geographical isolation kept it in the political backwater of western Europe. The Germans who were the real founders of the new Europe were the Salian Franks. Located as early as the middle of the fourth century on the left bank of the Rhine as military allies of the Roman emperors, they loyally fought against Huns and against other Germans until the late fifth century when there was no longer any Roman emperor to fight for. Free then to shape their own political fortune in the troubled waters of Gaul, the Franks capitalized on their opportunity in a grand manner under their great leader Clovis who, with Alfred the Great and Charlemagne, fills out the trinity of great political leaders in early medieval Europe.

At first Clovis had been but one of many Frankish chieftains—the leader of the Sicambri tribe that had filtered westward by the middle of the fifth century to the Belgian area about Tournai. Due to his military ability and thoroughly unscrupulous and cruel character, vividly described by the sixth-century historian Gregory of Tours, Clovis soon became head of all the tribes that composed the Salian Franks. Thus did Clovis, a member of the Merovingian family whose mythical founder was Meroveus, establish the Merovingian dynasty over the Franks. Around 481 he embarked upon a career of conquest which was to win him three-fourths of Gaul before his death in 511. Married to a Burgundian princess, a Christian, he was persuaded to accept Christianity for himself and his people, an event that proved to be decisive in the history of the Franks, for it endeared them to the Papacy and gained them papal support for all their conquests on the grounds

not justified

that they acted only to preserve the true faith against heathen and heretic. The account of Gregory of Tours naïvely indicates how shrewdly Clovis employed the cross to further the sword. Gregory writes that Clovis, prior to his campaign against the Visigoths (507), gave the following reason to justify it: "It irketh me sore that these Arians hold a part of Gaul. Let us go forth, then, and with God's aid bring the land under our sway." At Poitiers, "King Clovis by God's aid obtained the victory," and soon thereafter "the Lord showed him such favor that the walls [of Angoulême] fell down of themselves before his eyes . . . then, his victory being complete, he returned to Tours and made many offerings to the holy shrine of the holy Martin."[1] Clovis devoted the last four years of his life to rounding out his possessions to the north, by deposing and assassinating in the most crude and blatant fashion all the remaining Frankish chieftains who were blocking his climb to power.

3. The Byzantine Empire

WHILE GERMAN KINGDOMS were replacing the empire in the West, the situation was different in the eastern part of the empire with its capital at Constantinople. German tribes as well as Bulgarians and Avars occupied the Balkan region but, fortunately persuaded or bribed to move to the West, they never took Constantinople or that part of Asia Minor extending east to the Taurus Mountains, the area which was to be the core of the eastern or Byzantine Empire. Because of its powerful defensive site Constantinople did not suffer the frequent fate of Rome; in the next thousand years it was captured but twice, once in 1204 by the Latin forces of the Fourth Crusade, and again in 1453 by the Ottoman Turks who put an end to the Byzantine Empire. A more important cause for the survival of the Byzantine Empire than luck and location was its economy which, always on a higher level than that of the West, did not decline. Trade and industry prospered, there was no shift from a money to an agrarian economy, and the development of Constantinople into a great capital stimulated more intense economic activity. Queen of the Mediterranean for the next thousand years, Constantinople became one of the richest cities of the world and enjoyed an international trade. The Byzantine government, buttressed by a healthy economy, could collect the revenue needed for sustaining efficient administration and supporting a strong army and navy to defend the vital territorial core in the Balkans and Asia Minor. Despite repeated crises when it seemed that Constantinople would fall and the empire

---

[1] Trans. by Ormonde Maddock Dalton, *The History of the Franks by Gregory of Tours* (Oxford: Clarendon Press, 1927), II, 75, 77, 78. By permission of the Clarendon Press, Oxford.

end, gifted emperors and generals, imbued with the imperial tradition and determined that the Byzantine Empire should not die, retrieved the situation.

The history of the Byzantine Empire began when Constantine moved his capital in 330 to Byzantium on the Bosphorus, renamed it Constantinople, and worked to make it a second Rome. By this move the eastern part of the empire gained a capital and within a few years was permanently separated from the empire in the West. Theodosius the Great (379–395) was the last emperor to rule over a united empire. At his death it was divided between his sons Arcadius and Honorius and was never again united. During the fifth century the emperors spent most of their time defending Constantinople and keeping such German tribes as the Visigoths and Ostrogoths moving westward, but in the sixth century the Byzantine Empire entered the phase that would transform its institutions and make its culture distinct from that in the West. Also in the sixth century Latin began to be replaced by Greek, and soon men were to speak of the Latin West and Greek East.

JUSTINIAN

Ascending the throne in 527 was the great Justinian who ruled until 565 and who was the last Byzantine emperor who was Roman in thought and Latin in speech. Contrary to the unfavorable opinion of the contemporary historian Procopius, Justinian was obviously intelligent, ambitious, gifted as a military leader, and imbued with a sense of imperial grandeur that inspired him to embark upon the lofty project of reconquering the West and restoring the Roman Empire. He was ably assisted by his beautiful and remarkable queen Theodora who, after an early career as a performer in a circus, as a woman of loose morals sought after by the powerful, and as Justinian's mistress, became his devoted wife and loyal companion. Throughout the crises of Justinian's reign Theodora sustained his courage and at times saved him from ruin. Under this gifted team the Byzantine Empire flourished.

After gaining complete mastery of Constantinople, shoring up the defenses in the Balkans and in the east against the Persians, and assembling a well-trained army of heavy cavalry (*cataphracti*) equipped with bows and arrows, Justinian was ready to launch his campaign to reconquer the West. Under his brilliant generals Belisarius and Narses it seemed for a while as though Justinian would restore imperial unity. In 533 Belisarius with a small army completely defeated the Vandals and restored northern Africa to the empire. The conquest of Ostrogothic Italy, which was the next goal, proved incredibly difficult against stubborn resistance that reduced much of Italy to shambles, and Justinian could not truly claim Italy until 552. Turning then to Visigothic Spain, he reduced only the southeastern coast, and yet proudly boasted by 555 that he had restored the empire. His achievement, however remarkable, was at best hollow and transitory; his conquests ringed the

THE EMPRESS THEODORA AND HER COURT. This brilliant mosaic showing Theodora in majestic imperial attire is from the church of San Vitale at Ravenna which was completed in 548.

Mediterranean but did not penetrate far inland. The defensive forces in the East had been depleted and the resources of the empire overstrained by the effort. Within a short time most of the conquests were lost and Justinian left behind him an exhausted empire to meet new and deadly threats from the Persians and Arabs.

PERSIAN AND ARABIC CHALLENGES

After Justinian's death the Byzantine Empire met reverses from all sides. In the West the Visigoths regained all Spain and the Lombards moved in and conquered all of Italy except for areas on the coasts. The Avars and Slavs occupied the Balkans and threatened Constantinople. Meanwhile the Persians, pushing into Syria, took Damascus, Antioch, and Jerusalem, and proceeded into Egypt and Asia Minor. As the fall of Constantinople appeared imminent, the emperor Heraclius (610–641), infusing his subjects with amazing spirit, virtually accomplished a miracle. In 622, leaving but a small force to hold Constantinople against the Avars, Heraclius led a spirited army straight into Persian territory, forcing the enemy to regroup its forces for defense. By late 627 Heraclius reached the Tigris at Nineveh and there won a great victory. Soon the Persian king was overthrown by a rival in civil war and the Persians sued for peace, agreeing to return Byzantine territory and the Holy Cross which had been taken from

Jerusalem. When Heraclius returned as a hero to Constantinople in 629, neither he nor his grateful subjects could know that within a few years another menace from the East would undo all his triumphs.

This new threat came unexpectedly and swiftly from the Arabian peninsula. No one could foresee that from this huge desert, quiescent for centuries, ignored by the Greeks and Romans except for some trade with the Hejaz on the Red Sea, and populated by disorganized nomadic tribes of Semitic origin, could come such a storm. But the Arabs, inspired by the new faith of Islam proclaimed by their prophet Mohammed in the late sixth and early seventh century, and hungry for better climate and richer lands, burst forth from their peninsula after the death of Mohammed and established a new empire around the Mediterranean. They then constructed a fleet with which they plundered the islands, the European coast, and Asia Minor. In 655, after destroying a Byzantine fleet, the Arab fleet proceeded to Constantinople while an army moved through Armenia and Asia Minor to cut Constantinople off from supplies and manpower. Still Constantinople held and the Arab fleet was pushed back with the assistance of the mysterious "Greek Fire" (a highly inflammable compound). But other assaults kept Constantinople in jeopardy. In 717 with a joint naval and land force the Arabs tried for twelve months to reduce Constantinople but were finally repulsed by the emperor Leo III the Isaurian (717–741) whose courageous leadership won him recognition as saviour of the Byzantine Empire. Never again would the Arabs threaten Constantinople. Barred at the gate to Europe, they concentrated their efforts in the East and eventually established their capital at Baghdad.

However, the Arabs reduced the territory of the Byzantine Empire to the fringes of the northern Mediterranean coast, perhaps the most significant result of the Arab conquests for the West. The heart of the Byzantine Empire now became and would remain Asia Minor. The Arabs cut effective ties with the West, thereby forcing Byzantium to face eastward. Although East and West had been drifting apart since the reign of Constantine, the split was not complete until late in the seventh century when the Latin element in Byzantine culture rapidly disappeared and was replaced by the Greek. The religion of Byzantium was to be that of the Greek Orthodox church headed by the Patriarch of Constantinople rather than that of the Roman church headed by the Pope at Rome. The late seventh century marks the beginning of the history of medieval Byzantium.

4. The Rise of Islam

BEFORE RETURNING TO THE WEST and the vicissitudes of the new German states, we must examine the rise of the new faith of Islam and its influence on the history of the Mediterranean world. Because the vast Arabian desert had been ignored and

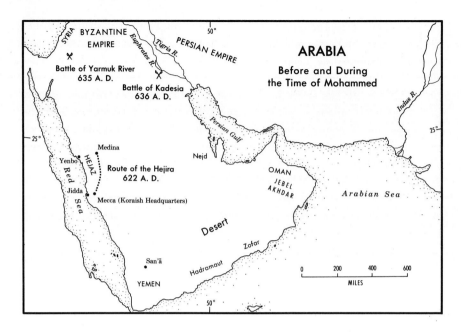

mostly isolated from the higher civilizations of the Mediterranean, the nomadic Arabic tribes lived simply and were chiefly concerned with adequate water and pasture for their flocks. They fought for good land and water holes. Most of what they knew came from oral tradition handed down from generation to generation. Their religion was primitive. They revered sacred rocks, trees, and wells and had great respect for the evil spirits (*jinn*) that brought calamities of the desert. Only along the coast of the Red Sea in the Hejaz and in northern Arabia was life more civilized, undoubtedly because these two areas had come into contact with Persian and Graeco-Roman culture through sea trade and the overland trade of caravans. Arabs in these areas certainly had been exposed to the teachings of Persian Zoroastrianism, Judaism, and Christianity.

MOHAMMED

Born into the tribe of Kuraish at Mecca in the Hejaz between 570 and 580 was <u>Mohammed</u>, whose religion of Islam transformed the Arabs and upset much of the civilized world. There was nothing remarkable about Mohammed's early life. Son of a poor family and orphaned at the age of ten, he had to support himself by working for a trading caravan, an occupation that gave him commercial experience and undoubtedly familiarized him with the religious beliefs of the Jews and Christians. As a successful trader, Mohammed came to the attention of Khadija, a wealthy widow of Mecca, who hired him as her business agent and later, when he was about the age of thirty, became his wife. His life was greatly changed. He now had the leisure and the means to speculate about life and to devote himself to religious and moral problems that had apparently troubled him for some time.

As Mohammed's meditations evolved into thoughts which he came to express, he concluded that Arab polytheism was wrong, that there was but one God (Allah), the creator of the world and man. To attain salvation when the fearsome day of final judgment came, man must live righteously and obey various precepts which Mohammed formulated. The man who so lived went to a joyous land of paradise, later described by Mohammed as a Utopian place; the man who did not, would go to the fiery land of hell to suffer awful torments. Much of what Mohammed proclaimed was taken from Hebraic and Christian beliefs, although he denied the divinity of Christ, regarding Him as just another of the Jewish prophets. Mohammed's chief innovation was to regard himself as the sole and true prophet of Allah the Almighty. He, Mohammed, was the only intermediary between God and man.

Eventually Mohammed began to have visions or religious experiences during which the Angel Gabriel spoke to him and delivered messages that became the foundation of his new religion. Most of what is known about Mohammed's faith comes from the *Koran,* a collection of his pronouncements, which dates from soon after his death in 632. Most of the one hundred and fourteen chapters of the *Koran* were written down by Mohammed and his close followers. The *Koran* has come down to us as magnificent and beautiful poetry. In it the religion of Mohammed is referred to as *Islam,* meaning submission to God; those who submit become members of the Moslem faith which states that "There is no God but Allah, and Mohammed is His prophet." To this profession of faith were added other moderate requirements, such as praying five times daily while facing toward Mecca which became the holy city of Islam, making one pilgrimage to Mecca in one's lifetime, giving alms for charitable and good causes, and fasting from sunrise to sunset during the sacred month of Ramadan. The moral precepts of the new religion were modified restatements of existing custom. Although polygamy and slavery were retained, Mohammed exhorted the faithful to ameliorate the condition of females and slaves. Sexual promiscuity was strictly forbidden, blood feuds between families were frowned upon and compensation substituted for revenge, and restrictions were put on food, drink, and daily routine that were eminently sensible and reasonable. Islam was a religion all could follow without too much personal sacrifice.

It seemed at first that Mohammed would only secure the conversion of his wife and his cousin Ali to the new faith. The Meccans overwhelmingly regarded the new prophet as an upstart and fraud who would only upset the status quo and even harm business by his attack on traditional spiritual beliefs and social practices. Making no headway in Mecca, Mohammed finally accepted the invitation from a group of Judaized Arabs living at Yathrib to come there and become their prophet and Messiah. In 622 with a small band of followers Mohammed made the trip to Yathrib, renamed Medina (The City of the Prophet). Known as the Hegira (Emigration), this event became the year 1 in the Islamic calendar. At Medina Mohammed worked feverishly to convert the rest of the population as well as the outlying tribes. Meanwhile Medina and Mecca became embroiled in a commercial war which was to benefit Mohammed. Now acting as an inspired religious leader Mohammed promised victory to Medina under the guidance of Allah and himself. In a series of victories after 624 the Medinans advanced to Mecca and occupied it. With the victorious forces went Mohammed who returned to his birthplace in triumph. The first holy war of Islam had been won.

Acting with moderation, Mohammed wisely introduced his religion without disrupting greatly the normal Meccan routine. His principal change was the purification of the famous temple known as the Kaaba (the cube), whereby he cast out the idols but shrewdly retained a sacred black stone revered by all. The Kaaba with its sacred stone became the focus and center of the Islamic faith, and Mecca the place that true believers faced when they performed their daily prayers. Soon Mecca became the center of pilgrimages that understandably contributed to the local economy. When Mohammed died in 632 his faith prevailed from Medina to Mecca and in much of the Hejaz; but would Islam remain dynamic without its founder?

THE KAABA AT MECCA. A sacred shrine even before Mohammed, the Kaaba is visited annually by over a hundred thousand Moslem pilgrims, and daily more than 450 million Moslems turn toward it to pray.

1. MESOPOTAMIAN SCULPTURE. Found in a temple dating from about the middle of the third millennium B.C., at Tell Asmar in Iraq, this figure carved in veined gypsum probably represents a priest, since it is beardless and its head is clean shaven.

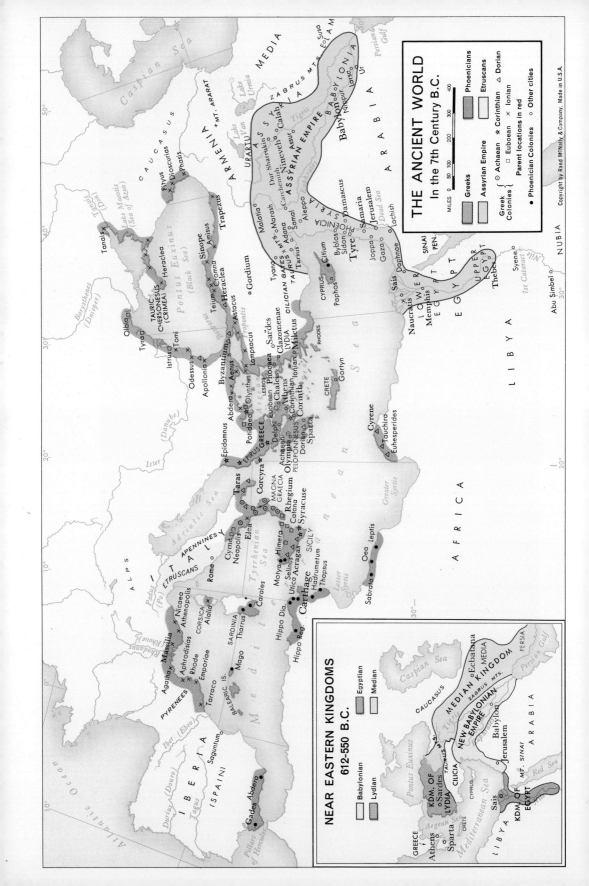

THE ANCIENT WORLD
In the 7th Century B.C.

MILES 0 50 100 200 300 400

Greeks | Phoenicians
Assyrian Empire | Etruscans

Greek Colonies: ⊙ Achaean ★ Euboean □ Corinthian ⊡ Ionian △ Dorian ✕ Ionian
□ Parent locations in red
● Phoenician Colonies ○ Other cities

Copyright by Rand McNally & Company. Made in U.S.A.

NEAR EASTERN KINGDOMS
612–550 B.C.

Babylonian | Egyptian
Lydian | Median

KDM. OF LYDIA — Sardes
CILICIA
TAURUS
CYPRUS
MEDIAN KINGDOM — Ecbatana
MEDIA
ZAGRUS MTS.
PERSIA
NEW BABYLONIAN EMPIRE — Babylon
Jerusalem
KDM. OF EGYPT — Sais
MT. SINAI
ARABIA
LIBYA
NUBIA
GREECE
Athens
Sparta
CRETE
Aegean Sea
Pontus Euxinus
Mediterranean Sea
Red Sea
Persian Gulf
Caspian Sea
CAUCASUS
Tigris
Euphrates
ARMENIA

MEDIA
URARTU
Lake Urmia
MT. ARARAT
Lake Van
ARMENIA
ASSYRIAN EMPIRE
ZAGRUS MTS.
ELAM
Susa
Ur
BABYLONIA
Babylon
Nippur
Larsa
Nineveh
Assur
Calah
Dur Sharrukin
Carchemish
Arpad
Marash
Samal
Aleppo
Adana
Tarsus
TAURUS MTS.
CILICIAN GATES
Tyana
Malatia
Gordium
LYDIA
Sardes
Clazomenae
Phocaea
Miletus
Ionian
Damascus
Samaria
Jerusalem
Dead Sea
Lachish
Joppa
Gaza
Dophnae
SINAI PEN.
LOWER EGYPT
Memphis
Naucratis
Sais
UPPER EGYPT
Thebes
Syene
1st Cataract
Abu Simbel
Nile
NUBIA
LIBYA
AFRICA
ARABIA
PHOENICIA
Byblos
Sidon
Tyre
CYPRUS
Citium
Paphos
RHODES
CRETE
Gortyn
Cyrene
Tauchira
Euhesperides
Greater Syrtis
Lesser Syrtis
Leptis
Oea
Sabrata
Thapsus
Hadrumetum
Carthage
Utica
Hippo Reg.
Hippo Dia.
Tacapae
SICILY
Syracuse
Catana
Acragas
Selinus
Himera
Motya
Rhegium
Cyme
Neopolis
Taras
MAGNA GRAECIA
Corcyra
Epidamnus
ITALY
ETRUSCANS
Rome
APENNINES
ALPS
Tyrrhenian Sea
Adriatic Sea
SARDINIA
Carales
Tharrus
Mago
CORSICA
Alalia
Aleria
Nicaea
Antipolis
Athenopolis
Aphrodisias
Massilia
Agatha
Rhode
Emporiae
PYRENEES
Tarraco
Saguntum
IBERIA (SPAIN)
Tagus
Durius (Douro)
Iber (Ebro)
Gades
Abdera
Mago
Pillars of Hercules
Atlantic Ocean
BALEARIC IS.
Mediterranean Sea
Pontus Euxinus (Black Sea)
Lake Maeotis (Sea of Azov)
Tanais (Don)
Borysthenes (Dnieper)
Danube
Ister
Rhodanus (Rhone)
Padus (Po)
TAURIC CHERSONESUS (CRIMEA)
Tanais
Pityus
Dioscurias
Phasis
Trapezus
Cerasus
Amisus
Sinope
Heraclea
Teium
Heraclea
Astacus
Byzantium
PROPONTIS
Lampsacus
LESBOS
Aenus
Abdera
Olynthus
Potidaea
Chalcis
EUBOEA
Athens
Delphi
Corinth
PELOPONNESUS
Sparta
Olympia
ACHAEA
DORIAN
EPIRUS
GREECE
Odessus
Apollonia
Tomi
Istrus
Tyras
Olbia
Gordium
Sardes
LYDIA
MEDIA
GREECE
CAUCASUS
Caspian Sea

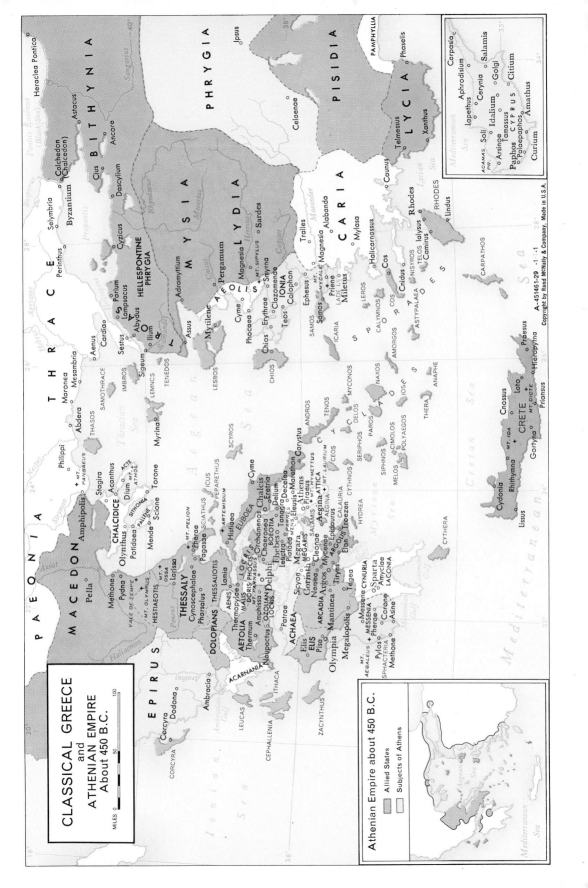

CLASSICAL GREECE
and
ATHENIAN EMPIRE
About 450 B.C.

MILES
0   50   100

Athenian Empire about 450 B.C.

Allied States
Subjects of Athens

A-451461-29 -1-1-1
Copyright by Rand McNally & Company, Made in U.S.A.

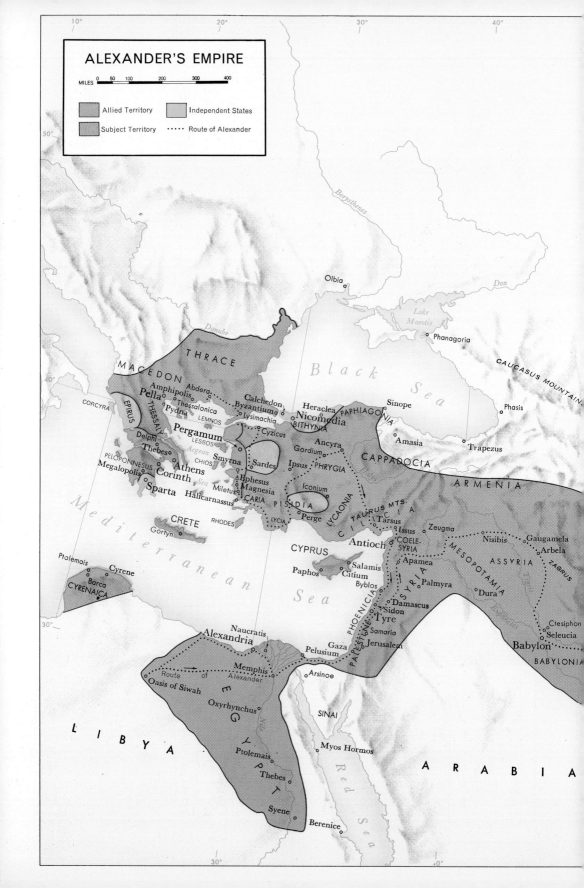

ALEXANDER'S EMPIRE

MILES 0 50 100 200 300 400

Allied Territory   Independent States

Subject Territory   •••••• Route of Alexander

Borysthenes

Danube

Don

CAUCASUS MOUNTAIN

Lake Maeotis

Olbia

Phanagoria

Black Sea

THRACE

MACEDON

Abdera

Amphipolis

Pella

Thessalonica

Pydna

LEMNOS

Calchedon

Byzantium

Lysimachia

Cyzicus

Heraclea

PAPHLAGONIA

Sinope

Phasis

Nicomedia

BITHYNIA

Amasia

Trapezus

CORCYRA

EPIRUS

THESSALY

Delphi

Thebes

Corinth

PELOPONNESUS

Megalopolis

Sparta

Pergamum

LESBOS

CHIOS

Smyrna

Sardes

Ephesus

Magnesia

Miletus

Halicarnassus

CARIA

Ancyra

Gordium

Ipsus

PHRYGIA

CAPPADOCIA

ARMENIA

Aegean Sea

Athens

PISIDIA

Iconium

LYCAONIA

TAURUS MTS.

C I L I C I A

Tarsus

Issus

Zeugma

Nisibis

Gaugamela

Arbela

ASSYRIA

ZAGRUS

RHODES

LYCIA

Perge

CRETE

Gortyn

CYPRUS

Paphos

Salamis

Citium

Antioch

COELE-SYRIA

Apamea

Palmyra

Dura

MESOPOTAMIA

Mediterranean

Ptolemais

Cyrene

Barca

CYRENAICA

Sea

Byblos

Damascus

Sidon

Tyre

PHOENICIA

Samaria

PALESTINE

Jerusalem

Ctesiphon

Seleucia

Babylon

BABYLONIA

Naucratis

Alexandria

Pelusium

Gaza

Route of Alexander

Memphis

Arsinoe

Oasis of Siwah

Oxyrhynchus

E

G

Y

P

T

SINAI

Myos Hormos

L I B Y A

Ptolemais

Thebes

Red Sea

A R A B I A

Syene

Berenice

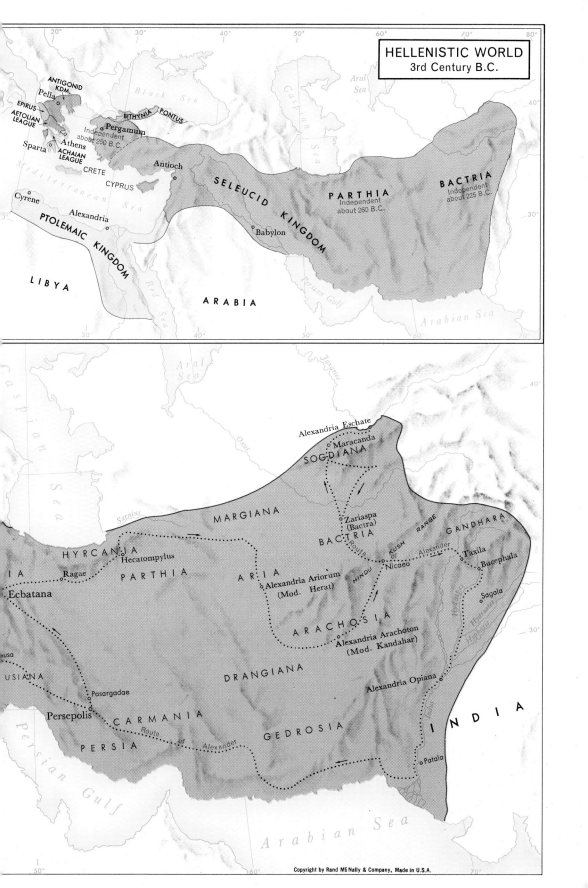

HELLENISTIC WORLD
3rd Century B.C.

Aral Sea

ANTIGONID KDM.
Pella
Black Sea
Caspian Sea
EPIRUS
AETOLIAN LEAGUE
BITHYNIA
PONTUS
Pergamum
Independent about 250 B.C.
Sparta
Athens
ACHAIAN LEAGUE
CRETE
Antioch
CYPRUS
SELEUCID KINGDOM
PARTHIA
Independent about 260 B.C.
BACTRIA
Independent about 225 B.C.
Cyrene
Mediterranean Sea
Alexandria
Babylon
PTOLEMAIC KINGDOM
LIBYA
Red Sea
Persian Gulf
ARABIA
Arabian Sea

Aral Sea

Caspian Sea

Alexandria Eschate
Maracanda
SOGDIANA
Oxus
Jaxartes
Sarnius
MARGIANA
Zariaspa (Bactra)
BACTRIA
KUSH RANGE
GANDHARA
HYRCANIA
Hecatompylus
PARTHIA
ARIA
Route
HINDU
Nicaea
Alexander
Taxila
Bucephala
Ragae
Alexandria Ariorum (Mod. Herat)
Ecbatana
ARACHOSIA
Sagala
IA
USIANA
usa
Pasargadae
Persepolis
CARMANIA
Route
DRANGIANA
Alexandria Arachoton (Mod. Kandahar)
Alexandria Opiana
of
Alexander
PERSIA
GEDROSIA
INDIA
Persian Gulf
Patala
Hydaspes
Hydraotes
Hyphasis

Arabian Sea

Roman City Names and Modern Equivalents

ROMAN NAME	MODERN NAME	ROMAN NAME	MODERN NAME
Ancyra	Ankara	Londinium	London
Aquincum	Budapest	Lugdunum	Lyon
Arelate	Arles	Lugdunum Batavorum	Leiden
Augusta Treverorum	Trier, Treves	Lutetia	Paris
Augusta Vindelicorum	Augsburg	Malaca	Malaga
Augustodunum	Autun	Massilia	Marseille
Bononia	Bologna	Mazaca Caesarea	Kayseri
Burdigala	Bordeaux	Mediolanum	Milan
Caesar Augusta	Saragossa	Moguntiacum	Mainz
Camulodunum	Colchester	Nemausus	Nimes
Carales	Cagliari	Olisipo	Lisbon
Colonia Agrippina	Cologne	Patavium	Padua
Deva	Chester	Salmantica	Salamanca
Eburacum	York	Thessalonica	Salonika
Emerita Augusta	Merida	Toletum	Toledo
Gades	Cadiz	Tolosa	Toulouse
Hispalis	Seville	Valentia	Valencia
Lindum	Lincoln	Vindobona	Vienna

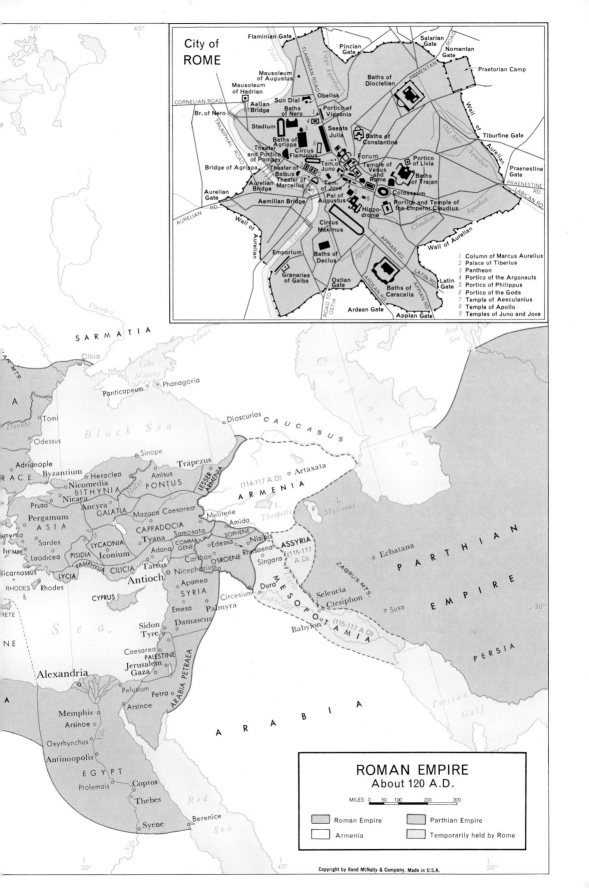

City of ROME

Flaminian Gate
Salarian Gate
Pincian Gate
Nomentan Gate
Praetorian Camp
Mausoleum of Augustus
Mausoleum of Hadrian
Baths of Diocletian
CORNELIAN ROAD
Sun Dial
Obelisk
Aelian Bridge
Br. of Nero
Baths of Nero
Portico of Vipsania
Tiburtine Gate
Stadium
Saepta Julia
Baths of Constantine
Baths of Agrippa
Theater and Portico of Pompey
Circus Flaminius
Forum
Temple of Venus and Rome
Portico of Livia
Bridge of Agrippa
Theater of Balbus
Tem. of Juno
Baths of Trajan
Aurelian Bridge
Theater of Marcellus
Tem. of Jove
Colosseum
Praenestine Gate
Aurelian Gate
Pal of Augustus
Portico and Temple of the Emperor Claudius
Aemilian Bridge
Hippodrome
Wall of Aurelian
Circus Maximus
Emporium
Baths of Decius
Wall of Aurelian
Granaries of Galba
Ostian Gate
Latin Gate
Baths of Caracalla
Ardean Gate
Applan Gate

1 Column of Marcus Aurelius
2 Palace of Tiberius
3 Pantheon
4 Portico of the Argonauts
5 Portico of Philippus
6 Portico of the Gods
7 Temple of Aesculanius
8 Temple of Apollo
9 Temples of Juno and Jove

SARMATIA
Olbia
Panticapeum
Phanagoria
Tomi
Odessus
Dioscurias
CAUCASUS
Black Sea
Adrianople
Byzantium
Heraclea
Sinope
Trapezus
LESSER ARMENIA
Artaxata
Nicomedia
Amisus
(114-117 A D)
Prusa
Nicaea
BITHYNIA
PONTUS
ARMENIA
Pergamum
Ancyra
GALATIA
L. Thospitis
L. Mantianus
ASIA
Mazaca Caesarea
Melitene
Sardes
CAPPADOCIA
Amida
Ecbatana
Laodicea
LYCAONIA
Tyana
Samosata
SOPHENE
PARTHIAN
hesus
PISIDIA
Iconium
COMMA-GENE
Adana
Edessa
Nisibis
ASSYRIA
icarnassus
PAMPHYLIA
CILICIA
Tarsus
Carthae
OSROENE
Rhesaena
(115-117 A D)
RHODES
Rhodes
LYCIA
Antioch
Nicephorium
Singara
EMPIRE
CYPRUS
Apamea
Dura
MESOPOTAMIA
Seleucia
SYRIA
Circesium
ZAGROS MTS.
Ctesiphon
Susa
PERSIA
Emesa
Palmyra
Euphrates
Babylon
(115-117 A D)
Sidon
Damascus
Tyre
Caesarea
PALESTINE
ARABIA PETRAEA
Persian Gulf
Alexandria
Jerusalem
Gaza
Pelusium
Petra
Memphis
Arsinoe
ARABIA
Arsinoe
Oxyrhynchus
Antinoopolis
EGYPT
Coptos
Ptolemais
Thebes
Red
Syene
Berenice
Sea

ROMAN EMPIRE
About 120 A.D.

MILES 0 50 100 200 300

Roman Empire
Armenia
Parthian Empire
Temporarily held by Rome

Copyright by Rand McNally & Company, Made in U.S.A.

PICTS

SCOTIA

SCANDIA
VISIGOTHS *OSTROGOTHS*

North Sea

ANGLO-
SAXONS
367-550

DIOCESE
OF
BRITAIN

547
York
Chester o Lincoln
C. 450
Caerleon o St. Albans Colchester
C. 500 London o
C. 449

ANGLO-
SAXONS

Atlantic Ocean

Elbe

FRANKS
Weser
Rhine
VANDALS
Oder

Tournay
355
Rouen
Soissons
Cambray
Treves
Cologne
BURGUNDIANS
Mainz
451
HUNS

486
Paris
Reims
Chalons
Metz
Orleans
Loire Tours
507
Poitiers
Autun
BURGUNDIANS
443
Lyon

452
Danube
452
DIOCESE
OF
ITALY
Salzburg
A L P S
452
Drave

DIOCESE OF GAUL

Milan
Pavia
Genoa
Aquileia

Bay of Biscay
Bordeaux

PYRENEES
412-507
Toulouse
Narbonne
Arles

Bologna
Ravenna
Pisa
Ancona
VISIGOTHS

Braga
Duero
Pamplona
VANDALS
Saragossa

DIOCESE OF SPAIN
VISIGOTHS
415
Toledo
Tagus
409-429
Merida
Guadiana
Seville
Cadiz
Cartagena
Guadalquivir

Barcelona
Tarragona
Tortosa
Valencia

568
Spoleto
489
Rome
410
455
Naples
Taranto

CORSICA

BALEARIC ISLANDS
SARDINIA

Ceuta

Mediterranean

Palermo
Reggio
Cose
Syracuse

DIOCESE
Hippo Regius
VANDALS
Carthage
OF
429
AFRICA

Tyrrhenian Sea

DIOCESE OF ROME

Tripoli

Routes of the Barbarians

Huns	Lombards
Visigoths	Ostrogoths
Vandals	Burgundians
Franks	Anglo-Saxons

375 —date people passed through region

200-375 —stop in region   507 —final occupation of region

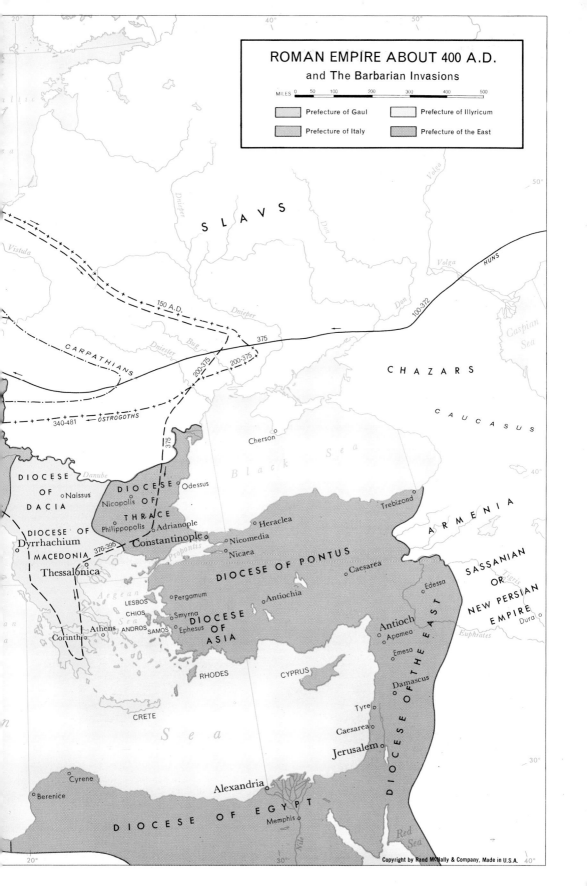

ROMAN EMPIRE ABOUT 400 A.D.
and The Barbarian Invasions

MILES 0 50 100 200 300 400 500

Prefecture of Gaul   Prefecture of Illyricum

Prefecture of Italy   Prefecture of the East

SLAVS

Vistula

Baltic Sea

Dnieper

HUNS

150 A.D.

Dnieper

CARPATHIANS

Dniester

Bug

375

200-375

200-375

100-372

Volga

Caspian Sea

CHAZARS

CAUCASUS

340-481 OSTROGOTHS

375

Cherson

Black Sea

Danube

DIOCESE OF DACIA

Naissus

Odessus

DIOCESE OF THRACE

Nicopolis

Philippopolis

Adrianople

Heraclea

Trebizond

ARMENIA

DIOCESE OF Dyrrhachium

MACEDONIA

376-395

Constantinople

Nicomedia

Nicaea

DIOCESE OF PONTUS

Caesarea

Edessa

SASSANIAN OR NEW PERSIAN EMPIRE

Thessalonica

Propontis

Aegean Sea

LESBOS

CHIOS

Pergamum

Antiochia

Tigris

Athens

ANDROS

SAMOS

Smyrna

Ephesus

DIOCESE OF ASIA

Antioch

Apamea

Euphrates

Dura

Corinth

Emesa

DIOCESE OF THE EAST

RHODES

CYPRUS

Damascus

CRETE

Sea

Tyre

Caesarea

Cyrene

Jerusalem

Berenice

Alexandria

DIOCESE OF EGYPT

Memphis

Red Sea

2. BUST OF CHARLEMAGNE. In the year 1000 the emperor Otto III disinterred the remains of Charlemagne and put them in reliquaries. This magnificent reliquary dating from around 1350 was made to hold the skull of Charlemagne. Although it may not resemble the real Charlemagne, it conveys the impact of the great emperor on subsequent ages.

tophæpe note þeht æphæpoe.þone opepme hehethon. ongealgan.Ða
þær iofepep fopfæftnyf afundoð ⁊þtah hpæþepe þæpa bynla
taldon fopgeat iofepep æptnoe·

Æften þam gapum phapao moette þæthéfttoot beanpe ta· ⁊him
þuht þæthége fápe gán up ofþam floor fífon fægpe óxan ⁊fpiþe

3. AN ANGLO-SAXON KING WITH HIS WITENAGEMOT. This illustration, which comes
from the Old Testament of the tenth-century English homilist Aelfric, shows the king
surrounded by the secular and spiritual members who comprise this aristocratic council.
They have just imposed the death penalty.

4. BIBLE OF COUNT VIVIAN. In this frontispiece from the Bible of Count Vivian, lay abbot of St. Martin of Tours, the monks are presenting a copy of the Bible to King Charles the Bald in 851.

ARABIC CONQUESTS AND THE CALIPHATE

Mohammed died without providing for a successor. Normally it would have been his cousin Ali who had married his only child Fatima, but Ali had little ability and was passed over for Abu Bakr, one of Mohammed's first converts and the father of Mohammed's favorite wife Aïsha. An assembly of those faithful to Islam elected Abu Bakr as *caliph* (successor of the prophet). Under Abu Bakr and his friend Omar it was decided to prosecute the Holy War and convert all of Arabia. Except for Jews and Christians, who were considered people of the Book, whoever would not accept Islam was to be slain. Within two years the armies of Islam had conquered all Arabia and were pushing into Syria and Mesopotamia. Abu Bakr died in 634 and was succeeded by Omar who vigorously prosecuted the war. In 636 a Byzantine army was severely defeated and Syria fell to the Arabs. By 650 all of Persia had been taken. Omar meanwhile directed his armies into the Byzantine province of Egypt, which his troops easily occupied. They were, in fact, welcomed as deliverers by the discontented subjects ruled so long by the Greeks and Romans. By 658 Arab armies had secured the coast as far west as Tripoli. The victories of the Arabs, though a tribute to their courage, esprit, and generalship, came easily because of the widespread discontent of the people under Byzantine and Persian rule. The people aided the Arabs and generally accepted Islam. With their customary good sense the Arabs soon saw that Islam could and should be a faith for all people and should not be limited to Arabs. Those who held out against conversion were generally spared and forced only to pay taxes to their new masters.

When Omar was assassinated in 644, an electoral body of six promptly elected as his successor Othman, a member of a leading Meccan family known as the Ommiads. Othman was not, however, a strong leader and his authority as caliph was challenged by Ali and his supporters. During civil war Othman was murdered in 656 and Ali was hailed as caliph by some of the regions under Arab rule. The Ommiad faction continued to fight, however, under an energetic man known as Muawija who swept all before him. In 661 Ali was assassinated and Muawija hailed as caliph by all the Arab lands. Until 750 members of the Ommiad family ruled as caliphs. The Ommiad caliphate introduced some fundamental changes in government. Recognizing that Syria was a richer base of power, the caliphate transferred the capital to Damascus. Caliphs were no longer elected for their personal ability and leadership; instead, the Ommiads established a dynasty and transformed the Arab state from a republican to a monarchical government. The caliphs surrounded themselves with capable professional advisers. Territorial administration was modeled on that of the Roman Empire with provinces, governors, and tax collectors. The Arab conquests were consolidated.

The civil war and Ommiad reorganization only temporarily halted the Arab expansion. Building a fleet, the Ommiad caliphs took command of the eastern Mediterranean and, as noted, almost captured Constantinople. Arab armies, pushing into the region north of Mesopotamia, occupied Armenia and the land up to the Taurus Mountains. East of Persia expansion continued to the Indus River and even beyond. Some of the hardest fighting was in northern Africa where the warlike Moors had to be conquered, a feat accomplished in the late seventh century. The Arab conquerors welcomed the defeated Moors into Islam and considered them magnificent warriors for future campaigns. By 710 all northern Africa from the Red Sea to the Strait of Gibraltar was under Ommiad rule.

But the thrust of Islam was not yet spent. In 711 Moorish forces under the leader Tariq crossed the strait into Spain and, after flanking the rock that bears his name (Jabal Tariq—Gibraltar), proceeded to reduce the Visigothic kingdom. By 718 all Visigothic Spain had been conquered and Islamic forces had begun sweeping into southwestern France. By the middle of the eighth century the authority of the Ommiad caliphate extended from the Strait of Gibraltar to the valleys of the Indus and Oxus rivers and into Turkestan. An empire more vast than any before had been established in less time than any previous empires. Only by the great effort of its fleet did the Byzantine Empire hold on to a small part of the eastern Mediterranean and cling to Constantinople and adjacent territory. The Arabs securely held three sides of the Mediterranean and dominated its waters.

CONSOLIDATION OF RULE

Within this polyglot empire there was little resistance to the Arabs because it was soon learned that the new rule was reasonable and the faith of Islam tolerant. The Arabs adopted local administrative systems and customs. They preserved the ancient and proud cultures. At first believers in Islam were exempt from taxation but eventually all subjects became liable. No systematic coercion was used to obtain conversion. There was nothing homogeneous about this new empire. Arabic, to be sure, became the official language of government and Islamic law superseded Roman, Persian, Visigothic, and other legal systems. And, as was only natural, families from Mecca and Medina acquired a monopoly over central and local government offices and constituted themselves into an exclusive aristocracy. These, however, were the only unifying features of the empire and, ironically, they were responsible for the collapse of the Ommiad caliphate.

In 750 a revolt broke out in Persia with its core composed of supporters of the Abbasid family, descended from Mohammed's uncle Abbas and from Ali, who proclaimed that they were the only legitimate followers of Mohammed. The Ommiads were quickly swept from power and all were killed except one who escaped to Spain and became caliph there. Thus began the Abbasid caliphate whose long rule coincided with exceptionally rich intellectual and artistic achievement. Because their main support came from the lands east of Damascus, the Abbasids chose as a new capital Baghdad, a city on the banks of the Tigris River destined

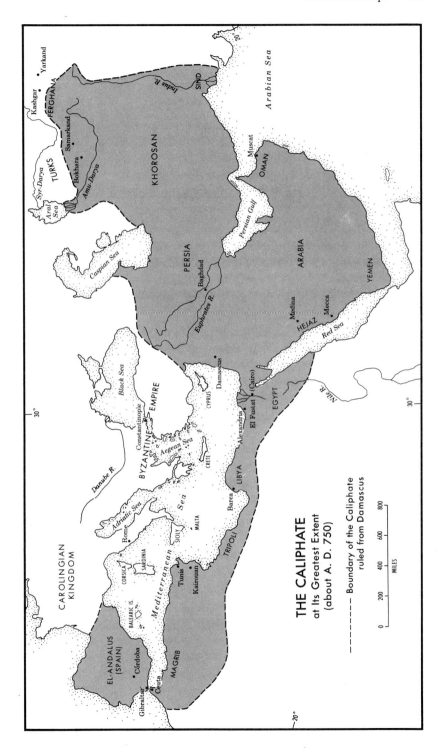

THE CALIPHATE
at Its Greatest Extent
(about A. D. 750)

– – – – – Boundary of the Caliphate
ruled from Damascus

MILES
0   200   400   600   800

to become celebrated in literature and legend as one of the richest and most exotic in the world. Later we shall explore the brilliant Islamic civilization that flourished in the following centuries and the new developments of Byzantine culture (see Chapter 6), but first let us see what occurred in western Europe in the lands now controlled by the Germans so that we can compare the civilization of the Latin West with that of Byzantium and the Islamic East.

5. The New Empire of the West

ACCORDING TO THE GERMANIC CUSTOM of inheritance, when the Frankish king Clovis died in 511, his realm was divided equally among his four sons. Although this partition weakened the Frankish kingdom through internal strife and jealousy, the ambitious brothers still carried on their father's policy of conquest. By 561 the Frankish kingdom had attained its widest expansion until the eighth century. The key to the amazing success of the Franks seems to have been that they never lost contact with their homeland, which remained their center of gravity. They did not migrate and lose their identity among a numerically superior populace; they conquered and added piece by piece to their lands around the lower Rhine, and maintained their political vigor and Germanic customs. After such a good beginning it is unfortunate that their custom of partitioning the land in each generation led to civil war and political decentralization.

Inevitably, political decline and splintering set in. By the seventh century there were four political divisions: Austrasia (east land), consisting of northeastern Gaul and the Rhine lands; Neustria (new land), consisting of northern and western Gaul between the Meuse and Loire rivers; Aquitaine; and Burgundy. Neustrian and Austrasian rulers fought for supremacy until kingship became a sham. Dagobert, who died in 639, was the last Merovingian king of any consequence, and his successors became puppets controlled by strong nobles and court factions. From a combination of these political events and strong racial and cultural characteristics, the territorial divisions that were subsequently to form France and Germany were already beginning to jell. On the one side were Burgundy, Aquitaine, and western Neustria, predominantly Roman in populace and Latin in culture, as against eastern Neustria and Austrasia which, in race and culture, were predominantly Germanic.

THE RISE OF CAROLINGIAN POWER

For a half-century after Dagobert's death the Frankish monarchy followed in the path of other unsuccessful German states. The Merovingian dynasty ceased giving any direction to its demoralized kingdom, and the various wearers of the crown became do-nothing kings (*rois fainéants*) who reigned but did not rule. All real authority fell to the principal officer of the court, who frequently but inaccurately has been called the mayor of the palace. In Austrasia a great landed aristocrat called Pepin I of Heristal attained this key position and won as well control over the royal finances and army. So firmly entrenched did Pepin become that he made the office hereditary, and his successors came to be known as the Carolingian House because subsequently the most distinguished representative was Charlemagne. By 687 Pepin's grandson Pepin II defeated the Neustrian mayor and wielded the supreme power in both provinces. This proved to be a master stroke, because by unifying the principal Merovingian territories Pepin made possible the revival of the Frankish kingdom. His son Charles Martel (the Hammer) quickly restored the boundaries to those of 561 and then turned to meet the threat of foreign invasion from the south. Having reduced all Visigothic Spain in the early eighth century, the Moslem Moors, as we have seen, crossed the Pyrenees and occupied land just to the north called Septimania. From this base of operations they began raiding southern France; it seemed only a matter of time before it would suffer the same fate as all the other lands absorbed by the Arabs during their great expansion in the seventh and eighth centuries. Charles Martel, however, took the field in 732 with a force of heavy-armed cavalry and decisively defeated the invaders between Tours and Poitiers. This was a great victory, for it threw the Moors back into Spain and transformed Charles into the defender and leader of western Christendom.

What was more natural than that the Pope, the head of the Christian church, should turn to Charles in his time of troubles? The papal lands about Rome—the

THE EARLY CAROLINGIANS

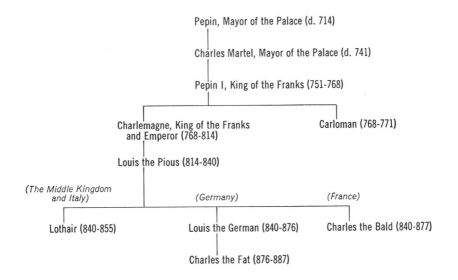

Pepin, Mayor of the Palace (d. 714)

Charles Martel, Mayor of the Palace (d. 741)

Pepin I, King of the Franks (751-768)

Charlemagne, King of the Franks and Emperor (768-814)   Carloman (768-771)

Louis the Pious (814-840)

(The Middle Kingdom and Italy)   (Germany)   (France)

Lothair (840-855)   Louis the German (840-876)   Charles the Bald (840-877)

Charles the Fat (876-887)

Patrimony of St. Peter—were threatened by conquest from the rejuvenated Lombard monarchy which had consolidated its authority over various principalities in the north and was pressing south against Rome. From the distant and weak Byzantine emperors could come no succor, so the Pope invited Charles to come south and save the spiritual head of the West. But Charles was not yet ready for a distant Italian adventure that might enmesh him in all sorts of political and spiritual difficulties; he politely refused, and left the Pope to continue fretting about the approaching Lombards. It was the son of Charles, Pepin III, who established that bond with the Papacy which was to form the basis for the establishment of the Holy Roman Empire. In 751, after the Lombards had captured Ravenna, an embassy of Pepin III asked the Pope a momentous question: What man had the best claim to the Frankish crown? The reply was that man who held the actual power. Immediately the Merovingian puppet was deposed and sent into a monastery to live out his life; a Frankish assembly solemnly elevated Pepin to be King of the Franks (751–768). Three years later Pepin marched to Rome; he was anointed king by the Pope, and appointed *patricius* of the Romans. Though lacking authority, the Pope by this appointment seemed to say in effect that the Byzantine emperor's power over the West was totally bankrupt and that western European political destinies would have to be directed on the spot by those with the power. In return for this papal favor, Pepin threw the Lombards back into northern Italy and by his famous Donation of Pepin created a belt of territory extending from Rome to Ravenna (the Papal States) to be ruled by the Pope.

CHARLEMAGNE AND HIS EMPIRE

When Pepin III died in 768 he left his kingdom to two sons; one son soon died and the whole inheritance went to Charles the Great, or Charlemagne, who presided over the affairs of western Europe until his death in 814. However one evaluates him, this giant deserves the rank of model ruler and takes a place beside the greatest of the Caesars. Thanks to the remarkable biography by his friend and secretary Einhard and to a good collection of administrative decrees which have been preserved, historians have found it possible to recreate a reasonably accurate and detailed picture of this genius and of his creation, the Carolingian Empire. Endowed with a tremendous physique and boundless energy, Charlemagne was further blessed with great military ability, a gift for administration, and an inquisitive and alert mind that sought to revive the spiritual and cultural life of western Europe. He transformed all that he touched. Although no detail of government escaped him, he never became bogged down in petty and routine planning; he always thought in terms of broad and high-level policies and thereby established the first real political structure of Europe since the third century.

We can only summarize Charlemagne's many conquests. In one campaign

THE GROWTH of the CAROLINGIAN EMPIRE

Kingdom of Clovis
Conquests of Clovis' Sons
Conquests of Charles Martel and Pepin I
Conquests of Charlemagne
Byzantine Empire

he completely subjugated the Lombard kingdom and assumed its crown in 774. Ignoring the complicated political mosaic to the south, he turned to the conquest of the heathen Saxons northeast of the Rhine. After a series of bitter campaigns, Saxony was reduced. Next, Charlemagne deposed the semiautonomous Bavarian duke, and from his land launched a great offensive to the east against the Avars, who had extended their empire west out of the Balkans. Reducing one great Ring (fortress) after another, Charlemagne had by the close of the eighth century drawn an eastern frontier that extended from the Adriatic to the Baltic Sea. All along the frontier were created military provinces called *marks,* or *marches,* which as buffer areas were to provide security and defense for the interior. To the south, Charlemagne was less successful. Apparently, he thought it possible to take Spain away from the Ommiad emir who had severed his political ties with the Abbasid caliphate at Baghdad on the Tigris River. In 778 he led an expedition through the passes of the Pyrenees onto the high Spanish plateau; meeting with no real military success, he withdrew to the north. It was while his army was filing through the pass of Roncevaux that part of it was ambushed by the fierce Christian Basques, an incident that inspired the glorious medieval epic *The Song of Roland*. Prudently Charlemagne contented himself with capturing Barcelona and organizing around it an area of defense called the Spanish March.

Having pushed outward the borders of the kingdom as far as his resources and ability permitted, Charlemagne looked to his authority within. By inheritance from his father Charlemagne was king of the Franks and *patricius* of the Romans; by conquest he was king of the Lombards. Although he exercised a real authority southward to Rome, and although he was the papal defender, he had no legal basis for such a role. In the year 800 Pope Leo III, having been driven from Rome by a rival noble faction, called upon Charlemagne for protection and took refuge with him. Charlemagne then marched to Rome and at a great assembly heard the charges pro and con on the conduct of Leo III. Finally, on December 23 it was decided that Leo should be the lawful Pope. On Christmas Day he conducted mass in the Basilica of St. Peter and, while Charlemagne was praying before the altar, Leo placed a crown upon Charlemagne's head. Then the congregation of people shouted: "To Charles Augustus, crowned of God, great and pacific emperor of the Romans, life and victory!"

Thereby was restored the Roman Empire in the West, but along vastly different lines. It was a Holy Roman Empire constructed by the Pope and Charlemagne, and it bore faint resemblance to the old imperial edifice. Fundamentally, Charlemagne's empire was crude and Germanic, as is so well borne out by his continued wearing of the customary German dress. Although Einhard avowed that the Pope's action took Charlemagne completely by surprise, it is obvious that the stage was carefully prepared and the complete drama willed by him. His new title was the logical capstone for his mighty achievements and proves how strong was the imperial idea of unity and peace even in those retrograde and primitive days. Although the Holy Roman Empire existed until put to rest after Napoleon's victory at Austerlitz (1805), it always lived more as a name and ideal for universal peace and unity than as a fact; it was, as the witty Frenchman Voltaire said, "neither Holy, nor Roman, nor an Empire." For the ceremony of Christmas Day 800, there was no legal justification inasmuch as the eastern emperor considered himself the rightful ruler of the West. But on the basis of power there was complete justification. This the notorious Byzantine empress Irene was induced to acknowledge by recognizing Charlemagne's title in return for his cession of a belt of territory along the northern and eastern shores of the Adriatic.

DISINTEGRATION OF THE CAROLINGIAN EMPIRE

However impressive Charlemagne's empire may have appeared to contemporaries, it is obvious to anyone who understands the political and economic conditions of the ninth century that it had been constructed only by virtue of Charlemagne's ability and that it could be maintained by no lesser man. Charlemagne himself had difficulty in holding his authority unimpaired and was constantly moving around his realm to keep local officers obedient. The lines of communication were too far flung and the economy too primitive to support such a vast structure. This was soon evident when Charlemagne died and was succeeded by his son Louis the Pious (814–840). Of high moral and spiritual caliber and graced with the best education available, Louis nonetheless lacked the essential political and military abilities. His empire was soon torn by civil war among his sons and threatened by foreign invasion.

When Louis died, three sons were fighting for supremacy. As the eldest, Lothair had been recognized as emperor and ruled over Italy. Arrayed against him were Louis the German, king of the East Franks, and Charles the Bald, king of the West Franks. These two, to cement their alliance, met in 842 and swore the famous Strassburg Oath wherein they promised total loyalty to each other. The historian Nithard tells us that Louis swore the oath in the French tongue so that Charles and his men could understand it, and that Charles followed with his oath in the German tongue. This alliance forced Lothair to conclude the Treaty of Verdun in 843. By its terms, Lothair retained the title of emperor and rule over a middle belt of territory extending from the south at Rome, up through Provence, Burgundy, Lorraine, Alsace, and Frisia. Charles received the lands to the west— roughly modern France—and Louis got the lands to the east—roughly the western half of modern Germany. A completely impractical arrangement, it doomed Lothair's middle kingdom to political impotence and disintegration. Such has been the history of this region to the present day, Belgium still lies insecurely between Germany and France, who have often competed for the rich lands to the south in Alsace and Lorraine. During the ninth century, by partition and war, the middle kingdom fell apart into a dozen small fragments, while the realms to east and west, at least on the surface, maintained their unity.

Simultaneously with this internal decay, the empire was forced to meet foreign invaders on all sides. The most serious menace came from the bold adventurers of the seas who pounced upon the coasts of Europe from their fiord homeland in Scandinavia. Whatever we call these intrepid sailors—Danes, Northmen, or Vikings (fiordsmen)—their adventures took them over much of the world. We have seen previously how they almost wiped out Anglo-Saxon England in the ninth century. Equally serious were their raids and expeditions on the Continent. Whether their widespread movement in the late eighth and ninth centuries sprang from lack of fertile land for a too abundant population or whether the defenseless state of the empire invited piratical raids, they came with a vengeance in the reign of Louis the Pious.

Crude, heathen, and bloodthirsty, the Vikings swooped down upon the coasts

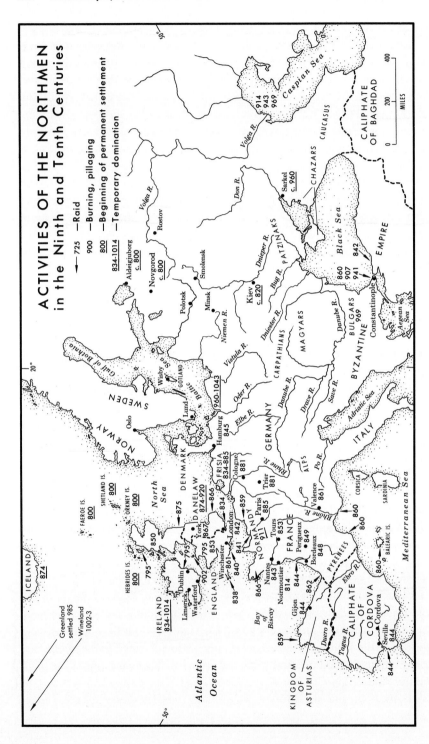

ACTIVITIES OF THE NORTHMEN
in the Ninth and Tenth Centuries

→ 725 —Raid
900 —Burning, pillaging
800 —Beginning of permanent settlement
834-1014 —Temporary domination

and up the streams in their long, sleek, open vessels, bent upon plunder and adventure. Usually in small bands, they looted and burned the churches and monasteries, put the clergy to the sword, and destroyed peasant, cattle, house, and crop. From the Low Countries and all around the French coast, through the Strait of Gibraltar, along the Mediterranean coast to Rome, and even to the Alps they went, striking terror into the hearts of all who chanced to cross their path. Across the stormy Atlantic they went to Iceland, Greenland, and North America perhaps as far south as New York. To the east turned those people who were called Varangians or Russians (Rhos by Byzantine writers) and who established themselves along the Dnieper River in Russia and forged a kingdom around Kiev.

Meanwhile, Moslem emirs from northern Africa launched raids from the south. Seizing such islands as Sardinia and Corsica, they jumped to Sicily and occupied it. Then they ravaged the coasts of Provence and Italy, even burning the church of St. Peter outside Rome and the monastery of Monte Cassino. For a time, it appeared that the Moslems might conquer Italy. To this misery of the empire was added another eastern scourge: this was a horde of nomads from Asia, the Magyars or Hungarians. Forced by some disaster to migrate west out of the Asiatic steppelands, they swept into the Balkans, occupied the area now called Hungary, and then drove through the feebly defended eastern marches. They sliced through Bavaria, Venetia, and northern Italy to penetrate in raids as far as the Rhine Valley and Burgundy.

While in all directions the empire was in deadly peril, Louis the Pious wrung his hands and prayed, his sons fought among themselves, and their successors among themselves. Only occasionally did they or local officials resist the raids which were increasingly taking the form of occupation. All central authority broke down. Local officers were left to defend their own regions, and actually became independent rulers; in them lay the only defense and security. The chance of succession briefly united the hapless empire under a son of Louis the German—Charles the Fat. But he proved his utter worthlessness and cowardice by avoiding the Vikings and bribing them with sums of money (*Danegeld*) to leave his land. He was swiftly deposed in 887, and with that event the Carolingian Empire came to a dismal end. Although there were other descendants they all had a sad fate; by 911 the German branch of the Carolingian House was extinct.

In the west various Carolingians survived for a hundred years, sporadically and unsuccessfully attempting to rule. The future of France, however, lay with the descendants of the valiant Count Odo of Paris whom the nobles elected their king in 887. He courageously threw the Vikings back from Paris and eventually, as we shall see, his descendants established the Capetian dynasty destined to rule in unbroken succession over France down into the fourteenth century.

Politically the Carolingian Empire had been replaced by a motley group of small independent German duchies and French counties in the north, by the

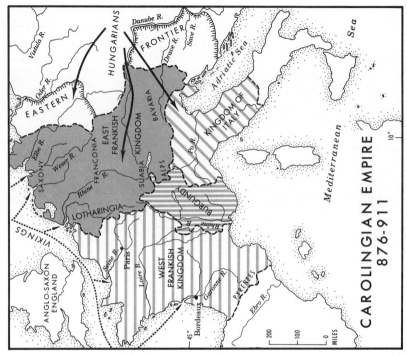

CAROLINGIAN EMPIRE
876-911

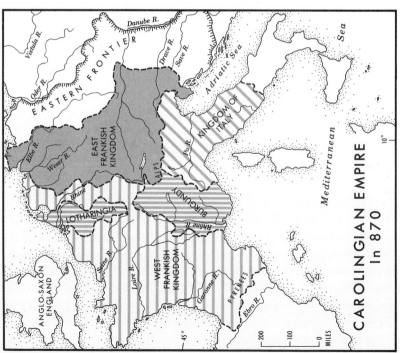

CAROLINGIAN EMPIRE
In 870

petty kingdoms of Burgundy and Provence to the south, and over the Alps by yet another complicated array of duchies. Political chaos ruled, and the powerful landed aristocrats usurped as much political and economic power as they could. All that can be said in defense of such local potentates is that someone had to rule and provide security, and that they were eminently successful in repelling the Northmen, with the exception of the northern French region of Normandy along the Seine River, which was ceded by the French king Charles the Simple to the Viking leader Rollo as a duchy in 911.

It almost seemed that Europe had sunk to a lower level of darkness than in the fifth and sixth centuries. The ninth century was an age of political anarchy when all hope of peace and security had vanished amidst a people whose civilization was close to the point of death. The only hopeful ray that glimmered feebly upon this rubbled society was the military strength and political stability gained here and there by various counts and dukes in their miniature states. From these bastions of strength, such as Flanders, Normandy, Anjou, Saxony, and Bavaria were to spring new political structures that were to be lasting and to provide the political stability needed for the birth of a new European civilization in the tenth and eleventh centuries.

6. Germanic Institutions

IN FOLLOWING THE DESTINIES of the various German tribes that occupied Roman soil between the fifth and ninth centuries, there has been no opportunity to describe their customs or their form of law and government. The first account of the Germans as given by Caesar in his *Gallic Wars* is too brief to tell us more than that they were fierce fighters and lived a pastoral life, moving about with their flocks, hunting, and fishing. Our picture of the Germans becomes much clearer about one hundred and fifty years later, thanks to the Roman historian Tacitus. Although his *Germania* tends to be a work of propaganda praising German morals, simplicity, and vigor as contrasted with Roman degeneracy, much of what he wrote was accurate. By his time, A.D. 100, the Germans had settled down to an agrarian life and lived in small villages encircled by fields, meadows, and pastures. Although there was a small exchange in money, livestock such as cattle and horses served commonly as money. Their food and dress were primitive. They lived principally upon fruit, game, and grain supplemented with a brew that was the forerunner of good German beer. The typical German was of large frame with blue eyes and reddish hair. Temperamentally he loved to fight and could endure much cold and hunger but had little inclination toward the daily routine of hard work. Hospitality was a code of honor with the Germans, and monogamy was the rule in family life.

German society was essentially aristocratic, being broken down into nobles, freemen, freedmen, and slaves. Land was distributed by rank and worked by the lower classes and by those individuals incapable of fighting. The typical German warriors fought and hunted; during intervals they slept, loafed, gambled, and drank. They were prodigious drinkers, sometimes continuing their bouts for days; so keen were they for gambling that a man might even stake his liberty on the roll of the dice. Thus we can observe that an aristocratic class of warriors rested upon economic dependents who supported them by performing all the necessary work in this primitive society.

The attainment of manhood by a German youth was marked by his investiture with a shield and spear in the presence of the tribal assembly. He was to use and guard these with his honor. The aspiration of all warriors was to join a war band (*comitatus*) led by a renowned fighter and consisting of a number of able followers. They fought for honor, glory, and booty. Each tried to excel the other; to survive the leader on the battlefield was the greatest disgrace. He who led the most rewarding expeditions had the greatest following. Such a chief was supported by the booty and land won; in turn he rewarded his followers for their brave and loyal services. The comitatus arrangement consisted of an aristocratic and honorable bond between warriors; eventually it was to provide an essential part of the feudal system that came to dominate Europe.

Political organization was rudimentary. Some tribes had kings, most of whom were elected; most tribes did not, being content to elect a war leader only during time of war. When tribal decisions were necessary, the freemen were assembled under the leadership of the principal aristocrats. Proposals submitted were accepted by loud clashing of shields and brandishing of weapons. The basic group of the tribe was the kindred group consisting of related families. In it every individual secured his right and status. The kindred group avenged injuries done to any member of the group through the blood feud or by exacting a compensation. Even homicide could be atoned for by the payment of cattle. Neither kings nor chiefs had any sovereign power in the making of laws or executing of punishments. The law was unwritten custom handed down orally from one generation to another and declared by the elder and sager men of the community. Local tribal government was equally primitive. The tribal lands seem to have been divided up into areas called *pagi* (comparable to counties) which consisted of so many families. Each pagus had its chiefs (*principes*) or leaders who controlled the primitive administration of law and government. They, in turn, had a weighty position in the tribal council. The Germans worshiped the native divinities and such gods as Woden and Thor. Except among those tribes that lived along the Roman frontier for a considerable time, Roman culture was unknown. Such, then, were the people who occupied the rotten imperial structure of the West in the fifth and sixth centuries.

EARLY GERMANIC GOVERNMENT

Once the Germanic states had been established we are better informed about their institutions. The Germans generally admired what they found remaining of Roman culture and preserved what they could of it. Those Germans who occupied the most Romanized provinces of the empire such as Italy, Gaul, and Spain became most Roman and earliest lost their Germanic identity. Of all the new states the Anglo-Saxon was most purely Germanic. Roman Britain had never been as romanized as the continental provinces, and the Angles and Saxons had had no contact with the Romans prior to their conquest of Britain. Here Roman institutions and law disappeared and were replaced by Anglo-Saxon.

In England the kings were almost absolute in their rule, although they did consult on important business in an assembly of nobles called the *witenagemot*. With the aid of their household officers, the kings directed all routine affairs of the realm and maintained relatively efficient control over a local government better organized than that of the Continent. England was divided into *shires* (counties) administered by sheriffs (*shire reeves*) who presided over the courts of justice, collected the royal taxes, supervised the royal estates, and assembled the men for military service. Each shire was subdivided into smaller districts called *hundreds,* which in turn were administered by officers called *reeves* whose work was similar to that of the sheriffs. The smallest units of organization were the agrarian villages, whose routine was purely economic and social, and the boroughs, which were military and administrative centers. Town life as it existed under the Romans had disappeared. Unlike the continental states, there were not two laws; there were only the Anglo-Saxon *dooms* which applied to all freemen. Except for the Frankish state under Charlemagne's tutelage, the Anglo-Saxon kingdom of the tenth century was the most efficiently governed and organized of western Europe.

CAROLINGIAN GOVERNMENT

Had Charlemagne's successors been capable of preserving the administrative machinery developed during his reign, the empire would have been capable of defending itself against attack and preserving internal order. Like his early Merovingian predecessors, Charlemagne held the sovereign authority; ultimately his will prevailed, although for important matters he assembled the chief men of the realm to get their advice and to promulgate edicts. Issued frequently in the absence of such assemblies, the edicts resembled instructions more than legislation. Called *capitularies,* they occasionally dealt with a single subject such as the management of the royal estates, but customarily they embraced a wide range of business running from military administration to church and educational reform. Charlemagne's principal tasks were to command the army, to carry out justice, and to protect the church; such work he did ably with the help of court or household officers who served as a sort of privy council or cabinet.

Carolingian local administration followed Merovingian precedents. The empire was broken down into provinces called *counties* administered by *counts,* who exercised judicial, military, financial, and executive functions on behalf of Charlemagne. The frontier areas were arranged into military *marches* which included several counties and which were commanded by superior officers entitled *marquises* or *margraves* (counts of the borders). All such officers were appointed by Charlemagne and were landed aristocrats who received donations of land plus a share of the royal revenue to remunerate their services. In such a large empire it was only natural that these local potentates tended to usurp royal privileges and to maladminister their districts. By constantly moving about his empire Charlemagne maintained his authority almost intact, but singlehanded he found this too much of a task and so resorted to a system of inspection first employed by the Roman emperor Diocletian. In a famous capitulary issued in 802, Charlemagne proclaimed that periodically there should be sent out from the court loyal ecclesiastics and nobles who as inspectors (*missi dominici*) were to conduct tours of inspection for groups of counties, to rectify grievances, to mete out justice, to communicate royal orders, and to carry back reports of local conditions. Although this was an excellent scheme for tying central and local government together, its effectiveness may be doubted, for with the passing of Charlemagne central government was not strong enough to enforce the system.

Practically all the public services that fall within the domain of the modern state and are now paid for by taxes were performed at that time by virtue of obligation to the crown. Military service, for example, was the obligation of all freemen; when summoned they had to serve at their own expense with weapons according to the wealth of their land and chattels. This system, called the *arrière-ban* (*ban* meaning *command*) on the Continent and the *fyrd* in Anglo-Saxon England, came to be supplemented in the eighth century by heavy-armed cavalry, a service, however, that had to be remunerated by granting large estates of land to noble warriors. In this step we see the beginnings of the feudal system which we will discuss later. In addition to military service the freemen of the empire also had to provide other varied services. They repaired fortresses, bridges, and roads, provided transportation, and did most of the work now paid for by taxes. Such a system was admirably geared to an economy with scarcely any money in circulation, and removed the necessity for direct taxation. Practically all the taxes were indirect, such as tolls from markets and bridges or tribute taken from subject peoples. Occasionally, contributions were demanded of the great men. But taxation as compared to Roman finance was extremely primitive; most of the revenue that came to Charlemagne took the form of natural produce such as grain or livestock. Seldom did any money change hands.

GERMANIC LAW

It is in the realm of law that one can see most clearly the sharp contrast between the Roman and the German levels of culture. For six hundred years a crude and highly irrational custom superseded the highly refined and rational system of Roman law. The German invaders permitted the conquered populace to continue living under Roman law compiled into codes by the various kings, while they themselves continued to be governed by the customs they brought with them. For a time, therefore, in all the kingdoms except the Anglo-Saxon there were two laws for two peoples, and as long as it was possible to make a distinction between Roman and German the concept of the personality of the law survived. But as the two peoples began to intermarry and fuse in custom and culture, it became impossible to keep the distinction. The practice of the *personality of the law* was then replaced by that of the *territoriality of the law*. A man living in Visigothic Spain was under the jurisdiction of Visigothic law; a man residing in Frankish Gaul came under the rule of Frankish law. Roman law, both in substance and procedure, disappeared and was almost forgotten except for those portions borrowed by the church and incorporated into its canon law.

German law henceforth ruled supreme until the revival of Roman law in the eleventh and twelfth centuries. And as no Germanic kingdom—not even Charlemagne's—was powerful enough to make a uniform custom prevail, law became localized and reflected the habits and ways of the countryside. In each community the most substantial landholders composed the court, supervised the primitive procedure, and declared the law. In the Frankish kingdom such men were called *rachimburgi;* in England, *doomsmen* because they *deemed* (declared) the *dooms* (laws). The giving of evidence, as we understand it, was non-existent and a man's guilt or innocence was determined by highly irrational, superstitious, and supernatural means.

Our best information on Germanic law and its procedure comes from the Anglo-Saxon dooms (collections of laws in the vernacular extending from 600 to 1040), the Salic Law (a code drawn up in Latin by Clovis for the Franks), and the capitularies. Though there was slight regional variation in Germanic trials, generally they were much alike. To bring suit against a man, it was necessary to summon him in the presence of witnesses to the local court to meet the charge. If the accused failed to appear in court, the plaintiff could take forcible action against him to rectify the wrong. If the accused appeared, then the plaintiff would accuse him according to a prescribed oath which, in turn, could be denied by a prescribed oath. Next the court—the doomsmen or rachimburgi—would set a date for the trial which customarily took the form of *compurgation;* in order to clear himself, the defendant had to swear a rigid oath of innocence that had to be supported as clean and pure by a definite number of associates or oath helpers (*compurgators*). If this was done he proved his innocence, but if either he or his associates so much as slipped on one word, or if he could not assemble the requisite number of oath helpers, he was declared guilty. If any oath helper swore falsely he lost all his possessions; consequently in small rural communities, which were the dominant form of social organization, it was extremely difficult for a man with the slightest shadow of guilt upon him to muster the required number of compurgators.

Men of evil repute, either plaintiff or defendant, were prohibited from undergoing compurgation and had to meet a sterner test. This was the *ordeal* which, because of its religious nature, was supervised by the clergy. Here, pure chance and superstition governed the mode of proof. The defendant would either plunge his hand into a pot of boiling water to retrieve a stone or carry a heated piece of iron so many paces. His hand would then be bound for a number of days. If, when the bandage was removed, his wound was clean and healing properly, the verdict was "innocent"; if the wound was festered, the verdict was "guilty." Another form of the ordeal was to toss a man into a pool of water which had been blessed; if the water received him and he sank, his innocence was established, but if he thrashed about on the surface, he was found guilty. Such trials by ordeal indicated to men of that age the will of God; to us of a more enlightened age, luck and the psychological element help to explain the outcome. Not far removed from the ordeal was

TRIAL BY ORDEAL. This illuminated manuscript shows a German empress walking over glowing embers in the presence of two bishops, in order to prove her marital faithfulness.

the Frankish trial by combat. Two men fought in armed battle; the vanquished was deemed guilty. The man of military and physical prowess found such a form of trial much to his liking, and many a bully went about winning all sorts of law-suits. Ultimately, all Germanic trials appealed to divine intervention; legal evidence such as a written document was seldom employed until the tenth century.

Where Roman law had arrived at a clear distinction between civil and criminal injuries, Germanic custom recognized none. Any crime—homicide, theft, assault—could be atoned for by paying a proper compensation to the injured party or his kindred. If a man was killed, his kindred had the right to demand the compensation called for by the dead man's rank. In Anglo-Saxon England the compensation or *wergeld* (man money) of an ordinary freeman was two hundred shillings; that of a noble, twelve hundred shillings. If the guilty party and his kindred did not pay the wergeld, a blood feud generally followed. Similarly, all offenses and physical injuries carried a tariff of compensations. The Salic Law, for example, declared that physical injury incapacitating the use of a hand, foot, or eye carried a compensation of sixty-three shillings. For stealing a sheep or goat the penalty was three shillings; for an ox or cow with a calf, thirty-five shillings. A woman slanderously called a whore received forty-five shillings. The Anglo-Saxon dooms had a minute list of compensations for injuries done to the eyes, ears, nose, toes, and teeth. For knocking out a tooth one paid from one to six shillings. A damaged thumbnail cost three shillings. The ancient rule of an eye for an eye and a tooth for a tooth prevailed, and few were the kings strong enough to make public justice supplant the justice and compensation exacted privately by the kindred. The best that kings could do was to exact additional fines as a share of the profits of justice and impose staggering fines for offenses done against them or against people and places put under their special protection. Eventually other social and economic bonds based on feudalism and manorialism were to weaken the kindred tie, but for much of the early Middle Ages it was the one social unit wherein the individual gained his recognition and security.

7. *Economic Stagnation*

Numerous explanations have been given, as we have seen, for the political and institutional decline of the Roman Empire. Although many help to explain the imperial death in the West, most historians have recognized the interdependence of the empire's political strength and its economy. When the economy of the city-state weakened, so did its political life, so did all phases of its life. Built upon the city-state, the vast imperial structure reacted to local repercussions and began its long downward path to destruction. We must conclude that however much the

Roman people lost their *esprit de corps* and their ability to be creative, or however much the barbarian Germans strained imperial military resources, catastrophic decline came only because the Roman economy fell apart. Without a thriving industry and commerce the brilliant city-state civilization could not continue. Fundamentally parasitical, the West had long lived upon the revenues and products drained off from the superior resources of the East; when finally Rome could no longer exact heavy tribute on the grounds of recent conquest and had to depend upon normal taxes to pay for its goods, there was not enough money. The money was now swiftly drained off to pay the East, until the balance was so lopsided that the West could no longer pay for eastern products.

While the eastern half of the empire lived on because industry and trade continued to thrive, the western half disintegrated. It was reduced to living upon its sole resource—land. Such economic degeneration was undoubtedly hastened by the German invasions and the later Moslem conquests. Already by the fifth century Vandal fleets had hindered commerce between the eastern and western Mediterranean, and when the Arabs conquered three sides of the Mediterranean in the seventh and eighth centuries, they almost put an end to trade between East and West. To be sure, a few Italian ports managed to maintain precarious relations with Constantinople, and we continue to hear of a few Syrians and Jews coming to such southern ports as Marseilles, but this trade was in luxury items such as incense for the church and costly cloth and jewels for the rich few. The *mare nostrum* of the Romans, which had provided the economic unity of the republic and the empire for five hundred years, had come to an end. As one Arab writer said, the Christians "can no longer float a plank on it." The West thenceforth existed until the twelfth century on an economy essentially agrarian.

THE AGRARIAN ECONOMY

From the fifth century onward the overwhelming mass of men in western Europe lived by agriculture. They fell into two classes. A very small number composed the landed aristocracy, predominantly barbarian, who controlled most of the land. The rest of the populace, perhaps as high as 90 per cent, constituted the unfree or semifree peasantry who worked the soil. Certainly, this economic stage had existed in the fourth century and was reinforced in the fifth by the Germans who had lived under a similar economic system. Without becoming involved in the argument as to whether the agrarian organization of early medieval Europe was essentially Roman or Germanic, we may say that the two systems were similar and fused. The Roman villa system was, however, so much better organized that the Germans—except for the Anglo-Saxons—used it as a model. The great Carolingian estates described by ninth-century sources closely resembled the vast imperial villas. The aristocracy gave its populace political, economic, and social security in return for economic labor. Retaining much land for their own use, the aristocrats divided out the rest among their dependents.

Legal distinctions no longer counted for much because a man, however free according to the law, could do nothing with his freedom; he was a slave of his economic condition. All peasants then, whether legally free or unfree, received uniform plots of land for their sustenance and had to perform about the same amount and type of service on the lord's land. They paid taxes and rent to the lord. They were triable in his court, which had its own peculiar custom. They had no choice; economic necessity dictated that they perform the lord's will or perish. Below these men who were called *coloni* (tenants) or *servi* (serfs) were those totally rightless individuals who were the slaves, so called from the Slavs whose lot it was so often to be sold into bondage. But gradually coloni, servi, and slaves fused to form that vast class of economic dependents—the medieval peasantry—which was to perform the hard labor of western Europe for centuries to come.

THE DECLINE OF COMMERCE AND TOWNS

If we possessed a ninth-century map of western Europe, we would see that hardly any towns appeared on it; Europe was but a vast countryside of landed estates with their little agrarian villages of peasants and their large fortified dwellings for the landlords. Urban life as known to the Romans and to us had disappeared. The essential supports of the ancient urban civilization—trade and industry—had declined to such insignificant proportions that the towns with their middle-class population of merchants and craftsmen could not survive. What trade and manufacture continued to exist were localized. Each estate became almost self-sufficient; each harbored a few artisans who fabricated the simple tools and supplied the needs of an agrarian community. There were, of course, local markets where agrarian produce was bartered, but such petty commerce was limited to an area of a few square miles and attracted no professional merchants from areas of great distance. So small was the need for money that Charlemagne coined only a silver penny called the *denarius* which could buy practically anything a man required. This coinage was not, however, uniform. Each region came to have its own coin as the great lords usurped regal rights and struck their own money, a practice that became more widespread as the Carolingian Empire disintegrated. Eventually, each region had a coin of different value and this heterogeneity added to the difficulty of interregional or long-distance trade.

Although some historians argue that town life never completely disappeared in the West, contending that administrative work and some small trade and industry supported a small resident bourgeois class, there is scarcely any evidence to substantiate this view beyond a few isolated cases such as the ports of southern France and Italy. To be sure, all western Europe was sprinkled with sites that bore

Roman names and were called *civitates* (city-states) or *castra* (camps) as, for example, Lyon, Cologne, and London. But this does not prove that such sites were true urban centers. Scrupulous examination of these places indicates that they had lost much of their population in the fifth and sixth centuries. Many became deserted ruins and were regarded as quarries where one could obtain building stone for fortified dwelling houses; others sheltered but a skeleton population generally concentrated in the corner of the walls most easily defended and fortified.

In the occasional Roman towns selected as administrative or ecclesiastical headquarters for count or bishop, there were a few soldiers, clerks, and various functionaries supported by peasants from adjacent estates. But in no respect were these administrative and ecclesiastical headquarters true towns; scarcely can they be distinguished from the rural communities. Economically they were not centers of production because there was so little commerce. Socially they were not marked off from the countryside by a population of bourgeois because there was no occupation to sustain such a class. Politically they had no municipal government because they were controlled by great lay or spiritual lords, who did all the governing required for a small body of servants every bit as much attached to their master as were his peasants. Real towns with bourgeois inhabitants were but memories in the sixth century and remained so until revived by the flurry of trade and industry that began in the eleventh and twelfth centuries.

8. The Christian Church

WHILE THE ROMAN EMPIRE was wasting away in the West, and while its once brilliant culture and institutions faded behind barbarization, the Christian church struggled forward. Successfully fighting for its life against persecution, paganism, heresy, political anarchy, and barbarism, it was the one Roman institution that survived the imperial death and thereby preserved what little Roman culture existed during the early Middle Ages. It is paradoxical yet significant that upon the eve of Odoacer's deposition of the last emperor in the West (476) the church had developed an efficient local and central organization that recognized the authority of one supreme ecclesiastic—the Pope in Rome. In addition, the church had vigorously disputed over its doctrine and hammered out a sacred tradition which became official throughout the West.

CHRISTIAN DOCTRINE

By the fifth century this tradition rested essentially upon the Christian Bible, a collection of authoritative books believed to have been written under divine inspiration. At first only the Old and New Testaments—the Scriptures—were accepted, but eventually other writings and church proclamations came to be added to the sacred law or tradition. The various collections of sacred writings such as the Old and New Testaments were called *canons* (laws) and these canons increased as the church added to its tradition and defined it more precisely. The Old Testament of the Christians consisted of a Greek translation of the old Hebrew books— the Septuagint—plus various books never written in the Hebrew. The New Testament recorded the custom and doctrine developed in the era after Christ and consisted of the Four Gospels, Paul's Epistles, the Epistles of the other apostles, the Acts of the Apostles, the Apocalypse, and other minor writings. To this core of tradition were added, as occasion demanded, church pronouncements and enactments. This authoritative law governed all orthodox Christians of the West.

While this church law was being collected and formulated there was also developing a group of beliefs held in common by the Christian communities. These beliefs provided the basis of Christian worship and helped to express the fundamental doctrine that God's son, Christ, had founded the earthly church to provide a way of salvation for all men. Salvation, it came to be believed, rested upon the Holy Sacraments which were outward signs of inward grace. The outward sign was a ceremonial act which symbolized the inward grace (the grace of God) transferred spiritually to man. Thus interpreted and believed in, a sacrament was a Christian mystery that produced a result attained by no other means. Eventually, the church came to recognize various sacraments that made up the sacramental system. Every child was baptized because *baptism* washed away the sin derived from its first parents Adam and Eve. The sacrament of *confirmation* followed baptism and admitted the individual to the church of true believers. Man and woman were united as husband and wife by the sacrament of *marriage*. When old enough to distinguish right from wrong, every individual was expected to confess his sins and, upon repentance, to receive absolution along with an appropriate penalty such as prayer, fasting, or a pilgrimage to some holy place such as a shrine; this was the sacrament of *penance*. All Christians partook of the communal service called the *eucharist* or mass. In this sacrament, the congregation of the faithful commemorated the last supper of Christ and by means of the sacramental bread and wine entered into a holy union with Him.

It was soon believed in the various communities that the ordinary man and woman were incompetent to administer these sacraments. The belief evolved, therefore, that such mystical powers had been reserved to a select group of men who formed the clergy and who had attained this elevated status by virtue of the sacrament of *ordination*. This sacrament rested upon the belief in Apostolic Succession. According to this theory, Christ had laid His hands upon the apostles and conferred upon them divine authority to continue His work of salvation. The apostles in turn commissioned others, and they others, and so the succession continued and still continues according to Catholic doctrine. Such men composed the ordained clergy and were entrusted with administering the sacraments and supervising the work of the church. Within the clergy there was, however, a difference in authority. Only a bishop (*episcopus*) received all the apostolic power; he then conferred some of the sacramental authority upon his subordinate—the priest (*presbyter*). Below the priests were lower ranks, such as the deacons, who held lesser powers.

ECCLESIASTICAL ORGANIZATION

Having developed a body of law and a doctrine administered by a divinely ordained clergy, the church recognized that such a system could be kept uniform only through an efficient territorial organization which, however, could not come until Christianity was officially tolerated and recognized as the sole legal religion in the empire. Signs of such organization appeared after Constantine's Edict of Toleration in 313, but real progress came only after Christianity was proclaimed the state religion by Theodosius in 392. Probably a combination of chance and custom influenced the clergy to model church organization after that of the empire. This decision gave the church a system tested by time and experience and perhaps explains more than anything else the phenomenal success of the church in western Europe. The basic ecclesiastical unit of government came to be the city-state which was called a *diocese* or *see* (*sedes,* seat); it was administered by a bishop who customarily located his headquarters and *cathedral church* (*cathedra,* bishop's chair) at the chief town. The diocese was subdivided into urban and rural *parishes* presided over by priests named by the bishop. In the early stages of this organization, informal assemblies of people had proclaimed clergymen bishops, but as bishops became more important and served as spiritual, political, and social leaders the office became a prize much sought after and often attained through the influence of great men or ecclesiastical factions. Eventually this unsatisfactory form of election was superseded by formal election by the diocesan clergy. Henceforth the ordinary populace merely confirmed the elected man.

It will be remembered that under imperial administration a number of city-states were combined to form a *province;* this system of centralization was also appropriated by the church. A group of dioceses was put under the supervision of a sort of superior bishop styled *archbishop* or *metropolitan* who enjoyed the privilege of consecrating all bishops within his jurisdiction. Normally an archbishop located his headquarters and church in an important town of the province which was called a *metropolis.* The next logical step, if imperial administration was to be followed, was to place a supreme ecclesiastic over all the church. Such a development had to wait until the emperors disappeared from the western scene, because as long as they wielded real power they regarded the church as a sort of department of state administered by the clergy under their authority.

Until the disastrous political events of the fifth century, the sovereign authority of the church in the West had rested in the body of bishops and archbishops who in general councils settled doctrinal and organizational problems and proclaimed canon law. The emperors would then give recognition to these acts by promulgating them in imperial edicts. When the emperors were no more, the system had to be changed.

For a long time many of the clergy had argued that Christian tradition had been handed down by the apostles and guarded in the churches they had established in such towns as Antioch, Alexandria, and Rome. Furthermore, they believed that Rome held a superior rank over other towns, even Constantinople, because it was here that the Apostles Peter and Paul had suffered martyrdom and here that Peter had been the first bishop of the church. The defenders of this belief developed, from the Gospel of Matthew, the Petrine theory, which supported the supremacy of the bishop of Rome as Pope. According to Matthew (16: 18–19), Christ had told Peter: "Thou art Peter; and upon this rock I will build my church. . . . And I will give unto thee the keys of the kingdom of heaven." The bishops of Rome and their supporters interpreted this passage as conferring supremacy upon the bishop of Rome and as initiating the doctrine of Apostolic Succession. Despite the appealing argument of this theory, and despite the repeated claims of the bishops of Rome to supremacy, other prominent bishops bitterly contested such a claim. Only slowly did a number of able bishops of Rome elevate their position above other bishops to eventual supervision over the whole church. Finally, with the distinguished Leo the Great (440–461) the supremacy of Rome was acknowledged by all the West. Henceforth, the bishops of Rome were truly the Popes, the fathers, of western Christendom.

For the centuries of political chaos that lay ahead, it was fortunate that the church obtained a central organization with a head who could speak out for it and give it a sense of direction. As the West became almost isolated from the East and lost all political unity, the Popes assumed not only the supreme spiritual leadership but also, by default, the political. Such was the situation until the eighth century, when the strong Carolingian House assumed direction of the political destiny of western Europe.

As one might expect, the problems of doctrine and organization were numerous and thorny for the growing church. In the East the clergy, Patriarch, and emperor vigorously disputed the spiritual supremacy of the Pope. And this conflict over spiritual and political power was fanned by doctrinal differences between East and West. Greek theologians of the East had long argued that the divine nature in Christ should be distinguished from the human, and that the Virgin Mary should be denied the title Mother of God. Some Greek theologians went so far as to attribute only one nature to Christ. It was finally decided in a church council held in 451 to uphold the view of Pope Leo I that Christ combined in Himself both a divine and a human nature. Despite this pronouncement, many of the eastern clergy did not adhere to it, and so the theological dispute continued, embittered by yet other differences as the political and ecclesiastical gulf between West and East widened. Here is the beginning of the famous *schism* (division) between the eastern and western churches which, with but a few interludes of rapprochement, continued into the twentieth century. Here is the origin of the Roman Catholic church of the West and the Greek Orthodox church of the East.

Besides these doctrinal problems, the church inherited others when it became a legally recognized institution and when it became the sole faith. No longer was it composed largely of the socially and economically downtrodden who adhered to their faith even though driven underground by persecution. When looked upon with favor, Christianity became popular in aristocratic circles, and men entered the clergy because there were fine opportunities for social, economic, and political advancement. All sorts of privileges, immunities, and bequests of money and land were lavished upon the church. By the late fourth century all men except Jews were compelled by law to embrace the Christian faith. In the rural areas, however, the inhabitants remained pagan at heart and in ritual for a long time; the church had to compromise and admit numerous pagan ceremonial practices and mystic beliefs in order to make itself appealing to simple rustics nurtured on soil that had been pagan for thousands of years. Even the educated and sophisticated classes often embraced Christianity more formally than out of real faith. In the fifth century a Christian was one by law rather than by belief. The church consequently had to be practical, to relax its primitive discipline and doctrine, and to accommodate itself to the masses of people who swarmed into its folds. When the church began tailoring its doctrine to meet the demands of the majority, it offended those who yearned for the primitive faith and simple social organization of the original apostolic Christians. These men, firm in their belief that the church had become too secular and materialistic, turned to a way of life devoted primarily to worship and meditation.

MONASTICISM

Christianity had a strongly mystical complexion and taught that truth was attained through divine revelation. Because many Christians believed that the ascetic life helped them in their quest for truth, the church in the West organized a routine of life for the clergy which included certain ascetic customs such as celibacy. All Christians were subjected to prohibitions at special periods such as Lent, when they were to forgo eating meat. Some Christians, although they were a minority, believed in a rigorously ascetic life that denied them all pleasure and inflicted severe hardships. They advocated celibacy, fasting, long periods of prayer, little sleep, and the simplest of food and dress. Men and women severed family and community ties to retire to isolated spots in the hills and forests where, in solitude, they strove after eternal truth and salvation. Women who vowed perpetual chastity and chose the ascetic life were called nuns. Those men who forsook the world, giving their goods to the poor, were called monks. Literally the word *monk* (*monachus*) means a man living alone, a hermit.

At first when we hear of such monks in Egypt and Asia Minor, they all lived the lives of hermits in the mountains or on the desert. Gradually it proved impractical to live alone, and then these like-minded men began to live communally and to share in the divine services and manual labor. During the fourth century St. Pachomius drew up a rule for governing such communities of monks and by the end of the century about seven thousand monks were living under the Pachomian rule in Egypt.

During the fourth century the Pachomian form of monasticism was adopted in various areas of the West. Persons from the most exalted positions of life renounced all their possessions in their quest after salvation and peace of mind. Particularly famous monasteries developed at Tours and Lérins in fifth-century Gaul. It was from Lérins that Pachomian monasticism was carried to Ireland by the exceptional St. Patrick (d. 461). Born in Britain, Patrick was captured as a youth by Irish pirates and held for six years until he escaped to Gaul where he became a monk at Lérins. There he conceived his life's work of Christianizing the heathen Irish, and in 432, after being consecrated a bishop, he set forth on his perilous mission. The rest of his life he gave to this work and, by the end of his career, he and zealous colleagues had Christianized the bulk of Ireland's populace. So strong did Ireland become in the faith that it was soon to send missionaries to Britain and northeastern Europe to further the good work.

The monastic system, however, that was destined to become standard for the Latin West was the Benedictine. It was named after St. Benedict (480?–543?) who, as a youth from a good Roman family, became disgusted with the fashionable and sophisticated society of Italian municipal life and became a hermit. His holy fame soon became so great that he found himself the leader of a large community of hermits who had sought him out. About the year 520 Benedict led his devoted followers to the top of a hill called Monte Cassino south of Rome and there built a monastery. Here he composed his famous rule for monks, intended not just for the monks of Monte Cassino but for monks all over the West.

Although it is impossible to summarize the famous rule, we can call attention to its most significant features. Moderation is the central theme, with emphasis upon communal living; Benedict believed that with the many pitfalls in a hermit's life each man needed a shepherd to help him follow in God's path. Before admission to a Benedictine monastery, a man had to renounce the world and swear to subject himself completely to the discipline of the monastery. Above all, he swore the vows of stability, chastity, and poverty, with the last emphasized over all. After a period of probation as a novice, the man was received as a full

member of the monastery. At the head of each monastery was a monk with superior powers; he was the *abbot*. The office was elective, and was to be filled by the
monk most virtuous and wise. The abbot made every decision, although the most
important were to be made only after consultation with all the monks. Still, the
abbot was to make whatever decisions were willed by God. Within his jurisdiction
were all appointments to office, and in him resided all disciplinary powers; nothing
was outside his care. It was essential, therefore, that able men be selected for abbots;
their ability determined the success of the holy community.

Each day there were about five hours of divine service beginning with matins
in the morning and ending with compline at dusk. Between the religious services, of
which there were eight, Benedict prescribed seven hours of work; this might be
farming, cooking, serving, building, clerical work, or the teaching of young monks
and boys of the vicinity. Some monks were always on duty to extend hospitality to
the weary traveler, for whoever knocked at the gates was to be received as if he were
Christ himself.

The dress of the monk was a simple tunic and cowl, in which he also slept.
His bed consisted of mattress, pillow, and blanket. Food was limited to vegetables
and fruit with a moderate amount of wine. Meat was permitted only to the sick.
The rule of St. Benedict was so sensible and practical that it survives today as a
principal form of monasticism in the Catholic church. In these monasteries that
sprang up all over western Europe was preserved what little remained of ancient
culture; from these religious centers learning spread and helped to restore light
once again to a dark and crude world. The Benedictine rule was adopted as the
official monastic rule by the Roman church. Henceforth, persons living under a
monastic rule (*regula*) were called *regular clergy,* while those ordained as bishops,
priests, and deacons were called *secular clergy* because they served God out in the
world (*saecula*).

THE TRIUMPH OF THE CHURCH IN THE WEST

The great vigor shown by the early Christian church in the centralization of its
organization, in its missionary zeal, and in the phenomenal growth of monasticism
was climaxed by the pontificate of Pope Gregory the Great (590–604). One of
the great Popes in the history of the church, Gregory, like St. Benedict, came
from a noble and wealthy family and received the best training possible in Latin
grammar and rhetoric. As a youth he witnessed the Lombard invasion of Italy,
and as a young man worked his way up the ladder of Roman municipal offices.
Suddenly, about 573, he tired of politics and worldly glory and retired to a
Benedictine monastery. His retreat, however, was interrupted by a mission as papal
legate to the court of Constantinople to secure military aid against the menacing
Lombards. After seven years there Gregory returned to Rome. The sole result of

his mission was to teach him that the Papacy could count on no help from the East but must assume a real political leadership of the West. He put this observation into practice when he was elevated to the Papacy in 590.

Possessed of the best training available and endowed with extraordinary common sense and wisdom, Gregory made Petrine supremacy an actuality and transformed the Papacy into a world power. Byzantine weakness, plus renewed Lombard advances, forced Gregory to assume political authority in Rome and the surrounding region. He finally concluded peace with the Lombards, recognizing their conquests. Although he could no more than assert his spiritual supremacy in the East, in the West he made it a fact, extending it to Africa, Spain, and Britain. Through his efforts the Papacy attained a universal authority that crossed over all political boundaries and gave the West the one bond of union it possessed. But realizing that to survive the Papacy must have a sound economic foundation, Gregory vigorously superintended the papal lands which, donated by pious Christians, composed the Patrimony of St. Peter. Over each estate he placed efficient managers. His correspondence shows that with all his international burdens he still maintained close touch with these men and busied himself with the minutest detail.

Undoubtedly the greatest accomplishment of Gregory was the conversion of the Anglo-Saxons. His concern with these people stemmed in part from misgivings about the Irish brand of Christianity which, under the stimulus of St. Patrick, was engaged in far-flung missionary activity. Irish Christianity had developed its own peculiar form of organization, wherein the clan was the basic ecclesiastical unit and monks were also priests who went about their Christian tasks out in the world. Their zeal was unflagging, and between the sixth and eighth centuries Irish monasteries attained great fame for their holiness, their missionary accomplishments, and their cultural attainments. Irish scholars were the leaders of western Europe. They possessed a good knowledge of Greek, and due to them many ancient writings have survived. In the last quarter of the sixth century the holy St. Columba began to convert the Celts, Picts, and Anglo-Saxons. In the seventh century one of his followers, the notable St. Columban, carried the faith across the English Channel to Brittany, then to Burgundy where he founded the famous monastery of Luxeuil, and then to the east among the Alamans where he founded the monastery of St. Gall. Finally, he passed into Italy and founded the monastery of Bobbio in the Apennines. Here he died in 615.

However much Gregory admired the pious and learned activity of the Irish monks, he was concerned about an organization so loose as to give complete freedom to the monk-priests. Less devoted men might abuse such liberty, and in any event the Irish organization was difficult to reconcile with the orthodox Roman system. Gregory, therefore, threw the weight of his immense prestige behind the Roman organization and Benedictine monasticism, with the result that the Irish

IRISH ILLUMINATED MANU-
SCRIPT. This beautiful illumination from the famous Book of
Kells dates from the eighth century. The interlaced pattern of
the frame surrounding the central
figure of the saint is typical of
medieval Celtic decoration.

brand of Christianity succumbed to the Roman on the Continent, and even lost
ground in Britain where Gregory launched a missionary project because, according
to legend, the sight of some Northumbrian boys in a Roman slave market imbued
him with the longing to spread the faith among the Anglo-Saxons. Whatever the
immediate cause, we may be certain that Gregory desired to win the Anglo-Saxons
to the Roman brand of faith, and he found his missionary project opportune when
the king of Kent married a Christian princess from the Merovingian House.

In 597 the Benedictine monk Augustine, leading a group of monks from
Gregory's old monastery, arrived at Canterbury, the capital of Kent. The king
and his people were soon converted, and from Kent the faith was carried to the
other Anglo-Saxon kingdoms. As soon as possible Gregory introduced the diocesan
organization and Augustine was installed as the first archbishop with his metropolis
at Canterbury. Throughout the next seventy-five years missionaries worked northward, adapting the faith to local needs and, where possible, incorporating pagan
ceremony into Christian ritual.

As the Roman faith spread northward in Britain it had to compete with Irish missionaries, and it was doubtful for some time which brand of Christianity would triumph. Finally Oswy, the powerful king of Northumbria and a strong adherent of the Roman faith, established his hegemony over much of the southern two-thirds of Britain. He assembled an ecclesiastical council at Whitby in 664 to determine which type of Christianity should be accepted. The council decided that Britain should be organized in the orthodox fashion under papal government, and the Irish missionaries departed from Anglo-Saxon England. The island was then divided into dioceses and put under two archbishops, one at Canterbury and the other at York.

The decision at Whitby was momentous for the future of the church. Thereafter the Irish influence waned on the Continent, until by the end of the seventh century all the Irish monasteries had adopted the Benedictine rule. Meanwhile, Anglo-Saxon monks took over Irish missionary work on the Continent with amazing success. About the end of the seventh century the monk Willibrord began converting the Frisians on the lower Rhine; he soon organized a diocese around Utrecht and became its bishop. Another Anglo-Saxon monk, Winfred, better known in history as St. Boniface (680–754), joined Willibrord and began to work along the eastern Frankish border, converting thousands of Thuringians. Receiving the support of the Papacy and the Carolingian House, Boniface founded monasteries and organized new dioceses. Eventually he became archbishop of the region with his metropolis at Mainz. Then in his seventies, he returned to work among the Frisians and was killed by heathen pirates in 754. Just as Gregory the Great and Augustine of Canterbury launched the church on a great missionary project among the Anglo-Saxons, so a century and a half later St. Boniface had carried the Christian faith into eastern Germany.

REFORM AND DECLINE OF THE CHURCH

Despite the spectacular achievements of the church in bringing the faith to the heathen and in expanding its territorial organization, the crude and chaotic times made it virtually impossible to staff its positions with intelligent and devout servants. There were too few schools and literate men to hold back the wave of ignorance and superstition. It is no wonder that, from the lowly priest on up to the proud bishop, the clergy was often debased. Many were illiterate and even ignorant of the simplest prayers and ritual. The vices of the bishops were enormous. Frequently from noble families, they considered their position simply a means of economic support and devoted most of their time to politics, war, hunting, and other aristocratic pastimes. Even the Benedictine monasteries were losing their zeal and became slack in the enforcement of discipline.

It was indeed fortunate that Charlemagne had the religious ardor and foresight to remedy this alarming condition. As we shall see, he established at his court a great palace school to which were lured the most distinguished scholars and teachers of the age. Here were trained promising young men whom Charlemagne then sent out to the bishoprics and monasteries, and who in turn were to look to the improvement of the discipline and education of their clergy. In reality Charlemagne went far beyond rejuvenating the clergy; the capitularies show him as the real head of western Christendom. He regarded himself as anointed by God to be a successor of the great Roman emperors who had wielded authority over church and Papacy. He asserted that the Pope was under his jurisdiction and, because of papal weakness and gratitude, there was no opposition to his claim. Charlemagne constantly issued capitularies dealing with doctrine and organization. He convened ecclesiastical councils and presided over them, sometimes telling the clergy how to settle a theological problem. He even controlled the episcopal and monastic elections by nominating men suitable to him.

Under Charlemagne's weak successors, who could not exercise this authority, the great ecclesiastics became independent potentates politically. The Papacy, along with the Carolingian House, suffered disastrous decline in the ninth and tenth centuries. Except for Nicholas I (858–867), who exercised a real spiritual authority in the West, the Popes were incompetent men who forfeited the leadership and respect of clergy and laymen. Most busied themselves in local Roman politics and fell so low as to become the puppets of selfish Roman nobles and their wives. By the tenth century it seemed that the work of such men as St. Benedict, Gregory the Great, and St. Boniface had been in vain. The Papacy was virtually unrecognized, and the church locally had lost sight of its mission. It seemed in imminent danger of falling victim to the unscrupulous power and ignorance of the age. But, as so frequently in its long history, misfortune called forth new zeal and activity, until by the end of the century the church was in the throes of a reform that was to elevate it to its greatest prestige and power during the Middle Ages.

9. The Decadence of Learning

THE SPIRIT OF DECLINE AND RETROGRESSION in the political and economic life of the early Middle Ages is apparent in the wasting away of the once magnificent Graeco-Roman intellectual achievements. The decay in Roman learning that began in the second century A.D. ended in almost total ignorance and illiteracy during the sixth and seventh centuries. What learning remained did so only because the church had to maintain a modicum of learning for the performance of the divine services. Of necessity, therefore, education and learning came under the control of the church and in the process were transformed to meet Christian requirements. In surveying the intellectual terrain of the fourth and fifth centuries, one finds that many Western scholars were ignorant of Greek and consequently of most of the advanced learning of the ancient world. Even Latin learning had become artificial and unimaginative to the point where scholarship consisted of but commentaries and texts upon the classics. The creative spirit had totally disappeared. In the disciplines of grammar and rhetoric—known today as literature and public speaking—the goal was to write and speak in a highly conventional manner about conventional subjects. Both the written and spoken word lost their vitality. Compositions and speeches became heavy and indirect, loaded with numerous and meaningless classical allusions. The complicated and ornate was preferred to the simple and plain. This was the age of the euphemism, the cliché, and the circumlocution. Such is the picture of the most elegant intellectual circles in Gaul at the end of the fifth century as drawn by Apollinaris Sidonius (d. 488), Christian prelate, politician, and writer of letters and poems.

In secular Latin literature the most outstanding composition was by the scholar Boëthius (480?–524) who graced the court of the Ostrogothic king Theodoric. While in prison waiting to be tried for treason, for a cause of which we are ignorant, he wrote his *Consolation of Philosophy,* which demonstrated in verse and prose the strength and consolation of philosophy during trial and tribulation. In addition Boëthius made valuable Latin translations from the Greek. He translated some of Aristotle's writings on logic, and they were all that western Europe knew of the great philosopher until the twelfth century. He also translated an introductory text on philosophy by Porphyry entitled *Isagoge.* These few words provided the basis of the most advanced education that could be obtained for the next five hundred years.

THE GREAT CHURCH FATHERS

It was but natural that, with the triumph of Christianity in the fourth century, ecclesiastical scholars should contribute most significantly to what learning then existed. And this learning, it should be emphasized, was of a simple and practical nature because it was meant to defend, define, and organize the faith and doctrine of Christianity. The most illustrious of such fourth- and fifth-century scholars were the great Latin church fathers, St. Ambrose (d. 397), St. Jerome (d. 420), and St. Augustine (354–430). Like many renowned early Christians, Ambrose came from a good Roman family, secured a sound education including a study of Greek, and entered the imperial service. In 374, when it was necessary to elect a new bishop of Milan, he was governor of that region and presided over the assembly of clergy and laymen. Legend has it that during the course of debate on possible candidates a child cried out "Ambrose bishop!" and in a burst of enthusiasm the crowd acclaimed him bishop. Within a week he was baptized and consecrated priest and bishop.

Ambrose never produced any great scholarly works but concentrated his writing on the practical side of religion. He is best known for his zeal in converting the pagans and for his eloquent and impassioned sermons. We are told that men from all stations in life accepted the true faith after having been captivated by the oratory of the fiery bishop. A strong defender of spiritual supremacy over temporal affairs and authority, Ambrose even forced the emperor Theodosius to beg forgiveness for permitting the cruel massacre of the populace of Thessalonica in 390. By this act, Ambrose emphasized that emperors are also men and, as Christians, subordinate to the church. This famous event, later heralded by defenders of papal and church supremacy over the state, occupied a prominent place in the investiture controversies of the eleventh and twelfth centuries.

In contrast to Ambrose, the practical church statesman, Jerome was the scholar. He has been one of the few Christian saints to be canonized for scholarly work. In his early life Jerome did not take the Christian faith very seriously; he was too captivated with the pagan classics to have much time for the Scriptures. Then a miraculous recovery from a serious illness caused him to put sinful rhetoric behind him and to serve the church. For a time he lived as a hermit and studied Hebrew until called to serve as secretary to the Pope. He retired later to a monastery at Bethlehem, where he died in 420. Throughout his holy life Jerome was engaged in scholarly work, some of which dealt with Christian archaeology, which stimulated him to make Latin translations from the Greek and Hebrew and thus prepared him for his great achievement—a Latin version of the Bible. When educated clergy realized that the various Latin translations of the Bible were unsuitable because of their errors and their reliance on bad texts, the Pope commissioned Jerome to do a new one. For the New Testament he employed the best Greek texts, but for the Old Testament he ignored the Greek Septuagint. With the aid of Hebrew scholars he translated the Old Testament directly from Hebrew texts, and so provided a new and accurate Latin translation that was declared the official Bible of the church and became known as the Vulgate.

The last of the trio of church fathers was Augustine who, by all agreement, was the greatest, and whose shadow still hovers over both the Catholic and Protestant churches. From his *Confessions*, a kind of autobiography written late in his life, emerge the principal facts of his life and intellectual and spiritual development. Born in northern Africa to a pagan father and a Christian mother, Augustine received a very good Latin education, probably because his father was a lawyer. While at Carthage studying law, Augustine developed a passion for rhetoric which he later taught, first at Rome and then at Milan where he held an imperial professorship. He meanwhile acquired a mistress with whom he lived for twelve years and by whom he had a child. In contrast to this side of his life was another of intense intellectual curiosity that drove him to seek answers to the fundamental questions of human existence. Soon realizing that satisfactory answers were not provided by pagan philosophy or religion, he turned to Neoplatonism and then to the

Christian heresy of Manichaeism which promised complete knowledge. But he was not satisfied, nor could he quench his desire for truth.

At this time he listened to the sermons of Ambrose and was so profoundly intrigued with the explanation that the Old Testament could be understood only through symbolic interpretation and that there could be agreement between the New Testament and Platonic philosophy that he immersed himself in the Scriptures. Hearing that the Christian hermits were achieving peace of mind and a vision of truth from their solitary lives of meditation, he spent hours brooding over problems that vexed him. Engaged thus one day in a garden, he suddenly seemed to hear a child's voice cry out: "Take up and read! Take up and read!" He did, and at random turned to Paul's Epistles to the Romans, 13: 13–14, which read: "Not in rioting and drunkenness, not in chambering and wantonness, not in strife and envying; but put ye on the Lord Jesus Christ, and make not provision for the flesh to fulfil the lusts thereof." In a flash Augustine understood that what he must do was believe in Christ and His message. He immediately abandoned rhetoric, broke with his mistress, dropped his plan to marry a woman of wealth, received baptism in 387, and began working for the Christian church. With his home in northern Africa converted into a monastery, he began to write on theological problems. Ordained a priest by the bishop of Hippo in 391, he soon became the bishop's assistant and later became bishop, an office that he held until he died in 430 as the Vandals were camped outside the walls of the town.

Augustine's ideas on theology dominated Christian thought down to Thomas Aquinas in the thirteenth century and still occupy a fundamental position in Catholic and Protestant doctrine. For centuries the core of Augustinian thought, that reason should be subordinated to faith, was the foundation of all medieval theology. Augustine so thoroughly digested Platonic philosophy, known to him by way of the Roman Stoics, and adapted it to Christian doctrine that it became theology's principal handmaiden until the introduction of Aristotelianism into western Europe in the twelfth and thirteenth centuries. In tracts against heresy and others explicating Christian truth, Augustine dealt with problems central to the Christian faith: predestination, the origin of sin, divine grace, human will, and the nature of salvation. The Augustinian doctrine that some men are predestined to salvation and others to perdition became one of the cardinal tenets of various Protestant groups.

In his most influential work *The City of God* (*Civitas Dei*), written to deny allegations that the sack of Rome in 410 resulted from the desertion of the pagan gods for Christianity, Augustine developed a teleological interpretation of history, arguing that history was determined by God for His own ends. The Christian church was "the march of God in the world" and through it God unfolded His plan of salvation. This interpretation of history prevailed throughout the Middle Ages. Augustine contended also that man was a citizen of two cities, that of his birth and that of God. The first city, a human creation with human laws, institutions, and rulers, was necessary, according to Augustine, to save sinful mankind from bestial anarchy. This city would end its existence only with the triumph of Christianity which would introduce the city of God, a Christian commonwealth that would bring about the culmination of the spiritual development of man. The Roman Empire was, therefore, an essential human institution that would be replaced by God's commonwealth. The *Civitas Dei* is a magnificent tapestry of man's knowledge, achievements, and existence as unfolded in the light of God's will. In the centuries that followed theologians whose thought attained the majestic level of Augustine's were rare. With Augustine centuries of pagan classical thought ended, and with him began centuries of new thought imbedded in the concept that only by subordinating human reason to Christian faith can man perceive truth and attain salvation.

LATIN LEARNING IN THE EARLY MIDDLE AGES

Augustine's death in 430 marked the end of an epoch in the decline of learning in the West. Into the fifth century all the men we have discussed knew their Latin well, some knew Greek, and all were steeped in the strong Roman grammatical-rhetorical tradition. By the sixth century no such generalization can be made. Only a few men were even stimulated enough intellectually to write, and of these but a handful could write decent Latin. The chaos of the late fifth and sixth centuries, although not quite destroying western learning, came close to it. Those historians who call the period from Augustine's death to Charlemagne the "Dark Age" of Latin learning are indeed justified. By the standards of learning of the second and the thirteenth centuries the period was dark. Proof of this is that during the sixth century Gregory of Tours (538–594), bishop and historian, was the most prominent author. His Latin was very poor. He frankly admitted that in rhetoric he was a "stolid ox," and that he had never mastered Latin grammar. As with many a modern schoolboy, genders, conjugations, and cases were meaningless to Gregory. He confused his endings; he had no sense of word order. Ablatives appeared in place of accusatives, and plural verbs accompanied singular subjects. To accentuate this abysmal ignorance, Gregory had no first-rate mind. He was totally naïve, superstitious, and prone to repeat all he heard. By normal intellectual standards he was merely a child, and yet we are grateful to him because his *History of the Franks* is one of the few written records we have of the early Frankish kingdom and its society. Passing all his life in Gaul, Gregory received what education was available to an aspiring clergyman and was ordained a deacon at the age of twenty-five. He went to Tours in the hope that the miraculous shrine of St. Martin would help cure his poor health. In 573 he was made bishop of Tours and held this position until he died.

Due to his ecclesiastical prominence, Gregory played a leading role in Frankish politics and knew the Merovingian House well; he was therefore qualified to write a history of the Franks. The chief attributes of his work, which extends from man's creation down to 591, are its honesty and enthusiasm, and the fact that Gregory was a contemporary of much sixth-century Frankish history. All who would like to know about the Merovingian degradation and the endless cycle of plots and assassinations at court should read Gregory's amazing account. But most important, a reading of Gregory imparts to one a sense of the whole decadence of sixth-century life. Society was brutal and crude, all men were subject to superstitious beliefs, hardly a man could read and write, and most men were even more naïve than Gregory. He defended all the treachery and murders of Clovis because they were for God's work. All events were caused by the intervention of God or Satan. The power of saints' relics could cure any known disease. At the shrine of St. Martin at Tours one could obtain any cure: for a stomach ache one mixed a drink from the dust of the shrine; for a sore tongue one licked the rail before St. Martin's tomb. One of the best scholars that sixth-century learning could produce, Gregory of Tours, accurately portrayed the dark age of which he was a captive.

Toward the end of the sixth and in the early seventh century Pope Gregory the Great contributed what little there was to sacred Latin learning. Practical administrator and world statesman, he still found time to write ecclesiastical works expressed simply in good Latin. His books were intended to be understood by any person who could struggle through Latin. His *Pastoral Care* was a handbook on the character and functions of a bishop. By writing down his sermons in a book called the *Homilies* he provided a model sermon book for his clergy. His sermons, unadorned and sprinkled with pious anecdotes to teach a moral, were brief discourses on scriptural texts to help explain the Christian way of life to a simple people. In a kindred book, the *Dialogues,* Gregory employed the technique of conversation and tales of holy men and women to explain the Christian faith and to emphasize the need of relying upon God to save oneself from Satan. Gregory also believed in the miraculous and superstitious lore of the age, and recounted a long list of extraordinary events caused by God or the devil. His chief theological composition was the *Moralia,* a commentary on the Book of Job. Here, he developed the idea that the Bible should be interpreted allegorically, an idea that came to dominate medieval biblical study.

To the west of Italy, in Spain, where Gregory had been primarily responsible for the Visigothic kingdom's turning from Arianism to orthodox Christianity, a somewhat higher level of civilization had endured. It is best expressed by Isidore, bishop of Seville (600–636), who during the course of his life wrote books on almost every conceivable subject. Toward the end of his life Isidore collected all his writings into a massive encyclopedia of knowledge called the *Etymologies* which for the next five hundred years served as the great book of knowledge for the western world. It, more than any work, represents what constituted learning in the Dark Ages. Isidore called it the *Etymologies* because he believed the essence of every subject and object could be found in its name. Once you understood the meaning of the name you could then define the object. As we might expect, Isidore's work is filled with weird etymology. Imbued with no critical ability whatsoever, he copied from any source, no matter how unreliable, plagiarized from other works, contradicted himself repeatedly, and produced a thoroughly unreliable book.

The most remarkable work of the eighth century came from Anglo-Saxon England which had benefited from its long contact with Irish erudition. Chiefly responsible for this was the Northumbrian monk Bede, who spent most of his life at the monastery of Jarrow, where he died in 735. Of all the scholars in the Dark Ages, he came closest to rising above its sublime ignorance. As a true believer, he used his erudition in the service of the Christian faith and quite naturally believed in divine miracles and cures. He was, however, a man with a highly critical mind who always tested his evidence as best he could. In all his various works he cited his sources, and frequently tells us how reliable he considered them. Author of works on varied subjects, he is best remembered for his treatise on chronology, which popularized the system of dating years B.C. and A.D., and for his *Ecclesiastical History of the English,* which was the best history written in western Europe from the fourth-century Roman historian Ammianus Marcellinus down to the twelfth century. For his *History* Bede consulted local archives and through correspondence collected material as far distant as Rome. He quoted in full charters and other pertinent records and critically analyzed written and oral evidence. Although his inclusion of miraculous and superstitious stories and beliefs may detract from its interest for the modern reader, one must realize that Bede's *History* was composed in excellent Latin, and that it was a thoroughly honest and intelligent history of early Anglo-Saxon England without which we would be left with nothing.

Except for Gregory the Great and Bede, learning in western Europe continued in its unhappy ignorance down to the end of the eighth century when for a brief interlude the great Charlemagne catalyzed a flurry of intellectual endeavor. Just in time did he attempt to revive learning in his empire, for it was in a desperate condition. The written and spoken Latin of even the educated was thoroughly bad; the grand old language was practically dead. As yet none of the vernacular tongues such as German and French were polished enough to be used for writing. The lowest point came in the last days of the Merovingian House when even the writing of the royal clerks was but a scrawl, and they had no knowledge of grammar. What education and learning there was resided in the clergy, and even this our skimpy records describe as mundane and degenerate. In the Benedictine monasteries a higher standard of spiritual discipline was maintained, but St. Benedict, it will be recalled, had not emphasized scholarly work in the daily routine. What learned activity was done in the various monasteries depended upon the tastes of the abbots. Where they were intellectually enthusiastic they encouraged the monks to copy manuscripts of some of the classics and to attempt some original writing. But such efforts were truly pitiful; there was little intellectual originality. At best, the richest monastic library consisted of a small chest of books. We are chiefly indebted to these monasteries for their copying of various classical manuscripts that otherwise would have been lost to us.

As for the secular clergy, it had sunk to an alarming depth. There were still no cathedral schools to offer an education to secular priests; what they got was secured informally or from the monasteries. Because they served out in the world, they became more tainted with worldly decadence and ignorance. Too many spent their time at politics and war rather than at prayer and learning. With an atmosphere so unconducive to learning, it is no wonder that there is scarcely a scholarly or literary work from the eighth century. Upon this situation Charlemagne gazed when he swore that the spiritual and intellectual life of his realm must be revitalized. Despite the inaccuracy of the phrase "Carolingian Renaissance" to describe the brief revival that resulted in the late eighth and early ninth centuries, there was a rebirth of a sort because western European thought and letters had, in reality, been dead.

THE CAROLINGIAN RENAISSANCE

From his capitularies and letters we learn that Charlemagne began to draw to his court at Aix-la-Chapelle the most renowned scholars and teachers of western Europe, to form a palace school where intelligent men could be trained for important ecclesiastical and administrative posts throughout the empire. To head his school Charlemagne secured Alcuin, the director of the cathedral school at York, who was trained in the intellectual tradition of Bede. Alcuin gathered about him scholars from all corners of the empire to begin the training of a new crop of learned men. To such men Charlemagne gave the choice church and state positions. They in turn set up local schools and improved the general level of learning. Although most were inferior to Bede, the Carolingian scholars far surpassed all others of the eighth century. Alcuin was essentially an organizer and teacher whose scholarly work was limited to treatises on the liberal arts and commentaries on the Bible.

Alcuin's best pupil was Rabanus Maurus (d. 856), who produced a book on the education of clergy and an encyclopedia based largely on the *Etymologies*. A more interesting writer, who came from the monastery of Monte Cassino and spent but a brief period at the school, was Paul the Deacon. He composed the *History of the Lombards* which, full of tall tales, is highly untrustworthy; yet it is the only record we have of these people. The finest member of the palace school, Einhard, received his training there and remained at the court as a clerk and close friend of Louis the Pious. His biography of Charlemagne ranks as one of the three or four best of the Middle Ages. Frequent contact with Charlemagne helped Einhard to paint a masterful portrait of his master at work, at play, at intellectual pursuits, and in familial relations. Basically his book is an honest description of the greatest man in the early Middle Ages; it should be read by anyone who hopes to understand the age.

Outside the confines of the palace school the most accomplished scholar was the Irishman, John the Scot. One of a handful who knew Greek, he knew it so well that he composed verse in it. His claim to fame, however, rests on his philosophical work, *On the Division of Nature.* Here John, while attempting to reconcile the ancient philosophy of Neoplatonism with Christian doctrine, demonstrated an intellectual vigor equal to that of the Latin fathers.

If the Carolingian Renaissance had produced only the handful of scholars just discussed it could not rightfully be called a rebirth. Its real achievement was in improving and spreading the general level of practical education. As organized by Charlemagne's reform of education, the monastic and cathedral schools offered a curriculum based upon the seven liberal arts. These disciplines were grouped into the *trivium* consisting of grammar, rhetoric, and dialectic, and the *quadrivium* consisting of arithmetic, geometry, astronomy, and music. Unfortunately, the curriculum sounded much more impressive than it was. The first objective was to learn Latin from the standard texts such as those by Donatus and Alcuin. Whoever advanced in this difficult task read some of the extant ancient classics and ended with an elementary study of the slim offerings in literature. Unlike the old classical-rhetorical training that had long been scrapped, a standard training in rhetoric, which consisted of reading some of the conventional handbooks and the *Homilies* of Gregory the Great, now aimed only at producing effective Christian speakers. There was no need for an ornate, complicated vocabulary; the simple and unadorned phrase sufficed. To be understood it had to be delivered in the vernacular. Dialectic, or what we would call philosophy, was restricted to reading Boëthius and his translations of Aristotle and the *Isagoge.* Except for one minor Platonic dialogue, nothing was known of Greek philosophy and science. As for the *quadrivium,* it existed but in name. Arithmetical problems were limited to the very simple ones, all of which had to be done in the complicated Roman numerals. Geometry was a lost art. In astronomy the most complicated task was determining the date of Easter. Music was not a subject of formal instruction.

The most we can say for the practical side of the Carolingian Renaissance is that it taught a limited number of men to read and write and thereby to appreciate the few classics available. These were copied and recopied, a boring occupation, but one that saved classical works from oblivion. Out of this copying mania also developed an efficient script that became the foundation of our modern letters. The Romans in their formal writing had used all capital letters, a system called the *majuscule.* In the later imperial era, however, smaller, rounder letters

CHARLEMAGNE'S CHAPEL AT AIX-LA-CHAPELLE (*left*). Connected to his residence, Charlemagne's chapel was a simple octagonal structure apparently modeled after the church of San Vitale in Ravenna.

BAPTISTERY OF THE CHURCH OF ST. JOHN AT POITIERS (*below*). One of the rare specimens of Merovingian architecture, the baptistery of St. John in debased Roman style dates from the seventh century and shows to what depths even the ordinary crafts had sunk.

became fashionable; this was known as *uncial* writing. As Mediterranean commerce declined and papyrus for paper became scarce in the West, parchment was substituted. The difficulty of producing enough suitable sheepskin caused scribes to economize with their letters and squeeze all they could on a membrane of parchment. This led to the development of the *minuscule* system which consisted of small letters with capitals inserted for beginning sentences, paragraphs, and proper names. Although there were several minuscule systems, including the Irish, Anglo-Saxon, Visigothic, and Beneventan of Italy, the Carolingian minuscule because of its superior clearness and simplicity came to dominate the scripts of western Europe. It was a truly beautiful hand. A manuscript so written could also include pictures and large capital letters done in brilliant gold, red, and blue; such artistic work was called illumination. Today a medieval illuminated manuscript is a costly collector's item which generally finds its way into a great museum or library. When printing was developed in the fifteenth and sixteenth centuries the Italian printers chose the beautiful Carolingian minuscule as a model for their type; it still dominates the printing press.

The Carolingian Renaissance extended only to the production of a few scholars and to some practical achievements in education. Nothing was written in Latin or the vernacular that could be called literature. In the fine arts, the techniques of architecture, sculpturing, and painting were equal only to constructing fortified dwellings and simple churches. The finest extant example of architecture is Charlemagne's chapel at Aix-la-Chapelle, a small octagon forty-seven feet across with a dome atop it, whose sculptured materials, including the blocks of stone, were filched from old structures in Rome and Ravenna. To compare this petty little building to the majestic structures of the Caesars is ridiculous. Neither the empire created in A.D. 800 nor its institutions and culture bore much resemblance to the proud empire of the Julio-Claudians.

10. Conclusion

ON THE EVE OF THE TENTH CENTURY western Europe, after five hundred years of ordeal, appeared on the surface to have lost its struggle to survive. Conditions seemed more desperate than in the fifth century when, despite military and political anarchy, the experience and wisdom of the empire could still be drawn upon by such rude chieftains as Odoacer, Theodoric, and Clovis. By 900 Roman civilization was barely a memory and men had to live by their own wits and exertions. But in the loss of Roman civilization lay Europe's salvation; a new Europe had to be constructed.

It would not do to go back, even if it were possible, to revive a culture that had proved itself incapable of advance. The Roman world was tired and uncreative; it needed new ideas and vigor. The ideas supplied by five hundred years of succeeding history, though few, were practical and provided a firm springboard for future progress. The Germans had injected an abundance of vigor. We can regard the eve of the tenth century, then, as a small incline that barely obscured rich valleys of achievement ahead. There in the small states resulting from the disintegration of the Carolingian Empire the hope of political stability and the foundation for future strong governments that could provide the security essential for the growth of the many components of a culture. The agrarian economic system kept the men of western Europe fed until the revival of trade and commerce in the eleventh and twelfth centuries could increase the standard of living. And the church, despite the depths to which it had sunk, was a common institution which, with inspired leadership, could give Europe a great spiritual life and at the same time be a nucleus for the revival and spread of a vigorous intellectual and artistic life. As history so often has demonstrated, before ages of new and dynamic progress there are frequently disheartening centuries of preparation and readjustment. Such were the early Middle Ages from which was conceived a new Europe.

Further Reading

The following collections of translations of medieval sources should be noted because of their scope and accessibility in paperback: *J. B. Ross and M. M. McLaughlin, *The Portable Medieval Reader* (New York, 1949); *R. Brentano, *The Early Middle Ages 500–1000* (New York, 1964); and *B. Lyon, *The High Middle Ages 1000–1300* (New York, 1964). Excellent surveys of the Middle Ages are by C. Stephenson and B. Lyon, *Mediaeval History,* rev. ed. (New York, 1962); J. R. Strayer and D. C. Munro, *The Middle Ages, 395–1500,* 4th ed. (New York, 1959); *R. H. C. Davis, *A History of Medieval Europe from Constantine to Saint Louis* (London, 1957); R. S. Lopez, *The Birth of Europe* (New York, 1967); and L. Genicot, *Contours of the Middle Ages* (New York and London, 1967).

For the vast literature on the end of the ancient world and the beginning of the Middle Ages see *B. Lyon, *The Middle Ages in Recent Historical Thought, Selected Topics,* 2nd ed. (Washington, 1965), pp. 1–12; and *The Origins of the Middle Ages: Pirenne's Challenge to Gibbon* (New York, 1972). The student may still read with profit *Edward Gibbon's *The History of the Decline and Fall of the Roman Empire,* orig. publ. 1776–1788, ed. by J. B. Bury (London, 1896–1902), Vols. I–VII. The most comprehensive treatment of the problem is provided by *F. Lot, *The End of the Ancient World and the Beginnings of the Middle Ages* (London, 1931). Other valuable surveys are by *M. Wallace-Hadrill, *The Barbarian West, 400–1000* (London, 1952); and *A. R. Lewis, *Emerging Medieval Europe, A.D. 400–1000* (New York, 1967).

The best source of Merovingian history may be consulted in O. M. Dalton, *The History of the Franks by Gregory of Tours* (Oxford, 1927). For Charlemagne and Carolingian history the chief source is Einhard's biography, *Life of Charlemagne,* trans. by S. E. Turner (New York, 1880). See also B. W. Scholz and B. Rogers, *Carolingian Chronicles: Royal Frankish Annals and Nithard's Histories* (Ann Arbor, 1970). For other Carolingian sources see *S. C. Easton and H. Wieruszowski, *The Era of Charlemagne* (New York, 1961). The classic work is, of course, *James Bryce's *The Holy Roman Empire* (London, 1904). It should be compared to F. Heer's *The Holy Roman Empire* (New York, 1968). Two other valuable books are those of *H. Fichtenau, *The Carolingian Empire* (Oxford, 1957); and D. A. Bullough, *The Age of Charlemagne* (London, 1965). For Carolingian institutions see *F. L. Ganshof, *Frankish Institutions Under Charlemagne* (Providence, 1968). The most stimulating social and economic studies of the period are by *H. Pirenne, *Economic and Social History of Medieval Europe* (New York, 1937), and *Mohammed and Charlemagne* (New York, 1939). A more recent account is that of *R. Latouche, *Birth of Western Economy* (New York, 1960). Still the most valuable survey of society is by *S. Dill, *Roman Society in Gaul in the Merovingian Age* (London, 1926).

The best introductions to the early Christian church are by S. Baldwin, *The Organization of Medieval Christianity* (New York, 1929); H. Daniel-Rops, *The Church and the Dark Ages, 406–1050* (New York, 1959); *H. Chadwick, *The Early Church* (Baltimore, 1967); R. M. Grant, *Augustus to Constantine: The Thrust of the Christian Movement into the Roman World* (New York, 1970). On the significance of the conversion of Constantine see *J. Burckhardt, *The Age of Constantine* (New York, 1949); and H. M. A. Jones, *Constantine and the Conversion of Europe* (London, 1948). For the writings of the church fathers see *F. R. Hoare, *The Western Fathers* (London, 1954). Excellent studies on the church fathers are those of C. C. Richardson, *Early Christian Fathers* (Philadelphia, 1953); *F. Van der Meer, *Augustine the Bishop: Church and Society at the Dawn of the Middle Ages* (London, 1961); and *P. Brown, *Augustine of Hippo: A Biography* (Berkeley, 1969). Early monasticism is best understood by reading the Rule of St. Benedict, but it should be supplemented with *H. J. Waddell, *The Desert Fathers* (London, 1936); E. C. Butler, *Benedictine Monachism* (London, 1919); and *E. Duckett, *The Wandering Saints of the Early Middle Ages* (New York, 1959).

An interesting account of the relations between Christian and Graeco-Roman culture is by *C. N. Cochrane, *Christianity and Classical Culture,* 2nd rev. ed. (New York, 1944). The most provocative interpretation of early medieval intellectual history is by *C. Dawson, *The Making of Europe* (London, 1932). Other classic accounts are by *H. O. Taylor, *The Classical Heritage of the Middle Ages* (New York, 1901); *E. K. Rand, *Founders of the Middle Ages* (Cambridge, 1928); and M. L. W. Laistner, *Thought and Letters in Western Europe, A.D. 500 to 900,* rev. ed. (London, 1957). See also É. Brehaut, *An Encyclopedist of the Dark Ages: Isidore of Seville* (New York, 1912). The best treatment of early medieval art is that of C. Morey, *Early Christian Art* (Princeton, 1953). Carolingian painting and sculpture are sympathetically discussed by *R. Hinks, *Carolingian Art* (London, 1935). For developments in architecture see especially *N. Pevsner, *An Outline of European Architecture* (Harmondsworth, 1953); and K. J. Conant, *Carolingian and Romanesque Architecture* (Harmondsworth, 1959).

Excellent short surveys of Byzantine history are provided by *S. Runciman, *Byzantine Civilization* (London, 1933); C. Diehl, *History of the Byzantine Empire* (Princeton, 1925); P. Lemerle, *A History of Byzantium* (New York, 1964); R. Jenkins, *Byzantium: The Imperial Centuries 610–1071* (London, 1966); *S. Vryonis, *Byzantium* *and Europe* (New York, 1967); and P. Whitting, *Byzantium: An Introduction* (New York, 1971). The principal source for early Byzantine history is Procopius, *The History of the Wars,* trans. by H. B. Dewing in the LOEB CLASSICAL LIBRARY (London, 1914–1928).

The best short account of Arab history is that of *B. Lewis, *The Arabs in History,* 4th ed. (London, 1958). Also valuable is *P. K. Hitti's *History of the Arabs from the Earliest Times to the Present,* 6th ed. (London, 1958); and G. E. Von Grunebaum, *Classical Islam: A History, 600–1258* (Chicago, 1970). Arab social history is well covered in R. Levy, *The Social Structure of Islam* (Cambridge, 1957). For the life of Mohammed and his faith see W. Watt, *Muhammad at Mecca* (Oxford, 1953) and *Muhammad at Medina* (Oxford, 1956); *H. A. R. Gibb, *Mohammedanism: An Historical Survey,* 2nd ed. (London, 1953); *Tor J. E. Andrae, *Mohammed, the Man and His Faith* (London, 1936); and *A. Guillaume, *Islam,* 2nd ed. (Harmondsworth, 1956). The most intelligent translation of the Koran is that of M. Pickthall, *The Meaning of the Glorious Koran* (New York, 1930).

CHAPTER 5

Seignorial ec system
and
Feudal Europe mil, pol, soc, system

*Commerce and industry were both reduced to insignificant pro-*portions in the economic stagnation that came with the fall of the Roman Empire in the West. Towns and their merchants and artisans disappeared when the occupations sustaining them no longer existed. Circulation of money never completely ceased but became so minimal that some historians have characterized the period between the fifth and twelfth centuries as an age of a *natural economy*. Actually, a more accurate description of these centuries, when practically all wealth was landed and when nearly all men lived in self-sufficient agrarian communities, is an *agrarian economy*. The countryside had no urban markets to produce for, because western Europe's population had moved to the land in order to survive. Here men lived under a system called *seignorialism*. By way of preliminary definition, we may say that seignorialism was an economic system of agrarian exploitation by which the inhabitants of Europe lived almost exclusively from the fifth to the twelfth century. It must not be confused with *feudalism*. Seignorialism, it must be emphasized, was an economic system; feudalism was the military, political, and social system of western Europe from the eighth to the thirteenth century. While occupied with definitions it is well to make a further distinction. Often historians, when speaking of this agrarian system, refer to it as *manorialism,* but this term is

156

not completely accurate; it is too narrow. Derived from the Latin word *manerium* meaning *manor,* it refers to an agrarian estate with its fields, buildings, and population. It does not include the relations between lord and peasants implied by seignorialism (from *seigneur,* lord), a more inclusive term and the one we shall use to describe the economic system.

When occasionally a stray record gives us a fleeting glimpse of the early medieval countryside, it shows that two forms of agrarian communities prevailed. Throughout northern Europe, with the exception of Scotland, Wales, and Brittany, small village communities of peasants predominated. In southern Europe and the three regions noted above, the hamlet (a small settlement of scattered houses) or isolated homestead was typical. Some scholars have concluded that the Germans were the creators of the village organization, but recent research suggests that the agrarian organization of Europe dates back before the Germans and Romans, and that the Alpine people lived in villages and the Mediterranean people in hamlets. As to why the north seemed to prefer villages and the south hamlets, there is no sure answer. Perhaps the two systems best fitted the requirements of northern and southern agriculture. Grain production prevailed in the north, and in the south, the grape and olive. Often hamlet areas were characterized by poor soil and a small population.

1. *Seignorialism*

ANOTHER PROBLEM is whether the villages we meet in the Carolingian period and after descended from the great Roman estates or from German agrarian communities. Previously we saw that the agrarian organization of the late Roman villa with its coloni and slaves was similar to that of the Germans and that the two fused. By the fifth century the peasants who worked the soil of the large Roman estate were economically and legally unfree, completely dependent upon the great landlord who held not only vast economic but also legal and political power. Numerous scholars, however, have argued that the German agrarian communities, though similar in their routine, were composed of free farmers who democratically ordered the economic, social, legal, and political life of their agrarian unit. However much we might like to trace our democratic institutions back to such Utopian communities, there is no sound evidence to support this theory propounded in the nineteenth century during the age of romanticism. Despite the argument that all Germans were originally free, only to sink in economic and legal status during the chaotic sixth, seventh, and eighth centuries, it is certain that both Roman and German agrarian organization was aristocratic—great warrior landlords held all the land which was worked for them by their economic and legal dependents.

The first lesson to be learned about seignorialism is that from the fifth century onward it was a system through which a very small percentage of men—the nobles and the great clergy—lived from the labor of the great mass of men—the peasants—who in return for a small parcel of land and survival were ready to perform necessary economic services. The second lesson to be learned is that the seignorial system, which today is associated with retrograde economies in backward countries, dominated western Europe into the twelfth century because no other economic system was possible. Until there were trade, industry, towns, markets, and bourgeoisie there could be no money economy. Only when they reappeared did seignorialism begin its slow retreat from western Europe.

CROPS AND FARMING METHODS

Despite the similarity of seignorial institutions throughout Europe, regional variations existed. Routine and custom were dictated by climate and soil. Products and techniques of flat land differed from those of mountainous or dune areas. The method of cultivation varied for grain field, vineyard, and orchard. The principal crop, grain, needed much preparation of the soil. In southern Europe, where the soil was light and sandy, the traditional Roman plow consisting of an iron bar attached to a wooden frame continued in use. Such a plow but stirred up the soil. For the heavier, richer, and more moist land of the north a durable wheeled plow was used. Oxen were employed to pull it because other draft animals with their primitive harness were incapable of such heavy work. The records state that a plow team consisted of eight oxen, though all might not be used at the same time. To rest them they were rotated in groups of two or four. No ordinary peasant could own such a team, so a group would share a team or use one supplied by the lord.

In our modern age of scientific farming, when the farmer with good land is disappointed unless he gets seventy-five bushels of corn and fifty bushels of wheat to the acre, medieval soil productivity seems unbelievably low. In England today the return is threefold that of a typical medieval manor. To sow the grain, it was broadcast as in biblical times. The use of manure was understood but it was not very effective because no community could support enough cattle to produce sufficient manure. The usual custom was to pasture cattle on a field lying fallow after the harvesting of its crop. Additional manure was secured from forest and wasteland where pigs were pastured. Until Europe's population began to grow in the eleventh century and markets for agrarian produce appeared, each community produced just enough to feed its populace. The hay from the meadow went to feed the ox teams, and little was left for the other cattle. Fortunate was the cow that did not starve in the winter after a summer spent on the skimpy pasture of a harvested field. Consequently, except for those needed for breeding, all cattle were slaughtered in the late autumn. Because of the impoverished diet, the meat was extremely tough and unpalatable. A medieval writer on agriculture said that if given a choice he would select the hide of a cow over its meat. The milk from the cows was always turned into cheese. Sheep were valued because of their wool. The cheapest and most durable animal was the pig. He took care of himself all seasons of the year and ate anything he could find. With the abundant forest land of early medieval Europe, it was simple for every community to maintain a sizeable herd of pigs that grazed on the nuts and acorns.

The typical peasant family held a plot of about thirty acres of tillable land plus meadow, pasture, wood, and fishing rights. In ordinary years this was sufficient to feed the family. But during war, which was all too frequent, and during drought and heavy rains it was difficult, and for many impossible, to survive. Neighboring regions might have enough food to share, but means of communication and transportation were so wretched that it could not be secured. Thus did the inhabitants of Europe live on the doorstep of starvation for centuries, constantly praying to God and the saints for a good harvest and vintage. Bread was the staple diet of the peasant, who supplemented it with fruit and vegetables from his garden. Only rarely did he enjoy the luxury of fish, chicken, or meat, and if meat, almost always pork. Down to the twelfth century, the typical community was self-sufficient. It produced its own simple food and clothing. Craftsmen such as smiths, millers, brewers, and the women at their hand looms supplied what had to be processed and fabricated. The only commerce consisted of exchanging so many chickens for a pig and so many measures of wheat for a bony cow.

AGRARIAN ORGANIZATION

The question that logically follows is how a typical agrarian community was organized so as to accomplish its work. In those regions where the isolated hamlet and homestead dominated, each peasant was responsible for his own plot of land. Except for cooperating with his neighbors on a large project such as clearing additional land, plowing, and harvesting—a custom still followed by modern farmers—such a peasant was not governed by a communal routine. His principal obligation was the payment of rent to the lord for his plot of land. We are therefore more concerned with the communal and cooperative village system, which dominated the richest lands and which was found in the leading states of medieval Europe—England, France, and Germany. But before proceeding to a description of one of these villages let us clearly distinguish the village from the manor. The manor was the basic unit of seignorial exploitation. It might consist of one village, its lands, and its peasants, but this was not general. Villages and their lands were usually divided among several lords whose portions were manors. Sometimes a group of villages formed a manor. At other times a manor was composed of several villages or parts of villages scattered over a large area. The great Carolingian monastery of Saint-Germain-des-Prés outside Paris had estates extending from Brittany to the Moselle Valley. The abbey of Saint-Trond in Belgium also held estates on the Moselle so as to have vineyards for its wine. In eleventh-century England great lords had lands scattered over a number of counties. What makes the pattern even more confusing is that in those villages divided among several lords the peasants were also divided, one belonging to this manor and another to that. One English historian has called this complicated skein "tenurial heterogeneity." Our conclusion must be that the manor was an artificial unit created for seignorial exploitation whereas the village community was the essential economic and social unit of agrarian life.

By the ninth century, when there are adequate records, one is impressed by the equality of peasant holdings and services. This is particularly evident in a ninth-century survey of all the possessions of the monastery of Saint-Germain-des-Prés. The following entry on the peasant Bodo and his household is typical of hundreds:

> Bodo a *colonus* and his wife Ermentrude a *colona,* tenants of Saint-Germain, have with them three children. He holds one free manse, containing eight *bunuaria* and two *antsinga* of arable land, two *aripenni* of vines and seven *aripenni* of meadow. He pays two silver shillings to the army and two hogsheads of wine for the right to pasture his pigs in the woods. Every third year he pays a hundred planks and three poles for fences. He ploughs at the winter sowing four perches and at the spring sowing two perches. Every week he owes two labour services (*corvées*) and one handwork. He pays three fowls and fifteen eggs, and carrying service when it is enjoined upon him. And he owns the half of a windmill, for which he pays two silver shillings.[1]

To be sure, this is a complicated passage, but in effect it simply says that Bodo holds so much arable land (about thirty acres), so much vineyard, and so much meadow. He owes so much rent and weekly labor services plus additional work when it is required. No matter how called—freedmen (*coloni*), serfs (*servi*), or freemen (*ingenuiles*)—the peasants all held the same amount of land and had the same obligations. Whether free or unfree, each was forced to work according to a strict routine, to perform common obligations, and to live from a standardized measure of land. Regardless of how many heads there were in a peasant household, each peasant held the same amount of land. The agrarian routine, it should be noted, had to be adhered to if lord and peasant were to survive. Cooperation, not communism, was the theme of the medieval village. The seignorial system was based upon cooperation and originated from economic necessity.

---

[1] Eileen Edna Power, *Medieval People* (London: Methuen, 1927), Ch. I, note B1.

The agrarian villages practiced an agricultural routine called the *open-field* system. It seems that with the wheeled plow it was more efficient for the peasants to cooperate in the cultivation of their fields. If each peasant household contributed to the common effort, then naturally each shared in the fruits. Experience had taught that it was unwise for a peasant to have all his arable land concentrated in one field, because he might suffer from having it located on poor soil or in an area frequently flooded. Each peasant's allotment, therefore, was scattered in strips over the arable land of the village. Because the strips were not fenced, this arrangement has been termed the open-field system. In some parts of Europe it is still possible to detect the remains of the open-fields, and the historian with the aid of aerial photography can almost reconstruct some of them. From the accompanying plan it can be seen that the open-fields were divided into fairly large sections determined usually by the contour of the land. These sections, called *shots*, were in turn broken down into *strips* approximately an acre in area. The strips were terminated by unplowed headlands upon which the plow team could turn about. In some areas the strips were separated by a ribbon of unplowed turf or a balk consisting of two plowed furrows thrown up against each other. The strips were a furlong in length

MEDIEVAL PEASANTS AT WORK. This scene of peasants harvesting wheat and shearing sheep is from the celebrated fifteenth-century illuminated manuscript, *Les Très Riches Heures* of the duke of Berri. In the background is the castle of Poitiers.

(furrow-long) and four rods in width (sticks for nudging along the oxen). This means that each strip was 220 yards long and 22 yards wide, totaling 4,840 square yards (one acre). Each peasant received what his strip produced. Other agrarian rights were shared in common. Pasture rights permitted the peasant to pasture so many animals on the fallow fields. From the meadow he got a share of hay, and from the woodland he could take a limited amount of brush and fallen timber for fuel and lumber. Here, too, he could pasture his pigs, a privilege called *masting* or *pannage*. Around his hut, each peasant had a small garden and yard where he grew his vegetables and kept chickens, geese, and bees. In addition, most peasants had a cart, some simple implements like the rake and hoe, and a few pieces of personal property.

Far back into the ancient world men had known that soil became exhausted from continuous planting. The Romans understood that soil exhaustion could be prevented by the use of fertilizer and by the planting of certain crops that put nitrogen and other minerals back into the earth. But because manure was scarce and the value of legumes was imperfectly understood, the Romans relied upon *field rotation* to keep their land fertile. They employed the two-field system, whereby each year half of the land was cultivated and the other permitted to lie fallow. This system continued throughout southern Europe in the Middle Ages and spread to those northern areas where the soil was poor. In most of northern Europe, however, the soil was rich enough to permit cultivating two-thirds of it annually while one-third lay fallow. Of the two-thirds cultivated, one-half was planted in autumn with wheat or rye and harvested in the early summer; the other half was sown in the spring with barley, rye, oats, beans, and peas and harvested in late summer. The pattern of rotation was such that the fall field lay fallow the next year, the spring field was plowed and planted in the fall, and the fallow field was planted in the spring. In this manner the three fields could be completely rotated in four years. The great advantage of the three-field system was that it permitted more land to be cultivated and facilitated plowing. It is reasonably certain that the greater productivity of this system and the use of the heavy wheeled plow accounted for the greater agricultural prosperity of northern Europe.

Of great importance in the agrarian community were the relations of lord and peasant. We have shown earlier how all western Europe came to be broken up into landed estates controlled by great spiritual and lay lords. Generally by the eighth century there was in every community a fortified dwelling or manor house where the lord, his family, his servants, and his retainers lived. The most powerful lords lived in imposing fortified structures called *castles* (*Burg* in German, and *château* in French). Surrounding such a building was a belt of land, often fenced or walled off, called the *lord's close*. Here were his garden, orchard, bees, fowl, barns, and stables. Here were stored his produce, animals, and implements. Customarily, although one cannot generalize, the lord shared the common meadow,

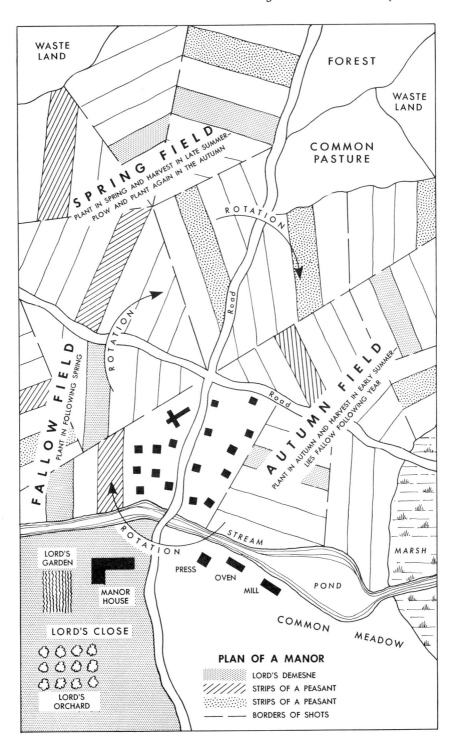

WASTE LAND

FOREST

WASTE LAND

COMMON PASTURE

SPRING FIELD
PLANT IN SPRING AND HARVEST IN LATE SUMMER—
PLOW AND PLANT AGAIN IN THE AUTUMN

ROTATION

Road

ROTATION

FALLOW FIELD
PLANT IN FOLLOWING SPRING

Road

AUTUMN FIELD
PLANT IN AUTUMN AND HARVEST IN EARLY SUMMER—
LIES FALLOW FOLLOWING YEAR

ROTATION

STREAM

MARSH

LORD'S GARDEN

MANOR HOUSE

PRESS

OVEN

MILL

POND

COMMON MEADOW

LORD'S CLOSE

LORD'S ORCHARD

PLAN OF A MANOR

LORD'S DEMESNE
STRIPS OF A PEASANT
STRIPS OF A PEASANT
BORDERS OF SHOTS

pastured his cattle on the fallow land, and held arable strips dispersed among those of the peasants. Of all these rights and land he had the lion's share, generally a third, known as the *lord's demesne* or *inland*. Because the lord's function in society was to fight, govern, and hunt, his arable land was worked by the peasants, a duty they must perform in return for their land and their very lives. To supervise this work the lord appointed a steward, who was assisted by officers elected by the peasants. There was a reeve assisted by the hayward who kept animals off the meadow, a plowman who directed the plowing, and a cowherd, swineherd, shepherd, dairymaid, and aletaster. The steward also presided over the seignorial court, in which all the peasants were triable, and he enforced the sentences. The law of the community was the custom stated by the older and better men.

SEIGNORIAL OBLIGATIONS

The principal obligation of the peasants to their lord was the performance of labor services. Generally these services were much the same for all the peasants, although the baser tenants sometimes had to perform more onerous tasks than those of a higher legal status. Labor services, it must be emphasized, were a matter of local custom. All sorts of petty rents had to be paid, and mostly in kind—so many geese, chickens, eggs, or pigs. The labor services, called *corvée,* consisted primarily of agrarian work done on the lord's demesne. The least free of the peasants were bound to do whatever was commanded at any time. The average peasant, however, owed weekly service for a specified number of days plus working extra days at plowing, planting, and harvesting seasons. This extra labor was called *boonwork* because it was considered a boon to the lord. Those peasants highest in the legal and economic hierarchy of the community had only to perform boonwork. Besides the usual agricultural services, the peasants also had duties of a political and public nature. They helped to build and repair castles, bridges, and roads, to provide transportation, and to accomplish the humdrum tasks of war such as digging fortifications and carting supplies. When their lord's land was attacked, they fought, or fled for their lives.

There were in addition to the routine services special payments and rights that the lord was entitled to and over which he had a monopoly. If a peasant's son desired to become a priest or monk he had to pay a set sum to the lord for this privilege because his departure reduced the manpower of the manor. If a peasant's daughter desired to marry a man outside the community, the lord gave his consent only upon receipt of a payment called *merchet* or, in French, *formariage.* Upon the death of a peasant, his family had to pay a sort of inheritance tax called *heriot* (*mainmorte*) in order to possess the land and its rights. The payment consisted either of the peasant's best animal, of some personal property, or of a nominal sum. Some of the more infamous exactions were the *head tax* (*chevage*) which recognized the dependence of the peasant and the *tallage (taille)*. This latter tax was levied on the whole community whenever the lord was in need of money and, in many areas, it became an unbearable burden. In the hands of some unscrupulous lords it was simply robbery. The lordly monopolies were almost endless. To hunt and fish, his permission had to be obtained and the catch shared, with the lord getting the biggest fish. In France he customarily got a pike when one was hooked. It was unfortunate for the peasant caught poaching. Permission was required to cut growing timber. Most lords exercised powers public in nature and possessed by virtue of royal grant or, when there was no strong central authority to halt the fragmentation of public authority, by usurpation. Numerous lords struck their own coins which they repeatedly debased. They exercised tight control over local trade through orders called *bans*. Official weights and measures of the lord had to be used in the market; tolls had to be paid on all goods displayed for sale; and the peasant had to have his wine pressed at the lord's wine press, his grain ground at the lord's mill, and his bread baked at the lord's oven. The fees were a certain portion of the wine, flour, and bread. These revenues were called *banalités*.

Closely associated with these monopolies was that of justice—the most highly regarded of all. From every case tried in the seignorial court the lord got a fee and, in addition, a fine for each violation of the law. The concern of medieval lords for law and order should deceive no one into thinking that justice was their chief goal and ideal. Their prime concern was to obtain the profits of justice. The greatest lords wielded a high justice which gave them jurisdiction over the most serious criminal and civil offenses. The rank and file enjoyed a low justice which entitled them to hold court for routine civil and criminal pleas. For all lords, the exercise of justice symbolized the high authority they held over their dependents. Proud was the lord when he could point to the gallows upon which he hanged culprits condemned to death in his court. As with other public powers, those of justice had either been obtained by regalian grant or through usurpation; unfortunately in the hands of many lords such power was an excuse for blatant extortion. In the age of seignorialism every man took and kept what he could.

It is impossible to total up seignorial income because so much of it was received in labor. The income was derived from the agrarian products of the demesne, labor services, special payments, monopolies, and the profits of justice. It supported the lord and his family and provided the resources necessary for him to fulfill his role as a member of the feudal system. It should be obvious by now that the feudal lord who possessed landed estates and wielded both economic and political powers over his dependents—the peasants—was concerned with his seignorial unit as a source of revenue and as a means of giving him the time to concentrate on the feudal tasks of fighting and governing. It follows, therefore, that feudalism rested upon seignorialism; the men who fought and prayed were supported by those who worked. Without seignorialism, feudalism could not have functioned.

PEASANT LIFE

But what was life like for the peasant who bore such a heavy burden? A quick answer would be that his lot was miserable and hopeless. And judged by the standard of living and degree of freedom enjoyed by the common man in vast areas of the world today such an answer is reasonably accurate. But in the light of what the ordinary inhabitant of the medieval countryside could expect it falls short of the truth. What perhaps 90 per cent of Europe's inhabitants desired, and all they could expect, was a minimum of security, enough food to repel starvation, and a hut to withstand a little of the cold and rain. Essentially the seignorial system gave this to the peasant and, although his heavy labor bore painfully upon him, he knew no other way of life and believed that God had ordained such an existence for most of His children. There was, to be sure, sporadic criticism and uprising, but they were the result of blind rage at a particular offense by a particularly evil lord; they came not from the conviction that society could be changed to give the peasants freedom and a share of the worldly goods. Such ideas came to the peasant only when a money economy returned to Europe and upset eight hundred years of living from the soil. Starvation, natural catastrophes, brigandage, and war, although feared and hated, were accepted as inevitable. Most lords, however, did what they could to keep their peasants secure, for they were essential to seignorialism; without them the land was worthless. In order to live the peasants accepted their legal and economic degradation. But there was, in fact, very little agrarian slavery in the Middle Ages. Although the medieval records speak often of servi (serfs), they were not the slaves or bodily property that they had been in the Roman Empire. A serf might still be recognized as unfree legally, but economically—and this was the essential test—he had climbed up to the level of the ordinary peasant whom the records term a *villein* (*villanus*) or a *rustic* (*rusticus*) and who legally was recognized as free. And yet there was scarcely any difference between the two, because the villein's freedom meant nothing to him. Seignorial custom and economic necessity bound both peasant and serf to the estate of which both were considered appurtenances not to be sold apart from it.

The peasant's life was indeed a busy one. When not working for the lord, he had his strips and those of the other peasants to cultivate. He was helped with this work by his wife and children, all of whom went into the fields. It mattered not who did the work so long as it was done. In every community we hear of those landless peasants called *cotters,* who held but a cot and a garden and eked out a living by working for the lord and peasants during the busy seasons. There were, too, always a few craftsmen such as the blacksmith, the miller, the shoemaker, mason, and carpenter, who along with the priest had their plots of land and through their skills fulfilled the corvée. Peasant, cotter, craftsman, and priest, all lived together in a cluster of miserable plastered mud and straw huts with thatched roofs, not far from the manor house. These cottages were arranged on either side of one or two dirt roads which might cross and form a sort of square; here generally were the parish church, an adjacent cemetery, and the mill and wine press if they were powered by human or animal labor. If there was a stream, the mill and press were located beside it for water power. Not far from the center of the village there would likely be a pond from which were taken fish and eels, a delicacy relished during periods of fasting. Surrounding the village would be the fields and meadow. Beyond was the woodland, waste, and sometimes marshland.[2]

In this physical environment the peasant lived out his humdrum life. Up before dawn, the peasant and his family retired with the setting sun. "Man went to bed early in those ages simply because his worthy mother earth could not afford him candles." Suffering from the bitter cold of the early winter morning and perhaps wishing for a better lot, the peasant dulled the pain of his existence by singing the lusty provincial tunes as he went from one task to another. Eventually there was a song for every task, season, and month. Full of the superstition inherited from the German and Roman worlds, the peasants watched the "old gods stalk up and down the brown furrows" and "muttered charms over their sick cattle . . . and said incantations over the fields to make them fertile." The church wisely encouraged such belief and taught the peasant "to call on Christ and Mary in his charm for bees." And thanks be to holy church, she provided the peasant with his numerous holidays on Sundays and saints' days. Although the church frowned on the peasant's indulging in amusement on holy days, there was no stopping him until the Reformation. He danced, sang, drank, and capered about in the churchyard to the accompaniment of "ribald love-songs," "wicked songs with a chorus of dancing women," or "evil and wanton songs and such-like lures of the devil." A poor priest of Worcestershire, England, was kept awake all night by peasants dancing in his churchyard to a song with the refrain "sweetheart have pity." Groggily saying the mass next morning he caused a terrible scandal by intoning "sweetheart have pity" rather than *Dominus vobiscum."*

It was a great day for the community when wandering minstrels and jugglers passed through and performed their bawdy, awkward songs and acts in return for hospitality, food, and a few *deniers*. On special days such as Christmas, or occasions such as marriage and knighting, the lord might fête the peasants with his good beer, mutton, and beef, and the good old custom held that everyone could drink all he could hold. Now and then a great lord, or even the king, might pass a night at the manor house and, despite the work involved, it was worthwhile because one snatched a glimpse of the great personage just come perhaps from a distant and romantic place such as Paris or Rome. In his aristocratic finery and shining mail he provided a memorable spectacle. Such an event, as well as perhaps a trip

---

[2] See the plan of a manor on p. 163.

twenty miles distant to some great fair at Saint-Denis or at Troyes, where a whole new world was opened up before the peasant, would be recounted for years and years to children and grandchildren.

These were the amusements and diversions of the humble peasant, whose inevitable fate it was to return to his miserable little cot with its rude table, bench, and bags of straw upon which he slept in indescribable filth. We know these pedestrian but essential things about the peasant, yet we will never know what he believed, thought, and aspired to. Invariably, and this is especially true in the Middle Ages, the common man and his thoughts pass unrecorded as the contemporary historian and writer describe the deeds, passions, loves, and aspirations of the rich, aristocratic, and powerful man. It is a shame we are so little acquainted with a medieval peasant, however dull the poor fellow was, because, as one historian has so aptly said, "history is largely made up of Bodos." This was never truer than in the Middle Ages between the fifth and twelfth centuries, when the seignorial system and its peasants fed Europe and enabled the feudal aristocrats to fight and govern.

2. Political Reconstruction

BY THE BEGINNING of the tenth century the Carolingian Empire was no longer a fact. As a result of internal anarchy and of Viking, Hungarian, and Moslem attack, central authority had disappeared, land was lost to the invader, and the empire was fragmentized into numerous small, independent states controlled by counts, dukes, and bishops.

GERMANY

With the death of the last Carolingian in Germany in 911, the nobles chose a ruler from their own ranks—Duke Conrad of Franconia—to govern the eastern kingdom of Germany. Conrad realistically saw that he should be content with the title of king and not attempt to exert authority beyond the borders of Franconia; actually, the dukes of Bavaria, Saxony, and Swabia equaled Conrad's power and ruled independently. Each fought desperately to stave off conquest by the threatening Hungarians. Conrad's successor was the Saxon duke Henry the Fowler (919–936), who contented himself with improving the defenses of Saxony. He had the good sense to protect the Elbe-Weser river area by constructing large fortified camps (*Burgen*) to obstruct the Hungarians. His strategy paid off in 933, when along the Unstrut River, a tributary of the Elbe, he decisively defeated the Hungarians and rolled them eastward. Although Henry also occupied Lorraine, he continued to permit the great dukes to rule their duchies like kings. By the middle of the tenth century there were established four powerful duchies—Saxony, Swabia, Franconia, and Bavaria—whose rulers were competent and able to provide some political stability and security for their subjects.

FRANCE

In the old middle kingdom of Lothair and to the west in France, political fragmentation was more severe. To defend the northern part of his kingdom against the Vikings, Charles the Bald had erected three military marches. Flanders was entrusted to a powerful and ruthless noble called Baldwin Iron-Arm. The duchy of Burgundy, given originally to a local count, fell into the hands of a branch of the French royal family during the tenth century. Because of its unfavorable location for trade, however, Burgundy was slower to develop. It did not become a strong state until the fourteenth century. The lands centering around Paris between the Seine and Loire rivers were assigned to Count Odo of Paris who, as we have seen, was elected king in 887, and became the founder of a strong house which established itself securely as the royal dynasty in 987 with the election of Hugh Capet, from whose name comes the word Capetian. But not until the early twelfth century were the Capetian kings able to begin the construction of a strong state. Their territory—the Île de France—was boxed in by too many powerful neighbors.

In this hundred-year period small states were springing up all over France. The county of Flanders, strategically located along the North Sea below the estuary of the Meuse and Scheldt rivers, expanded in all directions and became a strong state where the central authority was feared and obeyed. Just to the west the duchy of Normandy also became a power. This territory had been conquered by the Normans in the late ninth century, and Charles the Simple, recognizing a *fait accompli,* had granted it to the Norman leader Rollo, who swore allegiance to Charles and agreed to hold the duchy as a fief in return for military service. Under a line of strong-willed dukes the Normans developed efficient political institutions and quickly adopted Frankish culture. The neighboring duchy of Brittany remained barbarous and wild, overrun by anarchy. To the east of the Île de France the count of Troyes kept adding to his lands until he had formed the county of Champagne which, advantageously situated on the north-south trade routes, was to become an extremely wealthy feudal state. To the west of Paris was the county of Blois, and then extending along the Loire down to the Bay of Biscay was the county of Anjou which, under the remarkable Fulk Nerra, became one of the principal French states by the end of the tenth century.

The French states of the south, with their strong Roman tradition and distinct Provençal dialect, hardly seemed a part of France. The local rulers were completely

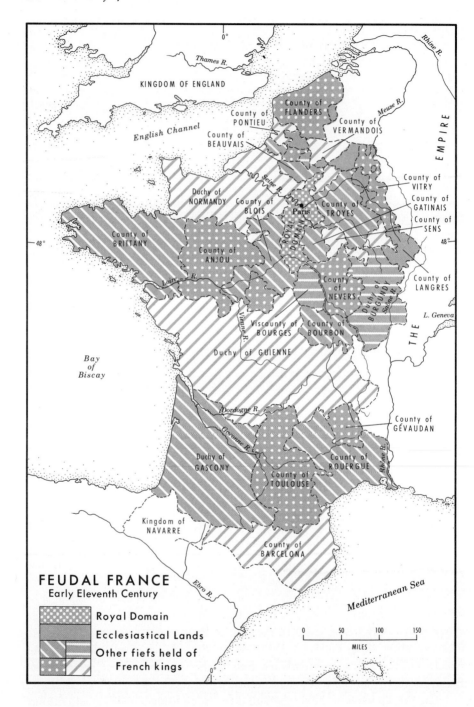

KINGDOM OF ENGLAND

Thames R.

English Channel

County of
PONTIEU

County of
FLANDERS

County of
VERMANDOIS

Meuse R.

County of
BEAUVAIS

County of
VITRY

County of
GATINAIS

County of
SENS

Duchy of
NORMANDY

County of
BLOIS

Paris

ROYAL DOMAIN

County of
TROYES

Seine R.

County of
BRITTANY

County of
ANJOU

County
of
NEVERS

Duchy of
BURGUNDY

County of
LANGRES

Loire R.

Vienne R.

Viscounty of
BOURGES

County of
BOURBON

Duchy of GUIENNE

Saône R.

L. Geneva

*Bay
of
Biscay*

Dordogne R.

Garonne R.

County of
GÉVAUDAN

Duchy of
GASCONY

County of
TOULOUSE

County of
ROUERGUE

Rhône R.

Kingdom of
NAVARRE

County of
BARCELONA

Ebro R.

Mediterranean Sea

FEUDAL FRANCE
Early Eleventh Century

Royal Domain

Ecclesiastical Lands

Other fiefs held of
French kings

0   50   100   150
MILES

THE EMPIRE

Rhine R.

independent; none recognized the Capetian kings. Of the numerous states which peppered the south only four were powerful. The principal one was the duchy of Aquitaine extending from the Loire to the Garonne and from the Rhône to the Bay of Biscay. Southward from the Garonne down to the Pyrenees was the duchy of Gascony. To the east along the Mediterranean were the counties of Toulouse and Barcelona. These, then, were the leading states of the tenth century which, along with Anglo-Saxon England, formed the core of western Europe. Below the Pyrenees all Spain was Moslem. So, too, were the principal Mediterranean islands such as Corsica, Sardinia, and Sicily. Italy was cut up into many small principalities that warred among themselves and set the precedent for centuries of Italian particularism. Papal power was so anemic that it could not be maintained even over the Papal States. In central and eastern Europe, running north and south, were the uncivilized Slavs, Hungarians, and Bulgarians. In the Scandinavian region were the pagan and retrograde kingdoms of Denmark, Sweden, and Norway.

RETURN OF POLITICAL STABILITY

Despite interesting and significant historical developments in the peripheral areas, the center of power in medieval Europe lay not around the Mediterranean basin, as it had during the Roman Empire, but in the northwestern part—England, France, and Germany—where a fertile and well-watered land abounding in natural resources was blessed by a mild but cool temperature that favored agrarian productivity. Here, given an opportunity, a large population could be supported and a brisk trade, commerce, and industry revived. In the late tenth century this opportunity came. The strong group of states that replaced the Carolingian Empire proved themselves capable of preserving reasonably firm government internally and of repelling the Viking attacks from the north, the Hungarians from the east, and the Moslems from the south. For the first time since the Roman Empire, men were able to devote some of their efforts to concerns other than war and the struggle to survive. They could interest themselves in trade and industry, in a higher standard of living, in a more elevated spiritual life, and in a richer culture. As a result of the political stability produced by the small states of western Europe, society recovered from the dark abyss of despair and put down roots for the flowering of medieval civilization in the eleventh, twelfth, and thirteenth centuries.

It is no wonder, then, that before historians began to explain historical phenomena rationally they developed an intriguing but untrue legend telling how medieval men believed that the end of the world would come in A.D. 1000 and waited for the fateful day in despair. But when the year 1000 came and passed and the world still continued monotonously on, men took hope, became ambitious, and wrought the great economic, political, religious, and cultural revival characterizing the following centuries. In the discussion that follows we shall be interested solely in the military, political, and social institutions that dominated these states and enabled their rulers to forge political structures capable of supporting stable and strong government. These institutions that developed in France and western Germany, and then spread to England and to many other areas of Europe and the Mediterranean world, we call feudal. Our task is to define the system of feudalism which dominated western Europe from the middle of the eighth century into the thirteenth.

3. Feudalism

SCHOLARS FIRST USED THE TERM *feudalism* after the French Revolution in the late eighteenth century; it referred to the institutions of the Old Regime overthrown by the revolutionaries. Since then, scholars studying the institutions of oriental countries have also used the term in writing about the history of Japan, Korea, India, and China. Today one frequently sees the word used to describe retrograde economic systems or any sociopolitical organization considered antiquated and backward. In the nineteenth century powerful American capitalists were called *feudal barons*. However picturesque such description and however much it suggests a few powerful men subjecting the masses to abject subservience, it is inaccurate. Feudal institutions existed on a full scale only in medieval Europe. As we have emphasized, *feudalism* does not refer to economic organization.

ORIGIN AND DEFINITION OF FEUDALISM

In searching for the elements that composed feudalism, most scholars have agreed that the highly honorable and personal relationship between noble men was fundamentally derived from the Germanic *comitatus*, wherein the celebrated chief led valorous warriors to military glory. The leader (*princeps*) and his followers (*comites*, companions) entered into a mutually honorable relationship whereby the leader promised glory and plunder and the follower, loyal support and service unto death. Such a relation was voluntary and involved no degradation for the follower. As an institution the comitatus was found throughout all the German tribes from the Goths to the Vikings, and the noble and illustrious relations and deeds it involved were glorified in such epic poetry as the Anglo-Saxon *Beowulf*. Although in the Late Roman Empire such an honorable relation cannot be found, there was a similar practice called *commendation*. To obtain the protection of a powerful lord or to secure a plot of land from him, the humble man would place his person and all his goods at the disposal of the lord. The latter would give protection and land to the dependent, who in turn offered his economic services. This practice continued under the Merovingians. Often we read of how an individual became the man (*homo*) of a lord (*dominus*), but this relation was unhonorable and degrading for the dependent because he was obliged to perform humble economic service. Here actually originated the dependent tenure of seignorialism between lord and peasant. The honorable personal relation in feudalism had a Germanic origin.

There was, however, another late Roman institution that did become a part of feudalism; this was the *precaria,* land granted during the pleasure of the donor. Governed by "precarious" tenure, such land could be repossessed at any time. Eventually, under the Franks such tenure was extended to a term of years or for life in return for services, customarily economic. The word *precaria* signified that land had been granted to a man as a result of his prayer (*preces*). Sometimes these grants were called *benefices* (*beneficia*) because the land had been obtained as a boon from the grantor; in such cases the benefices were agrarian estates (manors) received by aristocrats, who in turn were the lords of the peasants on the estates. It was under the Carolingians that the honorable relation of the German comitatus was fused with the benefice to form real feudalism. In the eighth century the Carolingian rulers and great nobles had followings of noble men who were styled *vassals* (from *vassus,* meaning military retainer).

The vassals of the Carolingians occupied an enviable position. They formed an elite who helped govern and who served as heavy-armed warriors mounted on horseback; they in turn led their own warriors to serve on the battlefield. To remunerate them for their services the Carolingians gave out the only wealth they possessed—landed estates which they granted from their own extensive lands or from those appropriated from the church. It appears that the first Carolingian to grant landed estates, commonly called benefices, to royal vassals in return for military service was Charles Martel. This military benefice gradually came to be known as a *feos* or *fief* in the Romance vernacular, a term derived from a German word meaning cattle or property. Later, the vernacular word was Latinized into *feodum* or *feudum* from which the French *féodal* and English *feudal* have come. The Carolingians, therefore, began the custom of granting military benefices or fiefs to vassals. But why? The reason seems to be that they felt the need of opposing the Moslem and Hungarian swift mounted warriors with heavy-armed cavalry, a type of military service that was extremely expensive and forced them to remunerate their vassals. The fief constituted the payment. It consisted not only of a landed estate, its appurtenances, and peasants, but of public powers called immunities which bestowed the right to hold a court, to tax, to raise military forces, and to exact services such as the building and repairing of roads. All royal vassals such as the counts, marquises, and bishops were granted fiefs and thus wielded economic and political authority. In such a manner, feudal tenure brought with it the exercise of political authority.

The essence of real feudalism was the combination of vassalage and fief-holding. A noble man (the vassal) entered into a mutually honorable relation with another noble man who granted him a fief primarily in return for military service. For centuries the Germanic custom of vassalage had existed but there was no feudalism because vassals were not awarded fiefs for military service. For centuries *precaria* or benefices had been granted to men but without specifically obligating them to perform military service and without involving the honorable contract of vassalage. Feudalism developed only when vassalage and fief-holding fused. Soon the day was to come when every vassal held a fief.

PRINCIPLES OF FEUDAL TENURE

Although feudalism spread across Europe, around some shores of the Mediterranean, and eventually to Syria where it was transplanted by the crusaders, it originated in western Europe and developed most fully in England and in the region between the Rhine River and the Pyrenees. The fundamental component of feudalism was vassalage; no man could receive a fief without being a vassal, and to be a vassal the man had to be a noble. The ceremony by which a man became a vassal was called *homage* (*homagium* from *homo,* meaning *man*). The man went before the lord, knelt, placed his hands between the lord's and became his man (*homo*), swearing *fealty* (*fidelitas*) and promising to fight for and protect him against all men who lived and died. The lord in turn accepted the homage and fealty, raised the vassal to his feet, and kissed him. Then on the Bible the vassal took a sacred oath to fulfill his promises. Homage, however, must not be confused with fealty; they were two separate acts. All the strong rulers of Europe exacted fealty, that is, an oath of allegiance from all their free subjects, whether or not they were vassals. Only when homage was done did a man become a vassal.

Thus were noble warriors united in an honorable relationship and bound in mutual obligation, the vassal to perform military and other service for the lord, and the lord to protect and honor his vassal. Should any lord attempt to reduce a vassal to servitude, commit adultery with his wife, or attack him, the vassal was justified in deserting the lord. If either defaulted on his obligations he was considered guilty of feudal perfidy. This noble relation is well portrayed in medieval vernacular epic poetry such as the Anglo-Saxon *Beowulf* and the French *Song of Roland*. Throughout the latter there runs the theme of loyalty unto death by Charlemagne's vassals, Roland and his friend Oliver. The treacherous Ganelon is the archetype of feudal perfidy; no fate was too cruel for him. The motif of this great poem is vassalage, a noble relation traceable back to the comitatus.

In the Middle Ages some land was always held in absolute ownership and entailed no service; this was *allodial land*. In extent it was insignificant when compared to the land governed by feudal tenure. When a lord granted his vassal a fief it was done through an *investiture* ceremony. To symbolize the transference, the lord customarily handed the vassal a stick, knife, or piece of turf. The vassal received possession, not ownership, and enjoyed possession only as long as he fulfilled his feudal obligations. Upon his death, his son could receive possession of the fief after becoming the lord's vassal and receiving investiture. He, too, enjoyed possession so long as he was a faithful vassal. By the tenth century, however, fiefs were becoming heritable and it was taken for granted that a son would inherit his father's fief upon performance of homage. When receiving the fief, the heir paid to the lord an inheritance tax called *relief*. This valued lordly right was called a *feudal incident*. Should the vassal die without heirs, then the *incident of escheat* applied, whereby the fief reverted back to the lord.

Although not used everywhere throughout Europe, the rule of passing the fief down intact to the eldest son (*primogeniture*) was found to be most efficient; it insured that a fief would not become fragmentized, thereby weakening the value of the military and political service attached to it. Under primogeniture one man— the eldest son—assumed the total responsibility for the fief. When a vassal left behind only an infant heir, a lord insured control over the fief by customarily exercising the *incident of wardship*. The lord supervised the rearing of the heir and administered the fief until the boy was old enough to become a vassal, to re- ceive investiture of the fief, and to fulfill his obligations. When there was only an heiress, the *incident of marriage* applied. Obviously a woman could not render the necessary military and political services, so the lord married her off to a suitable noble who did homage for the fief and performed the service.

The principal service entailed by the fief was military. From the eighth century on, a vassal holding a fief must provide the service of so many heavy-armed men (knights, *milites*) mounted on powerful war chargers. Gradually custom dictated that each fief owed a quota of knights who were to fight in the field every year for at least forty days at their own expense. In the early days of feudalism each vassal probably fulfilled this obligation by taking his military retainers to the lord. These warriors, fed and maintained in the vassal's household, were called *house- hold knights*. This arrangement, however, proved unsatisfactory for both vassal and household knight. The vassal found it expensive and awkward to maintain rough and tough fighters in his household; the warriors were discontented because they aspired to holding a fief which brought with it social, political, and economic prestige. It thus became standard practice for the vassal to grant some of his land in fief to these knights, who as his vassals held their fiefs in return for the perform- ance of a stipulated amount of military service. These vassals in turn could grant out some of their land in fief to other knights—their vassals—for military service; and the process could then be repeated. This was the system of *subinfeudation*. It has been estimated that in the twelfth century the count of Champagne was the vassal of nine lords and the lord of hundreds of vassals who in turn had *enfeoffed* (granted in fief) land to subvassals. By subinfeudation, the count of Champagne could muster a force of two thousand knights. Most fiefs obligated knight service, but there were some that entailed *castle-guard,* that is, providing so many knights to guard the lord's castle for a stipulated time. Some fiefs were held by the tenure called *serjeanty,* which meant that the holders rendered less than knight service. They furnished footsoldiers (serjeants), horses, or arms. And, finally, some lands were granted to churches and monasteries for the sole obligation of pious service such as praying for the souls of dear and departed relatives. This tenure was known as *free alms.*

Besides his military obligation the vassal had others of a pecuniary nature called the *feudal aids.* It was customary for the lord to collect standard contributions from his vassals whenever his eldest son was knighted, his eldest daughter married, and when, captured in battle, he required a ransom. The vassal was also expected to extend hospitality to his lord when the latter visited him; he was to lodge, feed, and entertain the lord and his establishment. This obligation was onerous and expensive, for the lordly household included the lord and his family, some retainers, servants, horses, and dogs. Another obligation was *suit to court.* The lord summoned his vassals to court for a variety of reasons. Sometimes it was to help celebrate a great festival or holy day, or the knighting or marriage of some of his children. At other times it was to consult with the vassals on a matter involving war, peace, or a treaty. If he required a pecuniary contribution not called for by feudal custom he had to secure the consent of his vassals.

For promulgating important laws vassals gave their advice and consent. The lord's court was a judicial tribunal where according to feudal law all differences among his vassals were adjudicated. Here any vassal could get feudal justice, because he was entitled to judgment by his feudal *peers* (social equals), the other vassals. The lord presided over the court, which was not like a modern court that listens to evidence, decides the case, and then determines the penalty. It heard the charges of the two parties and decided almost invariably that the dispute should be settled through trial by combat. The victorious individual was declared innocent. As for the vanquished, the court declared what the law was and what penalty applied. If a vassal failed in his feudal obligations he was summoned to court to answer for his misdemeanor and to be punished. If he failed to comply with the summons the court would declare him a feudal felon who had forfeited all right to his fief. The lord then could confiscate the fief. If the vassal thought himself powerful enough to contest the confiscation he would reply with a formal act of defiance, whereby he renounced his homage and fealty; then only war could settle the outcome. Feudal justice, it should be noted, was only for feudal aristocrats; it had no connection with seignorial justice which applied only to the peasant. Every lord had a seignorial court for his peasants, and all lords had courts for their vassals. But there were petty vassals at the bottom of the hierarchy who had no vassals, and they held only seignorial courts.

In the early Middle Ages all the great ecclesiastics such as bishops and abbots received fiefs for which they had to render military service in person. The German bishops acquired renown for military prowess. In the *Song of Roland* Archbishop Turpin died a hero's death on the field of battle. When the spiritual level of the church was at low ebb, this practice was quite acceptable, but with the revival of spiritual life in the eleventh century it became embarrassing to have bishops ride to battle with lance, sword, and battle-axe. The church prohibited such martial activity and attempted to restrict prelates to their occupation of praying. Faced with these restrictions, bishops and abbots resorted to subinfeudation to provide the necessary military service while continuing to render all other feudal obligations not connected with bloodshed. The chief distinction between ecclesiastical and lay fiefs was that the incidents of relief, marriage, and wardship could not be exercised with the former. To recoup himself for this financial loss, the lord received the income from the ecclesiastical fief in the interval between the death of the holder and the installation of a successor.

The principal modification of feudal tenure began in the eleventh and twelfth centuries. Prior to this time all homage had been simple homage, that is, a vassal owed all his loyalty to one lord. But gradually this vassal became the vassal of another lord and then other lords in order to increase his feudal wealth and prestige. Because for each of these fiefs he owed military service, this arrangement was confusing in case of war between two lords of the vassal; neither they nor he were certain which lord he should support. As multiple lordship grew, feudal law was modified to admit a higher loyalty called *liege homage*. A vassal became the liege man of one lord and owed to him his paramount loyalty and service. Customarily, he became the liege man of the lord from whom he had held his fief longest or from whom he held the richest fief. But even with liege homage, war brought on complications, and all sorts of precautions were inserted into feudal contracts so as further to define obligations. When in the twelfth century the kings of France and England fought in Normandy, their common vassal, the count of Flanders, so arranged his feudal obligations that both lords secured his service. To his liege lord, the king of France, the count rendered his personal service and a token contingent of fighters; to the English king he sent a sizable force of knights. Still, these precautions often collapsed, and then the vassal chose one lord to support, thus forfeiting one of his fiefs.

Feudalism was a rough, practical military and political system which was the only possible solution when all the functions of government and society had to be remunerated in land. Feudalism and seignorialism dominated western Europe until the returning money economy rendered them ever less essential, and finally vestigial. During its heyday, feudalism spread throughout much of Europe as the feudal aristocracy sought new land and military glory. It was carried by crusading knights into Spain and thence to Syria and the southern Balkans. Norman mercenaries and adventurers took it to Italy, Sicily, and England. To the east, the

Germans pushed it into central Europe. Eventually it got to Scandinavia. As feudal tenure spread there developed with it certain knightly practices and a code of conduct called *chivalry*.

4. Chivalry and the Feudal Aristocracy

FROM THE FRENCH WORD *chevalier* (meaning *knight*) has come the word chivalry. Simply defined, it means the customs and ideas of the feudal aristocracy composed of lords and vassals. Its derivation from *chevalier,* which also referred to a man who fought on a horse (*cheval*), indicates the importance of the horse for the feudal system. Until the eighth century no horse of western Europe had been strong enough to permit a heavy-armed man to fight upon it. Then, somehow, there came into western Europe by way of the Byzantine Empire a large oriental steed which proved capable of the task. Known first to the Parthians in Persia and then to the Byzantine Empire which used it with great success during the cam-

CAROLINGIAN KNIGHTS and A MEDIEVAL TOURNAMENT. These two scenes illustrate the advance made in medieval armor. In the manuscript on the *left* the Carolingian knights, who appear in a ninth-century psalter of Saint-Gall, are very simply protected, while on the *right* those shown participating in a fourteenth-century tournament in an illumination from the *Chronicles* of Froissart are completely covered with armor.

paigns of Justinian, this war horse (the *destrier*) was used to carry the victorious troops of Charles Martel in his battle with the Moslems at Poitiers in 732. Henceforth until the fourteenth century the mounted knight dominated the European battlefield. This fighting technique was costly and demanded a well-trained warrior; only richly supported feudal aristocrats could afford these expensive horses and acquire the skill to fight on them. The gulf was thereby widened between the feudal aristocrat and the peasant who fought on foot with scarcely any equipment. In fact, the true gentleman and aristocrat came to be the mounted knight. His elevated estate was completely out of the peasant's reach; the knightly class became a closed corporation with its special training, customs, and code of behavior.

EDUCATION FOR KNIGHTHOOD

Although some sons of noble families were marked out for high church offices, most were looked upon as candidates for knighthood and were introduced early to a rigorous training to give them competence in this profession. At the age of seven or eight a boy would be placed in the household of a renowned noble, often the lord of the boy's father. There he would learn to ride and care for horses, develop elementary fighting skills, become acquainted with the ways of aristocratic society, and develop a polite and respectful attitude toward noble ladies, whom he waited upon and helped in every way. While undergoing this education the youth was called a *page,* in French *valet* or *damoiseau* (little vassal or lord). At the age of fourteen he became a *squire* (candidate for knighthood) and entered upon a more rigid course of training. He became the assistant of a knight who was responsible for his martial skill. Under the knight's surveillance he practiced with sword and tilted with lance. The squires jousted among themselves and fought sham battles called tournaments. A sterner training came when the squire accompanied his knight to war. He guarded a spare horse and armor, helped the knight to dress in his mail, often rescued the knight when dismounted or wounded, and sometimes threw himself into the fray.

After the squire had proved his competence in training or on the field of battle he was accepted into the order of knighthood. This was accomplished by a ceremony called *dubbing to knighthood* (*adoubement* in French) which perhaps had as an antecedent the Germanic custom of admitting a boy to man's estate by presenting him with a sword and shield, or the Roman ceremony of recognizing manhood by giving a boy his *toga virilis.* Although any knight could bestow knighthood, it was generally done by the boy's father or a very distinguished warrior. If possible, the dubbing occurred on the battlefield where, perhaps, the squire had demonstrated his bravery. In a very simple ceremony the squire was presented with a sword, given a few words of knightly advice such as the obligation of being valorous and proud, and finally given the *accolade,* which consisted of a rough blow across the neck. This blow was to impress the new knight with the seriousness of his obligations and estate. All sorts of records and aristocratic literature tell of such dubbings. In 791 Charlemagne girded a sword upon his son Louis the Pious. The famous Bayeux Tapestry depicts Duke William of Normandy knighting Earl Harold of England. Most of the feudal epic poems—the *chansons de geste*—describe the ceremony in glowing phrases.

Of all the knightly virtues emphasized at the dubbing, that of prowess stands out. Repeatedly the young squire was admonished: *Sois preux!* This simple phrase embodied many virtues and accomplishments. The true knight was brave unto reckless daring and death. He was true to his friends and a devoted servant of the church. In his fighting he was to employ no tricks or unfair stratagems; open and equal combat was the ideal. A word pledged must be kept to the death. If a knight was captured and gave his word not to escape he must adhere to it. Only if rescued or ransomed could he honorably obtain freedom. A knight caught in a cowardly act completely lost face and was discredited to the end of his life. Any breach of these rules was interpreted as the grossest insult, resulting often in bloody feuds between noble families which continued until insult had been avenged.

CHIVALROUS CONDUCT

Gradually chivalrous conduct became formulated in a rigid code of etiquette governing the behavior of every true knight. Honor came to him who adhered to the etiquette; disgrace to him who flouted it. In the vigorous days of feudalism between the eighth and twelfth centuries, chivalrous conduct imposed no soft or unmilitary restraints upon the knight. Against his enemy he could be ruthless and violent; he could slaughter his foe's peasants, plunder his goods, burn churches, and even rob and rape. Knightly conduct pertained only to the other members of his caste, and woe be to all other individuals. Although a knight truly loved and appreciated his mistress, he valued his wife only as a companion to bear good strong children and manage the household. For such a work horse he had little time or affection. By decent and fair standards, chivalry was basically a selfish way of life for a small percentage of Europe's population. It signified nothing more than the mutual respect of knights; all other individuals were inferior and beyond the pale.

Real chivalry must be interpreted as a code of conduct for tough warriors; we must not view it according to fourteenth- and fifteenth-century sources when, with feudalism and knighthood degenerating, the feudal aristocracy, to save face, developed an elaborate mode of chivalrous conduct at which it play acted. In earlier centuries, although the church had managed to inject some Christian ritual into the ceremony of dubbing to knighthood, such as prayer and fasting before the altar, had composed a set of rules for high moral and Christian behavior, and had partially diverted the knight's martial activity into fighting holy crusades against the infidel, chivalry had not at all been anemic. The typical knight was not overly polite, and he did not often indulge in the composition of songs of love and epic adventure which he sang to the accompaniment of a harp. The women of the court with their fine ideals did not dictate to him, and seldom was he overwhelmingly and chronically in love. He was a practical, gruff, and able fighter who concentrated upon his profession. Mock tournaments, such as the Field of Cloth of Gold of Francis I of France and Henry VIII of England and the antics of Don Quixote, had no place in the eleventh and twelfth centuries with such figures as William the Conqueror of England and Louis the Fat of France.

5. Feudal Warfare

LET US NOW SEE how the knight armed himself, fought on the field of battle, and built his fortifications. Fortunately, the typical knight of the eleventh century is vividly depicted for us by a contemporary record—the magnificent Bayeux Tapestry—which is a band of linen cloth 214 feet long and 20 inches wide, embroidered in colored thread with scenes of the Norman Conquest of England in 1066. Any visitor to the tapestry's museum in Bayeux, France, can obtain a fine knowledge of knightly armor and combat.

MILITARY EQUIPMENT AND TACTICS

The typical knight wore a belted tunic, close-fitting hose, and, when not fighting, a cape that fastened about his neck. When preparing for battle, he replaced the mantle by a shirt of mail called a *hauberk,* which was a leather jacket with metal discs sewn upon it, or a fabric of iron links. The hauberk extended only to the knees and was slit at the crotch so the knight could straddle his horse. It had sleeves down to the elbow and a mailed cowl that protected the neck. Over the cowl went a conical metal helmet with a nosepiece; the rest of the face was exposed. Occasionally a warrior wore heavy leather gauntlets and mailed leggings. The final piece of defensive equipment was a kite-shaped shield constructed of a wooden base with a metal veneer. The weapons were a lance of about eight to ten feet and a cross-hilted sword. We know, too, that most knights swung a battle-axe. To carry this weight there were the great war chargers with their oriental style of saddle, reins, and stirrups. A study of this tapestry suggests that it was no mean accomplishment for a knight to hold the shield on his left arm, the reins with his left hand, his lance in the right hand extended straight to the front, and then to gallop at full speed towards the enemy and try to knock him from his horse. After the charge the knights engaged in hand-to-hand encounter with sword and battle-axe; the unhorsed knight was in desperate straits, his position similar to that of a modern infantryman with rifle pitted against an armored tank.

Throughout the twelfth century there was little change in the knight's armor. By the thirteenth century, however, the armor had become heavier and more cumbersome and continued to become more elaborate until finally the knight became top-heavy and could not mount his horse alone. When unhorsed, he was like a capsized boat, completely immobilized because of his weight. In time the armor became plated, and a barrel-shaped helmet with only narrow slits for the eyes was clamped over the head. Although this helmet gave him much protection it obstructed his view and hampered his maneuverability; he was rather like a horse with blinders. Covered from head to toe, he could not distinguish friend from foe once the battle had been joined, so he resorted to the device of *heraldry*. He emblazoned upon his shield a coat of arms which identified him and came to be the noble insignia of his family. By the thirteenth century all the great feudal families had their distinguishing coats of arms. The French kings used the *fleurs de lys;* the English kings, the leopards; and the Flemish counts, a lion.

Into the thirteenth century the feudal army was organized around the mounted knight, who was assisted by auxiliary troops such as archers and dismounted men-at-arms. Typical tactics called for the opposing armies to charge headlong at each other and to unhorse, kill, disable, and disorganize as many of the enemy as possible. The better disciplined armies were grouped into squadrons of vassals under their lord or a distinguished captain. They held their formations as long as possible, wheeling and charging together. Eventually every battle ended in individual encounter, and the objective was to take as many prisoners as possible because they were more valuable than corpses; they brought ransoms. A celebrated knight like William Marshal, vassal of the English kings in the twelfth century, made a fortune from ransoms and ended his life the greatest baron in England. Except in extraordinary cases the goal was to win an engagement with as little loss of life as possible. In the English battle of Lincoln in 1217, when five hundred knights fought in each army, only one knight was killed, and even this accident was deeply regretted. Few pitched battles developed; the standard engagement consisted of guerrilla warfare, raids, and sieges of castles.

THE CASTLE

The military architecture of the Middle Ages passed through many stages, each an attempt to provide better defense against improved siege weapons. Originally the word *castle,* derived from the Latin word *castellum* meaning fort, referred to any fortified stronghold. In the early Middle Ages the typical castle was large and primitive, not unlike the American frontier stockade. It consisted of approximately thirty acres surrounded by a ditch, an embankment of earth, and a wooden palisade. This type of fortress served as a refuge point for the inhabitants of the area and was frequently an administrative and ecclesiastical headquarters. Such was the English *borough* (meaning originally *fortification*) constructed in the

FEUDAL WARFARE. The Bayeux Tapestry, which was completed in the latter part of the eleventh century and measures a little over 214 feet long and 20 inches wide, depicts the conquest of England by William the Conqueror. We see here, at the *top,* Norman knights attacking a motte and bailey castle; at the *center,* Norman equipment and the knighting of Harold by William the Conqueror; and at the *bottom,* the Norman ships crossing the English Channel.

ROCHESTER CASTLE, KENT (*above*). The keep of Rochester Castle, 125 feet in height, is one of the largest Norman stone keeps and the tallest in England.

CASTLE OF FALAISE (*below*). Built on a commanding height, the Castle of Falaise in Normandy, whose donjon dates back to the late eleventh century, is a fine example of an early Norman stone castle.

tenth century against the Danes, and the German *Burgen* (castles) thrown up against the Hungarians by Henry the Fowler. The typical castle of later centuries was smaller and derived from a tenth-century French style of fortification. Its area was not over six acres, and it was divided into two parts—the *motte* and *bailey*.

The Bayeux Tapestry shows four such castles located in Normandy, Brittany, and England. Each had an artificial mound of earth surrounded by either a ditch or moat of water. On top of the mound (*motte*) was a wooden palisade which often enclosed a wooden tower called a *keep*. Thrown up around the motte was an earthen embankment and stockade, likewise surrounded by a moat. One crossed the moat by a drawbridge and encountered a gate barred by a heavy timbered grilled door called a *portcullis* which was raised and lowered by a windlass. The area between the motte and outer fortification was the *bailey* or courtyard in which stood barracks, stables, barns, the kitchen, and other such buildings. The first line of defense was the bailey and its fortifications. From here the defenders could retire to the motte and finally to the keep, which also served as a residence for the lord and his family. The first simple keeps were divided into stories. In the basement were a well and storage rooms; on the first floor, a storage room for arms and quarters for the garrison; on the upper stories, the lord's quarters partitioned into a great hall, some sleeping chambers, and perhaps a chapel. The roof was constructed for defense and lookout and was crowned by the lord's pennant bearing his coat of arms. From here rocks and arrows would fall upon the besieger. When the Normans conquered England they built five hundred of these castles throughout the island.

By the late eleventh century the powerful lords were constructing more durable castles out of stone. Essentially they were massive square stone towers with walls twenty to thirty feet thick. These were the *tower castles,* and they were surrounded by watered moats. A good example of such a castle is the Tower of London built by William the Conqueror. Meanwhile, in the twelfth century the motte and bailey castle was modified. Its various parts were being reconstructed in stone. First, the gate of the bailey was fortified in stone so as to form a massive gate tower. Provided with holes and slits to fire weapons through, and considerably more fireproof, the gate towers became a common feature of twelfth- and thirteenth-century castles. The next step was to replace the motte with a rectangular stone keep which served as fort and home.

Finally, the wooden palisades were replaced by masonry walls along which towers were strategically interspersed. A splendid example of such a castle is Rochester, located on the Medway River in Kent. Its keep, measuring 125 feet, is the tallest in England. But the greatest castle of western Europe in the early thirteenth century was Château Gaillard (Saucy Castle), so called because Richard I of England who built it is said to have exclaimed proudly: "Is not this a fine saucy baby of mine, this child of a year old?" It was constructed high over the Seine

BEAUMARIS CASTLE, ANGLESEY (*above*). On the Isle of Anglesey off the northern coast of Wales, Beaumaris Castle is a superb example of a concentric castle. Begun in 1295, it was never completely finished.

CARCASSONNE AND ITS RAMPARTS (*below*). Carcassonne is a good example of a concentrically fortified town. Located in the county of Toulouse, it was regarded as a strategic stronghold by the counts of Toulouse and the French kings, and in the thirteenth century its ramparts were greatly extended and strengthened by such kings as Louis IX and Philip III.

River in Normandy as a defense against the French kings. Incorporating all the newest features of military fortification and benefiting from the general European technological and economic advance, it was fundamentally one vast walled and towered fortress within another. The inside fortress was located on a height and was considerably higher than the exterior fort with its thick surrounding *curtain walls*. The whole structure had a commanding position on the Seine. Towers were located so that attackers could be engulfed in a deadly cross-fire of arrows. If the attackers broke through the outer defense they were virtually imprisoned between two walls of defenders. All about the walls and towers were walks, so that the defenders could swiftly concentrate to repel an attack; all towers and walls were capped by *machicolation,* that is, a parapet with openings between supporting *corbels* (projections out from the wall) for dropping stones or pouring boiling lead and pitch down upon the assailants. It seems certain that many features of this magnificent castle were borrowed by Richard from the fortifications he had seen in Syria while on the Third Crusade. There he saw castles with rounded walls and circular towers against which the stones of catapults glanced off harmlessly and the battering ram was unable to make a solid blow.

From a fortress like Château Gaillard it was but a short step to cylindrical towers placed regularly about walls. Such was the castle of King Louis IX of France at Angers and that of the Flemish counts at Ghent. The final creation was the most elaborate fortress of the Middle Ages—the concentric castle consisting of one massive castle within another. Edward I of England sprinkled these castles throughout Wales in the last quarter of the thirteenth century. No one who has the opportunity should neglect seeing Beaumaris Castle on the Isle of Anglesey, Carnarvon Castle, or Rhuddlan and Harlech castles. They are marvels of medieval engineering skill, and bear strong resemblance to the famous concentric castle in Syria, the Krak-des-Chevaliers, built by the Knights Hospitalers as a defense against the Turks. In France the most splendid example of such a concentric fortification is the town of Carcassonne, situated in the old county of Toulouse. Seldom did any of these complicated stone fortresses fall before an attack. They could be taken only through starvation or treachery. Castles dominated the countryside and life of western Europe until the fourteenth century, when gunpowder antiquated them. They then became palatial residences for the aristocratic; prime examples of this are the exquisite French *châteaux* along the Loire from Orléans to Angers, the prototypes of the castles drawn by artists for fairy tales and stories of medieval adventure.

ARISTOCRATIC LIFE

Although the stone castle has become a symbol for things medieval, it was only possessed by the great feudal nobles; the rank and file resided in unpretentious fortified manor houses protected by mere stockades. And even the great lords spent much of the year at various of their manor houses, gobbling up the produce of the estate, hunting wild boar in the neighboring forest, and hawking. Traveling from one manor house to another occupied much of the noble's life. While not traveling or fighting he hunted, banqueted, drank, gambled, and made love. When even these pastimes bored him and there was no war to fight, the knight made his own dangerous sport—the *joust* or tournament. The joust was an encounter between two knights. They charged with lance and attempted to unhorse each other. Wooden lances were often shattered, and then they fought with sword and battle-axe. The tournament was a mass mock battle between two groups of knights. At a herald's signal they would charge, break lances, and then fight at close quarters until one side had been pushed from the playing field. It was a deadly and bloody game but it kept the knight in top combat form, and gave him honor as well as ransoms when he disarmed and captured other knights. The only difference between the tournaments sponsored by the great princes and a real battle was that neutral spots were designated where a disabled knight could rearm, get another mount, or nurse his wounds; the captured were not placed in prison. Tournaments were held throughout western Europe at different seasons and festival days, and the good knights traveled from one to the other in quest of glory and riches. William Marshal made a business of this in the late twelfth century. He rode the tournament circuit just as today the American cowboy rides the round of rodeos in the western states. Not until the fifteenth and sixteenth centuries did tournaments degenerate into harmless pageants, where knights exercised in shining armor with blunted weapons before galleries of beautiful women who gave their handkerchiefs to be worn atop the helmets of their hero-lovers.

6. The Feudal State

POLITICALLY THE TENTH CENTURY saw the reconstruction of Europe into small kingdoms, duchies, and counties organized in accordance with feudal principles. We must now investigate the history of these feudal states to the middle of the twelfth century and learn how they employed feudal institutions in their government.

The logical area to begin with is France, where feudalism originated and where some of the strongest states arose. Between 987 and 1108 the history of the royal domain or Île de France was one of weakness and steady retreat before a circle of encroaching vassals of the Capetian kings. The counties of Champagne, Anjou, and Flanders, as well as the duchy of Normandy, robbed the Capetians of their land and flouted their royal authority. The great counts and dukes completely ignored their feudal obligation to serve and support their lord. Deprived of their vassals' military support, the Capetians were almost suffocated in their tiny realm consisting of a narrow strip of land from north of Paris down to Orléans. They were so weak they could not control vassals even within this area. Local lords built castles, usurped and defied royal authority, and plundered and pillaged. Repeatedly, such petty nobles defeated the kings. At one time a Capetian could not even pass safely from Paris to Orléans. The greatest humiliation was suffered when one Capetian was captured by a rebellious vassal and had to be freed by the ignoble footsoldiers of Paris. At times the kings were so destitute that monasteries took pity on them and supplied food and lodging. The nadir of Capetian disgrace came with the reign of Philip I (1060–1108), a completely disreputable character, recognized by none. It looked like the end of the house of Hugh Capet. And yet the Capetians survived, simply because their principal vassals preferred weak kings whom they could kick about at will, and were too jealous of each other to permit any to assume the royal title. Then, too, the church supported the Capetians because they represented legitimate authority, ruled by the grace of God, and supported law and order, always an ideal of the clergy. Finally, under feudal custom the Capetians were the supreme lords of the old western part of the Carolingian Empire, and this lent a certain amount of prestige to their kingship.

LOUIS VI AND THE FORMATION OF FRANCE

After the long and disastrous reign of Philip I, luck had it that he should be succeeded by the first of the great Capetians—Louis VI the Fat (1108–1137) whose reign inaugurated two centuries of constant increase in royal power and laid the foundations for the great state of France. It is only fair, however, to point out that the success of Louis was facilitated by the upswing in the economic and spiritual life of western Europe. The revival of trade, commerce, and industry, the reclamation of land for more cultivation, and the support of a revived Papacy and local church buttressed the financial and political power of Louis, permitting him to strike back at local and foreign opponents and to make the royal authority respected. Able to hire good soldiers with money derived from the taxes levied upon trade, and supported by the spiritual sanction of the church, Louis set about his arduous task.

Of exceptional mental and physical ability, Louis was also of exceptional size —so fat indeed, that hardly a horse could be found to carry him about on his weekly campaigns. His two objectives were to restore order within the Île de France and to make his feudal lordship respected outside. In this task he was ably supported by his chief adviser and minister, the famous Suger, abbot of the monastery of Saint-Denis where lie buried France's kings. Together, this well matched pair—the warrior and the administrator—waged an offensive against political anarchy. All vassals guilty of misdemeanors were summoned to court to answer the charges and submit; if they did not heed the summons Louis waged war on them and destroyed their castles. It took seven years to defeat the tough Hugh de Puiset, who rebuilt his castle almost seven times. But the most infamous resister was Thomas de Marly. This bloody robber, devoid of pity, killed and tortured men as he would the lowest animal. While riding through the fields he would dismount, cut off the legs of this peasant and blind that one. It took sixteen years for Louis to master Thomas. But when Louis died, after thirty years of war, he had completely reduced the royal domain and made it a land of law and order where royal power was respected. Over his royal castles he placed loyal custodians who used them to maintain peace and justice locally. The realm was divided into administrative districts headed by faithful officers called *prévôts* who collected taxes, headed local forces, executed royal orders, and administered justice. These vassals and officials were closely watched by Louis and Suger; few thought it worth the gamble to defy royal authority.

Outside his domain Louis found progress slower. The best he could do with Champagne and Normandy was to defend his realm against their attacks and play off the jealous count of Anjou against the equally jealous duke of Normandy. Farther afield he met with more success. In the duchy of Burgundy, he restored his nephew who had been removed by a local usurper. As far south as the county of Auvergne, he forced the count to restore the episcopal land and town of Clermont to its bishop. Although he interfered with a disputed succession over the Flemish countship, he had to retire. So famed had the reputation of Louis become that the dying duke of Aquitaine requested that his heiress Eleanor be put under the guardianship of Louis and married to his son. This unexpected request opened up southern France to the Capetians. When Louis VII mounted the throne in 1137 he inherited a secure domain, with an efficient feudal government respected throughout western Europe; the Île de France was on the threshold of phenomenal expansion in the next seventy-five years.

THE GREAT FRENCH FIEFS

Northeast of the Île de France lay the rich and powerful county of Flanders which, by the early twelfth century, was the wealthiest land of northwestern Europe. Well located on principal waterways and highways for trade and commerce, blessed with a fine climate for the woolen industry, and fortunate in having a long succession of hardheaded counts who followed an enlightened economic policy that encouraged trade, industry, the founding of towns, and the freedom of urban inhabitants, Flanders was a model feudal state. All the old regalian powers of the Carolingians had been usurped by the counts, to whom all the inhabitants of the region owed their first allegiance. The counts were the supreme military commanders and were entitled to the service of their vassals as well as that of all able-bodied freemen. Their castles dominated the countryside, and none could be constructed without their approval. Guardians of the peace of the county, the counts wielded a high justice that was paramount. All ecclesiastical establishments were under comital protection. Only the count could coin money, regulate commerce, and levy indirect taxes. Flanders was virtually a miniature kingdom. To enforce all these rights, the counts developed an efficient feudal administration. The county was broken down into military and administrative districts called *châtellenies* because they were organized about key *châteaux* at such places as Ghent, Bruges, Ypres, and Saint-Omer. Over each district was a *châtelain* who held the castle and exercised the comital powers locally. Although these officers were powerful feudal vassals who possessed extensive fiefs in remuneration for their service, and although their office became hereditary, Flanders was small enough that the counts could control them and maintain their loyalty.

The other powerful state of northern France was the duchy of Normandy which, by the late eleventh century, was the most thoroughly feudalized country of western Europe. It was powerful enough in 1066 to enable its duke, William the Conqueror, to defeat the strong Saxon king of England and conquer the island. Feudal tenure and custom in the duchy were highly uniform, because the land had been conquered rapidly by the early Normans. All the land was feudalized, and each fief owed a definite quota of knights. In the exercise of their powers the dukes resembled the Flemish counts; perhaps, in some respects, they copied from them. The dukes were the guardians of the peace and of the church; they nominated all important clergy to office; they regulated trade, the building of castles, and the coinage of money; they held a monopoly of justice over all major crimes and all warfare; they were the supreme military commanders. The dukes ruled Normandy through feudal lieutenants called *viscounts* who administered districts called *counties* (*vicomtés*).

The other French states were less orderly and powerful but most provided relatively stable government as, for example, the counties of Champagne, Aquitaine, and Toulouse. Particularly well organized was the county of Anjou which, like Flanders, was governed locally by *châtelains* whose headquarters were in the first stone keeps of Europe. The exceptions to the well-ordered feudal state were the duchies of Burgundy and Brittany which, in the absence of strong rulers and central control, were paralyzed by feudal warfare among the nobility.

ENGLAND AND THE NORMAN KINGS

Across the English Channel was the remarkable kingdom of England. Under the Wessex kings it had repulsed and conquered the Danes, and in the tenth century it had become a unified realm with a government superior centrally and locally to any of the continental states. At the end of the century, however, in the face of weak kings and renewed Danish invasions from the kingdom of Denmark, both government and resistance faltered; by 1016 Canute, king of Denmark, had been recognized as king of England and had established a North Sea empire. An astute ruler, Canute embraced the Christian faith, married the widow of the dead Anglo-Saxon king, and ruled as a true Saxon sovereign, accepting all the English laws and institutions. England prospered both politically and economically until Canute's death in 1035. Then in seven years his work was undone by two incompetent sons. In 1042 the throne reverted back to Edward the Confessor of the old Saxon House, who reigned until his death in 1066. He was, however, too pious and totally unfit in training and temperament for his responsibilities. His single contribution to English history was the founding of Westminster Abbey in 1051. Because the real authority resided with the earls of Wessex, upon Edward's death Earl Harold, a man of considerable military and political capacity, was elected king. But William, duke of Normandy, by virtue of certain nebulous relations with the Confessor, laid claim to the English throne. In a remarkable expedition, recorded on the Bayeux Tapestry, which called for the transportation of many fighters and supplies overseas, William defeated and killed Harold at Hastings, swiftly occupied England, and was crowned king, thereby founding the Norman dynasty in England. The Norman Conquest was, on the whole, beneficial for the island realm. It gave the English a strong line of kings and an efficient feudal system which was introduced in all its vigor. It also brought England into the main stream of European life.

The outstanding achievement of William the Conqueror (1066–1087) was to subdue England and to introduce strong central authority which was enforced on the lowest level of local government. That William was stern, ruthless, and overly greedy for money cannot be denied, but such faults were mitigated by his introduction of a peaceful and orderly government. The great monument to his efficient rule is *Domesday Book*, a royal record resulting from an investigation into the economic resources of the realm. No detail was omitted; all fiefs held of William were listed with all their appurtenances and incomes. The ultimate objective was a reassessment of taxation to bring William a larger return from his kingdom. The speed, efficiency, and ease with which this magnificent economic document was compiled is remarkable.

When William died of an injury sustained in a fall from his horse, the royal possessions went to his sons. The eldest, Robert Curthose (so called because his small stature required him to wear "short leggings"), became duke of Normandy while William Rufus became king of England (1087–1100). Both Normandy and England suffered under these men. Robert was a weak-willed, chivalrous ruler whose authority went unrecognized while the Norman nobility indulged in feudal warfare. William was a strong ruler whose authority was obeyed but who had only three interests—war, money, and Normandy. He used his father's efficient government to extort money from his subjects and schemed to take Normandy from his brother. He was a thoroughly unpopular man, and no one grieved when he received an arrow through the heart while hunting in the New Forest outside Winchester. None of his hunting party even halted to carry the royal corpse away and prepare it for a decent burial.

One of the party, William's youngest brother Henry, rode swiftly to Winchester, appropriated the royal treasure, and then had himself proclaimed king as Henry I (1100–1135). This diligent worker and astute man developed into one of medieval England's greatest kings. Robert, who opposed his succession to the throne, ended up by being deprived of Normandy in 1106 and spending the rest of his life in a dungeon writing poetry. Henry swiftly restored order to Normandy and kept Louis VI of France on the defensive. In England he concentrated upon improving both local and central administration and expanding royal justice. His great sorrow was that he had no male heir. His one son William met disaster on a stormy night in 1120. While crossing the English Channel he, his noble companions, and the crew of the "White Ship" were so drunk that the vessel crashed upon rocks and sank. Only a Rouen butcher survived to tell the sad tale. This left Henry with his daughter Matilda who was the wife of the German emperor Henry V. Upon her husband's death she returned to England, and Henry forced his vassals to recognize her as the next ruler of England. He then married her off to Count Geoffrey Plantagenet (so called from the broomflower he was accustomed to wear) of Anjou and she bore him a son—the future Henry II. This was an important union and birth, for out of it came the famous Angevin Empire of Henry II and his sons in the second half of the twelfth century. One day in Normandy, while doting over his little grandson and future heir, Henry I peacefully died.

NORMAN GOVERNMENT

However essential is a knowledge of the principal historical events under the Norman kings, such details become inconsequential when placed beside the Norman achievements in government. Under William the Conqueror, feudalism was introduced to England where its institutions provided the means of establishing an especially strong government. The Norman Conquest introduced the legal principle that ultimately all land was held from the king, to whom feudal services were due. Of the numerous royal vassals only a few received great public powers; these were the counts or earls who were appointed to the rule of military marches along the Welsh and Scottish borders. They exercised regalian powers in return for the heavy burden of continuous military defense. The rest of William's vassals were closely regulated and received no more than limited political authority. Judicial and military supremacy belonged to William. All serious offenses, called the *pleas of the crown,* were reserved for his court, and he wielded a monopoly over warfare and over the construction of castles. His financial, legal, and administrative powers were like those he held in Normandy, and were executed locally by sheriffs. These officers, comparable to their Anglo-Saxon predecessors, directed the administration of the counties. They were great vassals in possession of rich fiefs, yet they were appointed and dismissed at royal will.

One of the secrets of the Norman success was the close supervision of local government. During Henry I's reign, itinerant judges were sent out from the royal court through the counties on judicial circuits to try cases reserved for the royal justice. This legal innovation speeded up justice and inaugurated the process of expanding the royal law and making it common to the whole realm. In addition, these itinerant justices communicated royal orders to the sheriffs, and carried back reports on conditions of local government. They were the "roving eyes and ears" of the king and proved to be an effective check upon local officials. To improve the efficiency of his financial system, Henry developed a new treasury called the exchequer. Twice yearly the sheriffs had to come to Westminster to pay the revenues of their counties into this treasury. They had to render account before a board of treasury officials for every penny received and spent. Because the sums owed were computed on a table lined off like a checker or chess board, the treasury received the name *exchequer* (from *scaccarium* meaning *chess board*). This system of accounting was but an application of the principles of the abacus and it simplified adding and subtracting in Roman numerals, the only figures yet known in western Europe. This new department placed a rigid check over peculation and contributed to making the English kings the richest of north-western Europe.

The Norman kings were essentially absolute monarchs who, if they chose, could govern alone. Generally, however, for the weighty affairs of the realm and for extraordinary taxation they convened their vassals in a great feudal council to secure their advice and consent. No king, however strong, could continually ignore the feudal custom of suit to court or flout public opinion. To aid them in the daily routine of central government, the kings relied upon a court or household staff of personnel who looked after both private and public royal business. The chancellor, customarily a cleric, headed the writing office and supervised the drawing up of records, authenticating them with a great seal. The treasurer headed the exchequer staff. Two chamberlains kept the royal chamber in order and also managed the king's domestic treasury, which was used for paying household expenses. Constable and marshals had functions dealing with the care of horses and the royal sports of hunting and hawking. These officers plus other menial servants lived in the royal household where they were fed, lodged, and otherwise remunerated. When the king was absent in Normandy or too busy to accomplish all his tasks, a royal lieutenant called the *justiciar* acted in his name. Compared to other medieval governments, that of Henry I was a marvel of efficiency, proving as in Normandy and Flanders that feudalism could produce a strong state.

GERMANY UNDER THE SAXON KINGS

The history of Germany in the tenth and eleventh centuries was different from that of its western neighbors, principally because the German sovereigns became involved in grandiose adventures far distant from the duchies. If the Saxon successors of Henry the Fowler had been content to build up their power within the duchy of Saxony and then work to extend it over the other duchies, the development of Germany might have paralleled that of France where the Capetians gradually unified all the feudal territories under their rule. Henry's son Otto the Great left Saxony to be administered by subordinates while he attempted immediately to enforce his authority throughout Germany. Ultimately he was successful, but only after subduing revolts in Swabia, Franconia, and Lorraine, and appointing new dukes. Even the new rulers of these duchies, however, had to respect the strong regional feeling in their states and they often came into conflict with Otto. But Otto was an exceptionally ambitious and successful ruler who carried all before him. By 952 he had forced the king of Bohemia to recognize his lordship; he extended his authority to the Rhine by securing the allegiance of the king of Arles; and finally he added to his prestige in the old middle kingdom of Lothair by passing over the Alps, marrying the widow of an Italian king, and asserting his authority in this area. While Otto was absent from Germany, revolts flared up in the duchies and the Hungarians threatened in the east. Upon his return he ruthlessly suppressed the rebellion and then so crushed the Hungarians at the Battle of Lech in 955 that never again did they threaten Germany.

Unfortunately, Otto was not satisfied with his accomplishments in Germany; he felt compelled to interfere again south of the Alps. In 961, therefore, he accepted the invitation of Pope John XII, a completely unreliable and degenerate individual, to occupy Lombardy. Reducing this region with his army he took the title of King of Italy. Then in 962 he followed in Charlemagne's footsteps and was crowned emperor by the Pope, thus reviving the Holy Roman Empire. Armed with this authority, Otto deposed the unworthy John and had his own secretary elected Pope. For a while he made preparations to occupy the rest of Italy, including the Byzantine lands. He eventually dropped this project and arranged for his eldest son to marry Theophano, the daughter of the Byzantine emperor, who was to bring with her as dowry some of southern Italy. The few years left to Otto were spent in organizing the eastern part of Germany into bishoprics. At Magdeburg an archbishopric was authorized, which served as a base of operations for taking Christianity into the Slavic lands to the east. Otto the Great died in 973 and was succeeded by his son Otto II (973–983).

The consensus of historical opinion is that the imperial and Italian policy of Otto proved to be the bane of German politics. He set an example that German kings attempted to follow for two hundred years. It was the height of folly for them to emulate Charlemagne or mimic the imperial grandeur of ancient Rome. For ephemeral glory and a fruitless attempt to control the Italian peninsula, Otto and his successors forfeited the opportunity to forge strong central government and to expand German borders to the north and east. The duchies consequently remained strong and free of regnal authority; here began the pattern of German

THE SAXON AND FRANCONIAN KINGS

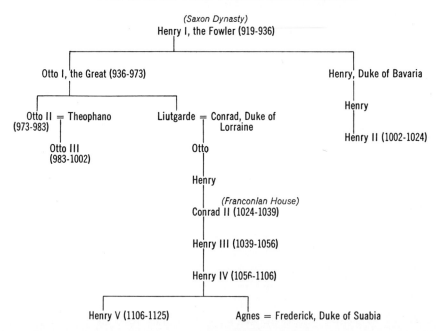

(Saxon Dynasty)
Henry I, the Fowler (919-936)

Otto I, the Great (936-973)

Henry, Duke of Bavaria

Otto II = Theophano
(973-983)

Liutgarde = Conrad, Duke of
Lorraine

Henry

Otto III
(983-1002)

Otto

Henry II (1002-1024)

Henry

(Franconian House)
Conrad II (1024-1039)

Henry III (1039-1056)

Henry IV (1056-1106)

Henry V (1106-1125)

Agnes = Frederick, Duke of Suabia

particularism and decentralization that kept Germany prostrate politically until its unification by Bismark in the nineteenth century.

The two successors of Otto the Great, Otto II and Otto III (983–1002), ignoring their great inheritance, frittered away their time in Italy. Otto II died while leading an expedition to enforce his claim to southern Italy. His son Otto III never knew Germany. Reared in Italy under the direction of his Greek mother Theophano and educated in the Byzantine tradition, he wasted his short life by pretending that he had restored imperial Rome. Meanwhile, Germany was bleeding with civil war between the great magnates. When Otto III died without heirs at the age of twenty-two the German nobles elected as king a man from a collateral branch of the Saxon House. He ruled as Henry II until his death in 1024.

GERMANY UNDER THE FRANCONIAN KINGS

Henry's death left the Saxon House without any male heirs by direct descent, so the German nobles chose as king Conrad, duke of Franconia (1024–1039), a descendant of Otto the Great on the maternal side of the house. Conrad was the first of the Franconian or Salian kings, who ruled Germany from 1024 to 1125. Although he went to Italy for a year and secured the imperial crown, he was an improvement over his predecessors. He restored a semblance of order in Germany, forced Poland and Bohemia to accept his lordship, and led some campaigns eastward against the Slavs. In 1032 he added a third royal title by assuming the kingship of Arles, a small principality in southern France along the Rhône River. Under his son Henry III (1039–1056), Franconian power reached its apogee. Henry consolidated his father's gains, extended German influence into Hungary, and followed the wise policy of maintaining peace while he looked to the reform of local and central government. He did remarkably well in maintaining his authority in Germany and Italy, a feat accomplished by governing through bishops, to whom he gave extensive political power. By so doing he escaped the danger of these key offices becoming the heritable possession of strong noble families and secured the support of the church which, with his sincere help, was undergoing a striking spiritual revival.

It was due in large part to Henry that able Popes were appointed and that their reform of regular and secular clergy was so successful. Unfortunately such a happy relation between church and state did not long continue. Although Henry was a devout son of the church and vigorously supported a strong spiritual organization, he still wielded the ultimate authority. He appointed and dismissed Popes just as he did bishops and abbots, who had to be suitable politically as well as spiritually because they were the nucleus of the royal administration. An invigorated church under the leadership of militant Popes and bishops could not endure this subservience. It remembered the lesson taught by Ambrose to Theodosius and fought bitterly to establish its independence. It was not content to be a department of state and to provide administrators for the Franconian emperors. The result was the investiture struggle which plagued the reign of Henry's unfortunate son Henry IV (see pages 233–236).

Until reduced to military anarchy by the investiture struggle in the last forty years of the eleventh century, Germany had no real feudalism. There had been vassals, but they did not hold fiefs in return for military service. Nobles had possessed large landed estates, but these were not feudalized. The Saxon and

Franconian emperors considered the great dukes their vassals, but they did not permit the office of duke to become a hereditary fief as it was in lands to the west. When strong enough, the emperors appointed and dismissed dukes at will. In each duchy they had numerous vassals, especially bishops and abbots, whom they used as a countercheck to the dukes and other powerful nobles. In this manner, the best of the German emperors maintained a central authority. But when with the investiture conflict military service became a prime need and the nobles enfeoffed their land to secure it, the imperial arrangement collapsed. By the end of the twelfth century Germany was completely feudalized; German knights and castles dominated the countryside. Strangely enough, Germany had just become really feudal when to the west feudalism was showing the first signs of decline. Unfortunately, the German sovereigns could not effectively use feudal institutions to develop strong monarchy. Having so long disdained to build up effective power in Germany, the kings forfeited a strong political base from which to expand their power. They degenerated into a harmless collection of men elected and permitted to hold the titles of king and emperor because they were politically weak. Disorganized and headless after the twelfth century, Germany continued to lead a splintered political existence to the end of the Middle Ages.

SOUTHERN ITALY AND SICILY

Beyond France, England, and Germany feudalism spread most successfully to southern Italy and Sicily. Although the German emperors asserted a sovereignty over all Italy, political life south of Rome was as it had been since the end of the Ostrogothic kingdom in the sixth century. Here scores of petty nobles, some of them Byzantine officials, feuded for power and reduced the Italian boot to a shambles. The anarchy was made worse by Moslem raids from Sicily. Such a situation was tailored to those men seeking military employment and possible political fortune. During the early eleventh century all sorts of crude warriors ended up in southern Italy fighting for the Italian nobles. Many came from Normandy where there was a long tradition of military adventure, and where there was not enough land for the younger sons. Especially was this true with the Hauteville family in which there were twelve sons. There was no choice but for them to go out into the world to seek their fortunes. Three quickly won military fame and land in Italy. William Iron-Arm fought himself up to a countship; his successor and half-brother Robert Guiscard (the Sly) began to master all the southern peninsula and in 1059 obtained recognition of his conquests. It was at this time that the Pope and the German emperor were engaged in the investiture conflict and the Pope needed all the military support he could muster. He therefore recognized Robert's conquests and proclaimed him duke of Apulia and Calabria.

Robert's brother Roger was also courted and was encouraged to conduct a holy crusade against Moslem Sicily. By 1091 Roger had reduced the island and was recognized as count of Sicily. He was succeeded in 1101 by his son Roger II, who opened up an amazing chapter of history in this area of the world. In 1105 he unified under his rule Sicily and the former possessions of Robert in southern Italy. In 1130 at his capital of Palermo he was crowned king of Sicily and Italy and inspired a brilliant flurry of economic and cultural advance. One of the proudest achievements of both Rogers was the strong government they founded. Recalling the political and military techniques in which they had been educated, they used the principles of Norman feudalism to construct their centralized state. Fiefs were granted for knight service, and all the other prominent features of feudalism found in Normandy and England were introduced. A group of house-hold officials served as intimate advisers and officers of state; for serious matters of state the great council was consulted. The kingdom was administered locally by officials comparable to the English sheriffs. In their treasury and customs system the kings of Sicily had a financial department that collected more revenue than any other state of western Europe. The English exchequer probably borrowed some of its procedure from Sicily. A blend of Norman determination, feudal institutions, Roman tradition, Byzantine culture, Arabic learning, and strategic economic location combined to make the kingdom of Sicily the most interesting and progressive state in twelfth-century Europe.

SPAIN

In Spain political weakness also invited feudal adventurers who, under cover of the cross, carved out for themselves new states and landed possessions. When by the early eleventh century the once powerful and brilliant Ommiad caliphate had been partitioned into a number of small independent emirates, it was simple for the Christians to push south of the Pyrenees. The old Spanish March of Charlemagne at the eastern end of the Pyrenees had become the kingdom of Barcelona. To the west, Basque mountaineers had thrown up the two small kingdoms of Aragon and Navarre. In northwestern Spain a group of Christians had managed to preserve their freedom in the mountains, and had formed the kingdom of León along the Duero River. Just to the east lay the Christian frontier land defended by a line of castles. From this forward position came the kingdom of Castile (land of castles). In the eleventh century these kingdoms pushed southward against the infidel. Piecemeal they occupied Moslem soil until in 1065 a great victory at Barbastro threw open the Ebro River Valley for conquest in the late eleventh and twelfth centuries. The success of the Spanish *reconquista* (reconquest) was due largely to the numerous French warriors who poured across the Pyrenees from Toulouse, Aquitaine, Gascony, and the northern states to join in the plunder. The church, eager to win Spain back to the cross, encouraged these warriors. The conquests were thus accomplished under the guise of a crusade; all men who embraced the holy cause and died for it were promised heavenly rewards. Many of these adventurers founded new principalities and established dynasties, as the Christian cross probed deeper and deeper toward the Strait of Gibraltar. In Spain, too, feudalism was introduced, and each of the Christian rulers secured military service by granting fiefs from land taken from the Moslem.

In other parts of Europe feudalism came later and was never as vigorous as in western Europe. It spread to Norway and Denmark, into eastern Europe, and, through the efforts of the Normans, into Scotland and across the Irish Sea to

Ireland. It was transplanted most successfully, however, into Syria by the crusaders in the eleventh and twelfth centuries. Having won a strip of land at the eastern end of the Mediterranean from the Seljuk Turks, the Christians established there four feudal states where the principles of feudal tenure helped to produce the fighting forces required to defend this Christian beachhead against the Turk.

7. *The Significance of Feudalism*

WITH A KNOWLEDGE now of feudal principles and institutions and the role they played in the leading European states between the tenth and twelfth centuries, we can gainfully discuss the value and significance of medieval feudalism. Traditionally feudalism has been regarded as the equivalent of political anarchy and as the cause of the disintegration of the Carolingian Empire into small political fragments. One American historian recently went so far as to compare lords and vassals to bands of gangsters and the war chargers to the armored car with its submachine gun and sawed-off shotgun. These observations are far from reflecting the truth. Perhaps the rise of the feudal system did coincide with the breakup of central authority in the Carolingian Empire, but this is no valid reason to conclude that feudalism was a destructive political force. To accomplish what was necessary in military and political services, feudalism was the only solution for a society living from the land. Whether or not there was feudalism, the Carolingian Empire was doomed to fall from its own weight; it was too vast to be held together by the primitive means available in the ninth century.

In France scholars have considered feudalism the cause for the anarchy and weakness of the royal domain but, strangely, both these evils rapidly disappeared when the first strong and capable king, Louis VI, mounted the throne; the royal domain then became a powerful and secure realm from which the royal authority expanded. Moreover, in all the other states examined, such as Flanders, Normandy, Anjou, Champagne, and England, strong government was founded upon feudal principles. We must admit, therefore, that feudalism was a most effective system when confined to small states where the principles of feudal tenure could operate and be enforced. Vassalage was a highly personal relationship and could function effectively only when lord and vassal were close to each other, the vassal in order to perform his services, and the lord in order to protect his vassal, hold his fidelity, and prevent him from usurping political and military powers. All the states where feudalism flourished were small, and it was easy for such men as William the Conqueror, Louis the Fat, and Fulk Nerra to keep alert eyes and strong fingers on their vassals, and to maintain the control that was the key to political strength and stability. For governing small states and for providing the essential military and political services the feudal system proved to be an excellent method. Feudalism, it must be emphasized, was a constructive, not a destructive, political force. The small states built upon it became strong and permanent; from them was to come the future political progress of western Europe.

Further Reading

The authoritative work on seignorialism is Volume I of *The Cambridge Economic History,* 2nd ed. (Cambridge, 1966). Other stimulating but rather technical accounts are by *M. Bloch, *French Rural History, an Essay on Its Basic Characteristics* (Berkeley, 1966) and *Land and Work in Mediaeval Europe, Selected Papers* (Berkeley, 1967). More elementary books on the subject are by H. Heaton, *Economic History of Europe,* rev. ed. (New York, 1948); *H. Pirenne, *Economic and Social History of Medieval Europe;* and N. Neilson, *Medieval Agrarian Economy* (New York, 1936). The various theories advanced on the agrarian structure of early medieval Europe are summarized by A. Dopsch, *The Economic and Social Foundations of European Civilization* (New York, 1937). An intriguing portrait of peasant life during the Carolingian era is contained in *E. Power's *Medieval People* (London, 1924), chap. I. Other good works on seignorialism are by *A. Luchaire, *Social France at the Time of Philip Augustus* (New York, 1912); and *P. M. Boissonade, *Life and Work in Medieval Europe* (New York, 1927). A description of life in an English agrarian village is provided by *H. S. Bennett, *Life on the English Manor: A Study of Peasant Conditions, 1150–1400* (Cambridge, 1948). A study from the sociological point of view is that of *G. C. Homans, *English Villagers of the Thirteenth Century* (Cambridge, Mass., 1941). For reference to more works see *B. Lyon, *The Middle Ages in Recent Historical Thought, Selected Topics,* 2nd ed. (Washington, 1965), pp. 12–21.

A clear and succinct introduction to feudalism is by *C. Stephenson, *Mediaeval Feudalism* (Ithaca, 1942). One should also consult his essays on the nature of feudalism in his *Mediaeval Institutions, Selected Essays,* ed. by B. Lyon (Ithaca, 1954). A more technical study is that of *F. L. Ganshof, *Feudalism* (London, 1952). The most comprehensive treatment of feudalism and its relation to medieval society is by *M. Bloch, *Feudal Society* (London, 1960). For discussion of the latest research on feudalism see *B. Lyon, *The Middle Ages in Recent Historical Thought, Selected Topics,* 2nd ed. (Washington, 1965), pp. 21–29. On the subject of chivalry the best book is by *S. Painter, *French Chivalry* (Baltimore, 1940). To catch the spirit of chivalry one should read C. K. Scott-Moncrieff's translation of the *Song of Roland* (London, 1920). A good collection of records on feudalism is found in *J. R. Strayer, *Feudalism* (New York, 1965). For a survey of warfare see *C. W. C. Oman, *The Art of War in the Middle Ages* (Ithaca, 1953); J. Beeler, *Warfare in Feudal Europe* (Ithaca, 1971); and A. V. B. Norman, *The Medieval Soldier* (New York, 1971). An excellent introduction to castle architecture as well as superb aerial views of English castles are provided by W. Douglas Simpson, *Castles from the Air* (New York, 1949).

Of the various histories on the early feudal states only a few can be noted. An elementary but superbly organized book on the principal feudal states is *S. Painter, *The Rise of the Feudal Monarchies* (Ithaca, 1951). The best study of France is *R. Fawtier, *The Capetian Kings of France* (London, 1960). A comparative study of France and England is that of *C. Petit-Dutaillis, *The Feudal Monarchy in France and England* (London, 1936). Two useful books on England in the eleventh and twelfth centuries are by *G. O. Sayles, *The Medieval Foundations of England,* 2nd rev. ed. (London, 1952); and F. Barlow, *The Feudal Kingdom of England, 1042–1216* (London, 1955). The political and military accomplishments of the Normans are vividly summarized by *C. H. Haskins, *The Normans in European History* (Boston, 1915). One should also see R. A. Brown, *The Normans and the Norman Conquest* (New York and London, 1969). On Germany the best modern study with new viewpoints on various political problems is that of *G. Barraclough, *The Origins of Modern Germany* (New York, 1948). For the conflicting views of historians on the Holy Roman Empire see *R. E. Herzstein, *The Holy Roman Empire in the Middle Ages: Universal State or German Catastrophe?* (Boston, 1966).

CHAPTER 6

Economic
and Religious
Revival

Primitive agrarian economy was the dominant economic feature of western European history between the fourth and eleventh centuries. The collapse of the Roman Empire in the third and fourth centuries was but the first of a series of disasters that forced men to live primarily from seignorialism for almost eight hundred years. The barbarian invasions throughout the empire introduced crude German warriors with their economic dependents. The main avenue of commerce between East and West—the Mediterranean Sea—was swiftly closed to the West. In the late fourth and fifth centuries, from their vantage point in north Africa the Vandals disrupted the flow of trade between the eastern and western halves of the Mediterranean. Meanwhile the West was drifting apart from the Byzantine Empire and was losing contact with the civilized stretches of Eurasia. Justinian's conquest of Ostrogothic Italy in the sixth century was ephemeral and wrought more destruction than political unity in the Mediterranean. This situation was worsened in the seventh and eighth centuries by the Arabs, who swept around three sides of the Mediterranean and made it their lake. There could be no trade overland to the east because of the fierce Hungarians. And the economic activity in the north around the estuaries of the Scheldt, Meuse, and Rhine rivers, that had flourished under the strong arm of Charlemagne, was snuffed out by internal anarchy and Viking attacks.

Western Europe, landlocked and paralyzed, had to rely principally upon land for its sustenance. There was scarcely any trade, there were no real towns, there were no bourgeois; man's existence was based upon the possession of land. The church, whose concept of man and the world fitted in admirably with these economic conditions, taught men not to complain about their earthly status. Whatever condition man was born into was divinely planned; man's lot was to labor and perform the obligations of his estate. His reward would come in the existence hereafter and eternal. In fact, the church at this time frowned upon the lending of money at interest (*usury*) and regarded trade and industry as worldly pursuits not provided for in God's omniscient scheme.

1. The Revival of Trade

IN THIS MILIEU few men dreamed that trade would once again make Europe vibrate with dynamic towns of industrious merchants and craftsmen. But there were, nevertheless, forces at work in northern and southern Europe preparing the way for the revival of trade.

SOUTHERN EUROPE

During the most difficult years of Arab domination of the Mediterranean, a few Italian ports had managed to maintain trade relations with Constantinople. One of these was Venice. To the security of the lagoons and marshes at the head of the Adriatic Sea refugees from the Huns, Ostrogoths, and Lombards had fled during the fifth and sixth centuries. There they built primitive dwellings on piles over the water and gained their livelihood from saltmaking and fishing. And so was founded Venice, destined to become one of the urban marvels of Europe. Forced to the sea and to trade because of their location, the men of Venice turned their backs upon the agrarian economy of the West and established trade relations with Constantinople, the capital of the Byzantine Empire. It was this link that made the development of Venice different from that of western Europe for almost three centuries. Constantinople was the bustling political and economic hub of the eastern Mediterranean, where trade and industry continued to support a thriving money economy. The great capital required the salt, fish, wheat, wine, and lumber that Venice could provide; in turn, it supplied the Venetians with finely fabricated products and spices from the Far East. Venice, therefore, contrary to the rest of

Europe, began its existence with a money economy and continued to live from trade. From the outset Venice, recognizing the political authority of the Byzantine emperors, directed its energies eastward.

By the eighth century the Venetians were the great provisioners of Constantinople. Their ships covered the eastern Mediterranean and their renown as shrewd merchants spread around the whole basin. Their desire for gain overshadowed what religious scruples they may have had about trading with the Moslems. During the ninth century they cemented commercial ties with Cairo, Damascus, and Palermo. Treaties were concluded giving them privileged economic status. By the early eleventh century Venice was an independent city-state republic whose wealth was the envy of the West and whose political and military power enabled it to clear the Adriatic of pirates and to establish commercial settlements the length of the eastern Adriatic coast. From the interior Venice obtained the lumber required for trade and for constructing its great fleet which dominated the Mediterranean to the end of the Middle Ages. Venice was lauded by contemporaries as Golden Venice (*Venetia Aurea*), the city "rich in money, rich in men."

The influence of Venice soon made itself felt in the Italian interior. By the tenth century Lombardy was stimulated to commercial activity and Pavia quickly attained renown as a trading center. The contagious disease of making money spread throughout northern Italy from Lombardy to Tuscany. In the early eleventh century Lucca began the fabrication of its fine cloths. In southern Italy, ports such as Salerno, Bari, Naples, and Amalfi that had retained tenuous political ties with Constantinople and had even managed to carry on a little trade fell in with the tempo of Venice and established economic ties with the Moslem emirates of Sicily and north Africa. Even Genoa and Pisa began to stir with economic activity. By the year 1000 they were sending out trading ships and were to the western Mediterranean what Venice was to the eastern. But unacquainted with the more reasonable and tolerant attitude of the East and farther removed from the Moslems, Pisa and Genoa refused to trade with the infidel. Imbued with the primitive Christian dread and hate of the Moslem faithful, they opened up the western Mediterranean to Christian shipping by force. In 1015 Pisa and Genoa attacked Sardinia. They then led raids against the North African emirates. Told by Pope and clergy that theirs was a holy cause and crusade, the devout Pisan and Genoese sailor and merchant ruthlessly moved against the infidel, until by 1087 they dominated the western half of the Mediterranean. The first successful Christian counterattack against the Moslem had been launched; it was to be climaxed by the First Crusade (1096), when fleets from the Italian ports joined with Christian knights to wrest the Holy Land away from the Turk.

By 1100 the Mediterranean had been reopened to western commerce from Constantinople to the Strait of Gibraltar, and the great boulevard of trade began to resemble its glorious days as the *mare nostrum* of the Romans. It was now left for the Venetians, Normans, Pisans, and Genoese to fight it out for commercial supremacy. From the highly sensitized economic center of Venice, trade had spread throughout Italy and along the shores of southern France. From southern Europe the economic revival gradually moved northward. Through the Alpine passes went the Italian merchant with his eastern wares. Once through the St. Bernard and Brenner passes he fanned out along the Rhine, Danube, Rhône, Meuse, and lesser rivers.

NORTHERN EUROPE

In northern Europe the economic revival did not come as rapidly nor as strikingly. Here trade appeared only after a degree of political stability had been achieved in the tenth and eleventh centuries. The role of the Vikings in furthering trade relations in this area was similar to that of the Venetians in the south. The Vikings swooped down out of the Scandinavian penninsula in the eighth and ninth centuries as pirates and at first wreaked havoc all along the coasts of the Continent and England. But gradually they shifted from piracy and conquest to peaceful pursuits. In England, after conquering much of the island, they were in turn conquered and fused with the Anglo-Saxons. In Normandy and other parts of northern Europe, they settled and absorbed Frankish culture. In the east, the Swedes swept south from the Baltic and down the Dnieper River until they made contact with the Byzantine Empire. Skillful sailors, the Vikings became the first great traders of northern Europe. As soon as the waters opened up in the spring their ships could be found from the Black Sea to Iceland. They served as the intermediaries of a northern trade that now tied England, Germany, France, and the Netherlands to Constantinople and the East by way of the Baltic, the Dnieper, and the Black Sea.

Although the Vikings helped to awaken commerce and to extend trade relations, the hub of the northern economic revival was Flanders. From this little county of the Netherlands, trade and industry radiated outward just as from Venice. The strategic geographical location of Flanders explains its prominence. Near to or crisscrossed by all the important waterways of northern Europe, it served as the crossroads for merchants, north and south, east and west. Here came Swedes from as far distant as Constantinople, English from York and Lincoln, Germans from along the Rhine, French from Bordeaux and Marseilles, and Italians from Venice and Genoa. Here they traded their products and then returned home for more. But Flanders was more than an international clearing house for trade; thanks to its gentle and humid climate, the sheep which grazed on the emerald-green meadows produced the finest-quality wool in the world. Already in Charlemagne's day, Flanders was famous for its high-quality woolen cloth. When the great Caliph Harun-al-Rashid sent rich gifts from Baghdad to Charlemagne, the emperor reciprocated with the finest present his empire could supply—exquisitely fabricated woolen cloth. By the year 1000 Flemish cloth was being carried all over Europe and soon raw wool had to be imported to keep the growing Flemish woolen industry supplied. By the early eleventh century the records refer to such places as Bruges, Ghent, Ypres, Lille, and Arras as centers for trade and industry. Soon these names would become synonymous with wealth and economic power.

With Flanders as with Venice, commercial activity spread rapidly to other regions located advantageously on waterways and intersections of roads. A busy commerce developed along the Scheldt up to Cambrai, along the Meuse to Dinant, along the Rhine at such centers as Cologne and Mainz, along the North Sea and English Channel, along Thames at London, along the Severn at Bristol, along the Seine at Rouen, along the Atlantic coast at Bordeaux and Bayonne. Inland, because of the lack of roads, the revival came more slowly except along the level routes that crossed the Champagne plateau and took the itinerant merchant from Rouen or Bruges to Venice, Florence, and Lucca. On these famous routes merchants from all over western Europe met and began to exchange their articles of commerce. So it was that in the eleventh and twelfth centuries trade revived throughout western Europe and spread to areas which had not known trade even during the height of the Roman Empire. And with trade came the circulation of money, the bourgeois merchants and artisans necessary to accomplish the functions of trade and industry, and the towns which afforded them protection, living quarters, and a place to fabricate and market their goods. The revival of trade in the tenth, eleventh, and twelfth centuries, a great revolution in itself, sparked an even more significant one—the revival of true urban life with its middle-class inhabitants and the social, economic, legal, and political privileges they required for engaging in trade and industry.

2. The Medieval Town

HISTORIANS ARE GENERALLY AGREED that urban life as known to the Romans or to men of the thirteenth century did not exist between the fourth and eleventh centuries in western Europe. What they do not agree upon, however, are the essential characteristics of town life. If by town life is meant urban communities with a bourgeois population of merchants engaging in local and long-distance trade and of craftsmen fabricating merchandise requiring training and skill, then there were no towns in these seven centuries. Nor were there towns, if by town life is meant urban communities with a bourgeoisie enjoying legal freedom, social and economic privileges, and political rights setting it above and apart from the peasants of the countryside. But if we understand towns to be fortified points serving as administrative and military headquarters for count or bishop with an assisting staff of soldiers and administrative personnel, then there were towns. If a deserted Roman town and camp or a castle are considered towns, then we may conclude there was true urban life.

THE ORIGIN OF THE TOWN

The essential problem for historians, therefore, has been to define a town. Despite all the various definitions, most historians have concluded that western Europe did not know real towns in the early Middle Ages. Except for isolated cases in southern Europe, Roman urban life ceased; all that remained of Roman towns or camps in the early Middle Ages was their name and the protection of their fortifications. So it was with Paris, Lyon, Mainz, Cologne, London, and Chester, places similar to the forts and the blockhouses that were prominent in American frontier history. So it was, too, with the castles and fortified refuge points like the boroughs and *Burgen* that feudal princes and lords threw up all over Europe. In all these fortifications lived merely some soldiers and humble civil servants whose status was hardly better than that of the peasants who supplied their food. Most of the land within the walls of the old Roman towns and camps was cultivated. Of trade and industry there was none.

Historians, having concluded that there were no real towns, were now confronted with explaining how towns arose. Numerous scholarly theories were propounded. One historian argued that towns arose from well-located manors, another found towns originating from the headquarters of bishops, another from local agrarian markets, another from fortified points of refuge, and yet others from guilds, from free agrarian communities, and from sites enjoying the special protection or peace of a great prince. But all these historians attempted to explain the origin of the town as a legal, religious, or military phenomenon. Such, of course, it was not. A real town had to be sustained by trade and industry. Only when and where these economic phenomena appeared did towns sprout up with their bourgeois inhabitants. Thus understood, the town was a social and economic institution which returned to Europe with the revival of trade in the late tenth and eleventh centuries. As trade and industry grew, so did the towns. It was but natural that towns started to develop first around fortified points which were strategically located on waterways and routes for trade and which could give the merchant protection. Around small castles and within the walls of old Roman towns and camps the merchant came to live. After him came the artisan for the industries that developed. Gradually but steadily the old fortification was surrounded by new houses and by extended walls until at last the original castle or camp had been absorbed and lost in the new town. Real urban life began in the settlements of merchants that grew up around the fortification. The latter merely contributed a good site, protection, and its name. This economic explanation for the origin of towns has been called the mercantile-settlement theory and it accounts satisfactorily for most of the urban development in Europe.

URBAN DEVELOPMENT

To comprehend urban evolution better it will be useful to study the origin of a few famous towns. In Germany along the Rhine River, the old Roman town of Cologne had been a rectangular fortress of 239 acres. After the barbarian invasions only a few stragglers remained clustered together in one corner of the walls. Because of its location Cologne was one of the first sites to benefit from the revival of trade. By the early eleventh century merchants had filled up the area within the old fortification and a new settlement of merchants had developed outside the wall nearest to the Rhine. A second wall protected this area down to the bank of the river. By 1100 three other settlements had sprouted up around the other walls and had been fortified. By 1180 new settlements had developed outside these suburbs and necessitated a wall around an area three times the size of that within the old town walls. All along the Rhine, at Roman and non-Roman fortified points, German towns sprang up in the eleventh and twelfth centuries.

In the county of Flanders urban development flourished early and centered about the castles of the counts which had been located at key points. In the tenth century, at the confluence of the Scheldt and Lys rivers, stood the comital castle of Ghent. It and the adjacent triangular walled area consisted of twenty-five acres

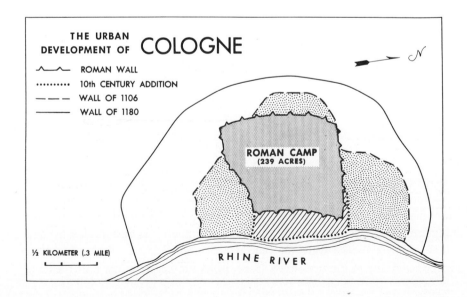

THE URBAN DEVELOPMENT OF **COLOGNE**

- ∿∿ ROMAN WALL
- ••••••••• 10th CENTURY ADDITION
- – – – WALL OF 1106
- ——— WALL OF 1180

ROMAN CAMP
(239 ACRES)

½ KILOMETER (.3 MILE)

RHINE RIVER

and was called the Old Burg. Soon trade and industry brought merchants and artisans who settled early in the eleventh century across the Scheldt River in an area called the New Burg or Port. By 1200 the new settlement encompassed two hundred acres, and during the thirteenth century new suburbs continued to push Ghent out into the countryside. This is not the place to become bogged down in detailed examples of similar town origins in England, France, Spain, Switzerland, and Italy, but it should be noted that at fortified points developed such famous towns as London, York, Nottingham, Magdeburg, Mainz, Constance, Paris, Lyon, Beauvais, and Cambrai. Just as American towns grew up around forts and stockades at Pittsburgh, Detroit, Chicago, and St. Louis, so, too, did European towns.

ELEMENTARY BOURGEOIS PRIVILEGES

It was not long until the more enlightened feudal princes, realizing what good revenues such towns could bring them, encouraged urban development and planned new towns (*villes neuves*) on land that seemed well suited for commercial or industrial development. Sometimes these projects turned out well and thriving towns developed, but often economic conditions were not propitious and towns failed to grow or at best became small market or agrarian communities. The most interesting aspect of these new towns for us are their charters of privileges given by the founding princes. To lure colonists to these new urban sites, the prince would lay out streets and fortifications and build a church. He would also promise to all settlers various social, economic, and legal privileges essential for those following the occupations of commerce and industry. Similar privileges, though existing

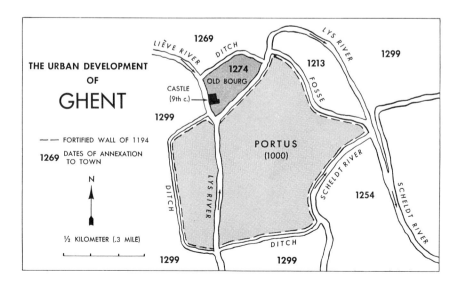

in all the older and better known towns, had been granted informally little by little to go along with the gradual urban development. Few of the old towns had charters, and we must turn to the charters of the new towns to learn what rights the typical bourgeois possessed. In Germany, one of the first successful towns was founded by Duke Conrad of Zähringen. In 1120 he created on wasteland near his castle the town of Freiburg-im-Breisgau. In a charter well publicized throughout southern Germany, Conrad promised each settler a plot of land for an annual rent of one shilling. This land could be inherited, bequeathed, and sold. Everyone living in the community was to be free from all seignorial obligations and tolls throughout the duchy. Because it was situated on the route cutting through the Black Forest from the Danube to the Rhine, Freiburg (free town) prospered. Throughout Europe similar foundations had equal success. In France, Lorris was founded by King Louis VI, and Montauban by the counts of Toulouse. In England, King Henry I founded Newcastle-upon-Tyne.

Hundreds of towns were thus encouraged in the Middle Ages. All enjoyed the same fundamental elementary bourgeois privileges consisting of certain social, economic, and legal rights. In all the men were legally free because the town was a privileged area set apart from the seignorial countryside. A merchant could not be bound to the soil and successfully engage in trade; he required, above all, mobility. The typical bourgeois held his ground freely, that is, for the annual payment of a nominal rent. He could inherit, will, alienate, and buy land. Holding land under such advantageous terms was known as *burgage* tenure. The townsman also enjoyed a special justice; he could be tried only within the town at a court consisting of fellow bourgeois. The law dispensed was totally different from feudal and seignorial law. It was the *law merchant,* which developed by trial and error to meet the economic requirements of litigation caused by disputes over sale, purchase, and contract. Developed upon the basis of experience, common sense, and hardheaded reason, this law was eminently practical and swift. It was standardized in most towns. In Germany the majority of the Rhineland towns followed the law merchant of Cologne, in northern France that of Rouen or Paris, in England that of London or Lincoln. Until towns obtained self-government the courts were presided over by officers of the prince who received a share of the profits of justice. Every bourgeois of a town enjoyed special commercial benefits. Unlike outsiders, who generally had to pay market tolls and fees, he could buy and sell freely in the town market. Often only local merchants had the privilege of buying and selling in the town, and they were usually protected by tariffs on imports. Obviously the lord profited from having as many prosperous towns as possible on his lands; from them he derived tolls, profits of justice, taxes, rents, and all types of revenues. In time of need, the townsmen could be summoned to fight or to defend their town. These, then, were the basic elementary economic, social, and legal privileges enjoyed by the urban bourgeoisie.

For the agrarian countryside the growth of the town and its freedom constituted a major social and legal revolution. Hordes of peasants escaped to these privileged islands of freedom to obtain emancipation. According to custom, if a peasant remained in a town for a year and a day undetected by his lord he automatically became free. All through Europe the old German maxim "Stadtluft macht frei" (city air makes free) could be seen in operation. Some peasants with markets now for their surplus produce sold it and were thus frequently able to purchase freedom from their lord. As the move from country to town increased and quickened, lords were compelled to meet the competition in order to hold enough workers to cultivate their manors. In return for nominal payments they began permitting their peasants to commute their labor services into money payments or rents, with the end result that the lord was transformed into a landlord and the peasant into a free rent-paying tenant. Many lords granted their peasants charters of privileges modeled upon those of neighboring towns, with the hope of retaining them and luring new settlers to convert forest and wasteland into productive agrarian soil supporting crops that could be profitably sold in the towns. An example of a free agrarian community that developed out of waste and forest was Lorris, founded in the early twelfth century by King Louis VI of France. It became a town of free farmers and wine merchants with privileges equal to those of great towns and developed into a center for the wine trade.

One cannot overemphasize the fundamental social and economic revolution caused by the revival of trade and towns; from it stemmed the long decline of feudalism and seignorialism. By creating once again a reciprocity of economic relations between town and country, it made possible the emancipation of the bulk of Europe's inhabitants by the end of the Middle Ages. The feudal aristocracy henceforth saw its political, economic, social, military, and legal dominance slip away as the bourgeoisie—the class of moneyed commoners—rose to the top and became a great European *estate* (class). But all these changes had only begun in the eleventh and twelfth centuries; centuries more were required to complete the process.

URBAN SELF-GOVERNMENT

Once having obtained his essential freedoms, the typical bourgeois began to anticipate the day when he would acquire political rights, those privileges generally associated with urban self-government. Having become experienced in the affairs of the business world and self-reliant as a result of his individual enterprises, the typical merchant chafed under the political domination of royal and princely officials whose whole mentality was yet feudal. The bourgeois had no love for these officials who presided over their courts, collected taxes, wielded administrative and military powers, supervised the market, and provided police protection. The townsmen resented outside authority and felt capable of exercising the duties of self-government. Already established in most towns was an institution through which the bourgeois could work and cooperate to achieve their cherished objective; this was the *guild merchant,* an economic association of the leading town merchants. Organized in the beginning to provide protection for itinerant merchants against robbers and, through numbers, to afford greater buying power and credit, the guild merchant developed into an economic and social organization which practically dictated the rules of life for the urban inhabitant. In order to sell or buy locally a merchant had to be a member of the guild. It controlled prices and the quality of the goods merchandised; it protected the merchant from outside competition; and it became a sort of social club where the merchant drank, obtained fellowship, and talked business. All guilds charged membership fees, used for varied activities. Pious and charitable causes were supported, churches and schools constructed, and funds set aside for the care of widows, orphans, and the sick, and the decent burial of the dead. But, above all, the guild merchant became the instrument through which the bourgeois negotiated with the political ruler on matters of trade with other states, taxation, and public works. In the guild was the seed of the future town council dominated by the wealthy merchant.

Political freedom came to the towns in various forms and under varying circumstances. In Italy, where there was no strong central political authority, the leading towns acquired self-government almost by default. The small feudal lords could not obstruct their march toward political independence. In Lombardy and Tuscany most of the principal towns became independent political powers resembling the Greek city-states. By the eleventh century Venice had become a republic with authority extending along the Italian and Yugoslavian coasts. The principal magistrate, the *doge,* was elected and ruled with the advice and consent of an aristocratic council of merchants. This executive body governed Venice like a sovereign power; it coined money, waged war, and concluded treaties. Although the form of government might vary in other towns, some being more democratic and others more oligarchical or despotic, all obtained self-government and a large degree of sovereign authority. Italy became a mosaic of small city-states, such as Genoa, Pisa, Siena, Florence, Lucca, Pavia, Milan, and Bologna; they fought jealously among themselves for economic and political gain and thus nurtured particularism—the bane of Italian medieval history. Only upon occasion did they bury their differences to fight against the German emperors from the north or against the Popes from the south. All these town governments were organized for the profit of the small governing clique of wealthy families who perpetuated themselves in power. The ordinary citizens had few rights and were already coalescing into the great urban estate of the proletariat; in no Italian town can it be said that democratic principles operated.

TOWN HALL OF SIENA. The tower of the town hall, typical of those dominating the market squares of Italian towns, was constructed between 1338 and 1348. The cornice above the shaft of red brick is of grey travertine stone and was based upon the design of the painter Ippo Memmi (1341).

The great towns of northern Europe acquired political freedom by other avenues. In Flanders a long line of enlightened counts saw the benefits of peaceably giving their towns self-government while still retaining the ultimate authority. During the twelfth century such towns as Saint-Omer, Ypres, Ghent, and Bruges obtained self-government through comital charters providing for town councils of magistrates who were to administer the town, assess and collect taxes, operate the courts, legislate for the citizens, provide protection, and act as intermediaries between count and town. In almost every case, the guild merchant took the lead in bargaining for self-government. The counts in turn secured the promise of higher taxes. Because the governments were, as in Italy, thoroughly oligarchical, there soon arose a deep chasm between the patricians and plebeians. The French kings followed a similar policy with their towns in the royal domain, and so did the Norman dukes, the counts of Champagne, and the English kings. But in northeastern France, particularly in Picardy, towns such as Beauvais and Cambrai generally had to fight to obtain political freedom from their masters, the bishops. A bloody series of uprisings was necessary in the eleventh and twelfth centuries before self-government was grudgingly granted by the proud prelates.

In southern France, notably in Toulouse and Provence, the leading towns such as Marseilles, Arles, Nîmes, Montpellier, and Carcassonne, obtained self-government peaceably. In Aquitaine and Gascony a like development produced such self-governing towns as Bordeaux and Bayonne. In Spain many of the towns resembled the Italian cities where the feudal aristocracy tended to live within their walls. Here towns were also forts because of the Moslem menace; they long retained the atmosphere of frontier posts and military headquarters. The principal Spanish town in the twelfth century was Barcelona, which became a leading Mediterranean port and banking center. In all the regions surveyed thus far—Italy, the Netherlands, France, England, and Spain—the self-governing towns were called *communes* because their bourgeois formed a body or community (from the Latin *communitas* or *communio*) that was a collective individual, a legal person. In a region like Picardy, the townsmen banded together in an association and *swore the commune;* that is, they pledged themselves to fight collectively for political freedom. And no matter how such freedom came—through peaceful means or war—all inhabitants of a town had to swear the commune and swear obedience to its government and institutions.

In Germany the towns winning self-government were called free cities. By the middle of the twelfth century Cologne was self-governing. It was followed by scores of other towns in the Rhineland during the next hundred years. In the Danube Valley Ratisbon was the principal free city; in eastern Germany it was Magdeburg. In the thirteenth century, when effective central authority disappeared in Germany, many of the free cities became virtually autonomous states like the Italian communes. Such were the famous northern ports and commercial centers which formed a commercial confederation in the thirteenth and fourteenth centuries called the *Hanse* (league).

Although at first political privileges and the right of local self-government were the objectives of the bourgeoisie, as this third estate became more numerous and wealthier it assumed a greater role in the politics of the state. Increasingly the medieval rulers had to ask it for taxes to meet the mounting costs of government in the face of declining feudal and seignorial incomes. In return for money, the bourgeois demanded certain national political rights and participation in the government. At this point the rulers began convening the bourgeois along with the clergy and feudal aristocracy in assemblies, called parliament, estates, diet, or cortes, and there they consulted with the king on matters of state and granted him taxes. This development was of major constitutional importance in the history of democratic government. Behind those men who finally came to sit in the Parliament at Westminster or in the Estates at Paris was a tradition and experience of three centuries in winning elementary social, economic, and legal bourgeois privileges, and in acquiring the art of local self-government. Let us not forget that the revival of trade created men of local substance and political experience, who in turn contributed largely to the development of constitutional government in western Europe.

3. Guilds, Markets, and Fairs

WHEN TRADE BEGAN TO REVIVE in the late tenth and eleventh centuries, the outstanding characteristic of the merchant was his itinerant life. The early merchant performed all the operations involved in merchandising his wares; he bought them, transported them, and retailed them. If ambitious, he was constantly on the road except in winter. He soon discovered that traveling alone was perilous in an area where there was little protection against violence, and so he banded together with other merchants and all moved from town to town in armed caravans. Armed with swords and bows, the merchants rode beside their pack horses and wagons loaded with boxes, barrels, and sacks. Often such a group had a standard-bearer and an elected leader—a dean—who wielded authority over the merchants bound in fealty to him and to each other. In this case the association would buy and sell in common and prorate the profit. Collectively they had more capital with which to operate and could act as surety for one another. These early associations, arising from the need for self-protection and economic and social gain, were conducting business over long distances by the early twelfth century. Merchants from the Netherlands could be found at the German mines of Goslar and at London. Italian merchants were coming to Ypres to secure its woolen cloth and to sell their eastern wares. For us it is important to observe that these itinerant economic associations were the first guilds merchant of Europe and that from them developed the guilds merchant of the towns.

THE GUILD MERCHANT

As business expanded and operations became more complicated, the merchant stopped doing all the work; he delegated buying and selling to employees or factors, and transportation to organizations specializing in land or water transport. The merchants became sedentary managers, supervising their businesses from fine stone dwellings or counting houses. Each town now began to have its own guild merchant that regulated the local business life and, in reality, the urban economy. The objective of the guild merchant was to preserve a monopoly over trade in the town market. The ideal of the guild was a stable price under stable conditions. Through a rigid code of specifications regulating price and quality of goods, the guild controlled urban trade. And when the leading towns became self-governing and the members of the guild merchant composed the town council, ordinances transformed these economic regulations into municipal law.

THE CRAFT GUILD

During the twelfth century the guild merchant was somewhat modified. Until this time it had included not only merchants who traded but also artisans who fabricated the commodities of commerce. Furthermore, the volume of trade had necessitated no specialization. By the twelfth century, however, all sorts of craft guilds began splitting off from the parent associations. In such regions as Flanders and northern Italy, where a number of towns were developing into industrial centers, scores of craft guilds arose. In the woolen industry, for example, there were the guilds of the weavers, fullers, and dyers. In every town there were the bakers, the shoemakers, the butchers, the fishmongers. In Dinant there were the copperbeaters. In Germany, where gold and silver were being discovered, gold- and silversmiths associated into guilds. Each guild elected officers, had its own set of regulations, and generally its own meeting hall. In every town around the central square or market place arose beautiful guildhalls in which the economic and social affairs of the guild centered. In such Flemish towns as Bruges and Ghent the market place and quays were rimmed by the magnificent halls of the merchant and craft guilds. The now famous Grand' Place of Brussels in the duchy of Brabant became a cobblestoned square bordered by Gothic stone lacery.

Each guild worked for its own interest and ruthlessly beat down internal or external competition. The weavers of Ghent and Ypres periodically went into the country nearby and destroyed the looms of farmers and weavers in small towns in order to obliterate any outside production of woolen cloth. Only through membership in a merchant or craft guild was urban existence possible. This was urban protectionism in its most perfect form.

As urban populations increased and ever more merchants and artisans joined the guilds, these associations tightened up entrance requirements and became more exclusive. The guild merchant now began requiring that a man possess so much property or have an annual income of so much before he was admitted. Increasingly, as its membership dominated municipal government, the guild merchant became aristocratic and oligarchic. In numerous towns membership eventually became heritable. The guild merchant had arrived at that point where it was the economic and political instrument of a few privileged families who used it to control the urban economic and municipal life for their own selfish aggrandizement. They despised the craftsmen and their guilds. Thus by the thirteenth century there was in many towns such as Ghent, Ypres, Bruges, Florence, Lucca, Milan, and Paris a constantly widening gulf between the bourgeoisie and the proletariat that

HÔTEL DE VILLE OF BRUSSELS (*left*). This hôtel de ville, the most impressive of numerous such structures in Belgium, is a fine example of the secular Gothic architecture in the Low Countries. The main facade, looking upon the open marketplace, was built during the first half of the fifteenth century. The slender and graceful belfry towers to a height of 320 feet.

CLOTH HALL OF YPRES (*below*). The cloth hall of Ypres is the largest and most imposing in Flanders. Begun in the early thirteenth century and finished in the early fourteenth, it testifies to the wealth and power of the great Flemish woolen centers. Although totally destroyed during the First World War, it has now been completely and faithfully restored.

was to foment bitter social and economic strife between these classes in the later Middle Ages.

Meanwhile, although on a more humble level, the craft guilds became equally exclusive. Almost from the outset each craft had three classes of members. Full-fledged members were the *masters* who knew their craft well and fully met the guild requirements. To become a master one had to serve an *apprenticeship* ranging from two to seven years. During this time, the aspirant lived with the master and learned his profession, as well as receiving a minimum education and some lessons in manners from the master and his wife. When finally the apprentice passed the rigid standards of the guild by suitably performing his tasks, he became a *journeyman*, which meant that he was entitled to work by the day (*journée*) for wages. After the journeyman had amassed sufficient capital and perhaps completed a masterpiece, he would generally set himself up in business and become a master. This system of training was an excellent means of ensuring quality craftsmanship, but unfortunately it was later modified so as to hinder and block men from becoming masters. Apprentices were forced to pay extremely large fees in order to obtain training. Standards for admission to the class of journeyman became outlandishly high and entrance fees so dear that few could afford to become masters. By the fourteenth century most craftsmen remained journeymen or wage-earners.

By the end of the thirteenth century both merchant and craft guilds had outlived their usefulness and had become associations or pressure groups working only for the interests of small groups. In most towns a new economic and social alignment was forming. The rich merchants were evolving into capitalistic entrepreneurs, who not only engaged in international trade but controlled all the operations involved in their commercial enterprises. Those merchants in the wool trade sold the woolen cloth all over Europe and also controlled the production of the raw wool and its manufacture into the finished product. The master craftsmen were slowly squeezed out of business by these new capitalists; most were glad to become supervisors or foremen over the various operations of manufacture. The great mass of men had become simply wage-earners employed by the week, totally dependent upon capitalist and foremen, and destined to be victims of the periodic business cycles.

However oppressive both merchant and craft guild had become by the fourteenth century we should not overlook their accomplishments. For a long period both were public spirited and considered foremost the well-being of their community. The rich merchants gave their town admirable government. From their pockets they contributed heavily to public buildings, roads, fortifications, schools, and pious and charitable causes. On a lesser scale the crafts followed suit. The magnificent medieval town halls, rich guild houses, cloth halls, belfries, hospitals, and glorious cathedrals that one can still admire in Europe were made possible

MEDIEVAL MERCHANTS. The butchers and clothiers portrayed here are from a stained glass window, executed around 1460, in the church of Notre-Dame at Semur in Burgundy.

largely through the civic spirit, labor, and generosity of the guilds. As one views in awe the magic of the stained glass windows of Chartres Cathedral he will notice that some of the most exquisitely executed windows were donated by local guilds and that the scenes formed by the stained glass often depict the craft's patron saint and type of work. The window which portrays the history of St. Anthony and St. Paul the Anchorite was donated by the fishmongers; that showing St. Thomas of Canterbury, by the tanners; and that depicting the history of Charlemagne, by the furriers.

MARKETS

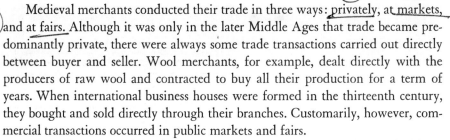

Medieval merchants conducted their trade in three ways: privately, at markets, and at fairs. Although it was only in the later Middle Ages that trade became predominantly private, there were always some trade transactions carried out directly between buyer and seller. Wool merchants, for example, dealt directly with the producers of raw wool and contracted to buy all their production for a term of years. When international business houses were formed in the thirteenth century, they bought and sold directly through their branches. Customarily, however, commercial transactions occurred in public markets and fairs.

Throughout the early Middle Ages, before the revival of trade, there had been local markets in which agrarian produce had been bartered; these markets continued to the end of the Middle Ages. When towns arose they, too, had their local markets where town merchant and artisan bought and sold and where the peasant brought his surplus produce and took home fabricated articles. Every feudal lord and every town could have a market which, as a clearing house, was most useful before trade came to be conducted all over Europe and the Mediterranean basin. Agrarian markets were weekly, but town markets were often held daily at designated market places and under detailed regulations. They opened and closed at specified hours; different products were sold at designated hours and places. The market was under the special protection of the lord or town who charged tolls, stall fees, and other indirect taxes, the proceeds of which were used to construct public market halls and to pave the streets. The principal purpose of the market was to handle the local trade of a town and surrounding area. The trade was almost exclusively between producer and consumer; there were few middlemen. In a county like Flanders or in the heavily populated Rhineland, there were hundreds of these small markets, often so close to each other that they were competitors.

FAIRS

Probably one of the most striking features of medieval trade to the end of the thirteenth century was the fair. Found throughout Europe, it was at its height while merchants were predominantly itinerant. The fair was the first manifestation of the international trade that swept over Europe beginning in the eleventh century. Although markets existed before fairs it is fallacious to derive the latter from the former; there was no link whatsoever. The markets were local, dealt principally in retail trade, were held daily or weekly, and could be held by almost any lord or town. Fairs were international in character; they were wholesale centers of exchange for all kinds of merchants from all over Europe. They were held but once or twice a year and were comparable to our world fairs and expositions. Only a powerful prince had the authority to hold fairs or to grant the right to lesser lords and towns. Both in size and kind of trade the differences were tremendous between market and fair.

The location of the fairs was determined by the principal trade routes. We find them, therefore, concentrated in the Rhine and Danube valleys, northern Italy, along the Rhône, in the Netherlands, and in southern England. The most famous fairs of Europe were in Champagne, through which ran at least six navigable rivers and across which went the chief routes between Italy and northern Europe. In addition, Champagne was about midway between south and north. Fairs were the most privileged commercial centers of Europe. They were under the special peace of the rulers in whose lands they were held; all merchants coming to the fairs were under a special protection. All business agreements were witnessed and sealed by fair officials in order to insure the legality and good faith of all transactions. All sorts of special dispensations were secured to expedite trade and provide comfort and amusement for the merchant. Card-playing and dice-throwing were permitted on saints' days and Sundays. There were feasts, plays, side shows, and dancing girls. But, most important, the ecclesiastical prohibition against usury was suspended.

Thanks to the enlightened economic attitude of the counts of Champagne who always seemed acutely appreciative of money, the fairs of that area became the leading centers for international trade between 1150 and 1300. The fairs were so arranged that there was a continuous cycle throughout the year. Each lasted for about six weeks. First there was the fair of Lagny-sur-Marne in January, followed in early spring by the fair of Bar. Next came the first fair of Provins in May, and in June the "warm fair" of Troyes. In September came the second fair of Provins, and finally the "cold fair" of Troyes in October. Because of the season, the fairs of Provins and the warm fair of Troyes were most important. To them came merchants from all over Europe. Here were the wool merchants from Flanders; the merchants from Italy with eastern wares and money for the Flemish woolen cloth which was sold in the Middle East; the German, French, Spanish, and English merchants. By the thirteenth century the merchants had built houses and headquarters for business, concentrated along certain streets according to their trade specialty or nationality. To facilitate trade, all sorts of comital officers supervised the operation of the fairs. The weeks of each fair were devoted to the sale and purchase of different categories of merchandise. For example, so many days each were allotted for the sale of woolen goods, leather, skins, furs, and of merchandise by avoirdupois weight.

But the Champagne fairs were more than international clearing houses for wholesale trade; they were also the money market for Europe. Here merchants cleared off debts previously contracted and entered into new business agreements, wherein they pledged themselves to meet obligations at a subsequent fair. This organization of credit, as we shall see, gave rise to all sorts of business techniques such as the promissory note (fair letter) and bill of exchange. Finally, it should be noted that each fair had a court to adjudicate the commercial disputes that inevitably arose. Here, under the supervision of the prince's representative, a group of merchants handed down decisions in accordance with a truly international law merchant. Justice was swift and practical and, at the most famous fairs, respected by all. In England, the fair courts were picturesquely termed *piepowder courts.* This name, derived from the French words *pied poudré* meaning "dusty feet," well described the itinerant nature of the merchant who came into the court with the dust of the road still on his feet.

By the end of the thirteenth century the fair had begun to decline. Merchants were becoming more sedentary, dealing directly with each other through branch houses and factors. Moreover, direct trade connections had been opened up between Italy, Flanders, and England; each year Italian ports sent fleets directly to such ports as Southampton and Bruges. After 1285, when Champagne fell under the rule of the French kings, the fairs were so unmercifully taxed that merchants were driven away. Then in the fourteenth century the Hundred Years' War dealt the death blow to these famous fairs.

4. *International Trade and New Business Techniques*

THE REVIVAL OF MEDIEVAL TRADE manifested itself principally along the old land and water routes of the Roman Empire. The main Roman roads had been constructed to connect the capital of Rome with the northern provinces. On both sides of the Apennines roads ran north to the Alps. In the west a main road ran from Genoa to Marseilles and then to Spain. In the east a highway ran from Aquileia to Trieste and the Balkan region. Between these two main arteries, less traveled routes fanned across the famous Alpine passes and connected up with roads running along the Rhône, Rhine, and Danube valleys. Other roads traversed the French plain and terminated at the North Sea and English Channel. In England

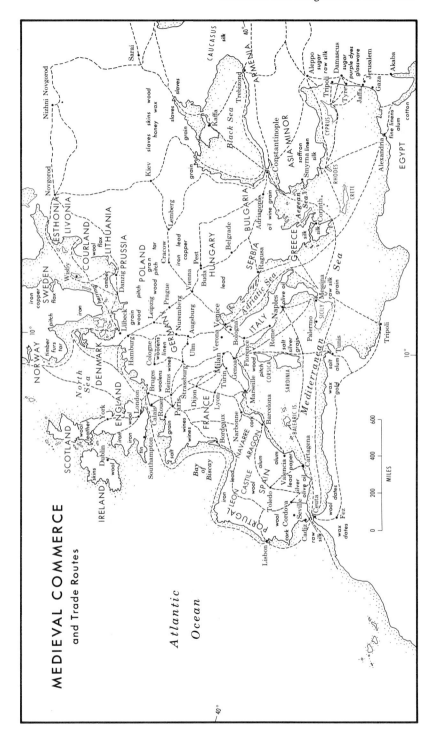

MEDIEVAL COMMERCE
and Trade Routes

the old Roman roads connecting the principal camps and towns carried most of the overland trade. Surprisingly few new roads were built in the Middle Ages; with the exception of the stone Roman roads, most highways were but dirt paths impassable during much of the year. Over these muddy quagmires passed the light two-wheeled carts and horses that carried the bulk of land cargos.

As though the physical obstacles to land transportation were not enough, the medieval princes and lords looked upon roads as a major source of revenue. All sorts of tolls and fees had to be paid at fords and bridges; in fact, one paid a toll merely for the privilege of slogging along a muddy path. Though some of the greatest communes secured freedom from toll for their merchants in certain lands, generally merchants were resigned to the payment of these onerous tolls that practically taxed them off the roads. In lower Austria, merchants who traveled a road in the Danube Valley had to pay seventy-seven tolls. In Flanders, the road between Douai and Rupelmonde, a distance of but sixty miles, was choked by twenty-two tolls. Rarely were any of these tolls used to repair the roads or build bridges.

BELFRY OF CLOTH HALL IN BRUGES. Often called the Venice of the North because of its numerous canals, Bruges was the principal center of commerce and banking for northern Europe in the thirteenth and fourteenth centuries. The belfry in the background, constructed in three stages between 1282 and 1482, is 266 feet high.

WATERWAYS

Under such circumstances it was but natural that the bulk of medieval trade was conducted by water. There were fewer tolls to pay, transportation was swifter, and boats could carry greater cargos. Besides the Rhine, Danube, and Rhône, the principal inland waterways were the Loire, Garonne, Seine, Somme, Scheldt, Meuse, Weser, Elbe, Ems, Thames, and Severn rivers. In such areas as Flanders, the counts and towns cooperated in connecting the numerous rivers and streams by canals. A fourteenth-century merchant could travel throughout Flanders by water. Beyond the inland waterways there were, of course, the Baltic and North seas, the Atlantic Ocean, and the Mediterranean. On rivers and canals clumsy barges powered by animals or men carried the cargos; on the high seas sailing ships were used. In the north the high rounded tublike *cogge* were employed; they carried large cargos but were extremely slow. In the Mediterranean, where the Venetians and Genoese dealt mostly in light luxury items, galleys were found to be the most efficient. Though they could not carry heavy cargos their swiftness more than outweighed this disadvantage. Most *cogge* carried from two hundred to six hundred tons, and some Mediterranean vessels were able to transport as many as one thousand passengers. By the early fourteenth century Venetian and Genoese fleets were regularly sailing to England and Flanders, and the vessels of the German Hanse could be found all over the northern seas. Compared to later maritime and commercial ventures, however, such achievements were quite limited. Few winter voyages were attempted, and until the compass came into general use few captains dared leave the sight of land. Piracy also obstructed voyages and necessitated that ships sail in convoys with armed protection.

COMMODITIES OF INTERNATIONAL TRADE

In the international trade that developed in the eleventh century the principal commodity was spices. Transported by caravan through the Middle East from India and China, the expensive spices were picked up by the merchants of Venice, Genoa, and Pisa and then distributed throughout the West. The spice trade formed the foundation of wealth of the Mediterranean ports and brought big profits from a minimum of labor and investment. By the thirteenth century the Italian ports were dealing in other luxury items. They imported citrus fruits, perfumes, dye-stuffs, silks, muslins, and other Arabian cloths, and traded timber, arms, and slaves in return for these fine eastern wares. During the twelfth century the Italians began selling the fine Flemish and Brabançonne woolen cloth they had purchased at the Champagne fairs. Soon the wool trade became the staple commerce of western

Europe and made such towns as Ypres, Ghent, and Bruges famous. Bruges became an international headquarters for merchants, who concluded their trade transactions there.

To the north and east of the Low Countries, trade was dominated by the German Hanse which came into prominence during the twelfth century. Under the leadership of Lübeck, such towns as Wisby, Rostock, Danzig, Riga, and Dorpat, and the famous towns of northern Germany and the Rhineland, formed an economic league so as to dominate northern commerce and to benefit from the economic privileges that could be won from princes by a large and powerful league of towns. In the principal towns of Europe, such as London and Bruges, the Hanse established factories or trading headquarters where it secured the fabricated goods of the south and sold such natural products as wheat, furs, tar, timber, and salted fish. In addition, it served as a trade intermediary between the West and Russia and the Byzantine Empire. In volume of trade the Hanse towns probably surpassed those of the Mediterranean, but in value and in profit the Italian ports outstripped the north.

Although England was blessed with a strong centralized government which could provide conditions propitious for trade, it remained basically agrarian and in the economic backwater until the middle of the fourteenth century. England's principal contribution to trade was raw wool, vied for by Low Country and Italian merchants. Some southern French towns such as Marseilles, Montpellier, and Narbonne participated in the Mediterranean trade, but they could not compete with the Italian ports. France, in fact, with the exception of the Champagne fairs, was not a great commercial center. Paris was an international cultural and intellectual center, never a commercial or industrial one. Throughout most of the Middle Ages France was primarily an exporter of natural products such as wine and grain. With wine the principal beverage of the feudal aristocrat and wealthy bourgeois, the fine Bordeaux and Burgundian wines became principal items of commerce from the twelfth century on. As the Spanish peninsula was reconquered from the Moslems, Spain became noted as a center for the manufacture and export of fine metal, leather, and woolen products. Barcelona specialized in the sale of Moorish slaves to the West.

One should note that, with the exception of woolen cloth, few manufactured products were important in international trade. A few German towns such as Nuremberg became known for metal-making, and Dinant in the valley of the Meuse gained an excellent reputation for its beaten copper ware. But the technology of metallurgy was not understood until the fifteenth century, and mining techniques were extremely primitive. Little coal was mined. By the end of the thirteenth century, however, all Europe from Spain to Russia and from England to the Mediterranean was the scene of a brisk trade that included the Middle and

Far East. Italy and the Low Countries were the centers of this trade, and from these regions came the development of new business techniques to facilitate commerce and credit.

MEDIEVAL MONEY

Although historians often speak of a natural economy dominating Europe from the fall of the Roman Empire down to the eleventh century, this is not completely accurate. The circulation of money did not entirely dry up, even though trading was conducted principally through barter. Down to the eighth century, in the Mediterranean region the Roman gold shilling (*solidus*) was in circulation and provided a stable coin for what little trade remained. When it disappeared the only coin that was used down to the twelfth century was the silver penny (*denarius*) struck by Charlemagne to serve as a uniform coinage in the empire. Struck at the ratio of 240 pennies to the pound, the penny was admirably suited for the limited trade transactions which took place down to the twelfth century. In this period a few pennies had considerable purchasing power. A weakness of the coinage, however, was that every prince came to coin these silver pennies and from feudal state to feudal state the penny varied greatly in value. Most princes debased their coins, continually restriking them at a lower value. In one German principality the coinage was debased by the ruler on an average of three times a year. Although this situation did not prevail in such strong states as England, Flanders, and Normandy, throughout Europe in the twelfth century there was a growing demand for a stable coinage and for a coin whose value was commensurate with the volume and value of trade. It was too burdensome to pay one's obligations in bags of silver pennies.

Quite naturally, the coinage reform began in the areas most advanced economically. In 1192 Venice struck a new silver coin called the *groat* that was worth twelve silver pennies (a *shilling*); immediately the silver groat became the chief coin of commerce. It spread north of the Alps and influenced rulers to imitate it. The English improved their sterling coinage, and in France a coin called the *gros tournois* (large Tours) was struck in the middle of the thirteenth century. About equal in value to the groat, it became the principal northern coin of commerce and was struck in most of the continental countries. Before long, however, there was need for a more valuable coin. In 1252 Florence coined the *gold florin,* and soon thereafter Venice followed with her *gold ducat.* These two coins corresponded in value to a *silver pound,* just as the groat had corresponded to the shilling. Thus the pound was transformed into a real coin and ceased being a term of account. Gradually the northern states followed with a gold coinage, and by the middle of the fourteenth century all Europe had gold coins; through the creation of the groat and gold coins the merchants were supplied with a stable currency which met the requirements of the expanded trade.

BUSINESS ORGANIZATION

In the twelfth century, when merchants began to settle down and conduct the bulk of their business from their homes or countinghouses, they found it necessary to cooperate with partners or agents who carried on the operations in other towns and countries. This inevitably increased the available capital and services and helped to expand the business. The favorite form of economic cooperation in the Middle Ages was the partnership. Sometimes one partner would supply all the capital and the other all the labor, such as making the trips for purchase and sale; the investor received three-fourths of the profits and the trader one-fourth. Under another arrangement, the working partner would supply one-third of the capital, and for this investment plus his labor would then customarily receive half the profits. This type of partnership was prominent in the maritime enterprises conducted by Venetian and Genoese merchants. These partnerships, however, were temporary and existed only for the duration of one trading enterprise. A lasting partnership occurred when close friends or relatives would agree to pool their money and labor for a stipulated number of years. Some partners managed the home office, some the foreign branches, and others took the trips. Generally such partnerships were dominated by a family or by a few closely related families. Great families, in fact, dominated large-scale medieval business. In Italy, by the thirteenth century numerous economic enterprises expanded beyond a partnership. For costly trading projects with the Far East, for the purchase of particularly expensive goods, or for the construction of a ship, dozens of men would invest money and then prorate the profits at the termination of a successful enterprise. With ships, numerous individuals would each own a fraction (*locum*) of the ship and receive an income proportionate to his share.

NEW TECHNIQUES IN FINANCE

Although improved coinage and new forms of economic association helped merchants extend trade, the greatest impetus was credit. The first extensive evidence we have of the development of credit comes from the Champagne fairs. There buyers and sellers canceled out obligations and concluded agreements to pay for goods at a subsequent fair. Sometimes such agreements were struck far distant from Champagne, but the parties would agree to settle their obligations there on a certain date at a particular fair. As banks of deposit emerged in the twelfth century, depositors gave verbal orders to transfer sums to creditors; eventually, depositors wrote orders (checks) to their bankers to pay a stipulated amount to the creditors.

But credit was facilitated most by the bill of exchange. Begun essentially as an acknowledgment of a debt to a merchant from another country and the promise to pay the debt in the foreigner's currency at a specified date, it soon assumed more complicated forms. A Genoese merchant, for example, rather than paying a debt to a Florentine merchant at Florence in currency of that state, would customarily pay the money to a Genoese creditor of the Florentine merchant, who was then credited with paying his Genoese obligation. In this manner debts were cleared between merchants all over Europe, with a minimum of currency changing hands. Another use of the bill of exchange was for a debtor to pay the sum to a local merchant who had an agent located at the town where the debt was payable. The debtor would receive a draft ordering the agent to pay a specified sum to the creditor. The draft would then be forwarded to the creditor and he turned it in to the agent who honored it. All the great companies of merchants handled such negotiations. They secured handsome fees for their services and eventually dealt in bills of exchange, making a profit from the differences in exchange rates between the various currencies.

Although the church had preached long and hard against the evils of usury, it was the first institution to make loans and charge interest. It made loans to impoverished nobles and took mortgages on their lands as security. When unfortunate debtors defaulted in their payments the church was not hesitant in foreclosing. Another prevalent method of securing loans was to pawn personal property for a certain term. Generally Jews dominated the pawnshops and collected as high as 40 per cent interest on small loans. Contrary to popular belief, however, the Jews did not dominate banking in the Middle Ages. The principal bankers were Italian merchants, who were replaced in northern Europe in the fourteenth century by native bankers. By 1200 banks of deposit were common and they were using the deposits to make loans at interest. The great Italian bankers such as the Frescobaldi, Bardi, Peruzzi, Scoti, and Pucci had banks located in the leading European towns and became international bankers dealing not only in private loans and bills of exchange but also in public finance. They became the principal lenders to the Pope, to great prelates, kings, princes, and towns. Loans were usually made on the security of future tax receipts; upon receipt of the taxes the bankers obtained both principal and interest. The princes became so dependent upon loans that they often permitted the bankers to take over the collection of taxes; sometimes the bankers were appointed officials in the treasuries and directed state finances. Although such loans netted lucrative profits, the risks were tremendous; it was a rare prince who would not renounce his obligations when pushed into a tight financial spot. Eventually all the Italian banking houses failed because they could not collect the tremendous loans outstanding to rulers; at this point native bankers and merchants were called upon to replace the Italians as moneylenders to the princes.

By the end of the thirteenth century the leading European merchants carried on international trade. Most conducted a specialized trade, and entered into various forms of associations or partnerships to facilitate their operations and expand their credit and buying power. To handle the increased volume and value of trade, Europe secured a new and sound silver and gold coinage. To expedite the payment of financial obligations and to provide increased credit, paper money in the form of checks and bills of exchange arose, a step that led to the development of international trading and banking companies to deal in these bills and to make private and public loans. During the course of the thirteenth century much of the European economy had become capitalistic; that is, the production and exchange of goods was carried on under a system of private enterprise and competitive conditions. With their profits the capitalists expanded business enterprises or invested in real estate, thereby adding to their wealth.

5. *The Cluniac Movement and the Revived Papacy*

THE DETERMINED EFFORTS made by Charlemagne to strengthen and reform the church ended, as did all his accomplishments, with his death; thereafter, the invigorated church degenerated into ignorance and corruption. Only seldom could a ruler such as Otto the Great or Alfred the Great stir the church out of its lethargy, so engulfed was it by the general economic and political misery. Popes and bishops, more secular than spiritual, flouted in their private lives most of the church canons. Typically the bishop was a feudal aristocrat whose ecclesiastical duties were performed—often incompetently—by underpaid subordinates. Most church offices were bought and sold, or were obtained through the patronage of a powerful lord. Most prelates greedily held a plurality of offices. Numerous clergy kept mistresses or were married and passed land and offices on to their heirs. Most of the clergy were abysmally ignorant, incapable of performing the simplest ritual. Like the Carolingian Empire, the church was rapidly fragmentizing into small units with no sense of central direction or cooperation. Life in the monasteries was equally degenerate. The Benedictine rule became a farce. Most monks with no thought of their vows of chastity and poverty lived luxuriously in their monasteries supported by the labor of their peasants. The abbots were like the bishops; the flush of the monastic ideal was seldom to be found. By the tenth century the church had become secularized and feudalized and most men, lay and ecclesiastical, accepted this situation as normal.

Somehow, as so often before in its history, the church found the strength to begin a reform movement. It started in the tenth century with a new monastic movement called the Congregation of Cluny. In 910, with papal sanction, William, duke of Aquitaine and count of Auvergne, founded in southern Burgundy the monastery of Cluny. According to the terms of its foundation, it was to be completely free from all secular and spiritual control except that of the Pope. The monks were to have absolute freedom in the election of their abbot. The old Benedictine rule was reaffirmed and was to be adhered to completely. Soon the abbey of Cluny became renowned for the piety and rigor of its life, and numerous old monasteries affiliated with it; they received new heads called priors appointed by the abbot of Cluny. The Congregation eventually numbered over three hundred monasteries and took the lead in crusading for the spiritual renovation of the church. The Cluniac reform program advocated complete celibacy, the independence of church from secular control, and the end of simony—the evil custom of buying church offices.

Alone the Cluniac agitation for reform would have made slight imprint upon European spiritual life; fortunately the emperor Henry III (1039–1056), eager to support the spiritual rejuvenation of the church, embraced its program. He moved quickly to stamp out simony and he forbade clerical children from holding church or state offices. But beyond this point Henry was unwilling to go. Like all eleventh-century rulers he regarded the church as a department of state and considered himself responsible for the Papacy. Perhaps his view of the Papacy was fortunate, for he finally ended a degenerate line of Popes that extended back to the ninth century. When he went to Italy in 1046 he found three men claiming to be Pope; he had all three deposed, secured the election of a worthy successor, and later nominated three of that Pope's successors. One of them, Leo IX (1048–1054), was responsible for the Papacy resuming its world power. He at once pushed the principles of Cluniac reform and held councils in Italy, France, and Germany to enforce canon law and to reestablish papal leadership over local churches. In the last year of his pontificate, Leo and the Patriarch of the eastern church broke irrevocably over matters of doctrine and ritual. Although the Patriarch caused the quarrel by condemning Latin usages and closing Roman churches in the East, neither side would compromise and the schism continued.

From 1054 to 1073 there were three Popes, but they rank as mediocrities beside Hildebrand who was archdeacon and chief papal adviser. During these years it was he who accomplished two key measures for the Papacy. He recognized the conquests of Robert Guiscard and his brother Roger in southern Italy and Sicily in return for their promise of military support against the German emperors, and, in 1059, he secured proclamation of the famous electoral decree stipulating that the Pope should be elected by the cardinal clergy of Rome. This was not a new law, but it applied to papal elections a practice employed at times to elect bishops and abbots. Its great significance lay in freeing the Popes from nomination or appointment by the emperors. Both in 1058 and 1061 Popes were elected freely by the Roman clergy because Henry III had left behind a small boy Henry IV (1056–

1106) who was in no position to uphold the traditional imperial rights. Then in 1073 Hildebrand was elevated to the Papacy as Gregory VII (1073–1085), and Henry IV recognized him. Although this recognition meant trouble for Henry he could not at the moment do otherwise, engaged as he was with suppressing a bitter Saxon revolt. When this was achieved he revealed his true feelings on papal independence.

6. *The Investiture Struggle*

IN THE FAMOUS STRUGGLE that ensued between Henry IV and Gregory VII, the former showed himself a skilled and tough fighter, but he was rash, violent, and unable to make graceful compromises. In Gregory he had to face one of the four or five greatest Popes of the Middle Ages. Possessing exceptional qualities of leadership and statesmanship, Gregory, by his whole-hearted and sincere devotion to church reform and to an independent Papacy, instilled this feeling in hundreds of leading churchmen and translated his fight into a grand moral struggle of Christian forces against worldly materialism and sin.

THE ISSUES

Fundamentally Gregory held to the view of all previous great Popes and the church fathers. He considered the Pope the successor of St. Peter, the designated representative of God on this earth. Not only was he to wield the spiritual leadership of God's church, but he was to supervise the secular institutions and their rulers. It was only natural, he thought, that as God's shepherd responsible for the salvation of His children, he should be supreme over emperor and kings whose task was but the maintenance of worldly order. In Gregory's mind, Pope and emperor should cooperate closely to bring the City of Man into line with the City of God, but he considered the imperial role subordinate. The emperor was like the moon that reflected the rays of light given off by the sun—the Pope. In support of his position Gregory could point to past tradition and history and could quote numerous papal writers on political theory. The independence and supremacy of the Papacy was evidenced by its strong position under Gregory the Great and by the historical fact that the emperors were crowned by the Popes. Furthermore, such writers as Augustine had argued that secular political institutions had resulted from the fall of Adam and Eve. Primevally there had been no need for governments with their armies and laws. They had come into being to suppress evil, and when this had been accomplished, they would disappear and give place to the City of God represented by the Papacy and church. Through the Pope, God exercised His authority and made known His will. Logically, so papal political theory ran, the Pope was the sovereign authority in this world.

But Henry could also point to historical precedent and quote imperialist political theory. Had not Charlemagne and Otto the Great appointed and deposed Popes, and had they not governed the church like a department of state? It was obvious, so the imperialists argued, that the emperor was directly responsible to God. Christ himself had said: "Render unto Caesar the things that are Caesar's." Yet in this statement lay the root of all the trouble. What properly were Caesar's things?

That Gregory VII was no bitter and uncompromising zealot is proved by his peaceful relations with other rulers, and by his moderate attitude toward pushing reform. Like Gregory the Great, he realized that progress came slowly and was built upon numerous small steps. With rulers such as William the Conqueror of England he concluded a *modus vivendi,* despite that ruler's claim to supremacy in the affairs of the English church, a difference Gregory was willing to forget in the face of William's enthusiastic reform of the church. Henry's violence and failure to keep faith with Gregory contributed to the bitterness of the struggle.

THE STRUGGLE OF GREGORY VII AND HENRY IV

In the first few years of his pontificate Gregory methodically moved against simony and clerical marriage. Opposed in this by some of the German bishops who had thrived on these irregularities, Gregory responded by removing those most stubborn. Then in 1075 he precipitated the break with Henry by prohibiting lay investiture. He forbade secular rulers to invest bishops with the spiritual insignia of their office. This struck at an old imperial custom and Henry, just victorious over the Saxons, was in no mood to obey the decree. When Gregory proceeded to threaten him with excommunication unless he respected the order, early in 1076 Henry replied by pushing his bishops into declaring Gregory a usurper and unfit to be Pope. Henry followed this act by sending a haughty letter to Gregory in which he called him a false monk and demanded that he surrender his papal power. The answer to Henry was indeed radical. In the tradition of Ambrose, Gregory declared that Henry had broken church law. He therefore pronounced the sentence of excommunication against Henry, released his subjects from obedience, and directed them to elect another ruler. This sensational stroke worked because it was supported by German internal politics. The German nobles, fearing the strong rule of Henry, were happy to revolt. They declared Henry deposed in the autumn of 1076, unless he could obtain absolution from Gregory within a year.

Completely taken by surprise with this swift action, Henry moved rapidly to make his peace with Gregory. Late in 1076 he set out for Italy, crossed the snowy Alps, and found Gregory early in January of 1077 at the Tuscan castle of Canossa where he had stopped while en route north for a meeting with the German nobles. Here, as a barefoot penitent clothed in coarse wool, Henry begged for absolution. After three days Gregory received the imperial penitent and granted him absolution. Happening as it did under such dramatic circumstances, the surrender of Henry at Canossa was looked upon as a glorious triumph of church over state. It seemed to signify that the Papacy had become a world power, supreme even over the emperors of the Holy Roman Empire. Indeed, it seemed to symbolize a magnificent future for the reformed and revived church.

The immediate victory, however, was secured by Henry. Having foiled the German nobility he proceeded to subdue the rebels, and by 1080 he was absolute master in Germany. Again he broke with Gregory, invaded Italy, and took Rome; in 1084 he installed another Pope, who crowned him emperor. Gregory took refuge with his Norman ally Robert Guiscard who marched north from Sicily and forced Henry out of Rome. After pillaging the city for three days, the Normans retired. Gregory felt so insecure that he accompanied them, and soon thereafter died as a bitter refugee at Salerno in 1085. Although it appeared that Gregory's glorious triumph at Canossa was completely neutralized by his sad end, the cause he fought for ultimately triumphed. By the early twelfth century the Papacy had established its independence and won recognition as the leader of western Christendom. Throughout Europe compromises were reached over the investiture struggle. In 1106–1107 Henry I of England and Anselm, archbishop of Canterbury, concluded an agreement whereby Henry surrendered his right to invest the bishops of his realm with their spiritual office; he continued, however, to invest the bishops with their secular fiefs and rights and reserved the right to approve the bishops elected by the cathedral clergy. In 1122 an almost identical agreement was concluded at the Concordat of Worms in Germany. Here Emperor Henry V and the Pope settled their differences by the same compromise. Although relations of church and state were never satisfactorily settled in the Middle Ages, and although many new issues continued to involve secular rulers in disputes with the Papacy, the most serious problems had been settled in the twelfth century. The apogee of church power came between the pontificate of Gregory VII and the end of the thirteenth century.

7. Byzantine Culture

By the end of the eleventh century in the wake of a remarkable economic, political, and religious revival western Europe was about to embark on a great offensive—a crusade against the infidel of the Islamic East. That an attack could be mounted against the East, the first for almost a thousand years, attests to the vitality of western Europe, a vitality that had been lacking for almost eight hundred years. Before examining this new involvement of Europe in the East, however, let us look at Byzantine and Moslem civilization in order to understand the dramatic differences between the cultures of East and West and to grasp the significance that renewed contact would have for Europe.

After Justinian's failure to restore Roman imperial unity around the Mediterranean and after the dramatic Arab conquests of the seventh and eighth centuries, Byzantine military and political power was largely restricted to Asia Minor, the Balkan area adjacent to Constantinople, and the waters of the eastern Mediterranean. We know, without getting involved here in the dynasties that preserved the Byzantine Empire against the Arab attacks and the Bulgarian and Russian threats from the north, that the defense was successful and that the territory in the Balkans was even increased. Not until faced with new attacks from tribes pouring west from the Asiatic plateau in the eleventh century did the defense fail and only then was there recourse to western military assistance. Later we shall see how Byzantine territory shrank until only Constantinople remained, but what should be understood now is that the political survival of the eastern part of the Roman Empire was vital because it fostered the continuation of a civilized life rich in achievement. When the West came into contact with Byzantine culture it would rediscover much of the classical learning forgotten since the Roman Empire in the West had disintegrated.

As the Mediterranean world of East and West drifted apart and regular contact ceased, Latin declined in the East as a written and spoken language and there was a return to Greek, the traditional language. Already under Justinian Greek was becoming the chief vehicle of expression. Although scholars and other educated men continued to read Latin, it was no longer the universal language. The last important Latin compilation was the *Corpus Juris Civilis* drawn up in the sixth century. To clear the confusion stemming from the numerous contradictory and duplicative laws and to make sense out of the divergent legal opinions of the jurists, Justinian ordered a massive study of the Roman law that resulted in two major compilations and a legal treatise. First the laws were sorted out and systematically collated to eliminate conflict and duplication. Some 4,652 laws were gathered into what was called the *Code*. Laws made after 529 were placed in a supplement known as the *Novels* (new constitutions). Eventually all new laws were written in Greek. By tremendous work legal experts sorted out the principal opinions of the Roman jurists, arranging them in one huge compilation containing 1,544 opinions by thirty-eight jurists. This work known as the *Digest* appeared in 533 and later wielded an authoritative influence on jurisprudence because it showed how the leading jurists had interpreted Roman law. To aid the lawyer and student to understand the *Code* and *Digest*, Justinian sponsored a textbook called the *Institutes* (533). Chiefly through these three works were the principles of Roman law preserved; from them were derived the legal systems governing all lands not under English common law.

Byzantine Greek, while never achieving the beauty or perfection of classical Greek, manifested an excellence in various forms of literary expression such as biography, history, treatises on government, and letters. Poetry alone was truly inferior, even though some of the hymn writers of the sixth century composed beautiful lines. To be able to read such authors as Homer and Thucydides, though an asset, was also frequently an obstacle to creative writing; many writers slavishly copied the style and thought of their classical predecessors until Byzantine Greek became lifeless and its thought arid. Even the flurry of scholarship and writing in the tenth and eleventh centuries produced works of little originality. Greek manuscripts were collected and copied. The learned Photius, the tenth-century Patriarch who was the center of a learned group of scholars, seemed incapable of original thought; he compiled the *Myriobiblon,* a vast encyclopedia of ancient and contemporary writers. In the eleventh century Michael Psellus wrote on a broad range of subjects and produced an excellent history of the Byzantine Empire. Such writing, which was typical of the period and which preserved, condensed, and provided commentaries and textbooks, was, however, quite different from and inferior to the work done by the Greeks of the fifth and fourth centuries B.C.; it had value only because it preserved a rich heritage that was eventually passed on to western Europe and that became the basis for the exciting intellectual advance of the Italian Renaissance. A comparison of such work, however arid, with that being done at the same time in western Europe emphasizes the pitiful state of learning in the West between the fourth and eleventh centuries.

Nor were Byzantine thinkers any more original in other branches of knowledge. Philosophers were content with further explication of Platonic and Aristotelian philosophy. Galen and Ptolemy had no real successors; advance in mathematical and scientific knowledge halted while men but digested what had been known for centuries. Although Leo the Mathematician, a noted teacher of mathematics at Constantinople in the ninth century, was given an imperial professorship, his contribution to learning was restricted to teaching. There was, it must be emphasized, no lack of support for learning. Some emperors even patronized a palace school; some were so well educated that they wrote valuable treatises on military tactics and civil administration. By way of contrast, no prince of western Europe was capable of this; indeed Charlemagne never even mastered the difficult art of writing.

Technologically and economically the Byzantine Empire was dramatically ahead of the West. Its economy remained based on money. Closely regulated by the government, industry and trade continued to thrive, and trade was even conducted on an international level. State factories employed many artisans who were organized into guilds. Ambassadors from foreign lands and also the crusaders were amazed at the richness of Constantinople, its fine houses, churches, and public buildings. The material level of civilization in Constantinople had not declined and perhaps had even surpassed that of the Greeks and Romans. Scientific knowledge produced work-saving devices such as cranes and implements of war like the catapult. The most fearsome weapon in the Byzantine arsenal was Greek fire, a highly inflammable material made from a naphtha base which, when placed in pottery containers hurled by catapults, proved to be a deadly weapon against ships and besieged towns. The early rise of Venice as an economic power certainly resulted in large part from its contact with Constantinople, a contact that brought familiarity with advanced economic practices and technology.

The Greek Orthodox church, as the eastern church came to be known, never made the theological contributions or produced the reform movements characteristic of the Latin church in the West. Unlike the Pope, the Patriarch of Constantinople was subordinate to the emperor and was considered an imperial official who headed an imperial department. Unfortunately the theological questions that concerned the clergy were not fundamental and served only to divide the church and alienate it further from the western church. In the eighth century the emperor Leo III the Isaurian, influenced by his contact with Mohammedanism and various unorthodox Christian sects, condemned the use of icons and pictures in Christian worship. He not only encouraged the clergy to preach against the worship of icons, but in 725 prohibited such worship and launched a campaign against it. This step seriously divided the Byzantine Empire and alienated the Papacy in the West. A schism (division) arose that ended only when images were again approved in 843. In the tenth century the Patriarch Photius stirred up another controversy by his condemnation of certain practices and doctrines of the western church. He condemned the eating of eggs during Lent, the use of unleavened bread in the mass, the shaving of priests' faces, and the doctrine that the Holy Spirit derived from the Father and the Son (*Filioque*). There was again internal dissension and another schism with the West. Indeed, the one real accomplishment of the eastern church was the conversion of the Slavic peoples and the Bulgarians during the ninth century, a feat accomplished by the missionary activity of two brothers of Slavic origin, Cyril and Methodius, who, after being ordained at Constantinople, preached the Gospel to the Slavs. To introduce the Christian Scriptures and liturgy to the Slavs, Cyril developed a modified Greek alphabet known as the Cyrillic alphabet that came to be used in such Slavonic languages as Russian. Through the efforts of Cyril and Methodius eastern Europe was introduced to Byzantine culture and has remained firmly tied to that tradition.

Byzantine architecture derived stimulation from two sources—Roman and Syrian. Byzantine architects, constructing buildings in Italy during the sixth century, were inspired by Roman forms. They chiefly constructed rectangular basilicas in which they used the semicircular arch and barrel vault. The arches in the basilicas were so designed that they sprang directly up from supporting columns.[1] The feature of Byzantine architecture most original and characteristic,

---

[1] For more details see pp. 294–296.

and one apparently adapted from Syrian designs, was the dome on pendentives, which consisted of placing a dome on four semicircular arches. The circular base of the dome rested primarily on the tops of the arches with the triangular spaces in the cones filled in. The spectacular church of Santa Sophia constructed by Justinian in Constantinople and the church of San Vitale in Ravenna are the finest examples of this type of architecture. In these and other Byzantine churches such as Sant' Apollinare in Classe outside Ravenna, the interior decoration was mainly brilliantly colored mosaics that covered the vaults, domes, walls, and floors. The figures in the mosaics are devoid of perspective but their primitive features contribute to the overall effect achieved by arranging the stones so as to catch and reflect light. The mosaics in San Vitale, which depict the court of Justinian, are probably the most celebrated. Any sculpture used was of plants, birds, and geometric designs. The real triumphs of Byzantine architecture and art, the dome on pendentives and the mosaics, were features that, except in Italy and Sicily, were little used in the West which preferred structures modeled upon the simple lines of the rectangular basilica.

8. *Moslem Culture*

NEVER SUCCESSFUL in capturing Constantinople and the territory adjacent to it, the Arabs had to be content with an empire that extended from the Atlantic Ocean to the Indus River. Expansion had come under the Ommiad caliphate and consolidation under the Abbasid caliphate which, as we have seen, supplanted the Ommiad in 750 and constructed the new capital of Baghdad farther to the east on the Tigris River. Under such caliphs as Harun-al-Rashid (786–809) the Arab empire attained great power and magnificence. Increasingly the Abbasids lived like oriental despots; they lost touch with their people and the lands they ruled. More interested than their predecessors in patronizing culture and cultivating a luxurious existence, they were less able military leaders and consequently various governors and generals gradually revolted and became independent rulers over large sections of the empire. Such was the course of Arab history in the ninth, tenth, and eleventh centuries until, on the eve of the First Crusade in the late eleventh century, the Moslem world was no longer united politically but divided into small emirates ruled by independent emirs, as in Spain, Tunisia, Morocco, Egypt, and Syria. The breakup of Arab political unity largely accounts for the success of the First Crusade. But the Moslem world, although split up politically, was still bound together by a common religion, language, law, and culture; there was a civilization common to the Moslem world, and even if one did not accept the Islamic faith he learned Arabic for its economic, social, and legal advantages.

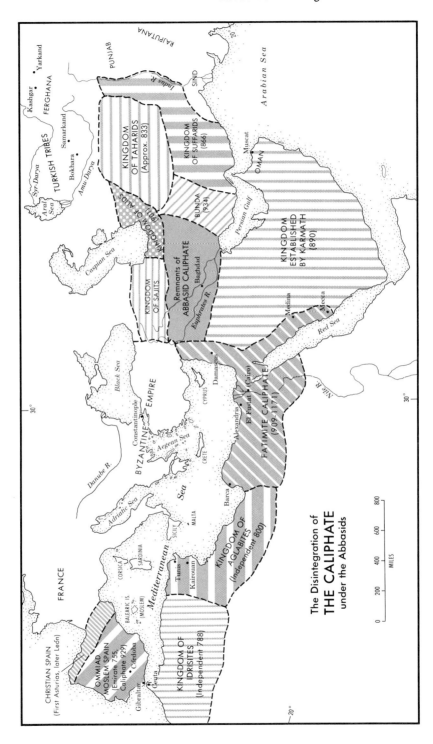

CHRISTIAN SPAIN
(First Asturias, later León)

FRANCE

Yarkand
Kashgar
FERGHANA
TURKISH TRIBES
Samarkand
Bokhara

Syr-Darya
Amu-Darya
Aral Sea

PUNJAB
RAJPUTANA
Indus R.
SIND

Arabian Sea

KINGDOM OF TAHARIDS
(Approx. 833)

KINGDOM OF SUFFARIDS
(866)

Muscat
OMAN

KINGDOM OF SAMANIDS (88)

BUNDA (934)

Persian Gulf

KINGDOM ESTABLISHED BY KARMATH
(890)

Caspian Sea

Remnants of ABBASID CALIPHATE
Baghdad
Euphrates R.

KINGDOM OF SAJITS

Medina
Mecca
Red Sea

Black Sea

BYZANTINE EMPIRE
Constantinople

Danube R.

Aegean Sea
CRETE

CYPRUS
Damascus

Alexandria
El Fustat (Cairo)

FATIMITE CALIPHATE
(909-1171)

Nile R.

Mediterranean Sea

Barca

Adriatic Sea

MALTA

SICILY

KINGDOM OF AGLABITES
(Independent 800)

SARDINIA
CORSICA

Tunis
Kairouan

BALEARIC IS.
(MOSLEM)

OMMIAD MOSLEM SPAIN
(Emirate 755,
Caliphate 929)
Córdoba

Ceuta
Gibraltar

KINGDOM OF IDRISITES
(Independent 788)

The Disintegration of
THE CALIPHATE
under the Abbasids

0   200   400   600   800
MILES

30°

30°

20°

20°

What characterized the Arabs after their conquests was their ability to ac commodate and adjust to different cultures. Tolerant of those they conquered, they preserved the rich cultural heritage of the Mediterranean basin and developed great respect for Graeco-Roman civilization which they assimilated and built upon. Eventually it was the Moslem world that introduced medieval Europe to elements of the Graeco-Roman civilization that had been largely forgotten for hundreds of years. Moslem scholars, after collecting all the great Greek classics and placing them in libraries such as that in Baghdad, then began translating them into Arabic. Plato, Aristotle, Galen, Hippocrates, and others were translated. By the end of the ninth century the Moslem world was familiar with the main body of Greek philosophy, science, medicine, and mathematics. From their contact with the lands to the east the Arabs also became familiar with Persian, Hindu, and Chinese learning. After a period of familiarization Moslem scholars began to write commentaries on this corpus of knowledge and to do further investigation. Moslem scholarship differed from Byzantine in that it was creative as well as assimilative.

We cannot pursue here a thorough discussion of Moslem learning but can only show briefly the magnitude of the Moslem contribution to various fields of knowledge. The Arab philosopher al-Kindi (d. 850) made a thorough study of Aristotle and began the reconciliation of Greek thought and Moslem theology. Averroës (d. 1198), who lived in Cordova and was the greatest philosopher, developed a rational and naturalistic interpretation of Aristotle that marked a break with a philosophical tradition which attempted to use Aristotle to support Islamic doctrine. Averroës realized that Aristotelian thought contradicted Islamic precepts and made no attempt at reconciliation. His writings, which were soon translated into Latin, profoundly affected the interpretation of Aristotle in Europe. From Ptolemy's *Almagest* the Moslems learned much trigonometry, geography, and astronomy. From Euclid they learned geometry and elementary algebra. Al-Khwarizmi (d. 850) wrote the first textbook on arithmetic, a work entitled *al-Gebra,* from which our word *algebra* is derived. From India the Arabs learned about the Hindu symbols which came to be called Arabic numerals. They apparently added a tenth symbol, the zero, which made the numerals invaluable for mathematical computation. Al-Khwarizmi described the use of the zero in relation to the other nine numerals. With this new mathematical knowledge the Arabs made advances in astronomy. They could more accurately observe and calculate the movements of heavenly bodies. They improved the astrolabe by which one could determine the position of a star and so locate exact latitude, a device that was extremely useful for navigation. Al-Biruni (973–1048) wrote a book contending that the earth rotates on its axis. The tenth-century scholar al-Haytham did research on light, color, reflection, refraction, and magnification.

In medicine the Arab achievements were equally spectacular. Hunayn-ibn-Ishaqu (d. 877), a skilled physician, translated the Greek works on medicine,

ARAB PHYSICIANS PREPARING MEDICINE. This early thirteenth-century painting, probably from Baghdad, shows one physician at work while another seems to be giving orders or advice. The picture appears on the leaf of an Arabic translation of the text of the Greek medical writer Dioscorides, who listed all the pharmacological samples known in his time.

composed a book on medical care, and wrote a scholarly treatise on diseases of the eyes. Al-Razi (865–925) wrote on all sorts of medical subjects, compiled a medical encyclopedia, and contributed a learned discussion of smallpox. As head of the hospital at Baghdad, he established courses in pharmacy, extended medical treatment to the poor, and initiated the licensing of physicians. The finest work in medicine, however, was done by Avicenna (d. 1037) who wrote a learned book known as the *Canon* which, embracing all known medical theory and practice, became the standard reference for Arab physicians and eventually, in translation, became known to European physicians. Although valuable, the Arab contributions to chemistry were too often devoted to such projects as transmuting base metals into gold. Also, many foolish ideas that were mostly astrological lore were taught as serious astronomical facts. Although in some areas Arab knowledge often did not proceed beyond the Greek, this was not the case in mathematics and medicine. How fortunate for the western world that the Arabs preserved and digested what they found, because during the twelfth and thirteenth centuries this knowledge, translated into Latin from Greek and Arabic, became a springboard for the amazing intellectual advance of these centuries and of the later Renaissance.

The superior civilization of the Moslem world is evidenced in its material life. Virtually masters of the Mediterranean for three or four hundred years, the Arabs dominated trade from the Strait of Gibraltar to India and China. They became the great middlemen between East and West. From the East they secured rare and precious goods. From contact with Russia they obtained slaves and furs. Probing deep into Africa and along its coasts, even to Madagascar, they procured ivory, slaves, and products that were never before known in the Mediterranean world. The Arabs became known as purveyors of exotic and scarce commodities. The lucrative international trade sustained large cities such as Baghdad, Damascus, Alexandria, and Cairo. The Arab coin, the *dinar,* became the international currency of Mediterranean trade and was for its time what the Roman *solidus* had been and what the British pound and American dollar would become.

Because of superior equipment Arab ships sailed almost anywhere, even across the Indian Ocean. The Arab sailors learned how to rig their ships with the lateen or triangular sail which permitted them to tack against the wind. They equipped their ships with the magnetic compass and could therefore navigate far beyond the sight of land. From China or India the Arabs learned about the windmill and its uses. Irrigation was so improved that arid lands produced rice, indigo, sugar, oranges, and lemons. The words *orange, lemon, spinach,* and *artichoke* are of Arabic origin. Intelligent treatises were written on the production of fruits and vegetables; indeed, the Arabs practiced scientific farming.

Arab craftsmanship was expert and beautiful. Superb fabrics were produced. Arab tapestries, carpets, rugs, brocades, and embroideries have never been surpassed. Arabic words taken over by the English language attest to the superior quality of Arab products: damask from Damascus, muslin from Mosul, fustian from the town of al-Fustat, and also cotton, satin, scarlet, and crimson. In metallurgy, glassmaking, the carving of crystal and ivory, leather-making, and ceramics, the Arabs became famous. Finely tempered steel swords came from Toledo, leather products from Morocco, metallic glazed pottery from Egypt, and the damascened armor from Damascus. In the West at this time few could afford the Arabic products with their exotic names that symbolized the wonders and riches of the East. Not until the thirteenth century would the West be able to import Arab goods in any quantity.

The Arabs had been almost wholly ignorant of architecture and building techniques until they saw what the Greeks, Romans, and Persians had constructed. At first appropriating and using for their mosques what buildings were available, they later adopted certain architectural features pleasing to them and created their own style. The earliest mosque employing new architectural principles was the Dome of the Rock at Jerusalem constructed in the seventh century. Here the architect designed a dome of timber and metal placed on a masonry octagon. The interior was decorated with mosaics. The mosque of Damascus erected in the eighth century, also decorated with mosaics, was designed both as a mosque and as a place for public assemblies. The interior is a medley of arches while the exterior has two arcades that delineate the two stories. Towering above all are the slender towers, the minarets, from which the *muezzin* called the faithful to prayer. Unfortunately most of the mosques constructed during the Middle Ages were destroyed by the Mongols when they swept into the Middle East in the thirteenth century. Only in Spain have most of the medieval mosques survived. At Cordova is a magnificent mosque with 1,293 richly decorated columns. During the thirteenth century emirs erected the celebrated palaces of the Alcazar at Seville and the Alhambra at Granada. These buildings with their horseshoe arches and bulbous cupolas typify the architectural style prevailing in northern Africa and Spain. Other regions preferred pointed, cusped, and flamboyant arches.

Forbidden by their religion to reproduce men and animals in art forms, the Moslems had to create other designs for decorating their buildings. Their principal inspiration was Persian. They designed exquisite patterns of flowers and leaves, produced beautiful calligraphy, and created what are known as arabesques by combining geometric figures and arranging them in intricate patterns. These artistic forms were created in mosaics, carved stone, paneled wood, colored stucco, and glazed tile.

That Byzantine and Moslem culture was on a level unequalled by western Europe until the thirteenth century or possibly until the Renaissance is indisputable. The Byzantines and Arabs were the teachers; the westerners were the pupils. The richest gift of Byzantium to the West was its preservation of Greek manuscripts with their keys to the knowledge of the classical world. To Byzantium the West

MOSQUE OF CORDOVA. Constructed in Spain between 786 and 990, this beautiful Arabic mosque is divided into eleven aisles, twelve bays long with interlaced horseshoe arches.

was also indebted for technological knowledge and advanced techniques in fortification. Learning advanced economic practices from Constantinople, Venice transmitted them into western Europe. The Arabs too preserved Graeco-Roman culture and also advanced beyond it in such fields as medicine, science, mathematics, and technology. This knowledge found its way into Christian Europe from Spain and from northern Africa by way of Sicily and southern Italy, a process that began in the eleventh century and was accelerated in succeeding centuries. While the Crusades may have revealed to many the superior civilization of Byzantine and Moslem lands, they did not inaugurate the economic and intellectual revival of western Europe; rather they were a manifestation of a revival already in process. The Crusades were at most merely catalysts.

Studying History 102
Einal 5/20/75

9. ⟨*The Crusades*⟩

THE GREATEST TESTIMONY to the revived power of the church was the launching of the great crusade against the infidel Seljuk Turks in the late eleventh century. There were four principal causes for this remarkable offensive of the West against the East. During the course of the eleventh century feudal adventurers and the

Italian ports had been wresting control of the western Mediterranean, Spain, Sicily, and southern Italy away from the Arabs. These limited offensives were a sort of prelude to a mightier undertaking; they proved that the Arab fighter was not invincible and also showed that much was to be gained commercially if all the Mediterranean basin could be conquered. Then, too, western Europe, in a high pitch of religious fervor as a result of reform and the leadership of the Papacy, was ready to be led in a great offensive against the infidel, who controlled all the holy places associated with the rise of the true faith. But the precipitating cause of the First Crusade was the rapid conquest of the Middle East in the eleventh century by the Seljuk Turks.

THE SELJUK TURKS

Sweeping out of the Asiatic plateau between the borders of China and Persia, these nomadic warriors reduced the Arabian caliphate in Persia and Mesopotamia and captured Baghdad. They then pushed westward to the shores of the Mediterranean, a move that brought them into contact with the Byzantine Empire. In 1071 the emperor rashly moved against the Turks in Armenia and was annihilated with his army at the Battle of Manzikert. In this one battle all Asia Minor was lost to Byzantium and the empire was deprived of those lands that had supplied its best soldiers. With practically all the Middle East lost to the Turks, who embraced the Islamic faith yet were much less tolerant of the Christian faith than the Arabs, the Byzantine emperors, despite their distrust of the West and the schism, were reduced to calling upon the Pope and western rulers to check the Turks and to save the holy places of Christianity from desecration.

THE FIRST CRUSADE

In 1095, when the Byzantine emperor Alexius Comnenus sent envoys to Pope Urban II asking for military assistance to help drive out the Turks, he received a more enthusiastic response than he bargained for. All he wanted was a force to recover Asia Minor; what he got was a European army whose goal it was to take all the Holy Land. Urban looked upon the plea for help as an opportunity for the Papacy to muster and lead the first great offensive against the East since the Roman Empire. There were, of course, other considerations. Urban had formerly been a noble of Champagne, and a great offensive in which the western knight could win glory against the infidel appealed to his chivalrous nature. Also, the martial instincts of the knight would be transferred to a good cause and would contribute to the peace and order that the church was laboring so assiduously to establish in Europe. Perhaps a successful enterprise undertaken by East and West might even heal the schism.

In the autumn of 1095 Urban proceeded to Clermont in south central France where he convened the great ecclesiastics and nobles of Europe. In an inspired address delivered in French, Urban called upon the nobles to bury their differences and to unite in a great holy crusade that would rescue the Holy Sepulcher from infidel hands. Moreover, there were rich lands and glory to be won; it was God's will. As Urban concluded his fervent sermon all the assembly was inspired to shout in a mighty voice, "God wills it!" Soon thousands enrolled in the sacred army, signifying their action by sewing a cross upon their tunics. So it was that the volunteer was called a *crusader* (*croisé*) and the expedition a *crusade*. The church gave assurance of all sorts of spiritual rewards to those who would make the great sacrifice and promised that all who died while on the campaign would immediately enter heaven. Clergy such as Peter the Hermit preached the crusade all over Europe and inspired large groups of humble and ill-armed men to march helter-skelter across southeastern Europe to Constantinople. Most perished before they arrived, and the rest rushed into Asia Minor where the Turks massacred them.

The main crusading armies began their trip east in the autumn of 1096. The principal leaders were Count Robert of Flanders; Count Raymond of Toulouse, who had fought in the Moorish wars in Spain; and Bohemund, the son of Robert Guiscard, a most experienced military leader who considered the expedition an

BATTLE BETWEEN THE CRUSADERS AND THE SARACENS. In this pen-and-ink drawing of about 1300 an unknown artist has given us a quick but vigorous sketch of the Crusaders and the Saracens fighting at sea; he has carefully blackened the faces of the Moslem warriors to distinguish them from his Christian comrades.

opportunity to carve out for himself a principality in the Near East. Marching and sailing by various routes the main armies arrived in Constantinople and, after some altercations with Alexius over an oath of fealty and the disposition of lands conquered from the Turks, crossed into Asia Minor in early 1097. Bravely an army of twenty to thirty thousand men pushed southward to meet the Turks. Early in the summer Nicaea was captured and by early autumn the crusaders were in Cilicia. But just as they arrived at the borders of the Holy Land, they began to fall out. They split up under rival leaders whose chief goals seemed to be the acquisition of land rather than the capture of Jerusalem. A nephew of Bohemund, Tancred, turned toward the Euphrates Valley and won for himself the County of Edessa. The main army, however, lay siege to Antioch and captured it in the summer of 1098, due to the generalship of Bohemund and the timely arrival of siege engines and supplies brought by a Genoese and Pisan fleet. At this point Bohemund cut himself off from the crusaders and took Antioch and the surrounding territory. For some time Alexius had ceased supporting the crusaders because they would not turn all their conquests over to him. Raymond of Toulouse became the bitter enemy of Bohemund because he, too, had coveted Antioch. As though such differences were not enough, the southern French attributed the fall of Antioch to the discovery of the lance that had pierced Christ while on the cross; it had been found by one of Raymond's followers, Peter Bartholomew. The Normans laughed at this claim, attributing the victory to the leadership of Bohemund. Finally Peter offered to settle the dispute through ordeal by fire. Barefoot he walked through a blazing fire of olive branches. Twelve days later he died. The Normans claimed the burns were responsible, while the friends of Peter said that he had suffered fatal injuries from the embraces of the fervent mob.

Despite such altercations, the army struggled south until it reached Jerusalem in the summer of 1098. Thanks again to Italian supplies, Jerusalem was taken after a six-weeks' siege and the Holy City was at last in Christian possession. Unfortunately Urban died just before the news of the conquest of Jerusalem arrived. Regardless of all the petty differences and the goal of many ruthless adventurers to win land and riches, the First Crusade was a glorious venture that reflected the revived spiritual, political, and economic life of the West. For the first time in eight hundred years, the West had mounted a successful offensive against the East and had brought most of the Mediterranean under its control. The Italian cities profited economically. Culturally and economically, thousands of westerners came into direct contact with the superior achievements of the East. The crusade accelerated all phases of European life.

As for the tangible gains of the crusaders, they carved out for themselves a group of states along the eastern shore of the Mediterranean. Running north to south there was the County of Edessa, the Principality of Antioch, the County of Tripolis given to Raymond of Toulouse, and the Kingdom of Jerusalem which had a theoretical sovereignty over the other states. On Christmas Day, 1100, Baldwin of Lorraine was crowned king of Jerusalem. The Latin States of the Crusaders had begun their precarious existence.

The First Crusade had been a success because of the immense fervor generated by an inspired Papacy, and because the Turks failed to unite against the crusading army. During the twelfth century the situation was reversed. The Turks united politically around the perimeter of the Latin States, while the crusading ardor flagged. The men who remained were content with their conquests, and only periodic reinforcements from the West enabled them to hold on to their lands. There arose, for example, in the late eleventh and twelfth centuries the Knights Hospitalers and Knights Templars, military orders of knights bound by monastic vow to protect the Holy Land.

THE SECOND, THIRD, AND FOURTH CRUSADES

In less than fifty years after the capture of Jerusalem, the Turks had united in Syria and retaken the County of Edessa. This event awakened Europe to a new offensive. The zealous preaching of the great St. Bernard stimulated Louis VII of France and Conrad III of Germany to lead the Second Crusade (1147–1149), but neither cooperated and the project was a dismal failure. As the Turks realized that the Christian knight was not invincible, they continued to press their attacks against the Latin States. Under the remarkable Saladin they almost swept the Christians into the sea. In 1187 Jerusalem fell; only Tyre, Tripolis, and Antioch remained. The fall of Jerusalem aroused the foremost kings of Europe to embark on a great offensive. But again disunity robbed the Third Crusade (1189–1192) of success. The emperor Frederick Barbarossa died before he arrived at the Holy Land; Philip Augustus of France had no sooner arrived than he returned to his kingdom, pleading ill health, although his real reason was to conspire against Richard I of England who remained in the Holy Land. Though imbued with a sincere desire to capture Jerusalem and though a gifted military leader, Richard I was only able to take Acre, win a few battles over Saladin, and conclude a treaty whereby Christians were promised peaceful access to the Holy City. The Third Crusade demonstrated that crusading ardor had vanished, and that rulers were primarily interested in western politics. Actually, only the Italian ports were interested in the East and their interest was motivated solely by commercial gain.

The last serious military expedition launched against the Moslems was inspired by the great Pope Innocent III whose ideal was to put the Papacy at the head of a common Christian undertaking as in the days of Urban II. This crusade, if it can be so called, was most peculiar. The only participants sure of their objectives were the Venetians. Few warriors knew where they were going or what they hoped to achieve. In the words of Villehardouin, participant in and historian of the Fourth

Crusade (1201–1204), it was "one of the greatest marvels and most wonderful adventures" of all history. An assembled force of French knights led by the counts of Flanders and Champagne marched to Venice which was to supply boats for the trip to Syria. Unfortunately, the crusaders had less than half the amount of money demanded by the Venetians. The doge of Venice then proposed a solution. If the crusaders would first go across the Adriatic Sea to the port of Zara, which just happened to be a commercial rival, and would capture it for the Venetians, the Venetians would then provide transportation to Syria. Although Zara belonged to the king of Hungary, a Christian, and although Innocent III excommunicated the crusaders for fighting other Christians and forgetting their primary objective, Zara was attacked and captured in late 1202.

Soon afterwards the son of the Byzantine emperor, who had just been deposed at Constantinople, approached the crusaders with another novel proposition. If they would first sail to Constantinople, capture it, and restore his father to the throne, he would then provide the money, supplies, and men to assure the conquest of Syria and Egypt from the infidel. After brief debate the main body of the crusaders agreed to the proposal. In the summer of 1203, defying the order of Innocent III to fight no more Christians, the crusaders captured the harbor and restored the deposed emperor to power. An immediate insurrection within Constantinople, however, which resulted in the death of the restored emperor and his son, rendered the efforts of the crusaders fruitless. They decided, therefore, to storm the city. In April 1204 Constantinople was taken, many of its defenders slaughtered, and its treasures systematically looted.

There was now a settlement between the Venetians and the crusaders over the remnants of the once majestic Byzantine Empire. The booty was equally divided, Count Baldwin IX of Flanders was elected emperor, and an allotment of lands was made. Venice secured a large section of Constantinople, all the strategic islands in the eastern Mediterranean, and a commercial monopoly throughout the empire. The great winners from these adventures were the Venetians who obtained economic hegemony of the eastern Mediterranean. The crusaders who chose to remain in the East secured fiefs in northwestern Asia Minor and in what is modern Greece. The Latin Kingdom of Constantinople was thus created and continued in existence until Greek rule was restored in 1261. The infidel in Syria and Egypt had long ago been forgotten. Despite his prestige Innocent III could not control the crusade he proclaimed; he had repeatedly to accept *faits accomplis* which he disliked. The Fourth Crusade dramatically illustrates the change in Europe during the century since the First Crusade. By the early thirteenth century political and economic considerations overshadowed Christian ideals and aspirations. The political and economic revival of western Europe had weakened ecclesiastical authority and initiated the secularization of thought. Gone forever was the time when a Pope could proclaim and control a crusade against the infidel.

Although a number of crusades were conducted in the thirteenth century by such men as the emperor Frederick II and Louis IX of France, they lacked real religious ardor and were unsuccessful. The age of the crusades ended with the Fourth Crusade. No amount of papal exhortation or threats could arouse the West to save the sinking states of the Holy Land. By 1268 Antioch had fallen, and with the capture of Acre in 1291 all the Holy Land had been reconquered by the infidel. Although the Latin States were lost partly because of the indifference of the West, it is no coincidence that they fell just as the church was entering a dismal path of decline in the fourteenth and fifteenth centuries. While the great accomplishments of the First Crusade seem to have ended in total failure, the crusades demonstrated that the West had achieved a dynamic economic, political, and military vigor and was no longer a barbarous and backward area. Through contact with the East it had been stimulated by the superior eastern culture, a culture which it rapidly proceeded to surpass.

10. *The Apogee of the Church*

THE GREAT AGE OF THE MEDIEVAL CHURCH lay between 1100 and 1300. The Papacy secured absolute spiritual authority over all the church and for a time exercised temporal supremacy over some of the greatest rulers. Despite some heresy and weakness in the church, these two centuries witnessed a series of spiritual reform movements which more than neutralized unorthodox religious currents and insured that the church would continue as a guiding spiritual force. Contributing to the strength of the church in this period was the systematization of an efficient administration.

As a world power the Papacy rose to its zenith under Innocent III (1198–1216), who belonged to a noble Italian family that contributed eight Popes. Innocent, bolder and even more ambitious than such predecessors as Gregory VII, employed every possible historical precedent and argument to bolster his claim to papal supremacy in spiritual and temporal matters. The tone of his whole pontificate was set in his first sermon delivered after his election as Pope. He declared: "The successor of Peter is the Vicar of Christ: he has been established as a mediator between God and man, below God but beyond man; less than God but more than man; who shall judge all and be judged by no one." On another occasion he wrote: "No King can reign rightly unless he devoutly serve Christ's vicar." The great difference between Innocent and most of the other Popes was that he made good his claims. Taking advantage of a fortuitous series of events in Europe, he triumphed over all the leading rulers. He humbled the emperors Otto IV, Philip of Swabia, and Frederick II. John of England made an ignominious capitulation whereby he even agreed to hold England in fief from Innocent. The shrewd Philip Augustus of France fared little better.

Meanwhile Innocent established his fullness of power (*plenitudo potestatis*) in the church. He made more efficient the collection of papal revenues. He empowered clergy of his court to act as papal legates and to travel all over Europe to accomplish his orders and make investigations. He encouraged judicial appeals to the papal court and regularly assembled ecclesiastical councils at Rome which passed legislation for the whole church. At the famous Fourth Lateran Council of 1215 (convoked in the Church of St. John Lateran at Rome), some rulers were deposed, procedure was devised to extirpate heresy, clergy were forbidden to participate in any trial involving bloodshed, and all clerics were declared exempt from lay taxation. Lastly the council passed two canons defining the doctrine of transubstantiation (the miracle in the sacrament of the Eucharist whereby the bread and wine are transformed into the flesh and blood of Christ) and prescribing the discipline of penance.

CANON LAW AND ECCLESIASTICAL ORGANIZATION

Another development of the twelfth century that tightened the organization of the church and defined its powers was the growth of canon law. The canons, or laws, consisted of the Scriptures, laws promulgated by church councils, and *decretals* (decrees) of the Popes. The weakness of canon law had been its lack of systematic codification. But with the revival of the study of Roman law in the eleventh and twelfth centuries, scholarly clerics developed an interest in collecting and systematizing the canon law. About 1140 at Bologna, the monk Gratian compiled a canon law code called the *Decretum* which became the official compilation and served as a text for teaching the canons. During the thirteenth century the Popes brought Gratian up to date by codifying the canons passed since 1140. The last great medieval codification came in 1317.

With its law well arranged and defined the church could more efficiently organize its legal jurisdiction. All clergy enjoyed *benefit of clergy;* they could be tried in both civil and criminal cases before an ecclesiastical court only. All infractions of the canon law were triable in spiritual courts, and eventually cases pertaining to marriage, adultery, dowry, and contracts were placed under spiritual jurisdiction. To enforce their sentences, church courts pronounced punishments similar to those of secular courts except that none involved bloodshed. Its two principal sentences were excommunication and the interdict. Pronounced by the Pope, archbishops, and bishops, excommunication barred an individual from the sacraments and services of the church. Often the sentence deprived a person of all Christian privileges and association, even forbidding burial in consecrated ground. Under the sentence of the interdict, a group of churches, people, or even a whole land could be placed under penalty. The interdict forbade any services in the church, which meant that none of the sacraments or services could be celebrated. Both these sentences were feared and avoided at all costs because it was taught that if men died while under sentence they went to hell.

In the twelfth and thirteenth centuries the administrative organization of the church greatly improved. At Rome the Pope was assisted in the government by the cardinal clergy (the College of Cardinals) which came to be composed of clergy appointed from all parts of Europe. These clerics plus numerous minor officials composed the papal court (*curia*) which performed various functions. It served as the highest court of the church; it had a chancery that drew up papal decretals, bulls, and corespondence; it had a treasury or chamber that received and disbursed revenue. Europe was divided into large ecclesiastical provinces governed by archbishops whose authority was conferred upon them by the Pope. Each province was subdivided into dioceses headed by bishops who customarily had their cathedrals at the principal towns of the dioceses. To help the bishop in his administration were several archdeacons who served as liaison clergy between bishop and lower clergy. Each diocese was arranged into rural deaneries headed by archpriests, and these in turn were divided into parishes with their priests. There was, then, a definite chain of command extending from the priest to the Pope.

THEOLOGY OF THE CHURCH

To insure its monopoly as a faith for all the inhabitants of western Christendom, the church labored industriously to construct a systematic theology. Until the late eleventh century theology had consisted of Augustine's thought as amplified by Gregory the Great. Early in the twelfth century the church pressed ahead with its theology and worked to harmonize sacred tradition and practice. The first such attempt was made in the second half of the twelfth century by the University of Paris theologian Peter Lombard. He composed the *Sentences* (*Opinions*) which became the leading theological textbook down into the thirteenth century, when the church finally constructed a unified system of theology and ritual.

Medieval theology was basically a gloomy system. Man's existence on this earth was merely a preparation for life eternal in the existence hereafter. Unfortunately, because of Adam's original sin, man's earthly life was beset by numerous sins and imperfections. Adam had destroyed a perfect state of existence, where man possessed free will to strive for good, and had caused God to impose an imperfect existence upon man. Through his children Adam passed on his sin to all men who from birth were tainted and doomed to an eternal death and suffering in hell. Only because of Christ's sacrifice for all men was it possible for a man to be saved from this horrible fate. This salvation was attainable only through God's grace and could be hoped for only by those who believed in redemption by Christ.

Until reworked by theologians in the twelfth and thirteenth centuries, the

5. CHALICE OF ABBOT SUGER OF SAINT-DENIS (ca. 1140). The sardonyx cup dates from Roman times, but Suger mounted it in silver and gold set with precious jewels and pearls so that it could be used in the celebration of the Mass at the royal abbey of Saint-Denis.

6. CORONATION ORB OF EMPEROR HENRY VI (1190–1197). The coronation orb with the cross mounted on a globe symbolizing the universe is one of the oldest symbols of the Christian empire. The sphere, made of six golden plates soldered together, is decorated with amethysts, sapphires, garnets, emeralds, and half-pearls.

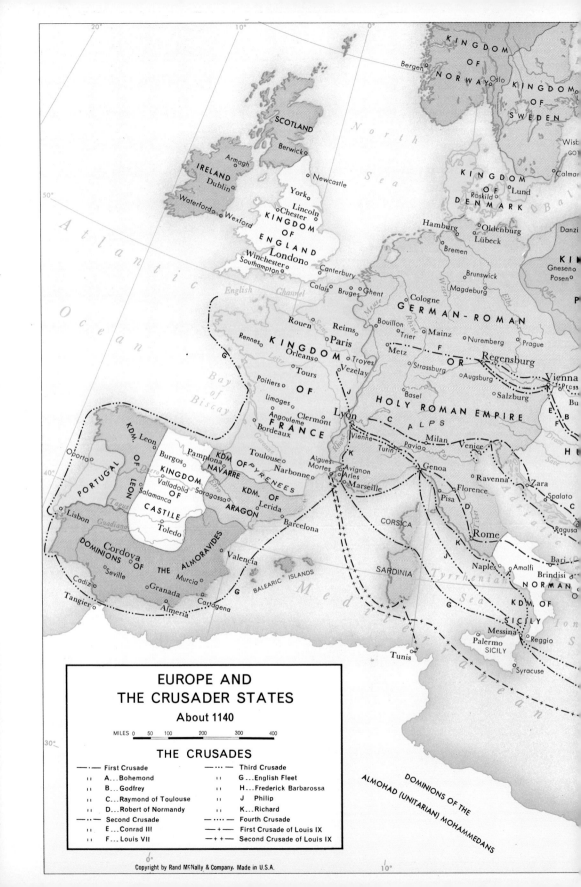

EUROPE AND
THE CRUSADER STATES

About 1140

MILES 0   50 100   200   300   400

THE CRUSADES

— · — First Crusade
  ‖ A...Bohemond
  ‖ B...Godfrey
  ‖ C...Raymond of Toulouse
  ‖ D...Robert of Normandy
— ·· — Second Crusade
  ‖ E...Conrad III
  ‖ F...Louis VII

— ··· — Third Crusade
  ‖ G...English Fleet
  ‖ H...Frederick Barbarossa
  ‖ J   Philip
  ‖ K...Richard
— ···· — Fourth Crusade
— + — First Crusade of Louis IX
— + · — Second Crusade of Louis IX

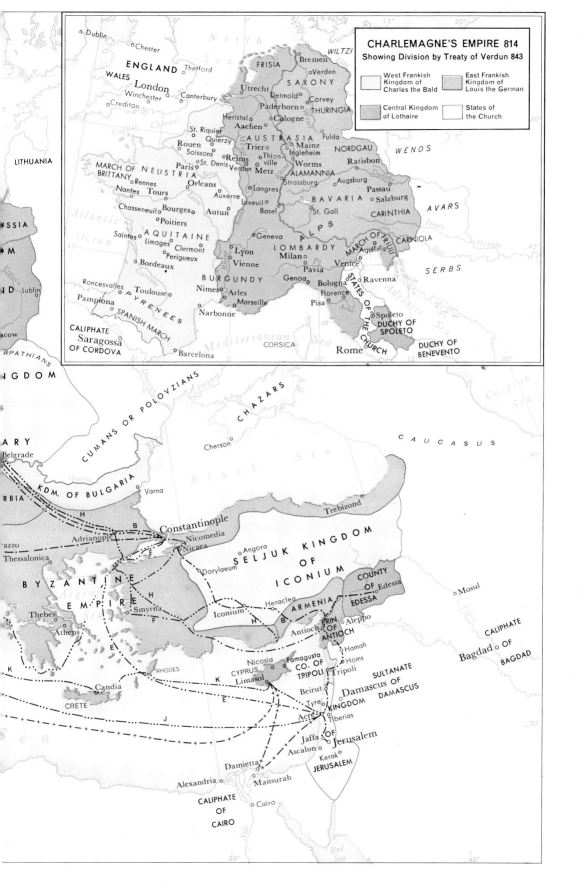

7. MONKS IN THE CHOIR. This miniature from the *Psalter of Henry VI,* king of England, dates from around 1430. Much of a monk's day was spent in the choir participating in seven regular services held from 2:30 in the morning to 7:30 at night.

8. APSE OF SANT' APOLLINARE IN CLASSE. Constructed in the sixth century by Justinian and Theodora, this church, just outside the city of Ravenna, is famous for its brilliantly colored mosaics. Seen here is Sant' Apollinare portrayed as the Good Shepherd among his sheep.

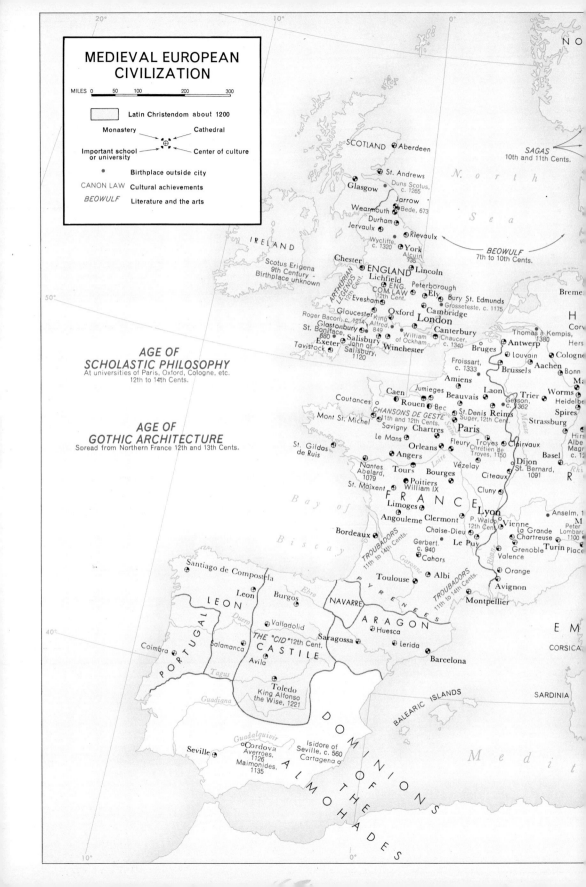

MEDIEVAL EUROPEAN CIVILIZATION

MILES 0   50   100   200   300

▭ Latin Christendom about 1200

Monastery ⟶ ⊕ ⟵ Cathedral

Important school ⟶ ⊕ ⟵ Center of culture
or university

● Birthplace outside city

CANON LAW Cultural achievements

BEOWULF Literature and the arts

NO

SAGAS
10th and 11th Cents.

SCOTLAND ⊕ Aberdeen

⊕ St. Andrews
Glasgow ⊕   Duns Scotus,
              c. 1265

Jarrow ⊕
Wearmouth ⊕ Bede, 673
    ⊕ Durham
Jervaulx ⊕   ⊕ Rievaulx
    Wycliffe,
    c. 1320   ⊕ York
              Alcuin
Chester ⊕   735
       ENGLAND ⊕ Lincoln
Lichfield ⊕
IRELAND   ⊕ ENG. ⊕ Peterborough
          COM. LAW
          12th Cent. ⊕ Ely
    ⊕ Evesham   ⊕ Bury St. Edmunds
                      ● Grosseteste, c. 1175
Scotus Erigena   ⊕ Gloucester ⊕ Cambridge
9th Century -   King ⊕ Oxford
Birthplace unknown Alfred, ⊕ London
Roger Bacon, c. 1214 849
⊕ Glastonbury   ⊕ Canterbury
St. Boniface,   680 ● Chaucer,
                      c. 1340
⊕ Salisbury ⊕ Winchester ⊕ Bruges
Exeter ⊕ William
Tavistock ⊕ John of of Ockham
         Salisbury,
         1120

BEOWULF
7th to 10th Cents.

Breme

H

Corv
Hers

Thomas à Kempis,
1380
⊕ Antwerp
⊕ Louvain ⊕ Cologne
    Brussels ⊕ Aachen
Froissart,   ⊕ Bonn
c. 1333   ⊕ Amiens   Laon ⊕ Trier Worms ⊕
                     Gerson,
Caen ⊕ Jumieges   1362 Spires ⊕
      ⊕ Beauvais ⊕ Reims
Coutances ⊕ Rouen ⊕ ⊕ St. Denis Strassburg ⊕
Mont St. Michel ⊕ ● Bec Suger, 12th Cent.
CHANSONS DE GESTE ⊕ Chartres Hirs
11th and 12th Cents.   Albe
   ⊕ Savigny ⊕ Paris   Magr
St. Gildas Le Mans ⊕ ⊕ Fleury ⊕ Troyes ⊕ Clairvaux
de Ruis   ⊕ Orleans Chrétien de ⊕ Dijon Basel ⊕
   Nantes ⊕ Angers   Troyes, 1150 St. Bernard,
   Abelard, ⊕ Tours ⊕ Vézelay 1091
   1079   ⊕ Bourges ⊕ Citeaux
St. Maixent ⊕ ● Poitiers ⊕ Cluny
   ⊕ Limoges ● William IX
         F R A N C E ⊕ Lyon ● Anselm,
   ⊕ Angouleme ⊕ Clermont P. Waldo, M
Bordeaux ⊕   ⊕ Chaise-Dieu 12th Cent. Peter
            Gerbert, ⊕ Le Puy ⊕ Vienne Lombard,
            c. 940   La Grande 1100
              ⊕ Cahors   Chartreuse Turin Piace
                         ⊕ Grenoble
   Toulouse ⊕ ⊕ Albi   ⊕ Valence
              TROUBADORS ⊕ Orange
   TROUBADORS 11th to 14th Cents. ⊕ Avignon
   11th to 14th Cents. ⊕ Montpellier

AGE OF
SCHOLASTIC PHILOSOPHY
At universities of Paris, Oxford, Cologne, etc.
12th to 14th Cents.

AGE OF
GOTHIC ARCHITECTURE
Spread from Northern France 12th and 13th Cents.

Bay of

Biscay

Santiago de Compostela ⊕
   Leon ⊕
LEON ⊕ Burgos
         NAVARRE
PORTUGAL ⊕ Valladolid
         ⊕ Saragossa
Coimbra ⊕ Salamanca ⊕ THE "CID" 12th Cent.
         CASTILE   ⊕ Huesca
         ⊕ Avila ⊕ Lerida
         Toledo
         King Alfonso ⊕ Barcelona
         the Wise, 1221

Duero
Tagus
Guadiana
Ebro
Garonne
Rhone

PYRENEES

A R A G O N

Guadalquivir
Seville ● ● Cordova
         Averroes,
         1126
         Maimonides,
         1135

D O M I N I O N S O F T H E A L M O H A D E S

Isidore of
Seville, c. 560
● Cartagena

BALEARIC ISLANDS

SARDINIA

CORSICA

EM

Medit

20°   10°   0°

50°

40°

10°

0°

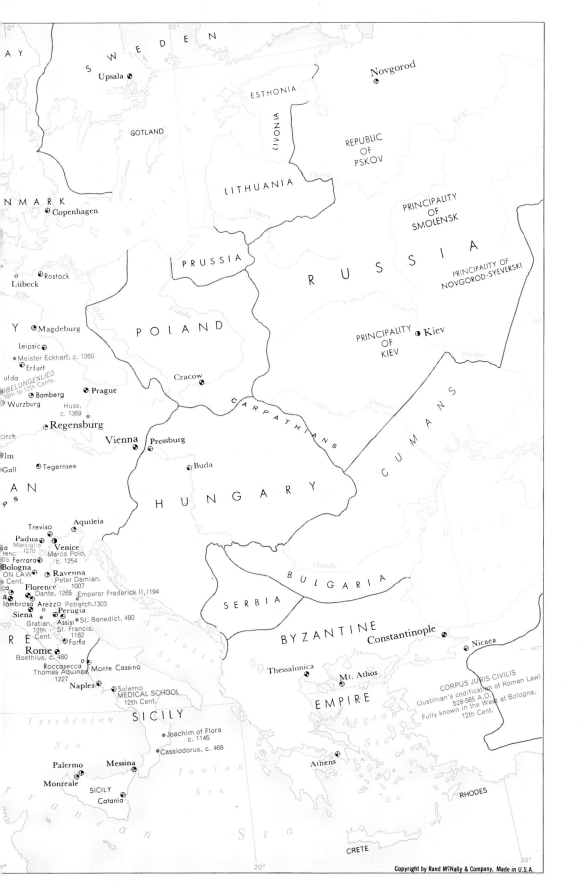

A Y

S W E D E N

Upsala ⊙

GOTLAND

Novgorod ⊙

ESTHONIA

LIVONIA

REPUBLIC
OF
PSKOV

NMARK

Copenhagen ⊙

LITHUANIA

PRINCIPALITY
OF
SMOLENSK

R U S S I A

PRINCIPALITY OF
NOVGOROD-SYEVERSKI

Rostock ⊙

Lübeck

PRUSSIA

Elbe

Y   ⊙ Magdeburg

Leipsic ⊙

• Meister Eckhart, c. 1260

⊙ Erfurt

ulda

IBELUNGENLIED
10th to 12th Cents.

⊙ Bamberg

⊙ Wurzburg

P O L A N D

Oder

Vistula

Cracow ⊙

PRINCIPALITY
OF
KIEV

⊙ Kiev

Dnieper

Huss,
c. 1369

⊙ Prague

C U M A N S

orch

• Regensburg

Im

Gall

Danube

⊙ Tegernsee

Vienna ⊙   ⊙ Pressburg

CARPATHIANS

Dniester

⊙ Buda

A N

P S

H U N G A R Y

Treviso

⊙ Aquileia

Padua ⊙

Marsiglio
1270

ranc

05 Ferrara ⊙

Venice ⊙

Marco Polo,
c. 1254

Danube

B U L G A R I A

Bologna
ON LAW
Cent.

⊙ Ravenna

Peter Damian,
1007

ca ⊙

Florence ⊙

Dante, 1265 Emperor Frederick II, 1194

SERBIA

lombrosa Arezzo Petrarch, 1303

Siena   Gratian, Assisi St. Francis,
12th   1182
Cent.

Perugia

St. Benedict, 480

BYZANTINE

Constantinople ⊙

⊙ Nicaea

R E

Rome ⊙

Boethius, c. 480

⊙ Farfa

Roccasecca
Thomas Aquinas,
1227

Monte Cassino

Thessalonica

Mt. Athos

EMPIRE

CORPUS JURIS CIVILIS
(Justinian's codification of Roman Law)
528-565 A.D.
Fully known in the West at Bologna,
12th Cent.

Naples ⊙

⊙ Salerno
MEDICAL SCHOOL
12th Cent.

SICILY

Tyrrhenian

Sea

• Joachim of Flora
c. 1145

• Cassiodorus, c. 468

Aegean

Sea

Palermo ⊙

Messina ⊙

Athens

Monreale ⊙

SICILY ⊙

Catania ⊙

Ionian

Sea

RHODES

a n

CRETE

Sea

Copyright by Rand McNally & Company, Made in U.S.A.

9. STAINED GLASS WINDOW FROM CHARTRES CATHEDRAL. Traditionally known as
La Belle Verrière, this window from the ambulatory of the cathedral at Chartres is a fine
example of early Gothic work in stained glass. The brilliant reds and blues used here
are typical of twelfth-century stained glass.

ideas of Augustine had dominated the doctrine of salvation. He had argued that God arbitrarily predestined some men to salvation and others to damnation and that nothing could set aside this Divine sentence. According to his doctrine of predestination, salvation could come only through faith and faith was predestined by God. Later theologians, considering such a doctrine overly harsh and arbitrary, modified it to declare that man had the free will to choose evil or good. Those who chose good could by faith and good works acquire salvation through God.

It has been noted previously that the early Christian church worked out the theory of sacraments, those visible signs of invisible grace which imparted God's grace and salvation to man. In the early Middle Ages the sacraments had been five—baptism, confirmation, marriage, penance, and the Eucharist. By the twelfth century the essential sacraments had been increased to seven. In the sacrament of *extreme unction* a man at the point of death was anointed by oil consecrated by the bishop. This ceremony was to assist in recovery or to prepare the man for salvation after death; it wiped away man's earthly sins and offenses. The sacrament of *ordination* or *holy orders* was administered by the bishop to all new priests. It officially conferred upon them their divine offices, empowered them to hear confessions and to forgive sins, and permitted them to accomplish the miracle of transubstantiation and the other sacraments. Ordination tied every priest to St. Peter, who had received his divine powers from Christ.

THE CHURCH AND SAINTS

Such, then, was the fundamental theology of the church. To the skilled theologian who never ceased arguing the fine points of Christian doctrine, and who had the education and intelligence to understand its complicated aspects, Christian theology was sufficient. This was not so, however, with the masses of ordinary folk who required their Christian beliefs to be explained in the simplest terms. Basically they were interested only in the significance of the appealing story of Christ's life, and in escaping hell and getting into heaven. For them the church therefore provided a religion based upon saints, martyrs, miraculous relics, and the Virgin Mary, Mother of Christ. The veneration of saints and their relics was a useful and simple device for teaching men how to follow in Christ's path and to attain salvation; but unfortunately the veneration of relics and their miraculous powers was greatly overemphasized. Men began making a business of dealing in relics. They collected all sorts of objects, supposedly true relics of some saint or martyr, claimed miraculous powers for them, and unloaded them upon naïve, unsuspecting people at fantastic prices. Tons of saints' bones were sold and anything from a tooth to a toe nail was venerated. King Louis IX of France built the exquisite Sainte-Chapelle in Paris to hold relics, particularly a thorn supposedly from Christ's crown of thorns.

By the twelfth century the Popes claimed sole power to canonize saints. A special court investigated the qualifications for sainthood. If it could be determined that a candidate was blessed and had been responsible for two miracles he was qualified. Each saint was believed to have special powers; images of saints were placed in every church, and people prayed to them to secure their miraculous help. But the Virgin Mary was prayed to for help more than the saints and more even than God and Christ. By the eleventh century the cult of the Virgin Mary had acquired a deep hold over the faithful, who prayed to this lovable and compassionate Mother to intercede with Christ for His help and salvation. The Virgin Mary was a figure all could love and understand because she was human, and not of the formidable nature of Christ who was the Son of God. The venerated position of the Virgin Mary was glorified in stone, glass, painting, and verse. Her cult almost obscured the story of Christ and His significance for God's children.

11. Reform and Heresy

HISTORICALLY ALL GREAT INSTITUTIONS have retained their vitality and usefulness to society so long as they have possessed the will and ability to reform and to progress. The medieval church was capable of this in the eleventh, twelfth, and thirteenth centuries. But because it lost this ability the church declined in the next two centuries. In contrast to the external agitation for reform in the later Middle Ages and in the sixteenth-century Reformation, reform during the great age of the church took place within the organization and was controlled by the Papacy.

NEW MONASTIC ORDERS

Just as the Cluniac movement had injected vigor and idealism into the old Benedictine houses during the tenth and eleventh centuries, so other monastic movements kept the monastic ideal alive when numerous Cluniac monasteries lost sight of their vows and fell into luxurious and lax habits. In the eleventh and twelfth centuries monastic reform came through the founding of orders of cloistered hermits. At first the most influential of these new monastic orders was the Carthusian, which took its name from the village of Cartusia (Chartreuse in French) near Grenoble in the western Alps where the first monastery was established. In all the Carthusian houses each monk lived in a cell with an adjoining garden. Here he ate and slept, prayed, contemplated, and copied manuscripts. Only for divine services and Sunday dinner did the monks associate. Today few people remember the Carthusians for their devout habits; they are associated rather with chartreuse, the famous liqueur with its distinctive color, made in their monasteries.

In the high Middle Ages the most influential monastic order was the Cistercian.

It was founded in 1098 at Cîteaux (*Cistercium* in Latin) in Burgundy by a certain St. Robert who, as a Benedictine abbot, had become disgusted with the laxity and degeneracy of that order. The man responsible for the impressive success of the Cistercians, however, was St. Bernard (1091–1153), the most prominent ecclesiastic in the first half of the twelfth century. With thirty followers he founded a monastery in 1112 at Clairvaux which became the center of the movement. From here, St. Bernard associated himself with all the leading events of western Christendom for the next forty years. Bernard was a fearsome figure indeed. His body was emaciated because of the severe ascetic practices he followed. He was a mystic who bitterly denounced all secular and material tendencies of the church. Nothing and no one escaped his scornful criticism. He hit out at the temporal power of the Pope, castigated the proud bishops, and criticized overindulgence in food and drink. He had no appreciation of art and leveled his harshest remarks at the fine Romanesque architecture of the Cluniac abbeys. Any theologian who departed however slightly from the traditional church doctrine was attacked by the strait-laced monk. This stern man dictated the stringent rules by which the Cistercians reformed the Benedictines.

The Cistercian rule was more severe than the original Benedictine. Manual labor was emphasized over all pursuits, and the diet was strictly vegetarian. The Cistercian monasteries were to epitomize simplicity; they were to have no ornamentation, not even stained glass windows. Each monastery had to live solely from its own income. Although the abbot of Cîteaux enjoyed preeminence and, along with the abbots of the four principal houses, made periodic inspections of the Cistercian establishments, each house enjoyed a large degree of autonomy and elected its own abbot. A later peculiar development of the Cistercian order was the admission of lay brothers who took certain of the monastic vows but never became regular monks; they were accepted to perform most of the agrarian labor. With these reinforcements, the Cistercians took the lead in reclaiming forest and wasteland for cultivation and established large granges dispersed over the European countryside. More than any other movement the Cistercians kept monasticism alive, but even this vigorous order declined during the thirteenth century. Fundamentally adapted to an agrarian society, monasticism inevitably had to retreat before the new urban civilization.

A prime task of the church in the twelfth and thirteenth centuries was to adapt its doctrine and organization to the requirements of the towns and their populace. Not until the thirteenth century, however, did the church come to grips with the problem. In the twelfth century the cathedral chapters of clergy (*canons*) had been invigorated by the foundation of two secular orders called the Augustinians and Premonstratensians. These orders gave the canons a rule and routine which improved their efficiency and brought them a sense of purpose. But this reform did not touch the ordinary layman who, in the cosmopolitan society of the town with its new ideas and cross-currents, was often influenced by religious movements unorthodox and heretical.

HERETICAL MOVEMENTS

The first major unorthodox movement was stimulated by the Italian Arnold of Brescia, who preached against the material interests and secular power of the church and advocated a return to early Christian poverty and humility. Such teachings, although not heretical, were intolerable to the Papacy when Arnold went to Rome and became associated with a revolution aimed at depriving the Pope of rule over the city. From 1145 to 1155 Arnold led the fight for urban liberty. Then he lost power, was tried and condemned as a heretic by the church, and turned over to the emperor to be burned.

Meanwhile, other apostolic movements were arising throughout Europe, all with a common goal—a Christian life that adhered rigorously to Christ's example and that of His disciples. In their fervor for reform and in their preaching the adherents often deviated from church doctrine. Toward the end of the twelfth century, in the towns of northern Italy, there arose a lay brotherhood of poor laborers called the *Humiliati* (the Poor and Humble), who followed a life of apostolic poverty and devotion to labor and criticized the church for its worldly interests. Although Innocent III recognized this order and attempted to employ it in the interests of the church, too many of its members refused to abide by amended rules handed down by the Pope and were openly critical of the Papacy. They were consequently proclaimed heretical and called upon to renounce their beliefs or suffer the consequences.

The largest heretical group arose in the towns and countryside of southern France. The adherents of this movement were called Cathari (the pure) or Albigensians (from the town of Albi in Toulouse). Ultimately, the Albigensian beliefs went back to the dualism of the Manichean heresy of the fourth century. The Albigensians firmly believed in a continuous battle between the God of Good and the God of Evil and held that eventually the former would triumph. Until this victory came, however, the God of Evil ruled over the world and its inhabitants. The church because of its secularism was but a servant of the God of Evil and consequently should be boycotted. Because the bodies of men were evil and begot more evil bodies through sexual intercourse, celibacy was urged upon those who would completely purify themselves. Inasmuch as only the most devoted and ascetic followers could hope to meet these severe standards, two classes of followers were organized. The "perfect ones" took and practiced all the vows—they remained celibate and became vegetarians. Some committed suicide rather than lapse back into evil. The rank-and-file Albigensians were "believers," who renounced the orthodox church and followed the injunctions of the perfect ones. These latter actually assumed the role of a clergy. This heresy had begun in the Balkans, spread into Italy, and eventually seeped into France where it centered in the county of Toulouse. Only a crusade proclaimed by Innocent III in the early thirteenth century and cruel employment of the Inquisition finally destroyed it. Supported even by the counts of Toulouse, the Albigensian heresy seems to have gained its strength in southern France out of protest against the blatant corruption of the clergy. However one regards this heresy, it must be admitted that it was a reaction against some of the flagrant abuses of the church.

Faced with the simultaneous rise of these heresies, the church became uncompromising and failed to distinguish between groups that were heretical and those that were non-heretical. In 1173, for example, a rich merchant of Lyon, Peter Waldo, gave up his riches and founded a lay order called the Poor Men of Lyon. The men of this order, soon called Waldensians, traveled in simple dress from town to town and administered to the poor and needy. They forsook all possessions and held all in common. An eminently useful and pious movement with the ability to reach the bourgeoisie, it was soon declared heretical and lumped with all the other heresies. The Waldensians, however, were never completely extirpated. They continued to exist in central Europe and contributed some of their ideas to the Hussites of the fifteenth century and to the Protestant Anabaptists of the sixteenth.

THE FRIARS

That the church held its own against heresy and established a relationship with the townsmen was not due to the efforts of the Papacy or of the clergy but to two orders of *friars* founded in the thirteenth century. Like the monks, these friars (brothers) lived by rules, but they associated with people and worked for their salvation. The friars were interested in their fellow men, whereas the monks tended to isolate themselves from society and to look after their own salvation. St. Francis of Assisi (1182–1226) founded the first order, known as the Franciscans. Like many notable religious figures, Francis in his early life had little concern for the ideals of Christianity. The son of a rich cloth merchant of Assisi, he led a dissolute life and became a soldier. He was captured in war and fell severely ill in prison, barely recovering. This was the turning point in his career. Returning to Assisi he renounced his former habits and wealth, dressed as a hermit, and looked to the care of the ill and lepers. He and some followers rebuilt churches in the Assisi area. His final step was to vow absolute poverty. Henceforth, he and the devoted followers who swarmed about him lived by charity and devoted themselves to preaching the Gospel and caring for the ill and needy. Francis and his followers did their best work in the towns. Through them the words and examples of Christ at last reached the ordinary inhabitant of the town. Few individuals before or after St. Francis have equaled his Christlike character. He loved all nature and all of God's creatures down to the humblest animal. He delighted in God's world and his creations and composed beautiful hymns praising God's work.

In the formal organization of the Franciscan order Francis had little part. Innocent III, shrewdly realizing the possibilities of this movement, recognized it and set up elaborate rules for its organization. The Franciscans were divided into administrative provinces with governing officials. At the head of the order was a minister general elected by general assemblies that met every three years. Within a short time the Franciscans could be found in every region of Europe.

The other order of friars was the Dominican, founded by St. Dominic of Castile. Having worked among the Albigensians, Dominic became convinced that the heresy could be conquered only by zealous and devoted missionaries. He, therefore, vowed his life to the work and attracted a devoted band of disciples. In 1215 Innocent III recognized this group and soon it had a constitution similar to that of the Franciscans. As the more educated and learned group, the Dominicans concentrated most on teaching theology and upon missionary projects. They were chiefly responsible for refuting heresies and winning heretics back into the fold, and became the leading inquisitors of the Inquisition system organized by Innocent III and his successors.

THE INQUISITION

Although heresy had been considered a crime by civil law since the early Middle Ages, there was no agreement on the type of punishment or on the procedure for bringing heretics to ecclesiastical justice. At the Fourth Lateran Council it was directed that bishops should appoint clerical investigators to ferret out heresy. Arguing that heresy was treason against God, Innocent III pleaded for stiff punishment. As a result, most states prescribed death by burning for those found guilty of heresy.

The Albigensian heresy was of such dimensions and so deeply ingrained in southern France that Popes of the thirteenth century authorized special tribunals of Dominicans to try cases of heresy. Responsible only to the Papacy and free from the restrictions of canon law, these courts of inquisition had their own procedure. The judges searched for and prosecuted all those suspected. Trials were secret, and the defendant could have no legal aid or any knowledge as to the identity of his accusers. Torture was employed to secure confessions. Those heretics who confessed and recanted generally received life imprisonment. Those who refused to confess or lapsed back into heresy were turned over to the civil authority for burning at the stake. However brutal such procedure, it must be remembered that the church attempted first to save heretics. The punishment and procedure were extremely cruel but so were customs and men in the Middle Ages; the church but reflected the age.

ST. DOMINIC. This portrait of the founder of the Dominican order, painted by Cosimo Tura about 1484, is a fragment of a polyptych on wood. Polyptychs consisted of four or more hinged panels. When religious subjects were painted on these panels, they were often used as altarpieces.

INNOCENT III. During his eighteen years as Pope, Innocent III reestablished papal authority over Rome and regained the Papal States. He encouraged papal supremacy over the temporal world when spiritual concerns were involved. He is shown preaching the crusade against the Albigensians.

The use of the Inquisition by the church was but one of numerous signs that the Papacy and great prelates were losing sight of their true duty. By force and authority they were bent on preserving their power and obtaining complete uniformity of belief. They ignored the example of Christ and of the other great Christian figures and overlooked the sincere and pious work accomplished by true Christian contemporaries. They seemed to forget that Christianity had become triumphant, that it had commanded the devotion of men because of Christ and the holy men who had practiced and preached His examples and precepts. In their pride they would not admit that the way to men's hearts and minds was through Christ and His teachings, although daily St. Francis and his followers proved the effectiveness of this way. Having obtained great power, the Papacy and hierarchy of clergy meant to perpetuate it by arbitrary force rather than Christian persuasion. In the late thirteenth century, confronted with the growing antipathy of the great states of western Europe to its international authority, the church toppled before the onslaught of temporal power. Lacking a strong inner spiritual force and purpose, Papacy and church began the gloomy trip down a road of decline and dissension. What the church desperately needed were men like Gregory the Great, Urban II, and St. Francis; what it got were Popes who concentrated on increasing their revenues and establishing their political hegemony over all Italy.

Further Reading

The most comprehensive survey of medieval trade and urban life is found in Volumes II and III of *The Cambridge Economic History* (Cambridge, 1952–1963). The best short study is still that of *H. Pirenne, *Economic and Social History of Medieval Europe* (New York, 1937). It should be compared to those of *R.-H. Bautier, *The Economic Development of Medieval Europe* (New York, 1971); *R. S. Lopez, *The Commercial Revolution of the Middle Ages, 950–1350* (Englewood Cliffs, New Jersey, 1971); and *A. Sapori, *The Italian Merchant in the Middle Ages* (New York, 1970). For the rise of the town see *H. Pirenne, *Medieval Cities* (Princeton, 1925). A discussion of the theories on urban origins is found in C. Stephenson, *Borough and Town* (Cambridge, Mass., 1933). Urban government is described by *H. Pirenne, *Belgian Democracy* (London, 1915). A history of a medieval commune is provided by *F. Schevill, *Siena, the History of a Medieval Commune* (New York, 1909). Good collections of sources on trade are those of R. S. Lopez and I. W. Raymond, *Medieval Trade in the Mediterranean World* (New York, 1955); and *H. L. Adelson, *Medieval Commerce* (Princeton, 1962). Urban records are found in *J. H. Mundy and P. Riesenberg, *The Medieval Town* (Princeton, 1958).

Full coverage of ecclesiastical developments is found in Volumes III, V, and VI of *The Cambridge Medieval History*. The best short book on the papacy is now that of *G.

Barraclough, *The Medieval Papacy* (New York, 1968). Excellent essays on the church are in *R. Southern, *The Making of the Middle Ages* (New Haven, 1953). On the investiture struggle one should consult A. J. Macdonald, *Hildebrand: A Life of Gregory VII* (London, 1932); *S. Williams, *The Gregorian Epoch, Reformation, Revolution, Reaction?* (Boston, 1964); and D. Knowles, *Thomas Becket* (Stanford, 1970). For the organization of the church at the apogee of its power see M. Baldwin, *Alexander III and the Twelfth Century* (New York and London, 1968); S. R. Packard, *Europe and the Church under Innocent III* (New York, 1927); L. E. Elliott-Binns, *Innocent III* (London, 1931); and *J. M. Powell, *Innocent III, Vicar of Christ or Lord of the World?* (Boston, 1963). The relations of church and state and of the political theory involved are discussed in G. Tellenbach, *Church, State, and Christian Society at the Time of the Investiture Controversy* (Oxford, 1940); C. H. McIlwain, *The Growth of Political Thought in the West* (New York, 1932); G. H. Sabine, *A History of Political Theory,* rev. ed. (New York, 1960); and J. B. Morrall, *Political Thought in Medieval Times* (London, 1958). On heresy and the inquisition see *H. C. Lea, *A History of the Inquisition of the Middle Ages* (New York, 1922), Vols. I–III; *S. Runciman, *The Medieval Manichee* (New York, 1961); J. R. Strayer, *The Albigensian Crusade* (New York, 1971); and J. B. Russell, *Witchcraft in the Middle Ages* (Ithaca, 1972). Sources on heresy are in W. L. Wakefield and A. P. Evans, *Heresies of the High Middle Ages* (New York, 1969). The best biography of St. Francis is by P. Sabatier, *The Life of St. Francis of Assisi* (New York, 1930). Many of the basic sources are translated in *B. Tierney, *The Crisis of Church and State, 1050–1300* (New York, 1964). *E. Emerton, *The Correspondence of Pope Gregory VII* (New York, 1932); and E. Lewis, *Medieval Political Ideas* (New York, 1954), Vols. I–II.

Of the extensive literature on the Crusades the most scholarly is the multivolume *History of the Crusades* appearing under the editorship of K. M. Setton (Philadelphia, 1955 ff.). Another excellent account is that of *S. Runciman, *A History of the Crusades* (Cambridge, 1951–1954), Vols. I–III. It should be compared to that of R. Grousset, *The Epic of the Crusades* (New York, 1970). D. C. Munro has studied the Crusader states in his *Kingdom of the Crusaders* (New York, 1945). For the debates of historians over the significance of the Crusades see *J. A. Brundage, *The Crusades, Motives and Achievements* (Boston, 1964). For a good source on one of the Crusades see *Robert of Clari, *The Conquest of Constantinople* (New York, 1969).

Supplementary to the books on Byzantine political and institutional history cited in Chapter IV are the following: E. Barker, *Social and Political Thought in Byzantium from Justinian I to the Last Paleologus* (Oxford, 1957); F. Dvornik, *The Making of Central and Eastern Europe* (London, 1949); and R. J. H. Jenkins, *The Byzantine Empire on the Eve of the Crusades* (London, 1953). Church history is well covered by G. Every, *The Byzantine Patriarchate, 451–1204* (London, 1947); F. Dvornik, *The Photian Schism, History and Legend* (Cambridge, Mass., 1948); and S. Runciman, *The Eastern Schism, A Study of the Papacy and the Eastern Churches During the XIth and XIIth Centuries* (Oxford, 1955). A good survey of Byzantine culture is by J. N. Hussey, *Church and Learning in the Byzantine Empire, 867–1185* (London, 1937). Also good is *C. Cavarnos, *Byzantine Thought and Art* (Belmont, Mass., 1968). For studies of Byzantine architecture and art see D. T. Rice, *Art of the Byzantine Era* (London, 1963); A. Grabar, *The Great Centuries of Byzantine Painting* (Geneva, 1953); and the Larousse *Encyclopedia of Byzantine and Medieval Art* (New York, 1963).

In addition to the books on Arabic history cited in *Further Reading* for Chapter IV see W. Muir, *The Caliphate, Its Rise, Decline, and Fall*, rev. ed. (Edinburgh, 1915); M. Gaudefroy-Demombynes, *Muslim Institutions* (London, 1950); T. W. Arnold and A. Guillaume, *The Legacy of Islam* (London, 1947); J. Schacht, *The Origins of Muhammadan Jurisprudence* (Oxford, 1950); and W. M. Watt, *Islamic Political Thought: The Basic Concepts* (Edinburgh and Chicago, 1968). A useful survey of Moslem culture is by G. E. Von Grunebaum, *Medieval Islam: A Study in Cultural Orientation*, 2nd ed. (Chicago, 1953). For the influence of Moslem philosophy and science see D. E. O'Leory, *Arabic Thought and Its Place in History*, 2nd ed. (London, 1939); and S. H. Nasr, *Sciences and Civilization in Islam* (Cambridge, Mass., 1968). A valuable study of Arab historical writing is by F. Rosenthal, *A History of Muslim Historiography* (Leiden, 1952). Arabic literature is surveyed in H. A. R. Gibb, *Arabic Literature: An Introduction* (London, 1926). Arabic medicine is well covered by E. G. Browne, *Arabian Medicine* (Cambridge, 1921). Architecture is dealt with in the definitive study of *H. A. C. Creswell, *Early Muslim Architecture* (Oxford, 1932–1940), Vols. I–II.

CHAPTER 7

The Medieval
Cultural
Achievement

People who know little about the Middle Ages commonly associate this historical age with ignorance, superstition, monolithic devotion to the church, and intellectual bankruptcy. Glib and popular writers delight in applying the term medieval to modern ideas and institutions considered backward and inept. Institutions are called feudal, underprivileged individuals are compared to peasants, and subpar or shoddy culture and learning are referred to as medieval or like that of the "Dark Ages." Such popular misconceptions about the Middle Ages have existed since Renaissance scholars of the fifteenth and sixteenth centuries reacted against what they labeled medieval culture and what they associated with Gothic barbarism. In addition to these popular misconceptions there are others more scholarly. Repeatedly one reads about the "medieval mind," the "medieval unity," and the "medieval harmony." Such descriptions, although traditionally used by historians to praise what they found in medieval culture, inevitably convey the idea that all medieval men acted, thought, wrote, painted, and built alike. This supposed uniformity in the Middle Ages could not be farther from the truth.

That the above conclusions and ideas are not characteristic of the Middle Ages will be obvious from the discussion in this chapter of medieval culture. A Dark Age there was in the early Middle Ages, but with the eleventh century began a lively cultural renaissance that stimulated solid achievement in the following centuries and prepared the way for even more significant advance in the fifteenth- and sixteenth-century Renaissance. Medieval Europe witnessed the growth of a new culture not at all dark, retrograde, and uniform, but bright, progressive, and diverse. The Middle Ages throbbed with the eager activity of men enthusiastically devoted to learning, writing, and the arts. Many of these men, individualistic, arrived at different solutions and conclusions. By the end of the thirteenth century medieval culture had not only attained but surpassed the level of Graeco-Roman civilization. Scholars constantly delving deeper into the Middle Ages are forcing the traditional view of medieval homogeneity to retreat before that of medieval heterogeneity.

1. *The Intellectual Revival*

THE SHORT INTELLECTUAL OUTBURST fostered by Charlemagne's reforms rapidly died out in the ninth century. For almost two hundred years the lamps of culture burned as low as before Charlemagne. Politically and economically Europe was incapable of providing the atmosphere conducive to cultural activity. What education and learning continued was due solely to the church. Having benefited from the Carolingian organization of monastic and cathedral schools, the church trained men for the clergy at its leading schools and there, too, manuscripts continued to be copied and preserved. By the eleventh century, however, the monastery schools had declined, and the work was carried on almost exclusively in cathedral schools at Paris, Chartres, Laon, Reims, and Liége. It was at these centers that intellectual life awakened in the eleventh century, when political stability and a revived economy made possible intellectual and artistic endeavor.

THE ROLE OF GERBERT

The first great figure associated with the revival of learning is Gerbert (940?–1003) who later was elevated to the Papacy as Silvester II. Of his early life we know only that he studied grammar at the French monastery of Aurillac and then went to Barcelona to learn mathematics. Eventually he attended the cathedral school of Reims to learn dialectic and remained there for a time as a master. At this early age he became renowned as a teacher of the *trivium* because he lectured directly from the classics rather than from the old textbooks. His most significant contributions, however, were in the *quadrivium*. Having learned much about Arabic science and mathematics while in Spain, he introduced this knowledge into Christian Europe. We are told that to illustrate the earth, stars, and constellations, he built two small spheres. One was solid and upon this he depicted the poles and other parts of the world. The other was an armillary sphere which consisted of metal circular bands that crossed, each apparently to represent the orbit of a planet. In the center of the sphere was a small ball—the earth; on the outside of the circles was a band picturing the signs of the zodiac. From the Arabs Gerbert had also learned about the abacus, a device that consisted of columns each representing a numerical value. By placing counters in a prescribed pattern upon the columns, it was possible to add and subtract very rapidly. When the principle of the abacus became widely known it was applied to practical problems and proved of great value. All sorts of manuals were written upon its use, and it was employed to facilitate accounting in the treasuries of states like England and Sicily. As yet in Europe only Roman numerals were used, and anyone who has attempted to do mathematical calculations with Roman numerals will understand how useful a device was the abacus. The Chinese and Japanese still use it, and we, too, have it in the form of a frame with metal wires and sliding counters to help children learn their arithmetic. We are certain that Gerbert also knew of the nine arabic numerals but not of the zero which made calculation to the base ten so simple. Whether Gerbert introduced the astrolabe from Spain into France is debatable, although quite likely. This instrument, essential for measuring distances and heights and the positions of celestial bodies, was soon in the hands of mariners.

Gerbert's importance for the revival of learning cannot be overemphasized. He laid the foundation for the study of mathematics, geography, and astronomy. From his teaching of grammar and dialectic at Reims he inspired numerous students to search for more of the old classics and to demand Latin translations of Arabic and Greek works. They in turn stimulated their students and so swelled the numbers eager to learn that universities began to develop around the cathedral schools in the twelfth century.

NOMINALISTS AND REALISTS

For the first time since St. Augustine, theologians in the eleventh century began to concern themselves with the serious study of the philosophical problems related to Christian theology. The prime concern of the eleventh and twelfth centuries was the fundamental nature of what scholars termed universals and particulars. Principally because of Augustine, who had digested and passed on to later ages much of Plato's thought, medieval theologians were convinced that particulars could not be understood nor have any reality unless associated with and partaking of the nature of their general ideas or universals. Actually these *realists,* as they came to be called, argued that a table cannot be recognized unless there is a general idea of what comprises a table; first there must be a universal idea of a table. According to them, therefore, ideas and abstractions preceded particular things. They adhered to the Platonic principle that only general ideas or universals are real.

Opposed to the realists were the *nominalists* who held to the Aristotelian position that universals had no real existence of themselves but were merely used to facilitate reference to abstract ideas. Only particulars—individual things—had reality. General ideas or universals were but names (*nomina* in Latin, from which the term *nominalist* was derived). The first exponent of the nominalist view was the theologian Roscellinus, who stated that universals were not real, or were not things, but were names and, as such, were no more than sounds. He was opposed vigorously by the famous theologian Anselm of Bec, who defended the traditional Platonic position. Roscellinus, though arguing that God, Christ, and the Holy Spirit were three distinct things or persons, denied that they were a part of the Trinity. Anselm's rebuttal was that all three partook of the Trinity and to deny this was to believe in three gods. Such nominalism, said Anselm, led consequently to heresy. In 1092 an ecclesiastical council compelled Roscellinus to retract his statements. Due to the efforts of Anselm, the Platonic-Augustinian tradition had won the first round but more debates were to follow.

ABELARD

The second stage of the nominalist-realist argument was dominated by the most accomplished scholar of the early twelfth century—the famous Abelard (1079–1142). Thanks to the survival of his autobiography—*The History of My Calamities* (*Historia Calamitatum*)—we are well informed about this exceptional man. Born into a noble Breton family, Abelard early in his life abandoned a knightly career for a scholarly one. As soon as possible he went from one cathedral school to another, studying with all the famous masters, but their answers did not satisfy the ambitious young student. He so ably refuted the realist position of the famous William of Champeaux in Paris that the local clerical authorities forced the upstart to leave the cathedral school. He then went to Laon, where he soon tired of the lectures of a shallow and boastful master. Again he outtaught and outargued the master and had to leave town. By this time, however, his scholarly fame was so great that in 1115 he was invited back to Paris to teach.

At Paris the rise and fall of Abelard was meteoric. A stimulating teacher and thinker of the first order, he quickly attracted the largest number of students to his lectures and became recognized as the leading scholar. But the charming master was soon enmeshed in a love affair that ended his brilliant career. He fell in love with the talented and beautiful Héloïse, the niece of a cathedral canon. Though only in minor orders and free to marry, Abelard was persuaded by Héloïse not to take this step because it would block his ecclesiastical career. She then became his mistress and bore him a child, and at this point Abelard secretly married her. In attempting to protect Abelard and his career Héloïse complicated her relations with the uncle who concluded that his niece had been mistreated and dishonored. With a gang of ruffians he attacked Abelard and castrated him so that further life with Héloïse or ecclesiastical preferment became impossible. He became a monk and Héloïse a nun. Isolated in a pathetically illiterate and backward Breton monastery, Abelard wrote his autobiography and languished for the academic stir of Paris. Héloïse, who had become the abbess of a group of nuns, discovered where Abelard was and initiated the most celebrated love correspondence of the Middle Ages. Still young and passionately in love with Abelard, she poured out her heart to him and pleaded for his sympathy, understanding, and expression of love. Abelard replied realistically but with words of consolation and underscored the futility of a love or life together. They must understand, he wrote, that however difficult, their only consolation and help could come from God. Anyone who hopes to understand the ideas and conventions of the Middle Ages must read the life of Abelard and his love correspondence with Héloïse.

Abelard left his abbey, just how or when we do not know, and returned to Paris where he began teaching. But his enemies soon prevailed upon a church council to declare his teachings heretical. Undaunted, Abelard set out for Rome to appeal the decision to the Pope. He fell ill en route, however, and died at Cluny. His body was returned to Héloïse for burial, and when later she followed him in death her body was placed next to his; at last the lovers had been united.

It was in philosophy that Abelard excelled and to which he brought radically new ideas. Basically a nominalist, he cleared up various misconceptions that had muddied this philosophical position. He insisted that one must differentiate between the sound and the meaning of a word because the sound is but the particular of the meaning—the real universal. What Abelard did was to introduce to philosophy the fundamental truth that logic consists in correct use of concepts, a philosophical conclusion that remains valid today.

Abelard's other contribution was in the field of theology. In a work entitled *Sic et Non* (*Yes and No*), he systematized and summarized the chief theological writings and their conclusions. His method was to present fundamental questions of faith and doctrine, and to answer them with the solutions provided by the Bible and the leading church scholars. To each question he attempted to give a satisfactory answer, but he truthfully admitted that there were often contradictions for which no reasonable solution could be found. Still, the scholar must not give up; he must strive to work out a satisfactory answer. Although Abelard emphasized the importance of reason in arriving at truth, he never contended that it was superior to faith. He but said that reason aided faith in attaining truth and concurred with the general church position that reason was the handmaiden of faith. The essential quality to note in Abelard is his doubting and inquisitive mind. In this respect he was far removed from Anselm of Bec who had stated: "Nor do I seek to know that I may believe, but I believe that I may know." Abelard's position is admirably summed up in his famous statement: "For by doubting we come to inquiry, and by inquiring we perceive the truth."

Stimulated by such men as Abelard and Anselm, theological and philosophical writings and arguments mushroomed during the rest of the twelfth century. The nominalists and realists refined and redefined their positions, while theologians, stirred by an argument going back to the eleventh century, hotly debated transubstantiation. Where church doctrine had traditionally held that in the service of the Eucharist the bread and wine were miraculously changed into the body and blood of Christ, now certain theologians denied this transformation, arguing that reason and common sense proved that the bread and wine remained unchanged. If pressed as to their ultimate conclusion these thinkers would have said that reason is superior to authority. However modern such a position, it smacked of heresy and involved many in conflict with the church, while St. Bernard and Hugh of St. Victor militantly upheld orthodox church doctrine. Both were essentially conservative and mystical. Both glorified faith and authority over reason. Hugh had no use for subtle dialectic; truth came from the revealed word of the Bible. The Bible should not be read literally but interpreted allegorically to fathom divine truth.

GREEK TRANSLATIONS

In intellectual disciplines other than theology and philosophy, men of the late eleventh and twelfth centuries were equally active. To counter the narrow concentration upon dialectic, the English scholar John of Salisbury (d. 1180) emphasized that true knowledge came only from the study of many fields of knowledge. Becoming a master at Chartres he made it the center for classical studies. Here the *trivium* was stressed, and young students learned to read and interpret the Latin classics. Here, under the stimulation of John and others, they gloried in the humane subjects such as literature. Men trained in this tradition soon yearned to read the Greek classics and Arabic works and clamored for translations. This helps to account for the rash of Latin translations made in the twelfth and thirteenth centuries.

Although many historians long attributed this feverish translation activity to the crusades, arguing that they introduced westerners to Greek and Arabic learning, there is little validity to this thesis. Few crusaders had scholarly tastes and very little translating was done in the Latin States of the Crusaders. Most was done in Spain, Italy, and Sicily, areas long in contact with Arabic culture, where there were Jews, Greeks, and Christians who had thoroughly learned Greek and Arabic. To these lands came scholars from all over Europe to learn the languages. These were the men who translated Greek and Arabic into Latin and opened up a vast new world of philosophy, literature, science, medicine, and mathematics to the West. During the course of the twelfth century, most of Aristotle's works on logic were translated and so, too, were the scientific and geographical books of Galen, Hippocrates, and Ptolemy. Latin translations of Arabic works were especially significant, because they introduced the superior Arabic learning on mathematics, science, and medicine to the West. The works of the famous Arabic mathematician al-Khwarizmi on arithmetic and algebra were translated. In medicine the studies of Avicenna were translated. Early in the thirteenth century the commentaries of Averroës on Aristotle's philosophy were put into Latin.

Such translations contributed immensely to the rich intellectual activity of the thirteenth century and set the mold for education and curricula for the remainder of the Middle Ages. The majority of translations were on philosophical, mathematical, and scientific works; they became the principal subjects of students training for law, theology, and medicine. These were the fields of knowledge most students hoped to enter, and so the study of Latin grammar and literature, though essential, came to be regarded as a means to an end. Such study produced the knowledge of Latin required to read the works prescribed for preparation in the trinity of law, theology, and medicine. Out of such training came the scholastic system of education that developed in all universities during the thirteenth century.

REVIVAL OF ROMAN LAW

Previously we have noted the contributions of Peter Lombard and Gratian to the systematization of the canon law, achievements that emerged from the revived study of Roman law in the eleventh and twelfth centuries. Although a knowledge of Roman law had completely disappeared from most of Europe, a few scraps had survived in Italy. Here it was in the eleventh century that the study of Roman law revived. Toward the end of the eleventh century, the *Digest,* a systematic explanation of the *Corpus Juris Civilis,* was discovered. Soon, at Bologna and other Italian towns, the substance and procedure of Roman law was studied under masters who lectured upon the *Digest* and more fully explained its content by writing *glosses* (commentaries) upon the complicated and conflicting legal principles. Because of this technique the masters were called *glossators.* Under their exacting training were produced those men who, with their fine knowledge of Roman law, used it in the service of canon law and the church, or became skilled administrators in the strong states developing in the twelfth century.

2. *The Rise of the Universities*

By the twelfth century masters and students had become so numerous at the noted cathedral schools that it became necessary to institute organization, rules, and academic requirements. The first step was for students and masters to combine into associations which eventually obtained legal recognition from municipal, church, and state authorities. The associations thus founded were called *universities* (from the Latin *universitas*) and were similar to the craft and merchant guilds. From such associations sprang the great universities of the twelfth century. Once a few universities had been organized, masters and students modeled others upon them, and later in the Middle Ages rulers constituted new universities by charter.

UNIVERSITIES OF BOLOGNA AND PARIS

Except for the famous medical university of Salerno which dated from the middle of the eleventh century, there were no universities until the twelfth century. The first ones arose at Bologna and Paris, and upon their organization most subsequent universities were modeled. At the outset of the twelfth century some famous glossators were teaching Roman law at Bologna and soon, thanks to the famous master Irnerius, Bologna became the leading school for the study of Roman and canon law. The first associations to appear there were those of the masters, who established rules regulating their affairs and the qualifications to gain admittance to their guild or college. The students copied the masters and organized associations that were called universities. During the twelfth century two student universities arose at Bologna, one comprising Italian students and the other all students from north of the Alps. Both acted together through representatives and came to be headed by elected rectors. The first objectives of the student universities were to win recognition from the municipal government of Bologna and to secure certain fundamental protections and privileges. By threatening to leave town, the students forced the townsmen to reduce their scandalous rents and to sell books at reasonable prices. They next worked for concessions from the masters. All sorts of regulations were imposed upon the masters, who received their income from student fees. The students' aim was to get their money's worth. Any master who had less than five students at a lecture was fined on the assumption that good lectures would draw larger numbers. Every lecture had to last the required time, and no difficult point could be skipped or glossed over. No master could leave town without student permission; for his wedding he got one free day. After contemplating the zeal of American students one can only conclude that the University of Bologna was the world turned upside down. Already trained in Latin grammar and literature, the Bolognese students were older than those of some universities and consequently were more serious. The masters' associations granted the degrees but the student universities had the authority and controlled the masters. Bologna was a students' university!

In northern Europe, the first university to develop was the cathedral school of Notre-Dame at Paris. Before the end of the twelfth century Paris was no longer a cathedral school but a university. Well located geographically and the political center of France, Paris early attracted hundreds of students. No doubt such brilliant masters as Abelard also contributed to the academic fame of the school at Notre-Dame. The early schools and lecture rooms were in the shadow of the great cathedral on the Île de la Cité. When this small area became too crowded, masters and students crossed the Petit-Pont to the Left Bank of the Seine. By the thirteenth century all the Left Bank was covered with quarters for students and rooms where the masters lectured. This area of Paris became known as the Latin Quarter because of the Latin language spoken there.

At Paris the associations or faculties of masters dominated the new university. This was but natural, because most students were quite young, having come there to study the basic subjects—the arts. Toward the end of the twelfth century these masters' associations began agitating for academic independence from the cathedral authorities and for self-government. After 1200 they rapidly acquired these. In that year certain royal officials had killed some prominent German students in a riot. In protest all the masters refused to teach and threatened to leave Paris. The king Philip Augustus immediately heeded their demands. He punished the royal officials and granted the masters a charter that freed them from all secular authority. It is with this charter, granted in 1200, that the University of Paris associates its official foundation.

The masters next bargained to secure their freedom from the local ecclesiastical authorities. By 1215 this goal had been achieved with papal assent. A set of regulations was promulgated for the governing of the university. Age and academic requirements were established for admittance to the guilds or faculties of masters. Students must enroll with masters, who were held responsible for their intellectual and moral well-being. Because Paris was the principal school where students went to learn the arts, the faculty of arts became the largest and most influential association of masters. It elected a rector who eventually came to be the accepted head of the university; the deans of the faculties of law, medicine, and theology recognized his superior authority. The only authority remaining to the chancellor of the Cathedral of Notre-Dame was the right to accept candidates for degrees recommended by masters of the various faculties. Most of the universities today, whether foreign or American, derive their organization from this academic cadre. Because the faculty of arts was so large and cosmopolitan, it underwent a peculiar development. It was subdivided into four groups or *nations*—the French (Latin people), the Norman, the Picard (consisting also of the Low Country people), and the English (comprised of people from England, Germany, and northeastern Europe). These nations elected the officials of the faculty of arts.

Derived also from Bologna and Paris were the academic degrees and the requirements for them. Bologna, which concentrated upon canon and Roman law, instructed advanced students with previous training in the arts; it consequently awarded higher degrees in law. At Paris a greater variety of degrees could be won, because the faculties taught theology, law, and medicine in addition to the arts. The faculties awarded the degrees. A student who had studied the arts for six years and had satisfactorily passed all requirements was admitted to the faculty of arts and awarded the degree of *Master of Arts* (A.M.). Such men often remained to teach the arts while they worked toward an advanced degree in theology, medicine, or law. When the candidate met the requirements of one of the advanced faculties he was accepted and awarded the appropriate degree. In law, he was awarded the degree *Doctor of Laws* (LL.D. from *Legum Doctor*); in medicine, the degree *Doctor of Medicine* (M.D. from *Medicinae Doctor*); in theology, the degree *Professor of Sacred Theology* (S.T.P. from *Sanctae Theologiae Professor*). The titles doctor, professor, and master actually meant teacher and signified that a man was competent to instruct in certain subjects. The degree *Bachelor of Arts* (A.B.) was a type of preliminary degree obtained after four years of training in the arts; an individual with such a degree could, if he chose, teach elementary subjects in the arts.

After the successful candidate had received his degree and a cap and gown signifying his academic specialty, he was ready to commence (thus the academic *commencement* ceremony) his career. Many chose to remain at Paris, teaching and earning a living from student fees. If the new teacher's lodgings were adequate he could give lectures there, but generally he had to hire a commodious room, preferably above a tavern. At Paris these lecture halls were concentrated along one street on the Left Bank, the Rue du Fouarre (straw), so called because the students sat on straw-covered floors as they listened and took notes. After the student had matriculated for the prescribed number of years, he underwent a rigorous examination for the degree. This was a much respected and feared hurdle, prepared for by intensive study. At Paris the examination was begun in the following manner: "Brother, what do you say to this question, what do you say to this one and this one?" From Bologna we hear of the "rigorous and tremendous examination" before learned doctors. The successful candidates threw victory banquets for all friends, and on such festive occasions there was much drink, food, and gaiety. Always there were the unsuccessful candidates, such as the one "who could do nothing in the disputation but sat in his chair like a goat." Those successful candidates who did not choose to teach found useful and lucrative positions in church and state, where their knowledge of theology, philosophy, mathematics, and Roman and canon law made them sought after as clerks and civil servants. Many entered into what we would call private practice and had successful careers as doctors and lawyers.

STUDENT LIFE

Thanks to the preservation of student letters and codes of university regulations, we are exceedingly well informed about the other major aspect of university life—non-academic or extracurricular pursuits. As in modern times, these records indicate the rich variety of experience afforded by university life. There were, of course, the serious and single-minded students who thought of and did nothing but study. Over such uninteresting individuals we may rapidly pass except for noting those who, being poor, froze or starved in rat-infested garrets or basements. We are all familiar with Chaucer's poor clerk of Oxenford who loved his Aristotle and gladly learned and taught despite his economic plight, and contemporary accounts frequently refer to "the misery of the poor and diligent scholar falling asleep over his books."

One gathers that the medieval extrovert, bent on having a real university experience, could not be surpassed even by today's student. We hear that students went "about the streets armed, attacking the citizens, breaking into houses, and abusing women. They quarrel among themselves over dogs, women, or what-not, slashing off one another's fingers with their swords." In the Latin Quarter were all the usual diversions. Taverns were numerous, women of ill repute abounded, and there was dicing, dancing, and singing.

For the student who really enjoyed himself university life was expensive. Like his modern counterpart, the medieval student wrote to his parents only when in need of money. So frequent and necessary were these medieval missives that professional rhetoricians sold letter models covering all pecuniary demands. Invariably the student emphasized the high cost of living at a university town and the expense of books and other materials. The clever and unscrupulous stooped to any device to secure the coveted money; they threatened that if it was not forthcoming they would have to cease their studies, they would not have enough to pay fees or buy books, they might starve or perhaps fall ill from too little wine and food. An Oxford student terminated a pathetic letter with the following lines: "Wherefore I respectfully beg your paternity that by the promptings of divine pity you may assist me, so that I may be able to complete what I have well begun. For you must know that without Ceres and Bacchus Apollo grows cold." An Austrian student wrote to his sister for 100 shillings, some sheets, and fine cloth. To touch her heart, he related that he slept on straw, had no shoes or shirts, and ate indescribable things. As might be expected, the reply was one of sympathy and a sum of money. Occasionally, however, there were those worldly fathers who knew about life in Paris, and instead of responding with money answered with reproofs. One father wrote that no money was forthcoming until the son reformed. And to drive home his point the father said that he had "discovered that you live dissolutely and slothfully, preferring license to restraint and play to work and strumming a guitar while the others are at their studies, whence it happens that you have read but one volume of law."

Not until the second half of the thirteenth century were attempts made to care for the hundreds of poor students who required assistance. Before this time they had barely survived, and many became ill or died from lack of decent food and quarters. The wealthy student could hire sumptuous lodgings and afford servants, but the son of a poor craftsman or peasant barely subsisted; he gave thanks to God for the opportunity to learn. Whatever we may say about stratified society in the Middle Ages, the university was one place where money and social prestige did not spell the difference between success and failure. Intellectual achievement counted for all, and both church and wealthy individuals came to look upon the support of poor and worthy students as necessary and pious work. Joining an order of friars solved the problem for some students but not for those who did not want to take vows. The solution for many of these students was the residential college. In 1258 Robert de Sorbon, confessor to the French king, endowed a hall for sixteen deserving candidates working in theology; in this manner was established the Sorbonne, the oldest residential college of which there is record. Rapidly other residential colleges were founded, and in Oxford and Cambridge they became the dominating feature of university life. Such famous colleges as Merton, Balliol, and Peterhouse date from the thirteenth century.

Such was the organization and life of the medieval university which, except for advance in knowledge, is fundamentally the same today. Our universities stem directly from the English, and many of our academic procedures from the German and French. Our universities are indebted not just to Paris and Bologna but to all medieval universities that took form between the twelfth and fifteenth centuries. In Italy, during the thirteenth century, some masters from Bologna founded Padua, and the emperor Frederick II created the University of Naples. In France emerged Montpellier and Orléans, both famed for the study of law. In the twelfth century some Paris masters migrated to Oxford, founding a university there, and from Oxford, Cambridge developed in the thirteenth century. In Spain the University of Salamanca was founded in 1220. Such German universities as Erfurt, Heidelberg, Prague, and Vienna did not appear until the fourteenth century. Meanwhile other distinguished universities sprouted up in France, Italy, Portugal, and Poland.

3. *Thirteenth-Century Learning*

ALTHOUGH BY THE FIFTEENTH CENTURY the word *scholasticism* connoted a system of learning devoted to arid and idle argumentation over subjects of no importance, during the thirteenth and early fourteenth centuries scholastic learning provided a sound education in the universities. Scholasticism was the medieval system of education to prepare men in the arts and professional subjects. It included such fields as mathematics, science, philosophy, logic, theology, and Roman and canon law.

This education was a tremendous improvement over any since the Roman Empire. At its best it forced the individual to analyze intellectual problems and to use his reason. The method of instruction required both master and student to argue and debate the subject matter. Such pedagogy contributed to the making of vigorous thinkers. The serious weaknesses of scholasticism were lack of emphasis on literature, ignorance of knowledge developing outside the university, and failure to appreciate adequately the empirical method, thus forfeiting knowledge provided by experience.

CONTRIBUTIONS OF THE SCHOOLMEN

Often the schoolmen have been criticized for merely assimilating classical and Arabic learning and being content thereafter to argue over inconsequential problems raised by the old learning. This is a partially correct but by no means totally accurate description of thirteenth-century intellectual achievement. Before scholars could advance they had to master the vast body of learning rediscovered in the twelfth and thirteenth centuries. When this was done there was significant advance in learning, much of it original. Early in the thirteenth century the mathematician Leonard of Pisa, patronized by the intellectually curious emperor Frederick II, was making original contributions. In close contact with Arabic and Jewish scholars, he summarized their mathematical knowledge in several books, and then went on to increase knowledge on algebraic and quadratic equations as well as to introduce new solutions to problems in trigonometry. In the field of medicine, although we are poorly informed, it is certain that experimentation resulted in better diagnosis and surgery, and that dissection was normal practice at the leading schools of medicine.

The principal scholarly arena in the thirteenth century was, however, devoted to philosophy and theology. These disciplines came to be the domain of Dominican and Franciscan scholars, who, lodged and fed in their numerous residential colleges, swarmed to the universities and dominated the faculties. Their pervading interest, supported by the Popes and great prelates, was to determine what changes in the traditional Augustinian-Platonic philosophical and theological position had been made by the Aristotelian philosophy and to define its place in Christian theology. In the twelfth century the church had been fearful of Aristotelianism because it seemed to contradict so much of what had been accepted for eight hundred years. The Popes and church councils attempted to ban certain of Aristotle's writings. In the thirteenth century the church became even more disturbed as numerous scholars, under the influence of the Arabic philosopher Averroës, accepted a naturalistic interpretation of Aristotle's premises and conclusions. Thus understood, Aristotle denied the existence of and necessity for God; all was determined by natural cause and effect. Sensing that Aristotle could not be banned from western Christendom, the Popes encouraged the Dominicans and Franciscans to attempt the reconciliation of Aristotelianism with the Christian faith and theology. Throughout the thirteenth century notable scholars attempted to write a *summa*—a compendium of all knowledge—that would accomplish this task.

ALBERTUS MAGNUS AND THOMAS AQUINAS

The first great summist was the German Dominican Albertus Magnus (1193–1280) who was trained and taught at the University of Paris. The works of this remarkable scholar, dealing with every conceivable subject, occupy in printed form thirty-eight quarto volumes. A great admirer of Aristotle, Albert contributed most significantly to scientific knowledge. Using the empirical method of Aristotle, he minutely observed animals and plants and produced amazingly accurate descriptions of them. Repeatedly, however, he demonstrated his independence by contradicting Aristotle's scientific observations and conclusions.

Albert trained the most renowned scholar of the high Middle Ages—Thomas Aquinas (1225?–1274). Coming from the Italian town of Aquino, Thomas studied six years at the University of Naples, became a Dominican, and then went to Paris to study with Albert. Here he won the doctorate in theology and taught until his death. Thomas, a theologian par excellence, devoted most of his encyclopedic learning to reconciling Aristotelianism with Christian dogma. His was the task of harmonizing the truth of reason with the truth of revelation. As Thomas viewed the problem there was but one truth; seemingly divergent truths must be meshed. Author of many works, his great triumph was the *Summa Theologiae* (*Summary of Theology*), which had as its main themes Christian salvation and ethics. His method for dealing with them consisted of asking 631 fundamental questions, and attempting to supply satisfactory answers by using canon law and syllogistic reasoning. On those occasions when he found it impossible to supply a good answer or to reconcile conflicting truths, he concluded that the revealed truth must be accepted because it came from God who was the Creator and embodiment of all truth. Although the truths of philosophy were generally valid, when they conflicted with divine truth they must yield. The purpose of philosophy was to clarify God's plan and His relations with the world of men.

The intellectual achievement of Thomas is one of the towering accomplishments of all ages. Through his labor, Aristotelian philosophy was placed in the service of Christian theology and the two harmonized in favor of the latter. Henceforth, the Thomist philosophical position supplanted the Augustinian-Platonic and still dominates the thought of the Catholic church. The *Summa* of Thomas Aquinas is now the official foundation for the teaching of theology in Catholic universities and colleges.

The Thomist philosophical and theological ideas dominated the University of Paris and prevailed throughout the Middle Ages but never to the exclusion of the traditional Augustinian position. Because Thomas was a Dominican, the Franciscans tended to embrace and defend the opposing view. At Paris vigorous disputations between the scholarly antagonists were normal. At Oxford the Franciscans ruled supreme, due largely to the intellectual vigor of Robert Grosseteste (d. 1253), who rose to be the leading lecturer, chancellor of Oxford, and bishop of Lincoln. The interests and training of Grosseteste were amazingly broad; he wrote on theology, philosophy, and science, and translated numerous Greek works into Latin. Through Latin translations of Arabic scientific works, he was familiar with the most advanced knowledge in mathematics and astronomy. He took special interest in optics and experimented with lenses and their powers of magnification. To Grosseteste should go the credit for stimulating the growing interest in experimental science. By emphasizing the need for always going back to the original sources and reading them in the original language, he also stimulated an interest in the classics and literature, thereby preparing the way for the Christian humanism that swept over Europe in the later Middle Ages.

ROGER BACON

Better known to subsequent ages was Roger Bacon (1214?–1294), a student of Grosseteste, whose fame is based in part upon much unreliable writing that has transformed him into the founder of modern science and a martyr to its cause. The accomplishments of the real Roger Bacon are solid enough without misrepresenting what he did. His academic life was normal and untroubled, and he was never persecuted because of radical ideas on science. Having studied at Oxford, he went to Paris for a master's degree and remained there to teach. He soon tired of the predominantly theological atmosphere and returned to Oxford where he joined the Franciscans and wrote and taught until his death.

While busily engaged on a *summa,* Roger received a request from the Pope to send him a copy because he had heard so much about the work. Roger, however, had just begun the compendium and so could only send the Pope a condensed outline of the contents. This work in itself was remarkable, and proved to be Roger's greatest book. He entitled it the *Opus Maius* (*Greater Treatise*), and later appended to it two supplementary parts. Briefly summarized, the principal points made by Bacon are the following: he accepted orthodox theology as the epitome of learning, while considering Aristotelian philosophy the best rational system to help explain divine truth. Like his master, he insisted that sources should be read in the original and urged scholars to learn Greek, Arabic, and Hebrew. Ignorance of these languages contributed, he said, to the backward state of science.

To facilitate learning Greek he composed a grammar. Finally, he made a plea for greater emphasis upon experimental science and herein made his most enduring contribution to medieval learning.

Bacon considered mathematics the foundation of most science and allied fields of knowledge. Experimental science he defined as the technique of arriving at conclusions through experience and experiment. It was while illustrating what he meant by experience and experiment that Bacon described wonderful mechanical machines, lenses, magnets, and explosive materials. However interesting and valid his observations and descriptions, most were not novel but derived from Greek and Arabic learning, from Albertus Magnus, and from Grosseteste. There is no reliable evidence that Bacon constructed the various machines and gadgets he described. His strength lay in the ability to describe and popularize scientific knowledge and in the realization of the significant advances in knowledge contributed by learning outside the university. He understood that the engineer, architect, and skilled artisan were in their manner contributing as much to knowledge as the learned schoolmen; later in the Middle Ages non-academics were to contribute more.

4. Medieval Latin

IN THE MIDDLE AGES the most significant literary achievements were in the vernacular languages. Evolving out of crude tongues at first suitable only for speaking, they had progressed by the twelfth and thirteenth centuries into rich languages which served as the medium for composition in prose and poetry. Yet the growth of the vernacular as a literary medium depended upon the achievements attained in Latin. The various literary forms that gained distinction in Latin served as the models for composition in the vernacular. Down to the twelfth century Latin was with few exceptions the only written language. And because few but the clergy could read and write, church literature dominated this period. All works dealing with theology, philosophy, sermons, and canon law were written in Latin. Throughout the Middle Ages all records of the church such as bulls, decretals, correspondence, and episcopal registers were in Latin. Although such Latin served as the model for some prose, it is to the clerks who had only vowed minor orders that we must turn to find literary compositions differing from the standard church prose and experimentation in various literary forms. These clerks, little attached to the church and usually employed as scribes and accountants by princes, nobles, and merchants, had greater freedom and were under no compulsion to adhere to any standard.

LATIN PROSE

Although Latin had sunk to abysmal depths during the early Middle Ages, by the twelfth century it had improved in both grammar and vocabulary. It was inferior to the fine Latin of Cicero or Caesar, but it satisfactorily fulfilled the requirements of church and state. To express the ideas of theologians, doctors, lawyers, philosophers, and the state, the old classical vocabulary had undergone radical innovation. Old Latin words were given new meanings and new Latin words were derived from the vernacular. To meet practical demands Latin became simple and direct. In so doing, it retained a vitality throughout the Middle Ages. No one can fail to be impressed by the Latin prose in the church liturgy or to catch the rhythm and style peculiar to the documents issuing from the papal and royal chanceries. The best Latin charters are works of style, clarity, and balance.

Seldom, even after the thirteenth century, did educated men write in any language but Latin; it continued to be the language of the intelligentsia. All works dealing with the arts and professional fields were in Latin. The complicated subject of political theory was invariably treated in Latin; even Dante, who almost singlehandedly made Italian into a great literary language, felt compelled to write his treatise on political theory, *De Monarchia,* in Latin. It was assumed that such a subject would be read only by educated men who expected or demanded that the language be Latin.

Practically all histories and biographies were written in Latin, not only because of their serious subject but because clerics generally wrote them. Most histories had as their theme the events of the world since Adam and Eve. Generally they were extremely unreliable, lacking both objectivity and perspective. Few historians really understood how to use historical evidence and uncritically repeated all that they heard or read. Usually their histories can be relied upon only for the contemporary events they record. Two notable exceptions were Bishop Otto of Freising, twelfth-century German historian, and Matthew Paris, thirteenth-century English historian. With Otto, historical writing attained its highest point. In his *Chronicle of the Two Cities* the history of the world is told from creation to 1146. Close to the emperor Frederick Barbarossa, who was his uncle, Otto wrote an extremely reliable account of German history in the twelfth century. The rest of his history, although less reliable, towers above others. In his writing Otto worked out a philosophy of history and critically analyzed various historical problems. The grand theme of his history was, as the title suggests, secured from Augustine. In Matthew Paris, monk of St. Albans monastery, Otto had his only serious competition. Matthew's writing dealt principally with English history, the best being the *Greater Chronicle (Chronica Majora),* which contains an excellent account of English history between 1066 and 1253. Using official records whenever possible, he wrote his history in a vivid style and with logical organization. His perspective on English history benefited from his rich knowledge of continental history.

LATIN POETRY

It had long been common for clergy and schoolmen to compose Latin poems on religious subjects; some of the great hymns are examples of such literary creation. Of more value for the development of vernacular literature, however, was the Latin lyrical poetry called *Goliardic* because it was composed by carefree students and clerks in minor orders who were dubbed the sons of Goliath (Philistines). Free from religious inhibitions or restrictions, these gay, irreverent, and witty individuals gave free expression to their emotions and ideas. They gloried in the wonders of nature and love and grieved over the sorrows and frustrations of men. The chief themes of the Goliardic lyrics were love, frivolous emotions, and drinking. Has there ever been a better drinking song composed than this?

> To you, consummate drinkers,
> Though little be your drought,
> Good speed be to your tankards,
> And send the wine about,
> Let not the full decanter
> Sleep on its round,
> And may unheard of banter
> In wit abound.
>
> If any cannot carry
> His liquor as he should,
> Let him no longer tarry,
> No place here for the prude.
> No room among the happy
> For modesty.
> A fashion only fit for clowns,
> Sobriety.[1]

And who can fail to be stirred by the following poem heralding the arrival of spring, the season of gaiety and love?

> Now the fields are laughing,
> Now the maidens playing,
> The face of earth is smiling,
> Summer now appearing,
> Joyous and lovely with all flowers beguiling.

---

[1] Helen J. Waddell, *Mediaeval Latin Lyrics*, 5th ed. (London: Constable, 1966), p. 185.

The trees again are green,
Budding the underwood,
And cruel winter passes.
O lads, be gay of mood,
For love Himself now leads you to the lasses.[2]

Not all the poetry was so full of joy, abandon, and love. There were the satirists who used their talents to sting the proud church and scathe the social order. Their poetry burlesqued all from Pope to priest, from king to peasant. Perhaps the most famous of all such writing was the *Gospel According to Marks of Silver*. While the poor man without money, seeking charity from the Pope, is coldly turned out because he does not know "the wisdom of cash," the rich clergyman, guilty of homicide, bribes the Pope and is absolved. To his cardinals the Pope says: "Brethren, beware lest ye be seduced by vain words. For lo! I give unto you an example, that even as I grab, so also shall ye grab." In such poems with their varied themes, vernacular literature found excellent models. And these gay, emotional, free-thinking, and frequently satirical poems show us again that the Middle Ages was not dominated by dull, unthinking, conventional, and sheeplike men.

5. *Vernacular Literature*

LATIN DOMINATED SERIOUS PROSE WRITING as it did church and state records. When, however, an increasing number of intelligent laymen learned how to read and write Latin and received training in both the arts and advanced subjects, vernacular writing began to appear. Speaking a vernacular tongue, these men naturally came to write in it. During the twelfth century laymen entered the government service of state and municipality, and by the early thirteenth century various records had begun to be written in the vernacular. This practice increased during the rest of the Middle Ages.

FRENCH PROSE

Although vernacular prose does not become prominent until the later fourteenth and fifteenth centuries, some very fine compositions, especially in French, appeared in the thirteenth century. The first excellent writing was by Geoffrey de Villehardouin, a prominent noble and marshal of Champagne. He wrote a vivid account of the Fourth Crusade. One of the leading figures of the expedition, he was an eyewitness to most of what he recounted. At the end of his famous adventure,

---

[2] *Ibid.,* p. 213.

he sat down and dictated in the French vernacular his version of the crusade. Ville-hardouin's *Conquest of Constantinople* is the first great prose work in French. Uncritical and devoid of deep insights, it is nevertheless a realistic, vivid, terse, and fast-moving account of an exciting historical episode, the closest thing to good journalistic writing produced in the Middle Ages. Repressing his own feelings, Ville-hardouin simply wrote down what he saw and heard.

An even more remarkable French prose work was the *Life of Saint Louis* by Jean de Joinville (1224?–1317), a prominent lord from Champagne, who was close to the famous French king. Sharing many of the experiences of his royal master, Joinville survived him and two of his royal successors. It was at the request of the French queen that Joinville, in his eighties, dictated his memoirs of St. Louis, which as biography is a classic. It deals primarily with the crusade of Louis, but at the beginning and end Joinville included sections on the personal life of the king; these are the intriguing parts because they afford one of the few intimate pictures of a medieval ruler. Although Joinville praised Louis for his Christian virtues, bravery, and sense of justice, he remained honest to his task, taking issue with and criticizing Louis when he felt warranted. The great Louis emerges from Joinville's masterpiece as a virtuous but human figure who, although less burdened with mortal shortcomings than most, still had to strive against the egoism and frailties of human nature.

EPIC POETRY

For some time before the vernacular was regularly used for prose, clerks and laymen had been composing and experimenting with it. Those who wrote Latin poetry found it natural to do the same in the vernacular. The written vernacular had a greater prominence in Anglo-Saxon England than elsewhere in early medieval Europe. Anglo-Saxon was used in the laws, charters, and other official records. Translations were made from Latin. The *Anglo-Saxon Chronicle,* which gives a yearly account of early English history, dates from the reign of Alfred the Great. In England, too, the first great vernacular poetry appeared. Perhaps as early as the seventh century was written the magnificent epic *Beowulf*—a heroic tale of martial prowess and adventure. Somewhat later appeared the moving elegiac poems, *The Seafarer* and *The Wanderer*. The subject matter of all this poetry was taken from the great Germanic sagas. The most famous of the German epics was probably the *Nibelungenlied* which supplied Wagner, the nineteenth-century composer and writer, with many of his operatic stories. Written about 1200, this grand epic was based upon traditional legends, some of which resemble the fine Icelandic and Norse sagas composed in the twelfth and thirteenth centuries. Dealing with the aristocracy these epics enlighten us on aristocratic ideas and customs.

But, as with much of the vernacular literature, the best epic poetry was French. The epics which first appeared in the eleventh and twelfth centuries are called *chansons de geste* (songs of great deeds). Less prone to borrow early Germanic legendary tales, the chansons de geste found a rich subject matter in Carolingian history or in classical antiquity and mythology. Whatever the source of the inspiration, these epics were written for the feudal aristocracy and expressed its code of behavior. The best known chanson de geste is the *Song of Roland*, composed in the late eleventh or early twelfth century by a Norman clerk. The poem with its theme of chivalrous conduct revolves around Charlemagne's Spanish expedition, especially around the ambush of his rear guard by the Basques in the pass of Roncevaux. Betrayed by the treacherous Ganelon, the courageous Roland and other brave and chivalrous vassals of Charlemagne fight to the death. Sung and recounted in feudal castle and court, this epic inspired the feudal aristocrat to his finest and most heroic behavior. To all, Roland was the archetype of the perfect knight. Hundreds of such epics were written in a typical long and dramatic style. Especially suited for chanting or singing, they became part of the repertory of wandering minstrels of low birth, called *jongleurs* (literally, jugglers), who eked out a living by entertaining at castles, markets, and fairs.

FRENCH FORMS OF POETRY

Along with the epic arose the vernacular lyric which, in contrast to the long poem, was short, simple, emotional, and composed to be sung to the accompaniment of a love melody. It was composed by *troubadours* (*trouvères*, composers) who typically were feudal aristocrats. One of the earliest was William IX, duke of Aquitaine, who lived in the early twelfth century. Originating in southern France, the lyric was composed in the dialect of that area—Provençal; until the thirteenth century Provençal was the recognized literary language of the lyric. Customarily this poetry was sung to the accompaniment of a guitar. What young maiden contemplating the beauty of the spring landscape from her chamber window would not be touched by the following lines composed by the famous troubadour Jaufré Rudel?

> Yet shall I know no other love but hers,
> And if not hers, no other love at all.
> She hath surpassed all.
> So fair she is, so noble, I would be
> A captive with the hosts of paynimrie
> In a far land, if so be upon me
> Her eyes might fall.

> God, who hath made all things in earth that are,
> That made my love, and set her thus afar,
> Grant me this grace,
> That I may some day come within a room,
> Or in some garden gloom
> Look on her face.[3]

The Provençal dialect dominated France and even Italy and Spain into the thirteenth century. Then poets began composing in the local vernacular, and henceforth one finds a rich variety of dialects in medieval poetry. In France, however, lyrical poetry became less human, simple, and natural, and more highly conventionalized around well-defined plots or situations. The lovers must be separated by a geographical barrier, their love must withstand the spells of evil wizards or complicated entanglements and also the test of innumerable heroic feats performed by the lover. The lines dripped with sentimentality, and all actions and emotions were overdramatized. This was the so-called *courtoisie* or courtly love poetry that depicted chivalrous virtue as having but one end—service for and glorification of the ladylove. Everyone is familiar with the love plots of this poetry because they dominate much of what constitutes love poetry today. After a night of lovemaking the lovers are reminded by the first light of dawn that they must cease; but no, they deny this news as a subterfuge to part them. In another typical situation, the handsome and chivalrous knight rides through the countryside and discovers a beautiful maiden tending her flock. He sings love songs to her, he praises her beauty, he conquers her.

Out of the troubadours' courtoisie apparently developed another literary form called the romance. Like the chanson de geste it was a long poem but written in rhyming couplets to be read rather than sung. The themes revolved around love and were derived from classical heroes and their adventures. Marvelous stories could be spun, for example, from the legends surrounding Achilles, Aeneas, Ulysses, and Alexander the Great, although, when reworked into the romance, the actors were portrayed as typical French aristocrats of the thirteenth century. Subject matter was also drawn from the exploits associated with King Arthur, mythical king of Britain in the fifth century. The Arthurian legend, preserved orally until the twelfth century, was then written down and embellished by the Norman writer Geoffrey of Monmouth (1100?–1154) who composed in Latin the *History of the Britons*. From this convenient source poets could now draw their material.

Famous for her compositions was the Frenchwoman Marie de France (late twelfth century) who was patronized by Queen Eleanor, the wife of Henry II of England. Twelve of Marie's romances have survived; few of their plots are new

---

[3] Helen J. Waddell, *The Wandering Scholars,* 7th ed. (London: Constable, 1966), pp. 225–226.

THE COURT OF LOVE. This fourteenth-century ivory box from Paris is carved with scenes showing the assault on the Castle of Love, a central theme from the courtly love poetry of the time. Thus, the knights, heavily armed and shown with war chargers and siege machinery, have baskets of flowers, and they are being rebuffed not with boiling oil but with roses, thrown upon them from the battlements above.

to anyone who has read *King Arthur and His Knights of the Round Table*. Somewhat more sophisticated were the romances of the poet Chrétien de Troyes (second half of twelfth century) who interspersed classical references into the Arthurian material. Apparently well versed in Ovid's *Art of Love*, Chrétien made his love affairs much more complicated and subtle.

But however well written and however amusing, these romances were superficial and circumvented the realities of life. Eventually the more discriminating reader and listener as well as the intelligent poet demanded more realism in their verse. This trend is represented by that fine thirteenth-century romance *Aucassin et Nicolette*. The theme is highly conventional. Aucassin, a young noble, falls in love with the humble Nicolette, a captive purchased from the Saracens. His father prevents the marriage and causes a series of unfortunate incidents for the lovers. Undergoing all manner of hardships, Aucassin searches after Nicolette who has fled; at length he finds her, she becomes a Christian, and they live happily ever after. Where this poem differs from the other romances is in its sardonic satire of aristocratic society. We see this when Aucassin loses his dog while passing through a dark forest and, after searching awhile in vain, breaks down into tears. In this unhappy state he meets a peasant who inquires about his misfortune. When Aucassin tearfully tells him about the lost dog the peasant turns upon him, declaring bitterly that he has no good cause for such sorrow; it is he, the peasant, who has real trouble. He then tells of his miserable existence; it is all work, not enough to eat, and unbearable housing. And, to make matters worse, some of his oxen have perished and for this he will cruelly suffer at the hands of his lord. By episodes like this the anonymous author repeatedly interjects criticism and satire into his romance.

For bawdy, humorous, and earthy satire, however, one has to read the rhymed poems, the *fabliaux* (stories or fables), composed for the pleasure of the bourgeoisie. Meant always to be humorous, the incidents and jokes were derived from subject matter that the typical merchant and artisan could appreciate. As in our society, there were particular stock individuals who bore the brunt of the jests and tricks—the rich and fat merchants, the priests and monks, and other persons in high places. The merchants are invariably depicted as stupid in matters of love, with wives untrue to them. Priests and monks are double-faced hypocrites; lawyers, dishonest tricksters; and knights, cowards. Fun is consistently poked at the church and its dogma. The composers of these fabliaux were most often the wandering clerks who invariably turned out to be the heroes of the verse. Clever and shrewd, they always turned a situation to their advantage and took from the merchant both money and wife.

In a similar vein of satire and humor were the poetic fables of animals and their exploits. Drawing upon a group of German folk fables about Reynard the fox and his animal associates, some French clerks developed them into the most amusing and popular romances of the Middle Ages. Arranged in a cycle of stories, this collection was known as the *Romance of Reynard*. Reynard is, of course, the rascal and villain who, although guilty of every conceivable crime, manages to hold one's sympathy because of his intelligence and clever tricks pulled off at the expense of the powerful and affluent.

Of a more serious tone, but not without a lesson or satirical barb, was the allegory. Long used to interpret the true meaning of the Bible, this device of describing one thing under the image of another was applied to literature. The result was a popular series of prose romances that reworked the standard poetical romances of such writers as Marie de France. A complete cycle of romances was written, for example, upon such Arthurian themes as the quest of the Holy Grail. Essentially religious and mystical, these romances remind one of Bunyan's *Pilgrim's Progress*. Another form of the allegorical romance criticized social and political evils. Of this type was the *Romance of the Rose* begun by the thirteenth-century writer William de Lorris. The Rose is a fair lady, courted by a lover whose task is advanced or obstructed by Reason, Idleness, Evil-Tongue, Fear, and other such qualities, each symbolizing types and professions of men with their various human weaknesses and strengths. This romance was continued in the fourteenth century in a highly bitter and satirical vein by Jean de Meung. When finished, the romance numbered 21,780 lines.

GERMAN AND SPANISH LITERATURE

Although most of the major vernacular literary developments occurred in the French language which set the style and standards for composition in other vernacular languages, we must not ignore some of the significant achievements in German, Spanish, and Italian literature. For the present, we may pass over the literature of England, because Anglo-Saxon disappeared as a literary language after 1066 and the English vernacular was not used for literature until the late fourteenth century. German writers were content with translating French literature or modeling their works upon the French compositions until the thirteenth century, when finally they began to demonstrate some originality. Such writers as Gottfried von Strassburg (ca. 1200), author of *Tristan,* and Wolfram von Eschenbach (ca. 1200), author of *Parzifal,* created a German form of the romance. Meanwhile, fresh, light, lyrical poetry came from the *Minnesänger*—the German troubadour. The most accomplished of such poets was the Austrian Walther von der Vogelweide (ca. 1200) who, as a wandering troubadour, was patronized by various princes including Frederick II. Walther is especially remembered for his exquisite love lyrics, of which *Unter den Linden* is best known.

Into the twelfth century Spanish literature remained under the shadow of the French. As in Germany, writers translated French poetry or mimicked the French models. Finally, in the twelfth century, arose the great Spanish epic *Poema del Cid,* which is comparable to the German *Nibelungenlied.* The epic centers about the famous legendary *Cid,* a brave knight who served both Christians and Arabs in the wars of the eleventh century and who eventually became lord of Valencia. Like Roland, Lancelot, and Galahad, the *Cid* is portrayed as a perfect Christian knight who fights for God and lord.

DANTE AND THE ITALIAN LANGUAGE

That of all the vernacular languages only Italian came to rival the French for literary composition was due to the towering genius of one man—Dante Alighieri (1265–1321). Of a prominent Florentine family, Dante received an excellent education, associated with the best minds in Florence, and took a leading role in politics. He became a member of that political faction called the Ghibellines who, throughout the city-states of northern Italy, opposed the political pretensions of the Pope and supported imperial rule. During a municipal revolution fomented by Pope Boniface VIII in 1301, the Ghibellines lost power to the papal faction— the Guelfs—who proceeded to exile their political enemies. Among those forced to flee was Dante, who first took refuge at Verona and then moved to Ravenna, where he later died. As with the great Athenian historian Thucydides, enforced leisure gave Dante the time to compose his magnificent works.

DANTE ALIGHIERI. In a rather badly preserved fresco entitled the *Paradiso* in the Bargello in Florence, we find this sensitive portrait of the great Italian poet, probably painted about 1300. The traditional attribution of the portrait to Giotto is doubtful, but the fresco is certainly the work of one of Dante's contemporaries.

Even before his exile Dante had experimented in composing love lyrics in Italian. In his book called the *Vita Nuova* (the *New Life*), Dante relates how he fell in love with the beautiful Beatrice, who unfortunately was already married. Although Dante spoke to Beatrice but once, he wrote of his love for her and glorified her forever in his famous lines. After her early death she served as an incentive for Dante to strive to become worthy of his idealized love for her. He then plunged into the works that made him famous. In the *Convivio* (the *Banquet*—a spiritual banquet) he combined Italian verse and prose into an allegory wherein he attempted to describe universal knowledge. In this work Dante demonstrated that Italian could be used for serious subjects; its composition served to stimulate others to popularize scholastic learning by writing about it in the vernacular. To convince the erudite that Italian was worthy of scholarly tasks, Dante addressed a book to them entitled *De Vulgari Eloquentia* (*On the Vernacular Tongue*). In scholarly Latin he pleaded for a standard Italian vernacular dialect for literature and convincingly proved that Italian was as suitable as Latin for learned writing. The only other Latin work of Dante was the *De Monarchia* (*On Monarchy*), a treatise on politics in which he argued for the supremacy of imperial over papal authority and made an eloquent plea for the particularistic Italians to unite into a national state.

It was in the vernacular, however, that Dante produced one of the world's masterpieces—the *Divine Comedy.* The literary form of the *Comedy* defies analysis; it is an epic, but much more. The central actor is Dante, who frequently interrupts the flow of events to interject his own opinions. In certain sections the poem reads like a lyric. In subject matter it resembles an encyclopedia, because it embraces all knowledge. At the outset of the poem Dante portrays himself lost in a forest. He is rescued by the Roman poet Virgil, who seeks him out and tells him that he has been sent there by Beatrice who is in paradise. Henceforth, Virgil acts as Dante's guide on the long trip to paradise. They begin at the bottom—hell— which in form resembles a cone or a child's spinning top. Here Dante sees all the figures who are barred from paradise. At the lowest point of hell and undergoing the most severe punishment are such men as Judas Iscariot and Brutus. Ascending upward in hell, he sees such figures as the lustful Cleopatra and Helen of Troy; at other levels are the slothful, avaricious, and false. Here some of the most prominent figures are Popes. Just above hell is a more agreeable place called *limbo,* where the virtuous pagans reside. Among them are Plato, Aristotle, Cicero, and Virgil. Dante next travels to purgatory, where absolved Christians must perform penance or labors in proportion to the sins committed on earth. From here he ascends to the Garden of Eden which is the earthly paradise. At this point Beatrice becomes his guide and leads him up through the heavens where he sees and talks with such famous figures as Thomas Aquinas, St. Benedict, Albertus Magnus, and Peter Lombard. At length Dante is examined by St. Peter and is then permitted to have a fleeting glimpse of God. In this work of genius Dante summarized the whole of medieval knowledge at the end of the thirteenth century. He also imparted such perfection to the Italian language that it remains basically the same today. Even Shakespeare did not accomplish this for the English language.

6. Drama and Music

MYSTERY PLAYS

Mystery plays grew up in the Middle Ages. With drama, as with literature, the origins are found in the church. There was no connection between classical and medieval drama; the latter developed out of the liturgy of the church. On special feast days such as Christmas and Easter, the liturgy came to be supplemented by other features. First, the choir might portray in song the story of the Nativity or that of the Resurrection. The next step was to act out the famous Christian stories; the choir donned costumes and performed with simple properties. In this manner developed the mystery plays. As long as they supplemented the liturgy they were performed in the sanctuary and in Latin, but as they grew more popular, a stage would be erected on one of the church porches or placed in front of the church so that a greater audience could witness the play. From here the play was often taken to the central market place or was performed a number of times in various quarters of the town. In Bruges it is still the custom for a modern mystery play entitled the *Jeu du Saint-Sang* (Play of the Holy Blood) to be performed every fifth year at the great market place before the medieval cloth hall. In Germany the famous passion play performed at the Bavarian town of Oberammergau is a survival of the mystery play. The final step in the evolution of the play was to substitute lay actors for clerics and to present the play in the vernacular so that all could appreciate it.

MIRACLE PLAYS

Most early mystery plays had as their purpose religious instruction and edification. In the twelfth century they were joined by the miracle plays which portrayed miracles performed through the intervention of the Virgin Mary or some famous saint. Perhaps the most popular of the twelfth-century plays was the *Mystère d'Adam* (*The Mystery of Adam*) that depicted the familiar story of Eve's temptation by Satan and of how she caused Adam's fall. Very humanly the plot is unfolded. Satan suggests to Eve that Adam is inferior to her and that he does not appreciate her ability or beauty. In fact, old Satan waxes most eloquent at one point and declares to Eve: "You are fresher than the rose and whiter than crystal, or snow that falls on ice in the vale." Eventually, of course, such plays dealt with more secular themes and even introduced political subjects. The plots were effectively presented to the audience in a direct and simple style.

MUSIC

The development of medieval music is also associated with the liturgy of the church. Apparently through Byzantium, the western church had inherited some of the Greek techniques used in choral music. Drawing upon this, the church developed what is called the plain chant for its liturgy, and it was soon made official. This chant is better known as the Gregorian chant because Pope Gregory the Great was considered the founder of this musical form. This was probably not the case; he merely supported it as the official musical style for the choir. The plain chant used a limited number of scales, and the notes could have any duration, being governed by the length of the Latin words in the liturgy. There was no instrumental accompaniment, and all the choir sang the same notes in unison.

The next step was the composition of polyphonic music. This technique seems to have been known since the ninth century. New voice parts were added at intervals of four, five, or eight notes from the main melodic part. This may have been done to accommodate those men of the monastic and cathedral choirs with high and low voices. At any rate the effect was most pleasing and softened the monotony of the plain chant. It then became evident to composers that these paralleled parts could be unified and brought into harmony with each other. They experimented with combinations of notes and soon produced harmonious chords. Many harmonious chords produced a melodious polyphonic composition.

As compositions became more advanced, simple paralleled parts were altered. Additional or decorative notes were added to the different parts for the sake of variety. At this point arose the need for measured music. In other words, with notes of various lengths added, it was most difficult for the parts to keep the same pace or time and to end the melody simultaneously. In the thirteenth century, thanks to Latin translations of Arabic works on the measurement of music, measured bars of music began to appear on the scores, and various notes were devised, each representing a length of time. In this manner were created the full, half, quarter, eighth, and other notes. By the thirteenth century both the principles of harmony and the measurement of music had been mastered; from this music has come our modern music.

Meanwhile, for secular music all sorts of instruments inherited from the Greeks and Romans were in use. There were harps, lyres, cithers, and various types of pipes and horns. The guitar apparently came into southern Europe from the Arabs. It was different from the lyre and harp in that, instead of fingers, a bow was applied to its strings.

7. *Romanesque Architecture*

WHILE DISCUSSING FEUDALISM we pointed out that until the late tenth or eleventh centuries castles were crudely constructed wood and earthen forts. Then stone castles appeared, but not before the second half of the twelfth century did they become massive, with complicated features of construction requiring skilled craftsmen with advanced architectural knowledge. In church architecture—the dominant medieval form—the great surge in construction did not come until the eleventh century. The principles of classical architecture had disappeared with the rest of Graeco-Roman culture in most parts of Europe. Here and there, a few crude stone churches were erected in the period between the fourth and eleventh centuries, but most churches were of wood. There was not the money, knowledge, or incentive to achieve anything greater.

From the commercial and political contacts of Italy with Constantinople, parts of Italy were familiar with Byzantine architecture, which was occasionally applied to western churches. This is seen particularly at Venice, where many churches reflect strong Byzantine influence. The best example is St. Mark's, constructed in the eleventh century, which had as its model the church of the Holy Apostles at Constantinople. But even in Italy Byzantine architecture had no pronounced vogue; as West and East drifted apart politically and religiously, so, too, did they drift apart architecturally.

THE ROMAN BASILICA

In the eleventh century, when the economic revival enabled the church to plan grander sanctuaries, it looked for design to the Roman basilica, a structure that had ordinarily been a public building. The basilica was a long rectangular structure divided by columns into a large central nave and two or more side aisles. At one end was the entrance; at the other generally a small half-circled section called the apse where, on a raised platform, the presiding officer would stand when assemblies were held. All the walls and columns were of stone but the gabled roof was of wood because, over the nave, it rested upon numerous columns between which were windows or openings for light; these openings formed the clerestory. A heavier roof of stone could not be supported by the columns. When the early Christians began to build their churches they followed the basilican plan, making only a few modifications. They placed an altar on the platform of the apse, constructed the building so that the front always faced to the west, and added a north and south arm near the apse so that the building resembled a cross. This addition was called the transept.

The finest example of a Christian basilica was the church of Sant' Apollinare in Classe outside Ravenna, constructed in the sixth century by the Byzantine emperor Justinian and his wife Theodora. Instead of copying the popular domed churches of his eastern empire, Justinian decided to have the church constructed in the basilican pattern. The prominent structural feature of this and other such churches was the disappearance of the traditional Greek entablature, the sculptured section of wall above the columns. The arches now sprang up directly from the columns. Within the church the walls, arches, and vaults (arched ceilings), especially in the apse, were decorated by brilliantly colored Byzantine mosaics. Skillfully arranging small pieces of marble and colored glass, the artisans attained beautiful designs and depicted well-known Christian figures and events. The mosaics in the apse of Sant' Apollinare portrayed St. Apollinaris as well as Christ surrounded by the famous four beasts of the Apocalypse. In the other fine Ravenna basilica of San Vitale, an exquisitely designed mosaic shows Abraham preparing to sacrifice his son Isaac.

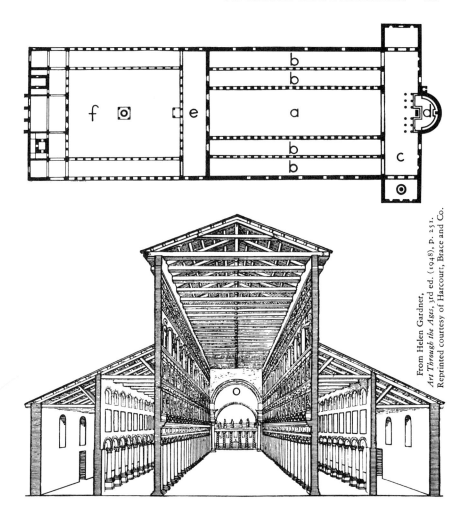

PLAN AND SECTION OF OLD ST. PETER'S AT ROME, A.D. 326
(Restored). *a*. nave; *b*. aisles; *c*. transverse aisle; *d*. apse; *e*. narthex; *f*. atrium.

THE ROMANESQUE STYLE

When the revival in building came in the eleventh century, the church copied these structures; the only feature that disappeared was the Byzantine mosaic. New features were added, however, as the architects experimented to replace the wooden roofs with stone. The conventional roof was too often the victim of fires that caused damage throughout the church. To raise a stone roof over the aisles and nave the architects resorted to principles employed by the Romans. From these experiments came what is called Romanesque architecture. One technique of raising a masonry roof was to use the barrel vault, whereby a half-cylindrical roof of masonry was placed upon the walls which supported an equalized weight. The other technique was to divide the roof area into squares or bays and throw over each bay two barrel vaults intersecting at right angles. This architectural principle, which was called the cross vault, concentrated the weight at the four corners formed by the semi-circular arches. It was relatively simple to provide for the outward-thrusting weight of the cross vault in the aisles, because on the interior they could be supported by the strong clerestory wall of the nave, and on the exterior by the outside wall which could be thickened or buttressed. Such supports were not possible over the nave, so there the architects had to be content with the massive barrel vault.

During the principal period of Romanesque construction, between 1000 and 1150, nearly all sanctuaries in western Europe had the same basic features. Because the walls had to support the tremendous weight of masonry barrel vaults and cross

ABBEY OF VÉZELAY. The Benedictine Abbey of Sainte-Marie-Madeleine was founded in 860 but its church dates only from the twelfth century. The Romanesque nave, broken into ten bays, was completed about 1140; the Gothic choir was finished in 1190.

vaults, they were thick, with few large windows. Inevitably, the nave was low and the interior gloomy with long walls of vast flat surfaces. To compensate for this dullness the walls and some of the vaults were covered by frescoes of religious scenes. But only when the sun is bright or there is artificial light do these frescoes show up to good advantage.

Limited as they were by such structural obstacles, the architects still managed to innovate in minor ways. At Sant' Ambrogio in Milan, which was rebuilt in the eleventh century, the nave was divided into five bays so that each equaled the area of two bays in the aisles. For variation, the architect managed to have three bays cross-vaulted, one barrel-vaulted, and the one over the altar capped with an octagonal tower with openings for light. In Germany few Romanesque churches had stone vaults; timbered roofs prevailed. On the exterior both German and Low Country churches had interesting features. Some had a western as well as an eastern apse with the entrances on the sides. The Germans also liked towers; on some sanctuaries, such as that of the monastery of Laach, there were three towers at the front and two at the rear. Another feature of some churches was a tower placed at the intersection of nave and transept to provide more light. The chief characteristics of Norman Romanesque architecture in the duchy of Normandy and in England are massiveness and fine proportions. The two most lovely structures in Normandy were constructed at Caen. They were the two abbeys—the Abbaye-aux-Hommes and the Abbaye-aux-Dames—founded by William the Conqueror and his wife. In addition to their massiveness, one is impressed by the facades. The naves end in gables, below which are the characteristic rounded Romanesque portals and windows. On each front corner is a massive tower. In England, Durham cathedral is the finest example of Romanesque architecture. Built on a commanding hill, its two western Norman towers give the effect of exceptional height.

In France notable features came to characterize Romanesque architecture. The churches were all placed and constructed so as to highlight the facade. Around the apse small half-circular chapels were added to form what is called the *chevet*. With architectural innovation this part of the church became one of its glories, often resembling the designs seen in large snowflakes. One of the first chevets of this type is found on the great Romanesque cathedral of Saint-Sernin at Toulouse. The church of Notre-Dame at Clermont-Ferrand is a classic example of French Romanesque design. On the outside the roof is gabled at the ends, while inside it is barrel-vaulted. Thick walls buttress the weight. Over the side aisles are quadrant vaults of heavy masonry to buttress the thrust of the nave's heavy barrel vault. By common agreement, however, the structure with the most beautiful Romanesque features is Saint-Trophime at Arles in southern France. Although some of the church dates back to the eighth century, most of it was constructed in the eleventh and twelfth centuries. Its two great glories are the inspiring facade and the peaceful cloister on the south side with its celebrated sculptured columns.

CATHEDRAL OF SAINT-SERNIN AT TOULOUSE (*above*). Saint-Sernin was begun in 1060 but most of it was constructed during the twelfth and thirteenth centuries. Note the semicircular ring of chapels which constitutes the ambulatory.

ABBAYE-AUX-HOMMES AT CAEN (*right*). The Abbaye-aux-Hommes was founded by William the Conqueror in 1064. The facade of the Romanesque church, completed about 1081, is one of the most imposing Norman works.

ABBEY CHURCH OF MARIA LAACH (*below*). The church of Maria Laach is an excellent example of German Romanesque architecture. Note the towers at both ends of the church and the lantern tower at the intersection of the nave and transept.

ROMANESQUE SCULPTURE

In many Romanesque churches, the dreariness of the interior was compensated for by exquisite sculptured decoration on the exterior. At the west portal of Saint-Trophime the sculptured stone told Christian stories to the rank and file who could not read or understand the Latin service. Above the portal, on the tympanum, is a sculptured story showing Christ flanked by the four beasts of the Apocalypse, a favored theme of Christian art. According to Revelation 4: 6–8, around the throne of God were four winged beasts with shapes like a man, a lion, a calf, and an eagle. The church taught that these beasts represented the four evangelists—Matthew, Mark, Luke, and John. They were pictured according to the manner in which they supposedly opened their Gospels. The church also taught that when Christ assumed human form the Incarnation was symbolized by the man, the Passion by the calf (the sacrificial animal), the Resurrection by the lion who had the power of restoring his cubs to life, and the Ascension by the eagle who could fly into the sun.

On either side of the portal just above the columns were numerous sculptured figures. On the far left, for example, was depicted a procession of those individuals

DANIEL IN THE LIONS' DEN. This twelfth-century Burgundian relief sculpture from the capital of a column, possibly from the abbey at Coulombs, indicates the narrative power of non-representational Romanesque art; the central figure of Daniel is given prominence by its size, while the fury of the lions, turned upon themselves, is graphically suggested by the curving patterns which they form.

elected to go to heaven. Between the columns were sculptured representations of famous saints. From left to right were St. Bartholomew, St. James the Minor, St. Trophime with two angels holding the bishop's mitre on his head, St. John the Baptist, St. Peter with the keys to heaven, St. Paul, St. Andrew, St. Stephen being stoned while two angels are taking his soul from the body and carrying it to heaven, St. James the Major, and St. Philip. Each time the faithful entered the sanctuary they passed by these Christian scenes and were reminded of the significance of the divine service within. All about the figures, on the tympanum and on the columns, were various carvings or markings, each being symbolic. A plain nimbus, for example, represented a saint, wavy lines represented water, and an angel looking down from a tower represented heaven. Most Romanesque churches had such sculptured facades and portals and passed on the beautiful custom to the Gothic churches.

8. *Gothic Architecture*

THE GREAT SHORTCOMING in Romanesque architecture was the inability to achieve height and light. The barrel vault was too heavy to be pushed toward the sky and to be supported by walls with enough openings for adequate light. These deficiencies were finally resolved when some architect or craftsman discovered that by pushing the buttresses outward from the walls—by making them fly through the air—a tremendous thrust could be supported. With the application of this structural principle Gothic architecture was born. In addition to the flying buttress two other structural devices were perfected in order to attain the majestic height of the Gothic cathedral. One was the rib and panel vault. The Romanesque architects had found cross-vaulting impossible to use for an elongated rectangular area; it was too difficult to make two barrel vaults intersect at the same height. But some architect experimented and discovered that, when arches are pointed, they can be raised to any desired height without affecting the width of their base. The other device which strengthened the vault was the addition of diagonal arches or ribs placed at the groins of the cross vault. Such ribs (comparable to steel girders) added strength to the vault and permitted the use of much lighter stone to fill in the spaces between the ribbed arches.

These architectural advances combined to make the Gothic cathedral quite different from its Romanesque predecessor. Basically a Gothic church consisted of a stone framework terminating in a series of pointed, groined vaults, all supported by flying buttresses. Thick walls were no longer required. Except for the masonry material and the flying buttresses the Gothic cathedral resembled a modern steel skyscraper filled in with glass. Light and height had been won. In design the

Gothic church resembled the Romanesque. There was the great nave flanked by side aisles. Facing the west was the facade, with its windows, sculptured portals, and towers. On the east was the apse, with the chevet which became more intricate and lacy in design. The transept remained, but it was pushed closer to the center of the cathedral. Within the sanctuary were three levels or horizontal sections between the floor and the top of the vaults. First there was the arcade, then the triforium, and finally the clerestory.

FRENCH GOTHIC

Most medieval cathedrals that date back to the twelfth and thirteenth centuries are not purely Gothic. Frequently Romanesque churches were modified by Gothic changes, and Gothic churches were modified by later medieval, Renaissance, and Baroque additions. In the Île de France, however, are found the purest and most

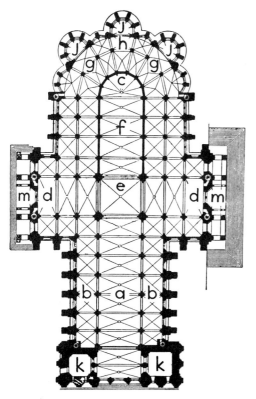

CHARTRES
CATHEDRAL

Plan of a Gothic Cathedral
  a. nave
  b. aisles
  c. apse
  d. transept
  e. crossing
  f. choir
  g. chevet
  h. ambulatory
  j. apsidal chapel
  k. tower
  m. porch

From Helen Gardner, *Art Through the Ages*, 3rd ed. (1948), p. 339.
Reprinted courtesy of Harcourt, Brace and Co.

glorious Gothic structures. Towns and bishops competed with each other to build the most magnificent and towering churches which, like the great town halls with their belfries, expressed civic and religious pride.

In each church structural and artistic experiments varied the architecture and made of each an individual creation with its peculiar characteristics. The best known are Notre-Dame at Paris, and the cathedrals at Reims, Amiens, Chartres, Beauvais, and Laon. Located on the Île de la Cité, Notre-Dame can be admired from any angle. As one wanders along both sides of the Seine, pauses at the book-stalls along the quai, or sits at a nearby sidewalk café, he can drink in the wonders of this lovely lady. Along the sides and out from the apse are the buttresses which appear to fly into infinity. There is the intricate and delicately designed chevet. High at the ends of the transepts and along the clerestory are the stained glass windows. At the front are the two gracefully proportioned towers and the great facade with the sculptured portal and great west window. These parts combine to form a harmonious, simple, and gracefully proportioned whole, an architectural achievement that stands up against the greatest of the Athenian buildings and yet epitomizes the fundamental difference between classical Greek civilization and that of the thirteenth century. Within this stone and glass marvel one is captured by the richness of light diffused by the stained glass windows, especially the great west window when the late afternoon sun streams through it. But perhaps the most remarkable effect is that of height, attained by the columns running along the nave. Each is a large circular shaft with four equally spaced small shafts attached. These small shafts make the columns (called *piers*) look slim and create the effect of the columns running unbroken from the floor to the vaults. It is true that Notre-Dame symbolizes the heart and soul of medieval France.

Almost as lovely is Chartres cathedral, with its harmonious proportions and its stained glass windows that surpass all others. The rose window in the facade is a work of genius, well deserving the eloquent praise bestowed upon it by Henry Adams in his book *Mont-Saint-Michel and Chartres.* The cathedral of Amiens is distinguished by the lovely sculpturing on its facade and by its balanced design. At Laon, perched high above the town, one sees a church with Romanesque columns but with perfect Gothic vaulting and flying buttresses. Reims, where the French kings were crowned, has a magnificent exterior dominated by the triple portal of the facade, the great sculptured figures just under the towers, and by the portal of the north transept. The interior shows to good advantage the groined vault, the clerestory with its stained glass windows, and the columns which pull the structure upward to heaven. Though never completed, Beauvais cathedral immediately conveys an impression of how tremendous it could have been. The nave is the highest in France—approximately 159 feet. Before the great spire collapsed it towered 500 feet.

CATHEDRAL OF NOTRE-DAME AT PARIS. In this view of Notre-Dame note how all the elements of the Gothic cathedral—the west facade and its towers, the nave, the south arm of the transept with its stained glass window, the crossing tower, the choir and the beautiful flying buttresses, and the chevet—contribute to the unity and harmony of the exterior design.

GERMAN AND ENGLISH GOTHIC

All over Europe Gothic architecture spread. It was least popular in Italy where a bright, warm climate did not make men long for light and airy structures, and in Spain where Arabic architecture wielded great influence over the style of Christian churches. Because in Germany the Romanesque style prevailed down to the fourteenth century, the Gothic structures subsequently constructed never equaled the excellence of the Romanesque. The cathedral of Cologne is very ornate. Strassburg cathedral is perhaps the finest example of German Gothic. Towering above all other buildings, it is one of the most impressive European cathedrals. The

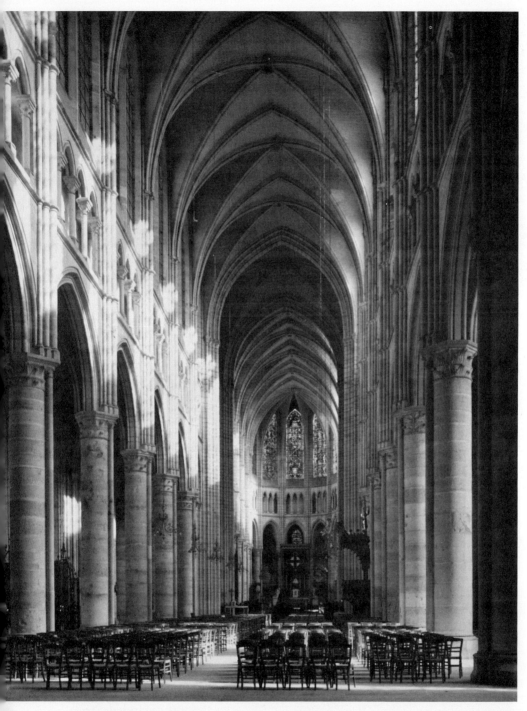

CATHEDRAL OF SOISSONS. The cathedral of Soissons designed by Bernard of Soissons was begun in the early thirteenth century. This view of the nave shows the pointed Gothic vaults and the vertical tripartite division into arcade, triforium, and clerestory.

CATHEDRAL OF AMIENS. This Gothic structure has one of the finest sculptured facades in France. Note the three sculptured portals and the tall figures across the front above the portals. Most of the facade was constructed between 1220 and 1236.

facade is dominated by three fine portals with sculpturing that fuses the traditions of the Île de France and the Rhineland. The long and clean nave is a marvel, with its high triforium pierced by seven great windows on each side. The great towers, though impressive, date from the fifteenth century. If the German Gothic structures never attained the beauty of the French, it must be remembered that they date mostly from the fourteenth century or later, when the Gothic style was becoming overornate and heavy throughout Europe.

In England the best of the Gothic churches are quite beautiful. Almost all have the pointed arch. Two of the purest Gothic structures are Lincoln cathedral and Westminster Abbey, the latter like the French cathedrals consisting of a skeleton of ribs, pillars, and buttresses, with large areas devoted to windows. Many English cathedrals were, however, modified Romanesque structures. Gothic clerestories and groined vaults were placed atop massive Romanesque walls that required no flying buttresses. An example of this is Salisbury cathedral. Most English cathedrals dating from the twelfth and thirteenth centuries also lack height because of their low vaults.

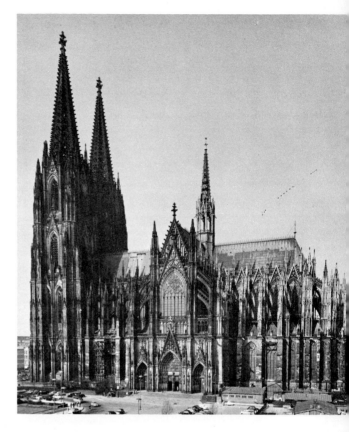

CATHEDRAL OF COLOGNE (*right*). This side view of the cathedral of Cologne suggests why it is sometimes considered pretentious. The choir was begun in 1248 and completed in 1322. This cathedral shows a strong high Gothic influence from France.

LINCOLN CATHEDRAL (*below*). Lincoln cathedral, begun in 1192, combines both Romanesque and Gothic features. The lower facade is Romanesque while the main complex of the building is early and high Gothic.

STAINED GLASS AND SCULPTURE

The decorative art that contributed most to the glory of the Gothic cathedral was the staining of glass, a process no modern artisan has been quite able to duplicate. Obtaining exquisitely brilliant colors in their glass, the medieval artisans composed their pictures of glass by placing small pieces of glass within outlines formed by the lead strips holding them in place. This work was done on large tables upon which the desired picture or design was sketched. For the large round rose windows in the facades, and for those in the ends of the transept, the glass was generally arranged in a geometric pattern formed by lead and stone so as to produce variegated colors within the church. The windows of the nave and aisles, which could be seen at close range, contained pictures telling stories of the Old and New Testaments and of the saints. At Chartres cathedral two of its finest windows portray the history of St. Eustace and the parable of the Good Samaritan, and the west rose window, contrary to the generalization above, tells the story of the Last Judgment rather than forming a geometric design of glass. Most Gothic cathedrals also had fine stone sculpturing, but with the large amount of space available for windows it was the stories in glass that primarily taught the common man much of his Christian knowledge.

As for Gothic sculpture, many of the Romanesque themes prevailed; over the portals of numerous churches there continued to be placed the four beasts of the Apocalypse or the Last Judgment. Saints and holy people were depicted and, down to the thirteenth century, the style was highly conventional and stiff; few of the figures looked human. In the twelfth-century facade of Chartres, however, one can observe a tendency to change. The figures are still stiff and monotonously alike, but some of their faces look human and have a marked individualism. During the thirteenth century sculpturing lost its stiffness and became natural and human; the various Christian figures portrayed began to resemble real men and women. This humanizing process may be studied with good results at the cathedral of Amiens which has one of the loveliest facades of all cathedrals. No one who has seen the Angel of the Annunciation or the portal of the Saviour with the Apostles can fail to admire the natural, human, and individualistic qualities of the various figures. On the porches of Chartres cathedral and all around the cathedral of Reims, artists obtained similar results. At Reims even the sculptured capitals of the pillars have naturalistic designs taken from the countryside. The artist was beginning to express his own feelings, tastes, and personality; he was also beginning to observe the world about him and to praise its beauty. Man's primary interest was shifting from heaven to this earth. When the artist was commissioned by princes, municipalities, and wealthy bourgeois to execute a building, a statue, or a picture, he bacame free to show even greater independence and flexibility in his choice of subject matter and his treatment of it.

symbolism

CATHEDRAL OF CHARTRES. Shown here is the tympanum of the Royal Portal completed in the twelfth century. The lower sculptured row represents the twelve apostles grouped three by three. At each end is a New Testament character. Above is Christ in the act of blessing, surrounded by the symbols of the four evangelists. In the archings above appear angels and the elders of the Apocalypse.

9. *Practical Learning and Craftsmanship*

INTO THE ELEVENTH CENTURY the skills of the artisan, as well as his tools and implements, were extremely primitive. Almost all the Greek and Roman technological advances had vanished; what survived were a few simple Roman tools such as the plow, sickle, rake, spade, hoe, and crude mallets, saws, and adzes. Lacking mathematical and engineering knowledge the early medieval builders could construct nothing but the humblest and crudest of buildings. Not until the West could read about and observe the highly skilled knowledge of the Arabs and Byzantines, and not until there was money to finance something more than a crude fort or small church was there any significant advance in architecture or the crafts.

SKILLS AND EQUIPMENT

Previously noted was the evolution in castle construction from wooden and earthen forts in the early Middle Ages to stone castles in the eleventh century and then to highly complicated fortifications during the twelfth and thirteenth centuries. To design these castles and to supervise their construction required skilled engineers or master craftsmen. These men were in effect architects who learned their skills through practical experience and observation. By the twelfth century there were many men who had a good knowledge of construction techniques, of draftsmanship, and of science. Some of them could read and write, and they composed manuals on the crafts and architecture for the edification of others. Under the direction of these masters worked skilled carpenters, masons, sculptors, glassmakers, metalworkers, and painters. The oft-repeated story that civil and religious ardor inspired all the people of a town to cooperate enthusiastically en masse to build a glorious cathedral is a myth. Devotion and pride did inspire men to give money which paid for the labor and material. However, the complicated cathedrals required architectural plans and professional craftsmen, as well as machines and devices such as cranes, molds, and scaffolding. Such skilled knowledge and building equipment were equally essential for the secular construction and engineering projects that characterized the twelfth and thirteenth centuries and busied every thriving town and port—beautiful *hôtels de ville,* cloth halls, guild houses, belfries, campaniles, vast walled fortifications, docks, canals, dredged harbors, and bridges.

Skills besides those of architecture and the building crafts showed equal progress. From its increased contact with the East, the West obtained knowledge of military fortification and siegecraft. All sorts of new weapons appeared, such as the improved battering ram, the accurate Italian crossbow, and the *trébuchet,* a device which hurled stones at considerable distances with great force. Metalworkers learned how to forge a tough steel that contributed to improved swords, spears, and armor. By the thirteenth century the armorer was capable of producing the complicated plate-armor suits of the knight. Much of his knowledge about steel must have came from the Arabs who had long been renowned for their Damascus blades of steel. Metalwork in the arts also progressed: pewterers, goldsmiths, silversmiths, and copperbeaters produced beautiful *objets d'art* for the church and for the nobles and rich bourgeois. The wood, stone, glass, pottery, and cloth crafts kept pace. The techniques employed, such as dyeing and weaving in the wool industry, were highly perfected.

 From its contact with the Byzantine Empire and the Arabs, the West especially benefited in agriculture, industry, and navigation. Irrigation was learned from the Arabs and was applied with great skill in southern France, Italy, and Spain. It seems certain that in the twelfth century the windmill came from the Arabs. The windmill and an improved water mill not only powered devices for milling and for the wool industry but also aided in the task of draining marshes and inundated land in northern Europe. The picturesque Dutch windmill dates from this period. By the twelfth century Europe knew about the magnetized needle and how, as a compass, it could guide ships across the seas. In the middle of the thirteenth century a military engineer, Pierre de Maricourt, wrote a remarkably detailed treatise on the compass, describing its various uses.

THE ARCHITECT VILLARD DE HONNECOURT

One of the finest records of medieval architecture, technology, and craftsmanship is the sketchbook of the thirteenth-century French engineer and architect, Villard de Honnecourt. In his book are complete designs of the leading French cathedrals, with detailed plans of their various parts such as the chevet, portals, and flying buttresses. We know that Villard traveled extensively about France to observe the cathedrals in construction and so to improve his knowledge of architecture. While he watched, he sketched. In his book are plans of the towers of the cathedral of Laon, the chevet of Reims cathedral, and the rose window at Chartres; there are designs of windows and drawings of pillars, portals, and sculptured figures. Of Villard's competence there is abundant evidence. He designed the cathedral of Cambrai and was hired by the queen of Hungary to design and direct the construction of various churches. He had a good command of geometry, surveying, and science, and his figures are drawn in geometrical proportions. He describes the process of determining the height of a tower, the distance across a pond, or the center of an area. His instructions on how to vault a roof and to construct the other complicated sections of a cathedral omit no step or detail. He was completely familiar with machines and devices to facilitate construction. He knew how to arrange scaffolding to the best effect. He described and sketched such machines as a hoisting machine operated by screws, a sawmill, and a machine for cutting piles under water.

The sketchbook of Villard de Honnecourt is an admirable description and reliable indication of the advanced state of architecture, technology, mathematics, science, draftsmanship, surveying, and craftsmanship in the later thirteenth century. We may be certain that he did not stand alone, that there were hundreds of men who possessed the same knowledge. His sketches and accompanying comments are undeniable proof of the dynamic character of medieval life in the eleventh, twelfth, and thirteenth centuries. In whatever field of culture or learning one delves he finds great and accomplished artists and thinkers. These were the centuries of the medieval university, of Gerbert, Peter Lombard, Abelard, Albertus Magnus, Thomas Aquinas, Grosseteste, Roger Bacon, and those wandering scholars—the clerks and Goliardi—who produced the admirable Latin and vernacular literature. How foolish it is to call the Middle Ages the "Dark Ages," to speak of the deadly medieval conformity, or to synthesize in terms of the "medieval mind." What we have studied in this chapter is a phenomenally rich cultural advance and diversity that catapulted medieval Europe ahead of the Graeco-Roman world.

Further Reading

The principal study of the medieval intellectual revival is by *C. H. Haskins, *The Renaissance of the Twelfth Century* (Cambridge, Mass., 1927). More recent studies are those of *C. Brooke, *The Twelfth Century Renaissance* (New York, 1970); and *R. W. Southern, *Medieval Humanism and Other Studies* (New York, 1970). For the opinions of historians on the nature of the twelfth century see *C. W. Hollister, *The Twelfth Century Renaissance* (New York, 1969). For theological and philosophical problems as well as the development of scholastic thought there are some excellent studies, of which the following are the most valuable: E. H. Gilson, *Reason and Revelation in the Middle Ages* (New York, 1938) and *The Spirit of Medieval Philosophy* (New York, 1936); *F. C. Copleston, *A History of Medieval Philosophy* (New York and London, 1972); *G. Leff, *Medieval Thought* (Harmondsworth, 1958); and *D. Knowles, *The Evolution of Medieval Thought* (London, 1962). The celebrated story of Abelard and Héloïse is best told by E. Gilson in his *Héloïse and Abelard* (Chicago, 1951). H. Waddell has written a charming novel, *Peter Abelard* (New York, 1933). The story of the love affair between Abelard and Héloïse can be read directly from their *Letters*, trans. by C. K. Scott-Moncrieff (New York, 1926). Selections from medieval philosophers have been translated in R. McKeon, *Selections from Medieval Philosophers* (New York, 1923–1930), Vols. I–II.

There is a delightful account of medieval universities by C. H. Haskins entitled *The Rise of the Universities* (New York, 1923). Haskins also gives a good insight into university life in his *Studies in Mediaeval Culture* (Oxford, 1929). A more specialized study is that of *G. Leff, *Paris and Oxford Universities in the Thirteenth and Fourteenth Centuries: An Institutional and Intellectual History* (New York, 1968). Translations of sources on medieval universities are found in L. Thorndike, *University Records and*

Life in the Middle Ages (New York, 1944); and *H. Wieruszowski, *The Medieval University* (Princeton, 1966). The most stimulating synthesis of medieval intellectual history is still H. O. Taylor's *The Mediaeval Mind,* 4th ed. (London, 1925), Vols. I–II. Medieval science is covered by *A. C. Crombie, *Medieval and Early Modern Science,* 2nd rev. ed. (New York, 1959), Vol. I; and *E. Grant, *Physical Science in the Middle Ages* (New York, 1971). A brief sketch of Roman law in the Middle Ages is that of P. Vinogradoff, *Roman Law in Medieval Europe,* 2nd ed. (Oxford, 1929).

For a sensitive appreciation of Latin poetry see H. J. Waddell's *Mediaeval Latin Lyrics,* 5th ed. (London, 1948). Equally good for the Goliardic and vernacular poetry is her book *The Wandering Scholars,* 7th ed. (London, 1949). The most comprehensive survey of Latin literature is by *E. R. Curtius, *European Literature and the Latin Middle Ages* (New York, 1953). The medieval romances are available in a number of translations, including several volumes in the *EVERYMAN LIBRARY and *THE PENGUIN CLASSICS. Of the studies devoted to Dante the most valuable is by K. Vossler, *Medieval Culture: An Introduction to Dante and His Times* (New York, 1929), Vols. I–II. On literature in Germany see P. Salmon, *Literature in Medieval Germany* (New York, 1967). The clearest explanation of medieval music is that by G. Reese, *Music in the Middle Ages* (New York, 1940).

A sample and concise description of medieval architecture is found in *N. Pevsner's *An Outline of European Architecture* (Harmondsworth, 1953). Also useful is H. Gardner, *Art through the Ages,* 3rd ed. (New York, 1948). Although occasionally inaccurate, the book which best expresses the spirit of medieval architecture is by *H. Adams, *Mont-Saint-Michel and Chartres* (Boston, 1933). Other excellent interpretations of medieval architecture are by *O. G. von Simson, *The Gothic Cathedral: The Origins of Gothic Architecture and the Medieval Concept of Order* (London, 1956); and *E. Panofsky, *Gothic Architecture and Scholasticism* (New York, 1957). Three books dealing with the construction of medieval cathedrals are by J. F. Fitchen, *The Construction of Gothic Cathedrals* (New York, 1961); *J. Gimpel, *The Cathedral Builders* (New York, 1961); and J. Harvey, *The Medieval Architect* (New York, 1972). Books on art and sculpture are by *E. Mâle, *Religious Art in France* (London, 1913); *C. R. Morey, *Medieval Art* (New York, 1942); and J. Evans, *Art in Medieval France* (London, 1948). Translations of the writings of medieval artists and architects are in *E. G. Holt's *A Documentary History of Art,* Vol. I (New York, 1957). The *Album* of Villard de Honnecourt has been edited with the inclusion of fine illustrations by R. H. Hahnloser (Vienna, 1935). Excellent photographs of medieval buildings are found in the volumes of THE PELICAN HISTORY OF ART.

CHAPTER 8

Medieval Politics
and
Institutions

Until the eleventh and twelfth centuries the dominant theme of European political history was the struggle of rulers to make themselves and the central governments powerful enough to enforce authority over men living in land under their rule. We have seen how, given the proper ingredients, some rulers succeeded in forging strong states. By using the feudal system such princes as the kings of France and England, the counts of Flanders and Anjou, and the dukes of Normandy built strong governments that were respected locally and that endured. These and similar states were small enough for the rulers to enforce their authority personally. All benefited early from the revival of a money economy. Political stability and security were hammered out, efficient political institutions were developed, towns arose, trade and commerce flourished, the population increased, and the princes obtained a growing income from their prosperous lands. These achievements mark the first stage in the political recovery of Europe.

Our task now is to trace the political history of the principal European states during the twelfth and thirteenth centuries. This history is dominated by the incorporation of small states into a few powerful ones that continually expanded until finally there emerged the strong nation state, the typical political form in modern European and world history. As these states were evolving in the later Middle

313

Ages, there developed in them many of the political institutions upon which modern governments are modeled.

1. England

WHEN HENRY I DIED in 1135 he was succeeded by his daughter Matilda. A woman and of imperious bearing, she was unpopular and never won the support of many feudal lords. Instead most of the lords recognized as king Stephen of Blois, the son of William the Conqueror's daughter. There then followed twenty years of bitter civil war that undid much of what Henry I had accomplished. England was not to witness such internal anarchy again until the fifteenth century. Although more successful in his bid for the throne than Matilda, Stephen tired of the struggle after his son and heir died. He therefore concluded an agreement with Matilda's son Henry whereby he would reign until his death and then Henry would succeed him. In 1154, within a few months after his compact, Stephen died and Henry mounted the throne.

HENRY II

Henry II (1154–1189) was England's greatest medieval king; as a monument to his achievements stand some of England's foremost institutions. Blessed with luck in practically all his endeavors, Henry brought to them a powerful physique, tremendous energy, raging temper, and superior mind. Restless, he transformed all that he touched. Tremendously ambitious, he combined work with his favorite pastime of hunting and even jotted down orders and memoranda while listening to the mass. Such a man was the founder of the Angevin dynasty who, before becoming king, was already an important continental prince. He had inherited Anjou from Geoffrey, his father, and Normandy from Matilda, his mother; he then acquired the great duchy of Aquitaine in southewestern France through a lucky marriage to Eleanor, its heiress. Eleanor had been the wife of Louis VII of France but the two were incompatible. The simple Louis had prevailed upon the Pope to absolve him from the marriage and by this foolish move both lost a territory much larger than the royal domain and made it possible for Henry to surround him with Angevin possessions. With his subsequent acquisition of more continental land and the struggle to hold it against the French kings, Henry had to devote most of his energies to affairs across the Channel. In effect until the reign of John the English kings were primarily continental princes.

THE NORMAN AND ANGEVIN KINGS

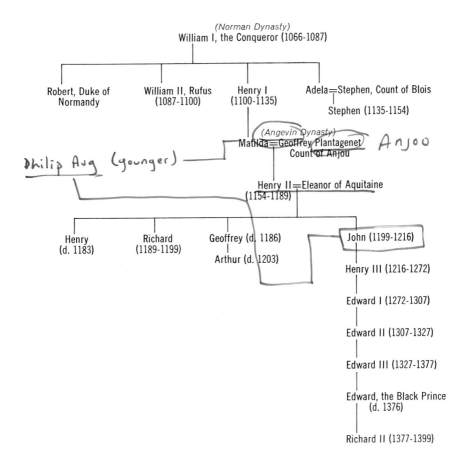

Although a warrior of ability, Henry preferred to win his ojectives through diplomacy. Within a few months of his accession he had reduced all the castles of the hostile barons and restored order to the kingdom. Through a show of force and skillful negotiation, he brought peace to the Welsh border and forced the Scottish king to acknowledge his lordship. In Ireland Henry interfered with a group of adventurous barons who had reduced the area around Dublin, and he forced both barons and Irish to acknowledge him as lord. On the Continent he was equally successful. By marrying his third eldest son, Geoffrey, to the heiress of Brittany he rounded out the Angevin empire in the north. In the south he forced the counts of Auvergne and Toulouse to render homage to him. By the marriage of one of his

daughters to the Guelf duke of Saxony, another to the king of Castile, and a third
to the king of Sicily, Henry spread his political net throughout Europe. By 1180
he was the most powerful ruler of western Europe.

The last years of Henry's life were clouded by the conspiracies of his sons with
the new king of France, Philip Augustus. Philip, whose goal was to destroy the
Angevin empire, cleverly fomented trouble between Henry and his sons who,
driven by greed, would stoop to any stratagem to secure power. Henry's one
weakness was in not realizing the pettiness and disloyalty of his sons. The eldest,
the Young Henry, was in constant revolt against his father until 1183 when death
put an end to his trouble-making. The next eldest son Richard, an easy victim
of the promises and lies of Philip Augustus, was a constant worry. Henry's favorite and youngest son John was the worst of the lot despite the rich lands lavished
upon him. Until 1188 Henry was able to hold Philip Augustus within the Île de
France and to smother the conspiracies of his sons. Then, becoming tired and old,
he was no longer a match for the combination of his sons and Philip. Defeated
in the field, he took to his bed and died in 1189; he had suffered his first real
setback. Just before his death he was forced to cede lands to Philip and to grant
Richard extensive authority in the Angevin lands. As he lay dying Henry gasped
out: "The four eaglets are my four sons who cease not to persecute me even unto
death. The youngest of them, whom I now embrace with so much affection, will
sometime in the end insult me more grievously and more dangerously than any of
the others." He was right; just before he died information was received that John's
name headed the list of the conspirators.

RICHARD I AND JOHN

As a warrior and leader who inspired devotion and loyalty, Henry's successor
Richard I (1189–1199) excelled; as an administrator and statesman he was a miserable failure. Interested only in war, chivalrous adventure, and hunting, Richard
gave little time to his English realm. During his reign of ten years he spent six
months in England; he regarded the island merely as a bank to finance his crusade
and his campaigns against Philip Augustus who conspired with John to undermine
his power in France. During Richard's absence able administrators governed the
kingdom. In 1189 he was in England for four months, to be crowned and to raise
money for the crusade. He did not return again until 1184 and then he remained
for two months in an effort to press more money out of his subjects for war against
Philip Augustus in Normandy. Until his death in 1199 Richard campaigned on the
Continent against his wily opponent. The complete master on the battlefield, he
was killed characteristically while besieging the castle of a vassal who, so it was
rumored, had discovered a rich treasure on his lands.

SCOTLAND

North Sea

IRELAND

Irish Sea

York

Lincoln   Humber

The Wash

Trent R.

ENGLAND

WALES

Ouse R.

Severn R.

London

Thames R.

Bristol   Canterbury

English Channel

Atlantic Ocean

48°

Rhine R.

FLANDERS

Meuse R.

THE EMPIRE

Rouen

CHAMPAGNE

Caen

Seine R.

NORMANDY

Paris

BLOIS   ROYAL
DOMAIN

MAINE

Le Mans

BRITTANY

BURGUNDY

ANJOU

Angers

Seine R.

Loire R.   Tours

Poitiers   TOURAINE

AQUITAINE

Angoulême   Limoges
Périgueux

0   50   100   150

MILES

Bay of Biscay   Dordogne R.

Bordeaux

Garonne R.

GASCONY   TOULOUSE

Rhône R.

NAVARRE   PYRENEES

Mediterranean Sea

2°

BALEARIC IS.

THE ANGEVIN EMPIRE

Lands ruled by Henry II

Land inherited from his father

- - - - Land acquired through
Eleanor of Aquitaine

French Royal Domain

The French Monarchy

Although married, Richard died without heirs. According to the custom of primogeniture the throne should have gone to the boy Arthur of Brittany, the son of Henry II's third son Geoffrey. But Arthur, a mere lad, could command no support from the English barons and officials who preferred a mature man. They joined Eleanor of Aquitaine in backing John who was immediately crowned. Philip Augustus, quite in character, supported Arthur and backed his claims to Angevin possessions on the Continent. John (1199–1216), though the most unsuccessful and degenerate of the Angevin kings, was not the least able. He thoroughly loved administration and devoted much time to it. He was responsible for numerous efficient reforms. His trouble was that he made the central government too efficient and oppressive. Although on occasion he could fight and demonstrate amazing bursts of energy, he was inconsistent and lazy. He too often failed to complete what he had begun and frittered away his time. Totally lacking in honor, he stooped to any deed or stratagem to secure money and power. Distrustful and fearful by nature, he was in turn distrusted by most. Ultimately he suffered disaster because he was a failure at war; to be successful a medieval king had to be an accomplished warrior who could win battles. This John did only once.

John secured recognition by Philip Augustus through certain territorial concessions and by doing homage for his continental fiefs and then spoiled it all by a foolish act that resulted in a disastrous war; he eloped with a pretty Poitevin girl who had been betrothed to one of his vassals. Immediately the enraged vassal appealed for justice to John's overlord Philip Augustus. John ignored Philip's summons to answer for his act, with the result that his fiefs were declared forfeited and were occupied by Philip. In a series of disastrous continental campaigns, John captured Arthur and had him murdered, but he lost all northern France. When war ended in 1205, Philip Augustus had gobbled up all the Angevin Empire except Aquitaine. Henceforth, the English kings devoted their energies to ruling England. English barons who held fiefs on both sides of the Channel had to forfeit their French possessions and became exclusively English in outlook. Separated politically from the Continent, England was launched on a separate course that helps to explain the peculiar development of its institutions.

Between 1205 and 1213 John was locked in conflict with Pope Innocent III. In 1205, when the archbishop of Canterbury died, the cathedral clergy secretly elected a man of their own choice rather than giving John the opportunity to influence the election. Infuriated, John tried to force his candidate on the clergy. The dispute was finally taken to Innocent III who refused recognition to both candidates and prevailed upon the clergy to accept the able Stephen Langton. John refused to accept Stephen and in revenge seized church land and incomes and drove out of office all bishops except one who was a favorite. Innocent replied by excommunicating John and putting England under interdict. For eight years, however, John successfully resisted the most powerful medieval Pope.

He had the support of a large number of barons simply because, with the revenue from the church, he did not have to tax his subjects. But suddenly in 1213 John had to make his peace with Innocent. Philip Augustus had readied an army to invade England and, to forestall this move, John offered major concessions to the church. He agreed to accept Stephen Langton, restore all lands to the church, make suitable indemnity, take England in fief from Innocent, and pay him a yearly tribute. Innocent now became John's protector and forbade Philip Augustus to proceed with the attack.

John had cleverly saved himself from Philip but shortly had to face even greater humiliation. Bent on reconquering his lost possessions, he levied heavy taxes on the feudal aristocracy and church and hired a large mercenary army to invade France. The barons balked under oppressive taxation and at the demand that they fight overseas. From 1213 on they were in a state of incipient revolt and John could not rely on them. Nevertheless, in 1214 he went to Poitou with the intention of attacking Philip Augustus from the southwest while his mercenary army, in conjunction with allied Low Country princes and the German emperor Otto IV, attacked in the northeast from Flanders. Due to his own military incapacity and to treachery in his forces, John retreated pell-mell. Meanwhile, in July 1214, Philip Augustus decisively defeated the allied forces at Bouvines in Flanders. This battle made France paramount in Europe, reduced Otto IV of Germany to impotence, and sent John home discredited to face a seething baronage.

The day of reckoning for John had finally arrived. Beyond a few loyal barons and mercenaries he had no support. Stephen Langton led the English clergy in a demand for reasonable and moderate reform. Using the old coronation charter of Henry I as a basis for reform, the barons and clergy hammered out a long list of proposals which they forced John to accept. In June 1215 at Runnymede, a few miles up the Thames River from London, John put his great seal to the famous Magna Carta, which has incorrectly been considered an early landmark in the struggle to obtain constitutional government. In 1215 Magna Carta was no such landmark. It was almost exclusively a feudal document which guaranteed that feudal custom and the time-honored rights of the feudal aristocracy would be respected; this class was practically the sole beneficiary of the charter. It was only much later, in the seventeenth century, that politicians and scholars transformed Magna Carta into a document of constitutionalism. Since then it has been wrongly interpreted as guaranteeing trial by jury, due process of law, no taxation without representation, and as extending constitutional rights and protection to all Englishmen. The one great principle that Magna Carta did proclaim in 1215 was that "the king is and shall be below the law."

Neither side intended to abide by the feudal agreement, and each resorted to arms. Civil war was waged on even terms down to October 1216, when John, overindulging in food and drink, died of dysentery and indigestion. With John re-

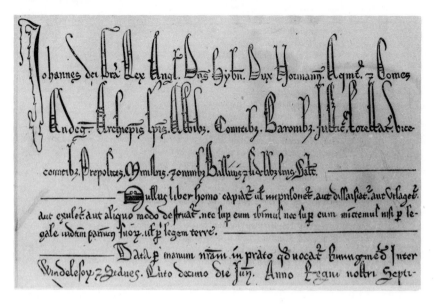

MAGNA CARTA. Reproduced here are a few lines of the copy of Magna Carta preserved in the British Museum. Lines four through six comprise the famous thirty-ninth clause which was concerned with due process of law. The Latin reads as follows: *Nullus liber homo capiatur, vel imprisonetur, aut dissaisiatur, aut utlagetur, aut exuletur, aut aliquo modo destruatur, nec super eum ibimus, nec super eum mittemus, nisi per legale iudicium parium suorum vel per legem terre.*

moved, the fire of baronial resistance faltered and within a year died out. John's nine-year-old heir, Henry III, received general recognition by the realm.

Although John appeared to have dissipated the magnificent achievements of Henry II, actually England lost only what would eventually have been lost even under a line of exceptionally able kings. In the Middle Ages it was physically and economically impossible to maintain an overseas empire and, in any event, the English could not have smothered for long the growing antipathy of the French to foreign domination. In the end it was better that most of the continental possessions were lost, for now the kings could govern as English sovereigns. Of greater value than their political and military exploits were the institutions erected by Henry II and his sons.

ANGEVIN GOVERNMENT

Under the Angevins royal power attained its zenith. Until John's fiasco, the kings were, in fact if not in theory, autocrats. Although they did not consistently flout baronial opinion, rarely did they take counsel and secure consent from the great feudal council of barons. Surprisingly little of what may be called legislation was promulgated with baronial consent; the kings preferred to govern with the assistance of the small court composed of state officials and loyal and intimate servants of the household. A great problem of English medieval history was to discover a means for controlling the king and rendering him responsible to the community of the realm. Only later when the royal subjects came to control the royal purse strings could they hope to limit the king's power.

The most important institutional developments occurred in the central government. By the reign of John, the *chancery* (secretarial office) had practically become a separate department with a staff and routine of its own. Its personnel were responsible for issuing most of the royal documents and authenticating them with the great seal. New types of records were devised, and an excellent system of record keeping was organized. In the realm of finance, the greedy Angevins were at their best. Henry II rehabilitated the exchequer and made it the most efficient treasury of western Europe. One of its treasurers, Richard-fitz-Neal, wrote a remarkably clear and detailed treatise—*The Dialogue of the Exchequer*—describing all the operations of this department, which had developed an effective and rational system of financial accountability and record keeping. While the traditional feudal revenues remained a major source of income, the Angevins looked to extraordinary taxation to meet their growing needs. They levied increased and more frequent *scutages* (payments of money in lieu of knight service). With the royal domain and towns they periodically negotiated for taxes called *tallages*. Both Richard and John assessed a new land tax called the *carucage* (levied on the *carucate,* the name for plowland), and all three kings experimented with a new tax on movable property consisting of a certain percentage of a man's yearly wealth. This tax subsequently became the accepted form of parliamentary taxation.

Of significance for the Anglo-American world, however, were the amazing legal innovations. We are especially indebted to Henry II for some of the most cherished and practical features of the common law system. Interested almost as much in law as in money, he devoted long hours to legal innovation. His principal goal, like that of his predecessors, was to make royal law and its procedure common to all England and snuff out feudal and local custom. To accomplish this he had first to make royal law more efficient, rapid, rational, and equitable; if it was to win over its rivals it must be a better product. Henry regularized the institution of the itinerant justices and sent them out annually on judicial circuits of the counties to hear cases triable only in royal courts. Constantly Henry and his sons reserved more and more criminal and civil cases for royal justice until there were few left for other courts. So popular had the itinerant justices become that Magna Carta insisted upon their making four judicial circuits a year. More than any other institution they spread royal law throughout the realm.

To provide for a more rational and just method for the trial of civil disputes involving the possession of land, Henry provided that they should be decided by a jury of good and lawful men empaneled from the neighborhood, a jury in other words that knew the facts about the land in dispute. The jury would declare under oath which party had the better right of possession and upon its answer depended the decision of the court. To secure this form of trial, however, one had to purchase a *writ* (royal order) directing such legal procedure. Rapidly there developed scores of judicial writs obtainable for a fee at the chancery; eventually a freeman could buy a writ applicable to any type of case. To mitigate the injustice suffered by many men when trial was by combat, Henry introduced the *grand assize*. Under this judicial procedure any freeman challenged by another to settle right to land by combat could purchase a writ ordering the question of right to be decided by a jury in a royal court. This was a great boon, because it kept unscrupulous bullies from accruing lands from lawful holders less skilled in combat.

For criminal justice, trial by jury did not begin until the reign of Henry III. Accused criminals were still tried by ordeal. Henry II introduced some radical changes, however, in this method. To bring criminals to justice he ordained that all men suspected of crime should be presented to the itinerant justices for trial by ordeal. To do this, local juries of twelve men were cmpaneled and asked under oath to name those suspected of crime. This was the origin of the *grand* (big) *jury* which brings *indictments* or *presentments* preliminary to criminal trials. After the trial by ordeal, the appropriate decision was handed down. But Henry distrusted this irrational mode of proof, and he ordered that all men of infamous repute, though cleared by ordeal, must leave the realm and forfeit all their possessions.

In dealing with the misdemeanors of the clergy Henry was less successful. Since the separation of state and church courts in the eleventh century, it had been customary to extend benefit of clergy—trial in a church court—to any clerk who could read a few lines of the Scriptures. Trial in a church court was much sought after because, even if found guilty, the clerk received a light punishment compared to what he could expect in a secular court. Canon law prohibited any sentence involving bloodshed, and therefore about the most severe punishment that could be meted out was imprisonment. Too frequently, as Henry knew, the church permitted criminous clerks to go free; such laxity contributed to much crime by clergy who were untroubled by the consequences. Henry's solution was that clergy be tried in church courts but, if found guilty, handed over to the secular arm of justice for punishment. In this Henry was strongly opposed by Thomas Becket, archbishop of Canterbury. The two contested this issue so bitterly that one day some of Henry's knights decided to relieve their royal master of this ecclesiastical pest and murdered him before the altar of Canterbury cathedral. This brutal deed outraged western Christendom and forced Henry to do penance and to drop his proposal. As a result, criminous clerks in England held on to their privileges throughout the Middle Ages.

In FR, Too

In general the most important cases were reserved for the king's own court—the *curia regis*. This court had so many functions, however, that it could not handle the cases which piled up. Also too frequently the king was on the move or out of the realm, and it was virtually impossible to get a case before the court. For some time cases of a financial nature affecting the royal revenue had been settled in the *exchequer court*. Henry now delegated more judicial powers. Members of his small council were designated members of a court to hear cases in the royal absence. In 1178 he instituted a permanent royal court at Westminster consisting of five judges who were to hear cases throughout the year. In this manner began the *court of common pleas* which adjudicated cases between private individuals. Cases that concerned the king continued to be tried in his *curia regis* or before a part of it empowered to try them. Eventually a separate court arose to handle these cases; this was the *king's bench*. By the thirteenth century there were four royal courts in which the royal—or common—law was practiced: the courts of the itinerant justices, the exchequer court, the court of common pleas, and the king's bench. Above all, however, was the *curia regis* which had the highest reserve of justice.

On the local level of administration the Angevin kings tightened their control. Henry II removed all the old sheriffs and replaced them with men of humble origin who loyally served the crown. Through the itinerant justices the king kept close check on local government. By using local juries for judicial and administrative purposes he established close rapport with the populace. During Richard's reign the office of *coroner* was created, to investigate and keep a record of accidents and violent deaths in the counties. By placing increasing reliance upon the local knights and squires the English kings were giving them valuable experience in government and were preparing them for the day when they would sit in a national parliament. By command the kings were forcing self-government upon their subjects.

ENGLAND IN THE THIRTEENTH CENTURY

It was a pity that after the bitterness of John's reign England did not receive a competent ruler. Instead it got Henry III (1216–1272), who failed in everything he touched. Quite like Edward the Confessor, Henry was totally unequipped for kingship. He was weak, vacillating, distrustful, spendthrift, unrealistic, unmilitary, and full of favoritism. Because the Pope had been his protector while he was a youth, Henry regarded the Papacy as his benefactor and became supinely subservient to its financial and political demands. Henry's sole virtues and accomplishments were an appreciation of the *beaux arts,* the reconstruction of Westminster Abbey, and fidelity to his wife. In foreign and domestic politics he was a failure. In a series of disastrous campaigns he failed to reconquer French territory and settled for a treaty in 1259 wherein he renounced claim to all lands lost by John in return for French recognition of English rule in Gascony.

During the 1250's when the Popes were trying to break German political power in Sicily and southern Italy, Henry cheerfully agreed to lend one of his sons as a candidate for the kingship of this territory and to pay the costs of the military campaigns necessary to destroy the Hohenstaufen power. This foolish promise, on top of his lavish support of foreign relatives and favorites, caused the barons to force reform upon him. In 1258 they set up a baronial council to help him govern and to serve as a control over him. But this solution was no happier than Magna Carta. After a few years during which both sides jockeyed for power, civil war broke out in 1264. Led by Simon de Montfort the barons won the first round and forced Henry to accept conciliar control. In 1265, to gain wide support and necessary taxes, de Montfort summoned *Parliament,* an assembly which included not only the barons and great prelates but also representatives from the counties and boroughs. Although de Montfort and his associates had no idea that they were creating Parliament, this assembly is significant because it became the model for subsequent Parliaments. In 1265 de Montfort was slain in battle and Henry resumed his customary authority wielded *de facto* by his son and heir Edward.

Edward I (1272–1307) was the last great English medieval king. An accomplished general, consummate politician, skilled administrator, and ambitious individual, he restored the prestige of the crown, made England's name respected once more in western Europe, and inaugurated far-reaching legal and institutional innovations. His achievements were least successful on the Continent. Pitted against the shrewd French king Philip IV, Edward barely retained Gascony. None of his campaigns launched against France from Flanders or from Gascony met with success. This he was to gain at home. Intent on reducing Wales, he began a series of campaigns that resulted in the conquest of Wales by 1284. It was incorporated into the English scheme of administration, and numerous colonists introduced English customs and culture. To the north in Scotland a disputed succession in 1290 afforded Edward an opportunity to intervene. Invited to study the claims of the leading contenders and to make a decision, he selected the candidate most likely to be subservient. Edward then made so many demands upon the new king and interfered so much in Scottish affairs that the Scots rebelled and repudiated Edward's claim to overlordship. Swiftly he marched into Scotland and reduced it. But the Scots were difficult to subdue, and he had to campaign against them again in 1298. This time skillfully employing the English longbow, he mowed down the Scots and won the great victory of Falkirk. Still the Scots were not prostrate. In 1307, while moving north to suppress revolt, Edward died.

He bequeathed to his son Edward II (1307–1327) a strengthened crown and a well-governed realm. On the other hand, he left behind a land almost bankrupt from supporting costly French, Welsh, and Scottish wars, and the imminent problem of the stubborn Scots who took advantage of the succession to throw off English rule and to invade the northern counties. Edward II, a complete failure as man and king, floundered as badly as Henry III. His principal accomplishments were wrestling with young favorites, playing with his pet lion, and drinking prodigious amounts of ale. Surrounding himself with useless sycophants he alienated the baronage, and he completely lost face when overwhelmed by the Scots at the Battle of Bannockburn in 1314. For the next three centuries the Scots remained independent. The barons, whose capacity for governing was no better than Edward's, forced conciliar control over him and attempted reforms similar to those forced upon Henry III. Edward and the barons muddled through to 1327, when a revolt led by his wife and her lover toppled him from the throne and replaced him with his young son Edward III.

COMMON LAW AND PARLIAMENT

As in the twelfth century, the significant events between 1216 and 1327 were of a legal and institutional character. During the reigns of Henry III and Edward I the common law system grew rapidly. Many new writs were devised to bring all manner of cases within the jurisdiction of the royal—*common law*—courts, which had a monopoly over justice by the end of Edward's reign. Feudal, borough, and local public courts were relegated to handling only very minor justice. To adjust the laws governing tenure of land in an age sloughing off feudal custom, Edward I enacted a series of great statutes that regulated such matters as the bequeathing, inheritance, and ownership of land. Some of the legal principles established by these statutes lie behind our modern property laws.

The thirteenth century also witnessed an expanded use of the jury. Already well entrenched as the most popular form of trial in civil cases, it was applied to criminal cases during Henry III's reign, a step necessitated by the action of the Fourth Lateran Council in 1215 which prohibited the clergy from participation in any trial involving bloodshed. This action ruled out trial by ordeal and forced Henry and his justices to substitute another type of trial. Early in his reign, therefore, Henry III ordered that criminal cases be tried by juries of twelve men. But because the criminal (*petty*) jury in its early stages was ordinarily composed of men from the grand jury or of men familiar with the background of the cases—individuals not at all impartial—jury trial for criminal cases was seldom used. It did not become popular until the middle of the fourteenth century, when royal statute forbade men of the grand jury to be empaneled for the petty jury. Throughout the Middle Ages, however, many men had to be forced to accept trial by jury, and some died in prison rather than accept it.

The most significant development of the thirteenth century was the rise of

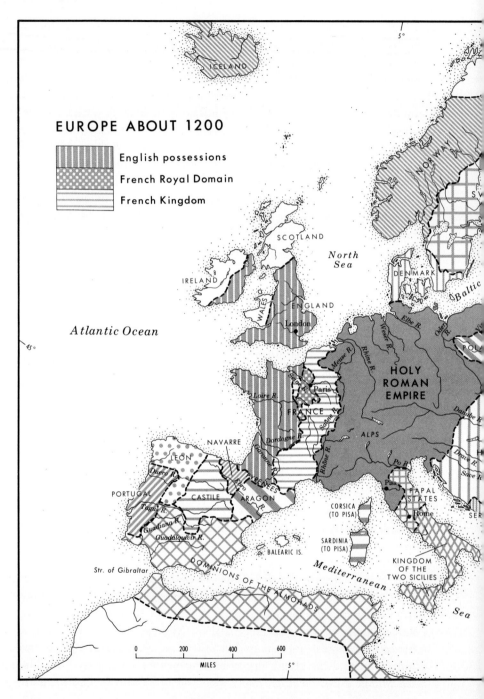

EUROPE ABOUT 1200

English possessions
French Royal Domain
French Kingdom

Parliament (literally, a "talking" or "discussion"). It had always been customary for the English kings to consult with the feudal *curia regis,* the great council, regarding extraordinary taxation and important affairs of state. Usually such consultation was only with the greatest royal vassals; for, although they had the right, seldom did the lesser ones attend. In the thirteenth century began the practice of summoning the great barons to national assemblies, or Parliaments, by individual writ. Eventually, the barons looked upon attendance as a heritable privilege; it became established custom for the eldest son, and for him only, to inherit his father's title and right to attend Parliament. This custom still prevails. By the fourteenth century the great barons so privileged were called lords and their assembly the *House of Lords.* In this manner arose one of the two components of Parliament.

Down to the reign of Edward I the baronial assemblies generally discussed affairs of state, voted extraordinary taxation, and served as the supreme court of the land. At this time the royal need for money caused enlargement of the baronial assembly. The kings had long been tapping the rich resources of the middle class merchants of the boroughs and of the knights and squires of the counties. Royal officers or itinerant justices had been sent out to negotiate for taxes in the form of tallages or percentages on movable wealth. This involved consulting the counties and boroughs individually. Eventually it was perceived that consultation on taxation could be carried on more efficiently in a central assembly at Westminster. The first Parliament, consisting of lords, burgesses of the boroughs, and knights of the shires was that of 1265 summoned by Simon de Montfort. Edward resorted to the same practice. To his Parliaments he summoned the great barons (lords), knights elected in the counties, burgesses from the boroughs, and representatives of the lower clergy. After the so-called Model Parliament of 1295, representatives from the lower clergy henceforth met in separate convocations in order to vote taxes to the king. This Parliament was composed of the lords, temporal and spiritual, and two burgesses from each borough and two knights from each county. In the fourteenth century all Parliaments came to be so constituted. Meanwhile the burgesses and knights, because of their similar economic status and community of interests, began to sit together at Parliaments. Because these men were commoners—not lords—their assembly was called the *House of Commons.* From the fourteenth century to the present the House of Commons has consisted of the representative element of Parliament; the House of Lords is the hereditary and privileged element.

Although on occasion Edward I passed legislation only with the advice of the lords and levied taxes without parliamentary consent, he generally made his laws and secured his taxes in Parliament. For the numerous taxes required Edward had to make concessions to the lords and commoners; from such bargaining developed constitutional government. A key advance in this direction occurred in 1297 during a bitter dispute between Edward and Parliament over excessive taxation. To secure a grant Edward swore to observe Magna Carta, to abandon unpopular customs and duties, and henceforth to levy no extraordinary taxes without the consent of Parliament. Here began parliamentary control of taxation, which was to grow in the next two centuries and to transform England into a limited monarchy.

The institutional and legal achievements of England in the thirteenth century were remarkable; no other state on the Continent could equal them. Although in some continental states it appeared for a time that assemblies similar to Parliament might transform the governments into constitutional forms, the fortunes of history and regional differences dictated otherwise. Only England emerged from the Middle Ages with a constitutional government. To understand this divergence, let us turn to the history of the other leading states.

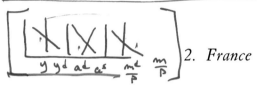

2. *France*

Louis VI left to his son Louis VII (1137–1180) a grand inheritance—a compact and well-ordered state, royal prestige, and marriage with Eleanor, the heiress of Aquitaine. Even an average ruler could have capitalized upon these assets, but Louis VII was not average. Devoid of common sense and perspective, he did all that a king ought not to do. He squandered time and money upon the dismal Second Crusade. During this venture the straitlaced Louis was so annoyed by the many flirtations of Eleanor, who had accompanied him, that he got rid of her, thereby enabling Henry II to acquire her and Aquitaine. In the first years of his reign Louis was saved from major pitfalls by the astute minister Suger, but after his death Louis struggled through one mistake after another. Louis, outmaneuvered by Henry II, was completely at his mercy; perhaps all that restrained Henry from invading the Île de France and absorbing it was fear that such action against his overlord might incite his own powerful vassals to revolt.

PHILIP AUGUSTUS

After much too long a reign the virtuous and stodgy Louis died and was succeeded by Philip (II) Augustus (1180–1223) who proved to be the real founder of France and one of its three great medieval rulers. Acutely intelligent and crafty, Philip Augustus was almost too modern for his age. A political realist, he had no sympathy for chivalrous adventure or impractical crusades. Suffering from poor health all his life and bald from an early age, he cut a pathetic figure on a horse. But this was of no consequence to him because it was not on a horse that he expanded the Île de France into a greater France; he accomplished this by his

THE CAPETIAN KINGS

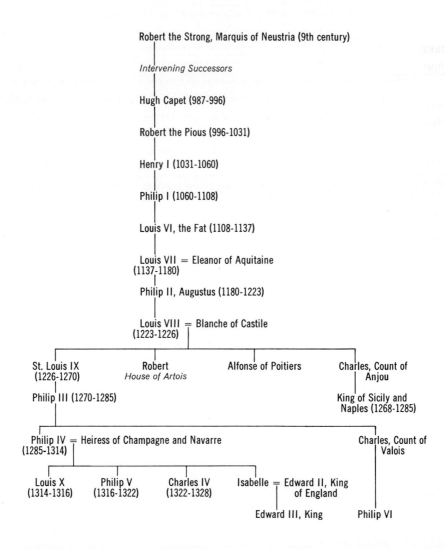

Robert the Strong, Marquis of Neustria (9th century)

Intervening Successors

Hugh Capet (987-996)

Robert the Pious (996-1031)

Henry I (1031-1060)

Philip I (1060-1108)

Louis VI, the Fat (1108-1137)

Louis VII = Eleanor of Aquitaine
(1137-1180)

Philip II, Augustus (1180-1223)

Louis VIII = Blanche of Castile
(1223-1226)

St. Louis IX (1226-1270) — Robert *House of Artois* — Alfonse of Poitiers — Charles, Count of Anjou

Philip III (1270-1285)

King of Sicily and Naples (1268-1285)

Philip IV = Heiress of Champagne and Navarre
(1285-1314)

Charles, Count of Valois

Louis X (1314-1316) — Philip V (1316-1322) — Charles IV (1322-1328) — Isabelle = Edward II, King of England

Edward III, King   Philip VI

intelligence and skilled political maneuvering. Philip, immediately throwing off the tutelage of the great nobles who had helped manage the government while he was a youth, asserted unchallenged mastery. Probing outward in all directions, he took advantage of every opportunity to expand his land. He was held in check by the equally able Henry II and by the military skill of Richard I, but he out-maneuvered John on every score and more than tripled the area of his kingdom. To the northeast he interfered in the politics of the rich county of Flanders and, by virtue of his victory at Bouvines in 1214, established his sphere of influence over

Henry II ⟷ Phillip Aug

that land. In the early thirteenth century he supported participation of his vassals in the crusade against the Albigensians in Toulouse and so prepared the way for that county's absorption into the royal domain. Looking eastward, he initiated what became a frequent objective of later French rulers—expansion to the Rhine. Although outwitted on a few occasions by Innocent III, Philip retained complete freedom of action and, unlike the English and German sovereigns, suffered no humiliation. Philip Augustus made possible the French hegemony in western Europe for the next hundred years.

ST. LOUIS

We shall dispose of the short and inconsequential reign of Philip's son Louis VIII (1223–1226) with the remark that he began the incorporation of Toulouse which was completed under his son St. Louis IX (1226–1270). Already informed by Joinville about the character of this remarkable king, we need here concentrate only on his political accomplishments. The first ten years of his reign were dominated by his mother, Blanche of Castile, who served as regent. A woman of ability, perhaps the equal of Eleanor of Aquitaine, she held France under firm control for her young son and presided over the occupation of Toulouse. So firm and stern was Blanche that Louis was afraid of her. Joinville hints that there was something of a mother complex in Louis that he did not lose even after his marriage to the attractive Margaret of Provence. In fact Blanche was so jealous of her daughter-in-law that she "would not suffer, in so far as she could help it, that her son should be in his wife's company, except at night when he went to sleep with her." During the day the young couple met at secret rendezvous to escape the old dowager.   *CONSOLIDATOR*

In 1236, old enough to assume rule, Louis found his kingdom in first-rate condition; it extended from the Channel to the Mediterranean. The English control in Aquitaine was restricted to a southwestern core, the land of Gascony. Of the French states remaining independent, Brittany and Burgundy were economically backward and politically weak; Blois and Champagne were ruled by friendly princes; and Flanders was still under French influence. Relieved of warfare against powerful neighbors, Louis was able to consolidate the territorial gains of the past fifty years, reorganize central and local administration, serve as the trusted moderator of disputes in western Christendom, and indulge in fruitless crusades to Egypt and Tunis. So weak from illness that he could not mount a horse when he departed in 1270 for the Tunisian crusade, Louis soon died from a pestilence that seized his hapless army.

Overly generous with his royal brothers, Louis granted them large territories out of the royal domain and permitted them to rule almost as independent princes. Charles, for example, received Anjou; and Alphonse, territory in Poitou and Toulouse. The granting of these lands (*appanages*) was to have fateful consequences for France in the fourteenth and fifteenth centuries. This generosity was one of the few foolish acts of Louis. His achievements in government were sound. He was a model of what a medieval prince should be in his high level of Christian conduct. He personified medieval Christianity. He was a man of peace and was deservedly canonized in 1297.

In French medieval history the rhythm of successful and then unsuccessful kings was continued by Louis' son Philip III (1270–1285), "the carbuncle sprung from that most precious gem of Christ, Saint Louis." Attempting to conquer the Spanish kingdom of Aragon, Philip met with military disaster and lost his life in 1285. His one successful stroke was to marry his son Philip to the heiress of the county of Champagne and thus pave the way for the acquisition of this rich area.

PHILIP THE FAIR

Philip's throne fell to Philip the Fair (IV) who ruled from 1285 to 1314. Along with Philip Augustus and St. Louis he composed the great trio of French kings. The historical riddle of Philip IV revolves around whether he was responsible for the notable institutional innovation and growth of royal power, or whether it was due to the intelligent and able ministers who surrounded him. Steeped in Roman law and power politics, these servants exalted absolutism and strove to convert into practice the old Roman legal maxim: "What is pleasing to the prince has the force of law." That Philip owed much of his success to able ministers is beyond debate. One day, parodying Christ's words, he said to his intimate councilor Peter Flote: "Thou art Peter, and upon this rock I will build my council." Another councilor, the political theorist Peter du Bois, argued for supremacy of royal power over spiritual authority. And another, William Nogaret, kidnapped Philip's ecclesiastical opponent Pope Boniface VIII. But ultimately a successful king is judged by his ministers and accordingly Philip, like Henry VIII of England, was a great king and his own master. Recent research has proved that he was an indefatigable ruler who loomed behind all the exceptional events of his reign.

Philip IV, like Philip Augustus, devoted most of his attention to expanding the borders of France. We saw how he tried to steal Gascony from Edward I. He employed similar subterfuges elsewhere. To the east, he acquired the French-speaking areas of Toul, Lyon, and Franche-Comté that lay within the borders of the empire. Exerting constant pressure upon the county of Flanders, he finally occupied it in the late thirteenth century. But here his success was short-lived. Rallying to the cause of their count, the Flemish masses in the towns revolted against the French and their allies, the Flemish nobles and rich merchants. In May 1302 the townsmen of Bruges rose up and massacred the French garrison and their sympathizers. This event, one of the glorious episodes in Belgian history, is known as the Matins of Bruges because the rising occurred in the early morning. Such action incited all Flanders to resistance, and when Philip IV sent a great feudal army to crush the Flemish he met with one of the great military debacles of the Middle Ages. At Courtrai in July 1302 the mightiest army of Europe was crushed by the Flemish pikemen. This was the first great victory of infantry over knights since the beginning of feudalism. In Flemish history it is called the Battle of the Golden Spurs because, so the report goes, the Flemish gathered three baskets of golden spurs from fallen knights. This setback had serious domestic repercussions for Philip and insured the independence of Flanders from French domination.

The repulse at Courtrai ended the major efforts of Philip for expansion, partly no doubt because he was deeply involved in a struggle with Pope Boniface VIII (1294–1303) and the Knights Templars. Boniface, the last of the powerful medieval Popes, had the energy and political ambition of Innocent III, but he lacked the latter's ability as a statesman as well as tact and common sense. Moreover, in his struggle with the secular powers of western Europe, he was pitted against states far more powerful than those arrayed against Innocent; a century had done much to secularize Europe. This change in attitude wrecked the papal position as head of western Christendom and influenced men to support their state against the papal international power.

PHILIP AND THE CHURCH

Seemingly unaware that theory could not always be translated into practice, Boniface issued the bull *Clericis Laicos* which forbade secular princes to tax the clergy without papal consent. This bull was directed principally against Philip IV and Edward I who were levying taxes on the clergy to help finance their wars. Boniface quickly learned that he was in no position to enforce the bull. Edward outlawed the clergy who refused to pay taxes, and Philip forbade gold and silver to leave the realm, thus depriving Boniface of much papal revenue. Boniface reversed his position and withdrew the prohibition. But soon at odds with Philip over the trial of clergy in secular courts, he revived his prohibition against taxation of the clergy and added insult to injury by claiming in the bull *Asculta Fili* (Listen, My Son) the right to interfere in the internal affairs of a state. Philip replied with a bitter defiance of these claims and backed it up by securing the support of the realm in a large assembly convened in 1302, composed not only of the clergy (first estate) and nobles (second estate) but also of the bourgeoisie (third estate). This was the first *Estates General* in French history.

Still incapable of sensing the dangerous terrain on which he trod, Boniface defended his actions in a long bull called *Unam Sanctam* which reiterated all the traditional arguments for papal supremacy and plenitude of power. The end of the drama provides a vivid commentary upon the rampant feeling of secularism and the sagging power of the Papacy as opposed to the strength of the national monarch in the early fourteenth century. While Philip was demanding the trial of Boniface before a church council, his minister Nogaret slipped into Italy in 1303 and, joining with some Roman nobles who hated Boniface, seized him at the town of Anagni. Although they shortly released the aged Pope, this crude blow and affront to his position broke him and he soon died. Philip then capitalized upon the fall of Boniface to reduce papal power further. He secured the election of a French prelate as Pope and then prevailed upon him to rescind all the decrees of Boniface. He also persuaded the new Pope to delay his trip to Rome. As Philip had hoped, the delay became permanent, and the Pope established his residence at Avignon along the Rhône River in Provence. Here under the influence of the French kings the Popes remained for most of the fourteenth century.

Philip's final act was his shameful attack upon the Knights Templars. With the fall in 1291 of the last Christian land in the Middle East to the infidel, the Templars had no good military reason for continuing their organization, and yet, recipients of pious gifts, they had become quite wealthy and had no thought of disbanding. Living in ease, they devoted their time to banking activities. With branches all over Europe and the Mediterranean area, they could readily handle international banking business and came to lend money and deal in letters of credit and bills of exchange. In France they became so powerful that they assumed the administration of the treasury; the French kings and nobles fell deeply in debt to them and became intensely jealous of these erstwhile crusaders become bankers. In 1307 Philip IV, who particularly coveted their money and lands, persuaded the Pope to investigate the order and its activities. Philip trumped up all sorts of false charges against them and then ordered all to be arrested and questioned under torture to secure confession of crime and financial dishonesty. The whole procedure was a farce, intended only to destroy the order. For seven years the Templars were persecuted, many burned at the stake as heretics. The Pope finally disbanded the order, and Philip at once confiscated all its movable property and land. Philip definitely was the precursor of a new type of ruler, one who had no moral or Christian scruples nor any respect for tradition or law. With him only success counted; the attainment of it justified any means. Philip spoke the language of the Renaissance despot.

MACHE

At his death in 1314 Philip left the French monarchy at its apogee of power; it was for all purposes absolute. He was succeeded, however, by three sons of mediocre ability who were plagued by revolts of the nobles chafing under the strong Capetian rule. To their lasting disgrace none produced an heir and so ended, after almost three hundred and fifty years, the rule of the Capetian dynasty. When the last son died in 1328, he was succeeded by Philip of Valois, a son of Philip IV's brother. It was the fate of the Valois dynasty to preside over the misfortunes of France during the next two centuries.

FRENCH GOVERNMENT (+100)

In general French institutional development resembled that of England; the principal difference was that the French lagged behind about a hundred years. Not until the reign of Philip Augustus is it possible to compare French and English central institutions. The rapid development under Philip owed much to the influence of English administration in the lands conquered in the early thirteenth century. Philip's utilization of his powers as the greatest feudal lord in France underlay his success in centralizing and invigorating the government. He insisted that all obligations be met by his feudal vassals. The great organ of central government was the *curia regis*, especially in its form of the small council which transacted all necessary government business. Like the English court, it soon began to split into departments with specialized functions. Always about the king was a household staff of officers and servants who looked after domestic needs. Some were skilled administrators, relied upon constantly for advice and delicate missions. These men, plus a group of trusted nobles, formed the small council that concentrated upon administration. For matters of great importance such as war and extraordinary taxation this council was supplemented by all the great nobles of the realm. Such an assembly was similar to the great council in England.

By the reign of St. Louis two departments had split off from the small council. One, the *chambre des comptes* (chamber of accounts), served as the central treasury that received and disbursed the royal income; it was comparable to the English exchequer though never as well organized. The other, the *parlement*, was the king's high court of justice. To handle the important cases about thirty men skilled in law were delegated as judges. This central court helped to standardize law in France and became a model for inferior provincial courts. Capetian taxation was similar to the English. Philip Augustus levied tallages (*tailles*) and his successors assessed aids on movable property which consisted of a certain percentage of the total yearly wealth.

The interest of St. Louis in just government led him to initiate a series of inquests into local government. Learning that local administration was corrupt, Louis did what Henry I of England had done almost one hundred and fifty years before; he created officers similar to the itinerant justices. Called *enquêteurs* (investigators), these royal officers were sent out periodically from the court to hear complaints, hold investigations, remedy abuses, try cases, and publicize royal orders and laws. They proved a most effective check on local officers, served as a bridge between central and local government, and helped to standardize law and institutions throughout France. Unfortunately Philip IV and some of his successors

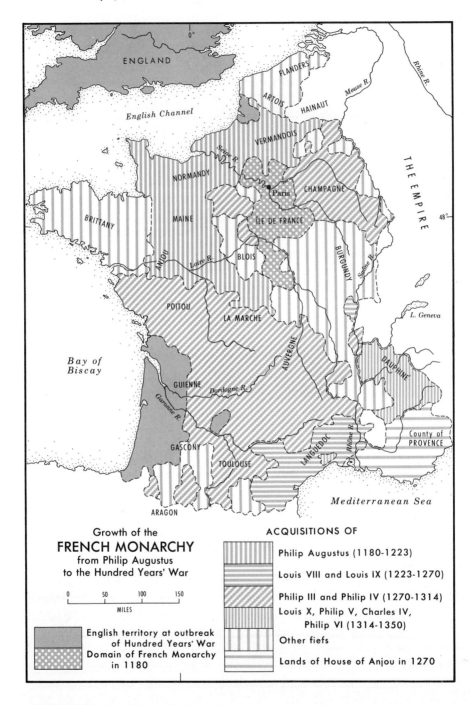

Growth of the
FRENCH MONARCHY
from Philip Augustus
to the Hundred Years' War

0   50   100   150
MILES

English territory at outbreak
of Hundred Years' War
Domain of French Monarchy
in 1180

ACQUISITIONS OF

Philip Augustus (1180-1223)

Louis VIII and Louis IX (1223-1270)

Philip III and Philip IV (1270-1314)

Louis X, Philip V, Charles IV,
Philip VI (1314-1350)

Other fiefs

Lands of House of Anjou in 1270

used the *enquêteurs* as agents of royal oppression rather than as royal guardians of justice.

On the local level of government the most significant change was the replacement of feudal administrators by non-feudal officers. The old feudal *prévôts* and *châtelains* had too often used their power to benefit themselves and their families and had fleeced both king and local inhabitants. Some time during the reign of Philip Augustus, they were replaced by officers appointed and liable to dismissal by the king. In northern France these officers were called *baillis* (bailiffs) and administered districts called *bailliages* (bailiwicks). In southern France they were called *sénéchaux* (seneschals) and headed *sénéchaussées* (seneschalships). Basically their duties were the same as those of the English sheriff.

However strong and efficient the French government had become in the thirteenth century, it never equaled the attainments of English government. Where England had been conquered as a whole by one stroke and had received institutions common to all the land, France had grown up slowly, adding territory after territory, each with its own institutions, customs, and laws which each province retained down to the French Revolution in 1789. There was no common law. The only institution common to all medieval France was the king, and even the French kings had to develop their powers gradually and force recognition of them province by province. For extraordinary taxation such as the tallages and aids the kings had to negotiate individually with province and town. Compared to England, France was very decentralized and therefore ill-prepared to resist strong kingship.

It was Philip IV who realized that asking for taxes from a national assembly was more efficient than individual negotiation with communities. For quite some time the first two estates of clergy and nobles had been summoned to great councils for their assent to taxation while the towns were consulted separately. In 1302, in addition to the first two estates, Philip summoned representatives of the towns— the third estate—to a central assembly. This, as we have seen, was the first Estates General of France. It was called to secure backing against Pope Boniface VIII and to get money for the Flemish war. Subsequent Estates Generals were held, but during the fourteenth century it became customary to consult with provincial estates such as those of Normandy, Champagne, and Toulouse. Central and common institutions had not progressed far enough for national assemblies to succeed as they did in England. Strongly provincial, the people had no sense of a bond of interests, no idea that as a united community of the realm they could resist autocratic rulers and control them. They consequently failed to realize the latent power of an Estates General while the kings, sensing that a central assembly, however effective for voting taxes, could be dangerous, dealt with their subjects region by region and skillfully kept the realm from coalescing against them. Herein lies the principal reason why France developed into an absolute monarchy and England into a constitutional monarchy.

3. *The Hohenstaufen Dynasty*

THE COMPLICATED HISTORY OF GERMANY in the twelfth and thirteenth centuries is so tortuous to follow and so barren of accomplishment that we need only concern ourselves with a few of the significant developments. Practically all that the history of Germany proves in these centuries is that this was a period of political retrogression as compared to political progress in France and England. This backward movement in medieval Germany is one of the chief causes of German particularism which lasted down into the nineteenth century. France and England emerged from the fifteenth century as nation states; Germany as a mosaic composed of dozens of petty principalities.

PROBLEMS OF ROYAL SUCCESSION IN GERMANY

When Henry IV mounted the throne in 1056, Germany was what it had been early in the tenth century—a sort of federation of a few great duchies. Although occasionally kings like Otto the Great and Henry III exerted real authority over these duchies, generally German rulers had to be content with their title and theoretical powers. A principal result of the investiture struggle and civil war

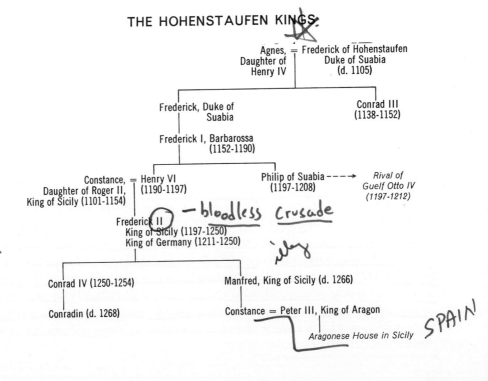

THE HOHENSTAUFEN KINGS

Agnes, = Frederick of Hohenstaufen
Daughter of   Duke of Suabia
Henry IV   (d. 1105)

Frederick, Duke of   Conrad III
Suabia   (1138-1152)

Frederick I, Barbarossa
(1152-1190)

Constance, = Henry VI   Philip of Suabia ---→   Rival of
Daughter of Roger II, (1190-1197)   (1197-1208)   Guelf Otto IV
King of Sicily (1101-1154)   (1197-1212)

                    — bloodless Crusade
Frederick II
King of Sicily (1197-1250)
King of Germany (1211-1250)

Conrad IV (1250-1254)   Manfred, King of Sicily (d. 1266)

Conradin (d. 1268)   Constance = Peter III, King of Aragon

                              Aragonese House in Sicily   SPAIN

(handwritten: Charles of Anjou)

during Henry's reign was to break up some of the large duchies into smaller feudal units and to produce a greater number of competitors for the crown. This fragmentation continued during the twelfth century, with the German kings finding it no easier to establish their authority over a horde of petty lords than over the great dukes.

Henry IV died in 1106 amidst a revolt in which his son was involved. But the son upon his coronation as Henry V (1106–1125) deserted his rebellious allies and fought as vigorously as his father to control them. He had little success, and his attainment of the imperial crown only added Italian problems. His one achievement was to settle the major differences of the investiture battle with the Pope at the Concordat of Worms in 1122. Henry died three years later without so much as leaving behind an heir. This of course contributed to the political instability of Germany and complicated the succession. With no close strong Franconian relatives to receive the crown, the electing princes therefore chose Lothair, duke of Saxony, who ruled as Lothair III (1125–1137).

This choice led to a bitter political feud which dominated German and Italian history for the next one hundred and fifty years. Lothair secured the throne due to his alliance with the dukes of Bavaria who came from the powerful Guelf family. This family supported Lothair in order to keep the throne from falling to their rivals, the dukes of Swabia who belonged to the Hohenstaufen family. The Hohenstaufen-Guelf conflict so embittered and weakened Germany that no permanent unification under a central government was possible. Immediately the seesaw battle for power began. The Hohenstaufen faction unsuccessfully revolted against Lothair. Upon his death the fickle nobles ignored the Saxon House and chose Conrad of Hohenstaufen, who ruled as Conrad III (1138–1152). The reign of this unhappy monarch was consumed in suppressing Guelf and Saxon revolts and participating in the Second Crusade.

FREDERICK BARBAROSSA

Fortunately when Conrad died the electors decided to keep the Hohenstaufen House in power and elected Conrad's nephew Frederick, commonly known as Frederick Barbarossa because of his great red beard. As a ruler Frederick I (1152–1190) ranks along with Charlemagne and Otto the Great. Of all the other German medieval sovereigns only his grandson Frederick II can be placed in the company of this distinguished trio. Frederick I followed in the tradition of Charlemagne and along with him has come down in German history and legend as one of the great national heroes. As a legendary figure he became *der alte Kaiser* who slept in a cavern high up in the mountains of Bavaria near Berchtesgaden and who one day would awake, come down out of his mountain retreat, and bring unity and peace to

Germany. During the nineteenth century at the height of German nationalism and romanticism, monuments were erected to Frederick and people made pilgrimages to his supposed tomb.

Dazzled by the magnificent imperial achievements of Charlemagne and Otto the Great, Frederick I immediately copied their Italian policy. In his case this decision was unfortunate; had he concentrated his exceptional political talents upon Germany he quite possibly could have laid the foundations for a united Germany. Instead he frittered away time and energy upon Italy. While Frederick was south of the Alps, his Guelf rival Henry the Lion, duke of Saxony and Bavaria, fomented revolt and, by marriage with the daughter of Henry II of England, cemented the powerful Angevin-Guelf alliance. Eventually Frederick allied himself with the Capetians and Europe was divided into two grand alliances. Meanwhile, his first Italian expedition in 1154 gained him imperial authority throughout Italy. Four years later he again went to Italy and at Roncaglia held a Diet and promulgated laws asserting his authority to name officials, tax the communes, and administer high justice. But the Italian communes of northern Italy—Lombardy—would not accept his authority and, led by Milan, they revolted. After a desperate siege Frederick took Milan and destroyed it. To offset Frederick's power in Italy, the Pope now allied himself with the Lombard communes and so forced Frederick to fight a combination of papal and urban power.

Working closely with the towns of northern Italy which organized the Lombard League, the Popes did all in their power to push Frederick out of Italy. The league rebuilt Milan, fortified towns, and allied itself with Henry the Lion. A series of campaigns followed, with the decisive battle at Legnano in 1176, where Frederick I and his German knights were routed by the Lombard footsoldiers (the clodhoppers). In 1183 Frederick concluded the Peace of Constance with the Lombard League. Formal recognition was given to the communes and to their traditional political rights; Frederick had to be content with a declaration of his imperial powers in Italy.

While the Italian policy of Frederick had ended in fiasco, in Germany respite from Italian wars enabled him to master Henry the Lion, who thereafter was never a threat to the imperial power. After Henry's fall the duchies of Saxony and Bavaria were never reconstituted as duchies but were subdivided into smaller states, as was the case with duchies in the late eleventh century. Reflecting the eastern colonization movement of the Germans in the twelfth century, new feudal states took form on the eastern borders of Saxony and Bavaria. In the north arose the margravate of Brandenburg and to the south, the duchy of Austria. The German movement eastward into central Europe during the twelfth and thirteenth centuries was much more significant than all the Italian campaigns of Frederick I. New towns such as Munich and Lübeck were founded, and they became the economic nuclei of flourishing trade and agriculture in the new lands.

Before Frederick I's last great campaign, the Third Crusade, during which he died, the old emperor achieved a diplomatic triumph by marrying his son Henry to Constance, the daughter of King Roger II of Sicily and heiress to that rich kingdom. At Frederick's death in 1190 Henry VI (1190–1197) acquired Germany, then the imperial crown, and finally the kingdom of Sicily. To round off his good fortune Constance presented him with a boy, the future Frederick II. By a simple marriage the Hohenstaufen had accomplished more than by all the wars of Frederick I. They now held Sicily and southern Italy and had boxed in the Lombard communes and the Papacy. The papal fear of being surrounded by the political power of one dynasty had become a reality. With perhaps a little more luck and common sense Henry VI might have achieved firm rule in Italy. But however shrewd and cruel, he was also so greedy for power and reputation that he became an impractical dreamer. He bargained with the Pope to make the imperial crown hereditary and laid plans to launch a great crusade that would make him master of the Mediterranean world and would restore the Roman Empire in the West. Suddenly in 1197, while preparing for this venture, Henry died; almost immediately the Hohenstaufen structure collapsed.

FREDERICK II

Henry VI left behind him to face the grim realities of medieval politics his three-year-old son Frederick, whose sole protector for the moment was his mother Constance. The German nobles refused to consider the young Frederick as king and instead elected Henry VI's brother Philip of Swabia who was opposed by the Guelf Otto of Saxony, the son of Henry the Lion. Through marriage and long-standing political agreements Otto had as allies the Angevin kings of England, while Philip of Swabia was naturally supported by Philip Augustus of France. As these lines were drawn and as civil war flared up in Germany, Pope Innocent III gladly became guardian of the young Frederick. Innocent then worked to separate the kingdom of Sicily from Germany and to destroy the Hohenstaufen power; he therefore supported the Guelf Otto. But only after Philip of Swabia was murdered in 1208 did Otto triumph. Ruling now as Otto IV and having received the imperial crown in return for renouncing any claim to Italy, he abruptly forgot his obligations to Innocent and proceeded to invade Italy in order to reduce the whole peninsula. Outraged, Innocent now reversed his policy and urged the German nobles to accept as their ruler the young Frederick who by this time had become king of Sicily. In 1211 Frederick was proclaimed king of Germany although he wielded no effective rule until Otto IV's power had been destroyed at the Battle of Bouvines in 1214. At this battle, it will be remembered, both Otto and John of England were crushed by Philip Augustus, the Hohenstaufen ally. In the kaleidoscopic politics of the early thirteenth century Innocent III had triumphed, but at a price;

he eventually had to back the Hohenstaufen Frederick, who was the bane of succeeding Popes until his death in 1250.

Frederick II, king of Sicily (1197–1250) and king of Germany (1215–1250), was a worthy successor of Henry VI and Frederick Barbarossa. Cognizant of his dependence upon Innocent III, Frederick at first deferred to the great Pope and assured him that he would never attempt to unite Germany and Sicily under one dynasty. He agreed to govern in Germany and to confer the rule of Sicily upon his infant son. But with the death of Innocent III in 1216 Frederick immediately broke his promises, becoming as obstreperous as the other Hohenstaufen. A clever politician, he repeatedly duped and defeated the less able successors of Innocent III. First he reversed his promise to Innocent, prevailing upon the German nobles to accept as king his infant son while remaining himself king of Sicily where he could more effectively concentrate on Italian politics. Then in 1220 he persuaded the Pope to crown him emperor. A thoroughgoing realist, Frederick scrapped his father's grandiose Mediterranean scheme and concentrated upon making himself master of Italy from the Alps to the tip of the boot. Quite frankly he was not interested in Germany; actually a stranger and infrequent visitor, he felt no sympathy for Germany nor did he understand its problems. He must indeed be held partly responsible for the political chaos that characterized German political life for the rest of the Middle Ages. Germany always played second fiddle to Italy. By 1225 it seemed that Frederick's domination of Italy would soon be a reality. His authority embraced most of the peninsula except for parts of Lombardy and the area around Rome.

Again, however, Lombard and papal resistance defeated the ultimate Hohenstaufen goal. As a youth Frederick had promised Innocent III to undertake a crusade to Palestine. Not intending to keep this vow, he repeatedly offered such excuses as ill health and the press of government affairs to postpone or circumvent the holy undertaking. But the Popes constantly bothered him and threatened excommunication if he did not fulfill his sacred oath. Finally in 1228 Frederick led an expedition to Palestine and, without spilling one drop of Christian blood, retook Jerusalem and a strip of land connecting it with Acre on the coast. He did this by shrewdly concluding with the various jealous and warring emirs a treaty that granted him what he wished in return for the promise that Moslems could worship freely in Jerusalem. The Pope was furious with this bloodless triumph secured on the basis of religious toleration and swore to destroy this unfaithful son of the church. Although Frederick remained master of Sicily and much of Italy until his death, even introducing a form of government resembling that of enlightened despotism, he had to fight continually against papal machinations and Lombard revolt. In 1237 he administered a crushing defeat to the Lombard communes at the Battle of Cortenuova and subsequently occupied most of the Papal States. But resistance continued and, while reducing more revolts in 1250, Frederick died.

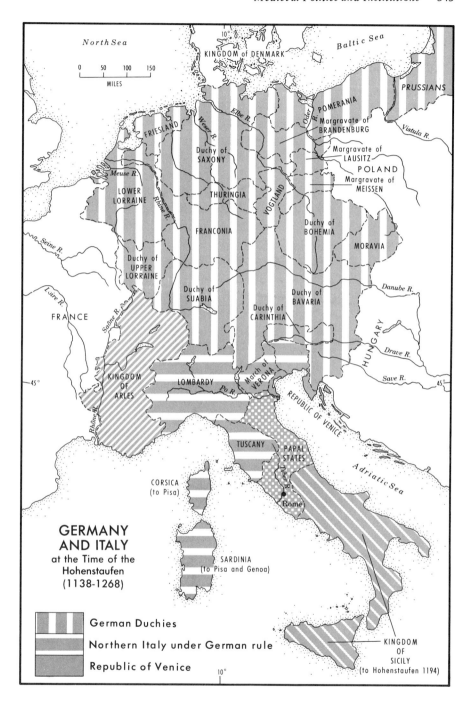

North Sea

KINGDOM of DENMARK

Baltic Sea

PRUSSIANS

POMERANIA

Margravate of
BRANDENBURG

Vistula R.

Elbe R.

Weser R.

FRIESLAND

Duchy of
SAXONY

Margravate of
LAUSITZ

POLAND

Margravate of
MEISSEN

Meuse R.

LOWER
LORRAINE

THURINGIA

VOGTLAND

Rhine R.

Seine R.

FRANCONIA

Duchy of
BOHEMIA

MORAVIA

Duchy of
UPPER
LORRAINE

Loire R.

FRANCE

Saône R.

Duchy of
SUABIA

Duchy of
BAVARIA

Danube R.

Duchy of
CARINTHIA

HUNGARY

Drave R.

45°

KINGDOM
OF
ARLES

LOMBARDY

Po R.

March of
VERONA

Save R.

45°

REPUBLIC OF VENICE

Rhone R.

TUSCANY

PAPAL
STATES

Tiber R.

Rome

Adriatic Sea

CORSICA
(to Pisa)

**GERMANY
AND ITALY**
at the Time of the
Hohenstaufen
(1138-1268)

SARDINIA
(to Pisa and Genoa)

German Duchies

Northern Italy under German rule

Republic of Venice

KINGDOM
OF
SICILY
(to Hohenstaufen 1194)

10°

MILES
0   50   100   150

THE ACHIEVEMENTS OF FREDERICK II

Like his predecessors Frederick had failed to forge an Italian kingdom; his achievements were, nevertheless, valuable. In government, economics, and intellectual interests and attitude Frederick demonstrated his genius and modern outlook. To standardize the law of his kingdom he compiled a secular code which rivaled that issued by Justinian. Incorporating feudal, Roman, Arabic, and Greek law, this code, the *Liber Augustalis,* contained 217 laws that reflect the dominant influence of Roman jurisprudence with its emphasis upon autocratic and centralized government. Central and local administration continued to be essentially that of Roger II of Sicily—a mixture of Norman, Greek, and Arabic. It is almost impossible to find an institution that can be called purely Norman or purely Roman. Men of various racial and religious backgrounds served in Frederick's government, and a limited religious toleration was practiced. Moslems, Jews, and Christians lived together without fear of persecution. Frederick, though encouraging the conversion of Moslems and Jews to Christianity, forbade the reverse process. Any Christian who left his faith was burned as a heretic. The limited form of religious toleration permitted by Frederick can be explained principally as a policy of practical politics; there were too many Moslems and Jews to kill them off, and the cultural and economic loss would have been catastrophic.

In economic matters Frederick was equally practical and progressive. He quashed all the cumbersome tolls and duties within the kingdom and substituted an import and export tax on all merchandise. At designated posts on the borders were warehouses through which all goods must pass and where customs must be paid. This department, called the *doana,* was comparable to the customs systems of modern states. Frederick not only facilitated trade and increased his revenue but also simplified the enforcement of embargoes during wars or diplomatic negotiations. To stimulate trade and commerce he founded a cycle of fairs like that of Champagne, concluded trade agreements with the Moslem states of northern Africa, and encouraged experimentation in more efficient agrarian techniques. He promoted scientific farming experiments upon his estates, bred new strains of cattle, and introduced new crops such as the date, cotton, and sugar cane. To handle the increased volume of trade, he coined the gold *augustales* which were equivalent to a pound and served as a precedent for the subsequent gold coinage of the communes of Lombardy and Tuscany. Fully aware that the bourgeoisie had benefited most from his economic reforms, Frederick had no qualms about levying heavy taxes upon this class and came to do so in central assemblies consisting of the great lords, prelates, and representatives from the towns. While he thus anticipated the French and English kings in the convening of assemblies which included the third estate, he was too absolute and the future history of Sicily too anarchical for the evolution of a parliamentary system.

Frederick's personality and intellectual interests were remarkable. He had no intellectual peer among his princely brethren. He was a sort of free thinker little bound by tradition or authority. He flouted custom and did what he willed. He loved the ease of oriental living and kept a well-stocked harem; he bathed at least once a week and did so on the Sabbath. He frankly admired the intelligence and attainments of the Arabs and patronized them at his court, the leading princely center of learning in western Europe. Frederick was no blind adherent of Christian faith; on occasion he uttered irreverent remarks and repeatedly demonstrated what philosophical and scientific learning was doing to his faith. Tremendously interested in science and experimentation, he constantly tinkered like the American inventors of the nineteenth and early twentieth centuries. Perhaps he did not realize it, but he was Aristotelian in his outlook and method; he was an enthusiastic empiricist. From all over the known world he collected a menagerie that apparently consisted of more animals than are found in most zoos today. There were elephants, camels, panthers, ostriches, and dozens of other non-European animals and birds. This menagerie was one of the wonders of Europe and amazed all those privileged to see it. Frederick and his court scholars studied the animals and wrote learned treatises upon them. Also Frederick wrote a most learned book *On the Art of Hunting with Birds*. In addition to discussing hawks and falcons and how

THE EMPEROR FREDERICK II. This portrait of Frederick II is from a miniature in his work on falconry, *On the Art of Hunting with Birds*. Note that the illustrator has included the falcon in the lower right corner of the illumination.

to train them and to use them on the hunt, he included a very scholarly and accurate section on ornithology with beautiful illustrations of all kinds of birds drawn by artists of his court.

The experiments and stimulating questions of Frederick are legend. Learned scholars all over Europe and the Middle East received inquiries. For example, Frederick asked why a stick appeared to be bent when plunged into water, and why the stars and sun appeared to be larger when near the horizon. Hearing that in Norway some geese were hatched from barnacles he secured some of the latter and discovered that this story was false. He investigated all sorts of rumors. Attempting to ascertain what language babies would naturally speak he had some reared in complete isolation. But he never completed the experiment because all the babies died.

Frederick was the greatest royal patron of artists, writers, and scholars in the Middle Ages. To his court came men of varied racial and religious backgrounds from all parts of western Europe and the Mediterranean world. Here worked Michael Scot, the famous Aristotelian philosopher and master of Arabic science. The mathematician Leonard of Pisa also enjoyed Frederick's patronage. Frederick founded the University of Naples as a center for the training of lawyers and continued to support the University of Salerno which specialized in medicine. An accomplished linguist who had mastered Latin, Greek, and Arabic in addition to German, French, and Italian, Frederick encouraged literature. The most distinguished court writer was Piero della Vigna, who was a skilled rhetorician and poet famous for his verse composed in the Sicilian dialect. Frederick may be compared to the later Renaissance princes who patronized cultural activity and contributed so much to humanistic learning in the fifteenth and sixteenth centuries. It is no wonder that in the thirteenth century he was truly "the amazement of the world" (*stupor mundi*).

THE END OF THE HOHENSTAUFEN DYNASTY

The death of Frederick II was a catastrophe for southern Italy and Sicily. In Germany his death caused hardly a ripple, so hopeless had his neglect rendered its political life. Frederick's eldest son, who had ruled Germany, died before his father and was succeeded by a second son Conrad IV who ruled until 1254 but never exerted any real authority over the kingdom of Sicily. At this point the Sicilians proclaimed Frederick's illegitimate son Manfred king. If permitted to rule without foreign interference, Manfred could have governed Sicily in a manner worthy of his father. He was, however, bitterly opposed by the Papacy whose goal was to annihilate the Hohenstaufen. The Pope searched all over the courts of western Europe to secure a candidate able and willing to conquer Sicily. We have seen how, as early as 1257, the Pope offered the crown to one of the sons of Henry

III of England. This scheme never got out of the planning stage due to strong English feeling against it. Finally in 1265 Charles of Anjou, brother of St. Louis of France, agreed to hold Sicily in fief from the Papacy and led an army against Manfred whom he defeated and killed in 1266. But Hohenstaufen resistance continued under Conradin, the sixteen-year-old son of Conrad IV. Bravely leading an army against Charles in 1268, he was defeated and captured and summarily beheaded in the market place of Naples. All remaining members of the Hohenstaufen family were then hunted down and killed by Charles who was warmly supported by the Papacy. And so ended the Hohenstaufen dynasty after more than a century of dominance in German and Italian politics.

Charles of Anjou, the new king of Sicily, was both able and ambitious, but cruel instincts and grandiose dreams combined to wreck his hold over the recently acquired kingdom. He had, moreover, become extremely devout and firm in his Christian faith, so much so that he lost all sense of humor and became a bigot in the cause of orthodoxy. Such a frame of mind won him few friends in Sicily where men of all religions lived without fear of persecution. Having completely reduced Sicilian opposition and having appointed oppressive French officials to the key administrative posts, Charles laid plans for a great crusade that would conquer all northern Africa and then roll on to occupation of the Holy Land. In 1282 the Sicilian Vespers rudely shattered his dream. Long chafing under French rule, the Sicilians suddenly broke out in revolt at Palermo on Easter Sunday while the bells pealed out for vespers. The French garrison and sympathizers were massacred and the revolt swiftly spread throughout Sicily. Charles never recovered from the disaster. As the revolt flared up, Peter III, king of the Spanish kingdom of Aragon, opportunely and obviously by previous plan, sailed to Sicily with an army and after occupying much of the island was proclaimed king by the Sicilians. Peter's claim to the throne was derived from his Hohenstaufen connection; he was the son of Manfred's daughter. Charles of Anjou retired to southern Italy and from there could not retake Sicily. When death came in 1285 to both Charles and Peter, Sicily remained in Aragonese hands and southern Italy in Angevin.

4. Italy and Germany

THE COLLAPSE OF HOHENSTAUFEN POWER and the death of Charles of Anjou ended any possibility of unifying Italy. In the south the Two Sicilies remained kingdoms on the maps of Europe into the nineteenth century while central and northern Italy were cut up into small city-states locked in intra- and inter-city warfare. For the next five hundred years Italy was the battleground of native and foreign states fighting for power. Seldom in the Middle Ages after the failure of Charles of Anjou did any power north of the Alps attempt to interfere seriously in Italian politics. The hodgepodge of small city-states and the Papacy were left free to fight among themselves for Italian hegemony. Although the names of Guelf and Hohenstaufen ceased to denote political factions supporting candidates from these two families, they continued in usage. Guelf came to designate those who supported papal power in Italy while Ghibelline, a corruption of the Hohenstaufen land of Waiblingen in Germany, came to denote those who still supported an imperial authority. For example, the Aragonese kingdom and the states of Florence and Milan were Guelf; the Angevin kingdom and the states of Pavia and Pisa, Ghibelline. But as the city-states constantly shifted their political alignments these labels ceased to have much significance.

THE ITALIAN CITY-STATES

Most of the leading Italian city-states in the thirteenth century were ruled by dictators who came to power by force or, as demagogues, were elected by the mass of the citizens. These dictators were the prototype of the Renaissance despots and ruled without respect for law or moral principles. In some states an oligarchy of the richest citizens controlled the government, but this was no improvement over dictatorship. It only meant that a few powerful men used public power to increase their private wealth and political prestige and employed their authority to enact ordinances that took political and economic privileges away from the rank and file of citizens. Ground down by intolerable political and economic conditions, the proletariat found strength in the late thirteenth and fourteenth centuries to revolt and overthrow their hated masters. The bitter class warfare in the fourteenth-century Italian city-state was duplicated only in the great industrial towns of Flanders. Dominated by an oligarchy, the republic of Venice was the sole state to retain political stability and municipal peace. Here membership in the city council was hereditary, enjoyed by only a few great families. How these few families held almost unchallenged mastery over Venice for centuries will always amaze the historian. One reason for the relative contentment of the masses seems to have been the good economic conditions and comparatively high standard of living which the Venetians enjoyed by virtue of their domination of Mediterranean trade, especially that with Constantinople.

GERMAN PARTICULARISM

Turning once again to Germany, we find that Frederick's indifference to politics there contributed to the worst kind of particularism. In practice Germany came to be ruled by the nobles. There continued to be kings, but their power was only theoretical; in general the men elected were too impotent to bother those who elected them. Some kings were not even German; they were foreigners who bribed the princes so that they could boast a title. One of these was Richard of Cornwall, the brother of Henry III of England, who visited Germany but once. The office of king was thus passed around until 1273 when the princes elected a petty noble, Rudolf of Habsburg (1273–1291). The Habsburg family had grown up and had gained lands on the eastern side of what is now Switzerland. Rudolf was a realist who knew that it was impossible to exercise royal authority in Germany and that imperial adventures south of the Alps ended in disaster. His sole aim was to use what kingly prestige he had to establish and build up the Habsburg fortunes in the lands around Austria. Moving against the king of Bohemia who refused to recognize him, Rudolf occupied much of what today forms Austria. Thus arose the Habsburg power in Austria and in the lands around the upper Danube, a power that remained until the abdication of the last Habsburg emperor toward the end of World War I.

After Rudolf's death in 1291 the kingship was passed around to insignificant princes until 1308, when the electors chose Count Henry of Luxemburg because of his poverty and political impotence. Henry VII (1308–1313) had ability as a politician and could have advanced the fortunes of his family much further if he had been content to labor patiently in Germany. At the outset of his reign he arranged the fortunate marriage of his son to a young noble woman who was being supported for the Bohemian crown against the Habsburgs. In 1310 when the marriage was celebrated, Henry recognized his son as king of Bohemia. This stroke established the Luxemburg dynasty at Prague and kindled a struggle for Bohemian power with the Habsburgs throughout the next century. Henry next fell victim to the Italian disease and led an army over the Alps. He reached Rome and was crowned emperor but soon had to retreat to the north. He died in the plague at Siena in 1314.

With the death of Henry VII we may for the moment halt our account of German history. Since the death of Frederick II Germany had been nothing but a geographical expression, a land subdivided into many petty states whose rulers owed theoretical allegiance to a king customarily weak and held in contempt. As for the Holy Roman Empire, it too had really come to an end. To be sure it continued its dubious existence until destroyed by Napoleon, but for centuries it was mainly a fiction; it had no force or reality. Perhaps it was kept because it symbolized to the later Middle Ages universal peace and unity, an ideal men strove for but never attained. By the early fourteenth century the Holy Roman Empire had so shrunk that it comprised only Germany; it was but a theoretical union of principalities and political associations.

GERMAN POLITICAL AND ECONOMIC ASSOCIATIONS

The rise of political and economic associations was the most important feature of German history in the later Middle Ages. Such associations sprang from the

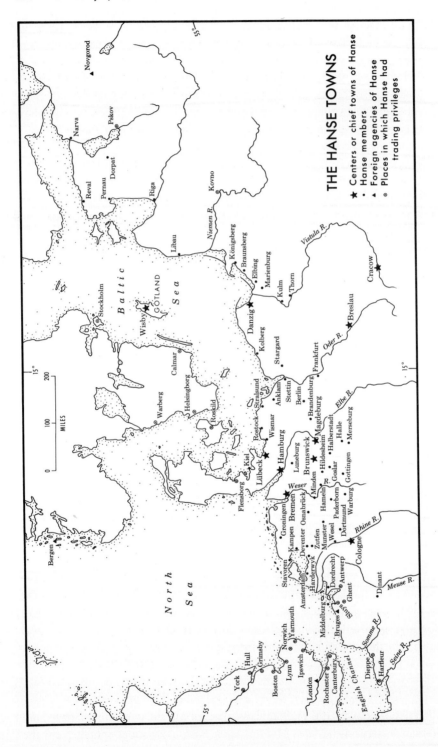

THE HANSE TOWNS

★ Centers or chief towns of Hanse
• Hanse members
▲ Foreign agencies of Hanse
⊚ Places in which Hanse had
    trading privileges

necessity for defense and for cooperation in attaining political and economic goals. We have previously seen that during the thirteenth century in northern Germany along the North and Baltic seas towns such as Rostock, Lübeck, and Danzig formed an economic association called the Hanse for the regulation and promotion of trade in northern Europe. By the fourteenth century the Hanse embraced dozens of towns united in an economic federation for mutual protection of their commercial interests. Eventually, they received the same political recognition in the empire as that enjoyed by the principalities. Another association developed in southern Germany in the mountainous area belonging to the Habsburgs just west of Austria and south of Bavaria. In 1291 men of the forest cantons of Uri, Schwyz, and Unterwalden formed the Swiss Confederation. These men, following the path of the great urban communes and the numerous rural communities of western Europe, swore an oath to fight against the Habsburgs and their oppressive rule and to win self-government. Ultimately the Swiss Confederation expanded to include seven cantons, freed itself from the Habsburgs, and obtained self-government and recognition of its political organization within the empire. Like the great German free cities, the Hanse, and the principalities, the Swiss Confederation held its liberties directly from the empire; this meant virtual independence.

5. *Central Europe and Scandinavia*

As of the year 1100 that part of Europe lying east of the Elbe River in Germany was comparable to the lands lying west of the Mississippi River in America around the middle of the nineteenth century. The Elbe marked an eastern frontier just as the Mississippi marked a western frontier. Beyond the Elbe lay a vast area sparsely populated with a people quite foreign to the inhabitants of western Europe. For over two centuries the Germans pushed the frontier farther east as they conquered peoples with a civilization much inferior to that of the West. As this region was opened up colonists poured in, cleared the forests, reclaimed land from marsh and sea, opened up rich land to farming, and founded thriving towns. Along with these political and economic activities went German culture. As America was dominated by the westward movement in the nineteenth century, so German history was dominated by an eastward movement. A great wave of colonization carried the frontiers of Germany from the Elbe to the Vistula River and along the Baltic Sea to the Gulf of Finland. The famous German *Drang nach Osten* (pressure to the east) began in the twelfth century.

In the early twelfth century directly east of the Elbe were a group of primitive states that had been organized by some Slavic tribes. East of Hamburg and along the Baltic were the Wends (Baltic Slavs), and east of them were the Pomeranians who had organized the duchy of Pomerania. South of the Wends and Pomeranians a larger tribe, the Poles, had formed a kingdom. South of Poland were the Bohemians and Moravians (Czechs). These Slavic peoples dominated central Europe, but there were also other peoples who had moved in from the east during the early Middle Ages and had conquered large areas of land. The Prussians and Lithuanians who spoke an Indo-European language had established themselves east of the Pomeranians along the Baltic. Beyond them were the Estonians, and then came the Finns around the eastern Baltic. All these tribes belonged to a linguistic group called the Baltic, a part of the Ural-Altaic group which originally had consisted of nomadic tribes living between the Ural and Altai mountains in north-central Asia. During their migrations some tribes had pushed into eastern and central Europe. To the south of Poland was the large kingdom of Hungary consisting of a Ural-Altaic people called the Magyars, or Hungarians, who had passed through the Pontic steppes in the ninth century and crossed over the Dniester River into southeastern and central Europe. During the tenth century the Hungarians threatened Germany, and it was saved only by the exertions of Henry the Fowler and Otto the Great. Halted in the west, the Hungarians settled down in the vast plain between the Carpathian Mountains and the Danube River.

THE KINGDOM OF HUNGARY

Although the peoples along the Baltic remained pagan, the rest of the Slavs and the Hungarians were converted to Christianity. In the east the Russians were converted by the Greek church, while the Roman church won Moravia, Bohemia, and Poland. The Hungarians turned toward the West for their religion and culture. Their king Stephen I (997–1038) was chiefly responsible for their Christianization and westernization. He enthusiastically supported missionary work, became the vassal of the Pope, and received from him the title of king in the year 1000. For his holy work Stephen was eventually rewarded with canonization. Unlike Bohemia and some other states east of the Elbe, Hungary was not conquered by the Germans, nor did it ever become a part of the Holy Roman Empire. Hungary blocked German colonization along the Danube and in the twelfth century was vigorous enough to push west to the Adriatic Sea and conquer Croatia. This move involved Hungary with the Italian states, chiefly Venice, which, jealous of its commercial interests, feared foreign penetration of the Adriatic or the Mediterranean.

THE KINGDOM OF POLAND

In the tenth century Otto the Great had established a tenuous control over the land between the Elbe and Oder rivers and had forced the Poles and Czechs to recognize his lordship. After his death, however, all this was undone. The Elbe again became the frontier and the Poles under their remarkable king Boleslav (992–1025) threw off German lordship and established a temporary empire consisting of Moravia, Bohemia, and Pomerania. But they could not hold this vast territory and in the eleventh century contracted to their original territory. Into the twelfth century, however, Poland remained a vigorous state that served as a buffer between Germany and Russia. The partitioning of Poland by numerous local princes during the twelfth century rendered it temporarily impotent and set in motion the first of a series of partitions that have repeatedly obstructed the national development of Poland. With the decline of Poland the Germans were once again able to push east and penetrate into Bohemia which was brought into the Holy Roman Empire. To the north they pushed outward all along the Elbe River. The Saxon dukes in particular promoted colonization projects and lured colonists from all over Germany and even from Holland and Flanders. They poured into the low-lying lands along the Baltic and reclaimed the land for agriculture. In the twelfth and thirteenth centuries the advance toward the Vistula River continued relentlessly. By the middle of the thirteenth century, Poland had been greatly reduced in size and power and was barely maintaining its independence. In the north, meanwhile, the Germans had overrun and colonized all the land—Pomerania and Mecklenburg—up to the Vistula River and were ready to spring across into Prussia.

THE TEUTONIC KNIGHTS

The next chapter in German conquest and colonization centers on the Teutonic Knights, a German religious order of knights founded like the Knights Templars and Hospitalers to defend the Holy Land against the infidel. The reconquest of the Crusader States by the Moslems, however, ended the military activity of the knights in the Middle East and diverted it to eastern Germany. This region, filled with heathen people, afforded marvelous opportunity for crusading, missionary, and economic projects. The Papacy warmly supported the conquest and Christianization of Prussia and in 1230 authorized the Teutonic Knights to carry out the holy task. Combining with another local military order called the Brothers of the Sword, they won great success. By the first quarter of the fourteenth century they had conquered all the Baltic coast area up to the Gulf of Finland. Over this land the Teutonic Knights wielded political authority and disposed of their conquests as they saw fit. They granted out fiefs of land to German nobles, settled German peasants on much of the land, and worked closely with the Hanse to develop the economic resources of the area. As a result the Baltic lands came under the German sphere of influence and Prussia became thoroughly Germanized.

THE SCANDINAVIAN KINGDOMS

North of Germany lay the Scandinavian kingdoms of Denmark, Norway, and Sweden. After the fall of the North Sea empire forged in the early eleventh century by Canute, king of England and Denmark, the history of the Scandinavian region is of little significance. The land was too barren and cold to nourish a dynamic political and economic life; the struggle to survive drained off most of the energy of the hardy Scandinavians. About all that can be said is that in the eleventh, twelfth, and thirteenth centuries the kings of Denmark, Norway, and Sweden fought unsuccessfully to conquer one another's lands, and finally united to resist the economic and political penetration of the North and Baltic Sea area by the German Hanse. Meanwhile, the feudal system found its way into these kingdoms and the more enlightened rulers began to emulate their southern brethren by founding towns and encouraging trade and commerce.

Records are so scarce that little can be said about Scandinavian institutions. We know that the kings were not strong and constantly faced revolt from their warlike and crude nobles in whom ran much of the adventurous Viking spirit. It is extremely doubtful that there is any truth to the view of some historians that democratic representative assemblies were a feature of Scandinavian government. This belief, like that in the democratic government of the early Germans, is but a romantic and unhistorical notion. Under the influence of the German church especially of the archbishopric of Hamburg the three kingdoms were converted to Christianity. Last to be converted was Norway. It came into the fold through the efforts of its kings Olaf I (995–1000) whose military exploits and famous adventures and travels gave rise to numerous legends, and Olaf II (1016–1028) who was canonized and became a national hero and patron saint of Norway. From Norway the Christian faith was carried to the distant colony of Iceland. Perhaps the most significant cultural contribution of these Scandinavian lands in the Middle Ages was their literature—the grand Icelandic sagas.

6. *The Mongol Invasions*

DURING THE TWELFTH AND THIRTEENTH CENTURIES the principal development in central and eastern Europe was the advance of the Germans. At moments, however, it appeared that new tribes from Asia might, like the Huns of almost a thousand years before, overwhelm central Europe and push into the western part. The menace this time was the Mongols or Tartars, as they were called, nomadic tribes that originally roamed the steppes of eastern Asia and whose history prior to the twelfth century does not concern us because it did not involve Europe.

They became a menace only under the famous Genghis Kahn (1162–1227) who united all the tribes and led them to the conquest of a vast empire that included all of China and stretched from the Pacific Ocean into central Europe.

Early in the thirteenth century while the main forces of the Mongols were reducing China, other forces began pushing westward through Turkestan toward the Caspian Sea, which they reached about 1220. A force then drove on from the Caspian into Russia and reached the Volga River where it disastrously defeated an army of Russian princes. With the death of Genghis Kahn the Mongol advance temporarily stopped, but it was resumed in ten years. In 1237 the Bulgarian state on the Volga was destroyed; by 1241 all the Russian principalities, even Kiev, had been reduced and all of Russia became a subject territory. Two columns next pushed into Hungary and Poland. The entire Hungarian plain was ravished and in 1242 the Mongols reached the coast of the Adriatic Sea. Even Austria was threatened when a force crossed the Danube River and sacked a village not far from Vienna. The other column, meanwhile, had sacked Cracow and defeated the combined forces of Poland and the Teutonic Knights. These were the deepest thrusts of the Mongols into Europe. At the death of the Mongol khan there was a scramble for power and the Mongols thereafter devoted their energies to controlling the vast continental region from the Volga River to the Pacific. Once again fortuitous circumstance had saved western Europe. Russia, however, was to remain a dependency of the Mongol state until the power of the khan was destroyed late in the fourteenth century by the princes of Moscow. This Russian success was possible only because the disintegration of the Mongol empire was at this moment hastened by the conquests of the great warrior Tamerlane (1335–1405). It was not from Tamerlane, as we shall see, but from the Ottoman Turks that the gravest threat to Europe and the eastern Mediterranean came during the fourteenth and fifteenth centuries.

7. *Spain*

SPANISH HISTORY up through the early thirteenth century revolves around the reconquest of the peninsula from the Moors. We have seen how such states as León, Navarre, Castile, Aragon, and Barcelona were formed in the eleventh century and began their "perpetual crusade" against the Moors to the south. The high point of the reconquest was in 1085 when Castile captured Toledo. After this Moslem resistance was stiffened with reinforcements of fanatical warriors from Africa. Not until 1118, with the capture of Saragossa by Aragon, was there further advance to the south. By taking this key point Aragon blocked southern expansion of the kingdom of Barcelona and was able to occupy all the Ebro River valley.

THE RECONQUISTA

In 1150 the ruler of Barcelona acquired the throne of Aragon through marriage and united the two kingdoms. Meanwhile the united kingdom of León-Castile had been torn apart by civil war over the succession. As a result León and Castile again became two separate kingdoms and during the strife lost territory to the west. Taking advantage of the civil war, the counts of Portugal won their independence and assumed the title of king. In their struggle for independence the Portuguese were supported by the Popes who treated their land as a papal fief and recognized it as a kingdom in 1179.

The Moors now took advantage of Christian disunity to reconquer much of their lost land. In 1196 a decisive Moorish victory pushed the Castilian House out of Toledo. While the infidel pushed north, war broke out among Navarre, León, Castile, and Aragon. Fearful that all Christian land below the Pyrenees would be lost, Pope Innocent III pleaded for harmony and preached a crusade. Thanks to his efforts the kingdoms of Aragon, Castile, and Navarre suppressed their differences long enough to win the greatest victory of the reconquista against the Moors. With the assistance of recruits from north of the Pyrenees, the three kingdoms crushed the Moors at the Battle of Las Navas de Tolosa in 1212. But immediately falling apart again, the three were not able to exploit their great victory. Only some fortunate successions kept the Spanish states from total anarchy. In 1217 the kingdoms of Castile and León were once more united under the able Ferdinand III (1217–1252), and Aragon fell to another exceptionally gifted ruler James I (1212–1276).

Spanish history in the thirteenth century centers upon the two states of Castile and Aragon. Under Ferdinand III and his successors Castile drove ahead with the reconquista. The campaigns were so successful that by 1270 only Granada along the Mediterranean remained in Moorish hands, and it so remained for the next two centuries. The kingdoms of Portugal, Castile, and Aragon now controlled most of the peninsula as well as the Atlantic and Mediterranean seaboards. Meanwhile the kingdom of Navarre fell under the power of a French house and left the Spanish orbit. We are not concerned with the complicated political history during the rest of the century; of greater significance was the development of certain Castilian and Aragonese institutions.

CASTILIAN AND ARAGONESE INSTITUTIONS

In Castile feudalism took a unique form. The nobles were divided into three classes, ranging from men with rights almost equal to those of the kings to men who were but simple knights. Unfortunately for the crown, these nobles were exempt from taxation and were in constant revolt. To offset aristocratic power the kings

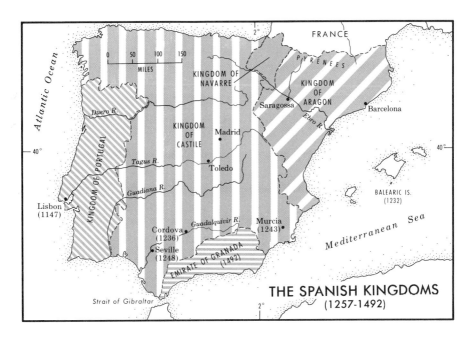

THE SPANISH KINGDOMS
(1257-1492)

in the twelfth and thirteenth centuries favored the growth of towns. They granted them liberal economic, social, legal, and political liberties, and many new urban sites were founded. Each town came to have its charter, or *fuero,* guaranteeing its privileges. Such royal support of urban self-government nurtured the growth of political competence and self-reliance. By the thirteenth century it was customary for these towns to band into associations or brotherhoods (*hermandades*) to preserve their liberties during times of military and political crisis. Gradually such unions became permanent and were recognized by the kings who found them valuable allies in their struggle against the unruly nobles.

It was undoubtedly royal need of money and support against the nobles that impelled the kings to summon national assemblies—the Cortes—which consisted of nobles, clergy, and representatives of the towns. Already in 1188 towns were represented in the Cortes of León, and in 1250 they were summoned to the Castilian Cortes. During the rest of the thirteenth century the Cortes, dominated by the representative element, won some striking privileges. It gained the right to grant all extraordinary taxation, a privilege that by the early fourteenth century had become written law. It also secured the right to petition the crown in matters of legislation. Winning still other privileges in the later fourteenth century, the Cortes, like the English Parliament, attained great power. But unfortunately all these privileges were lost before the onslaught of absolutism in the fifteenth and sixteenth centuries.

In Aragon the Cortes became prominent during the reign of Peter III (1276–

1285) who, as we have seen, also became king of Sicily after the Sicilian Vespers. The Mediterranean expansion of Peter taxed the resources of his realm, forcing him to make concessions to the Cortes in return for money. In a Cortes of 1283 the nobles and townsmen banded together and forced Peter to grant them the General Privilege which, in many respects, was like Magna Carta. Peter promised to govern according to the established laws, to punish no one except after due process of trial, and to force no man to serve in his army overseas. The General Privilege was more progressive than Magna Carta in that many of its rights extended to the bourgeoisie. The Cortes later won the right to appoint members to the royal council and forced recognition of the principle that it could depose and elect a king. Such radical concessions, however, did not become permanent and were suppressed by the middle of the fourteenth century. The principal difference between the Castilian and Aragonese Cortes was that in the latter the nobles had a dominant position and obstructed the growth of parliamentary privileges in the fourteenth century. The other peculiar Aragonese institution was a supreme judge (*justicia*) empowered to try all royal officials and cases between the king and his subjects.

In some respects constitutional growth in Castile and Aragon was ahead of that in England. But, as with France, constitutional progress ceased and succumbed before absolutism. Like France, Castile and Aragon had been built up piece by piece, each with its own customs and institutions. Too often the only common institution was the king. Although the Cortes provided an institution through which the community of the realm could express its will, the various elements of the realm did not coalesce into a tight union as did the English burgesses, knights, and lords. The Cortes was not powerful enough to oppose successfully the strong king. Behind it there had to be the middle class united in its interests and in the purpose of making the king rule according to the law of the land.

Further Reading

The titles that follow are but a few of the numerous good books on the political and institutional history of the high Middle Ages. The history of western and central Europe is treated in detail in the pertinent volumes of *The Cambridge Medieval History.* In addition to the books cited in Chapter V another standard work is that of *E. P. Cheyney, *The Dawn of a New Era, 1250–1453* (New York, 1936). For the influence of medieval states upon modern ones see J. R. Strayer, *On the Medieval Origins of the Modern State* (Princeton, 1970).

The two standard works on England in the twelfth and thirteenth centuries are A. L. Poole, *From Domesday Book to Magna Carta, 1087–1216,* 2nd ed. (Oxford, 1955);

and F. M. Powicke, *The Thirteenth Century, 1216–1307* (Oxford, 1953). Political history is interwoven into A. Kelley's good biography of **Eleanor of Aquitaine* (Cambridge, Mass., 1950). Studies dealing primarily with English constitutional history are the following: B. Lyon, *A Constitutional and Legal History of Medieval England* (New York, 1960); J. E. A. Jolliffe, *Angevin Kingship,* 2nd ed. (London, 1963); H. G. Richardson and G. O. Sayles, *The Governance of Mediaeval England from the Conquest to Magna Carta* (Edinburgh, 1963); and **A. F. Pollard, *The Evolution of Parliament,* 2nd ed. (London, 1926). Translations of pertinent records are in C. Stephenson and F. G. Marcham, *Sources of English Constitutional History* (New York, 1937).

There are few books in English on French political history. In addition to the books referred to in Chapter V the student should read **Joinville's *Life of Saint Louis,* trans. by F. Marzials (London, 1908). German history in this period is covered by **G. Barraclough, *The Origins of Modern Germany;* **J. Bryce, *The Holy Roman Empire* (London, 1904); F. Bauml, *Medieval Civilization in Germany, 800–1273* (New York, 1969); and R. Folz, *The Concept of Empire in Western Europe from the Fifth to the Fourteenth Century* (New York, 1969). German institutions are dealt with in G. Barraclough, *Medieval Germany* (Oxford, 1938), Vols. I–II. Valuable sources for Frederick Barbarossa are Otto of Freising, *The Two Cities,* trans. by C. C. Mierow (New York, 1928); and **Otto of Freising, *Deeds of Frederick Barbarossa,* trans. by C. C. Mierow and R. Emery (New York, 1953). For studies on Frederick Barbarossa see P. Munz, *Frederick Barbarossa: A Study in Medieval Politics* (Ithaca and London, 1969); and M. Pacaut, *Frederick Barbarossa* (New York, 1970). On the achievements of Frederick II there is the interesting but highly debatable biography by E. Kantorowicz, *Frederick II* (London, 1931). For the history of southern Italy and Sicily see **S. Runciman, *The Sicilian Vespers: A History of the Mediterranean World in the Later Thirteenth Century* (Cambridge, 1958); and D. M. Smith, *Medieval Sicily (800–1713)* (New York, 1968).

A general survey of Italian history is found in L. Salvatorelli, *A Concise History of Italy* (New York, 1939). For northern Italy there are the books of W. F. Butler, *The Lombard Communes* (New York, 1906); and F. Schevill, *History of Florence* (New York, 1936). The standard work in English on medieval Spain is still that of R. B. Merriman, *The Rise of the Spanish Empire* (New York, 1918), Vol. I. Useful for all aspects of Spanish history is R. Menendez Pidal, *The Cid and His Spain* (London, 1934). Also useful is H. J. Chaytor, *A History of Aragon and Catalonia* (London, 1933); and especially G. Jackson, *The Making of Medieval Spain* (New York, 1972).

CHAPTER 9

The Age of
the Renaissance
1300–1517

1. General Characteristics of the Age of the Renaissance

By the fourteenth century medieval civilization began to wane. Over the next five centuries a distinctively modern civilization emerged in Europe. Yet medieval ways did not vanish all at once, for no clear frontier sets apart medieval and modern. Indeed, although modernity usually implies something unmedieval, institutions and attitudes born in the Middle Ages are the basis for no small number of characteristically modern patterns of life. What gives the entire age from 1300 to 1815 its special quality is the blending of medieval and modern in simultaneous strangeness and familiarity. Obviously we can expect to find the medieval elements stronger in the earlier stages of this transformation while the modern will pre-dominate at the end.

It has become customary to call the first of these stages of the early modern era the *Renaissance,* a term that originally described the art and literature of Italy in the fourteenth, fifteenth, and sixteenth centuries. Some historians have sought to identify a single or a few central traits of the Renaissance—notably individualism, rationalism, and secularism—and to trace these outward from art, literature, and learning to all aspects of man's social life. Other historians, including the writers of this book, are wary of finding such a spirit of the times neatly identifiable in an "ism"; instead they see the Renaissance as an age when the life of the spirit was vigorous and rich, to be sure, but when economic, political, and religious institutions had their own patterns of growth. This is not to deny the interconnections among all these varied activities, some of which will be described in these pages, but only to emphasize their often-neglected autonomy.

2. An Age of Economic Recovery

THE ECONOMIC DEVELOPMENTS in the century and a half of the Renaissance were not marked by surging economic growth breaking out of medieval fetters, as was once believed, but by a slow, hesitant, and painful recovery from disasters in the mid-fourteenth century that shattered medieval prosperity. No longer did Europeans in the western and eastern regions alike seek out new lands to drain or clear for the plow. Population growth, for long so rapid, was reversed. The Black Death, as the recurring epidemics of bubonic plague were called, ravaged wide areas of Europe in 1348–1350, killing about a quarter of the population and accelerating an economic decline which had already begun. Wars, local and regional, remained endemic in European life, but the devastation wreaked by the soldiery was not as quick to be repaired and was more lasting in its consequences.

AGRICULTURE

Broad areas of the countryside especially in France were allowed to fall into neglect for decades. A shortage of agricultural labor held up recovery, although for the tillers of the soil who did survive private good came out of public disaster. In western and central Europe the peasants were able to obtain better rental terms and to achieve a very large measure of personal freedom. In eastern Europe, which was still sparsely populated, rulers and noblemen had to grant similar conditions to tempt immigrants from the west. In western Europe serfdom began to disappear as obligations to the manorial lords were commuted from payments in kind and labor services to fixed payments in currency. Since money itself was in turn subject to a long-term decline in value, the peasantry benefited by a reduction in their real payments. The manorial form of agriculture continued in general use but began to change character in western Europe; the lord of the manor more and more frequently rented out his holdings to peasants rather than having them tilled by serfs under obligations of labor service. In eastern Europe, on the other hand, estate owners preferred to operate their own farms. At first they employed hired labor, but from the fifteenth century onwards they began to use their rights of jurisdiction over the villages to compel peasants to provide increasingly burdensome labor services on the lands of the lords.

The two contrasting paths of development in agrarian life in western and central Europe were both the result of the same fundamental changes in economic life: growth of a money economy and decline in self-sufficiency of the countryside, expansion of commerce, increasing industrial activity, and continual growth of towns in western Europe. Farmers in such regions as northern Italy and the Low Countries were moved by the availability of the new urban markets to raise garden crops and industrial raw materials (notably flax and such dye plants as madder and woad) for sale. As we have seen in Chapter 6 (page 213), the presence of towns whose population was not ordinarily servile ("city air makes free") encouraged the emancipation of the peasantry in the countryside, where the vast majority of the population continued to reside, by providing an example of personal liberty and a place where one could go to gain it if need be. But, as increasing numbers of the farming population in western Europe turned their energies to cultivating cash crops instead of producing grain for their own use and for sale to the expanding population employed in commerce and industry, the need to import grain rose sharply. Some traditional sources of cereal foodstuffs—notably Sicily and the Black Sea coast (later to be called the Ukraine)—continued to supply much of the needs of Mediterranean countries; western Europe beyond the Alps had no such ready-made supplier and turned to the regions of northern Europe facing the Baltic, particularly Poland and the adjacent countries, for their surplus grain. This grain came not from stocks brought to market by free farmers but from large-scale shipments made by big landowners from the produce of lands tilled, as we have seen, by compulsory labor.

Another consequence of the agrarian transformation that followed in the wake of the new industries was the beginning of a centuries-long process of improving the techniques of agriculture—a process whose last stages, almost five hundred years later, would be called the *Agricultural Revolution*. These changes involved the replacement of the three-field system (in Mediterranean countries often the even less efficient two-field system) of restoring fertility to depleted fields by a system in which elaborate means were taken to maintain almost continuous fertility, such as heavy manuring (made possible by the increased flocks of dairy cattle and by the nearness of towns which supplied "night soil"), cultivation of leguminous crops, use of marl (limestone), more careful drainage, and use of improved plows and other farm instruments. It is notable, too, that these new-style farmers threw off the straitjacket of custom and adapted their operations to the needs of the market, changing crops according to price conditions. But these innovations were largely restricted to the Low Countries and, to a lesser extent, north Italy; elsewhere the transformation of agriculture was much slower or even totally absent.

INDUSTRY

Industry continued to be the occupation of only a small minority of Europeans. Agriculture provided the livelihood of a majority of the population even
in the Low Countries and north Italy where industry was most advanced. The
number of those engaged in making goods—notably cloth, leather products,
hardware, and, not least, arms and armor—was increasing, however, and the
towns these artisans inhabited continued to grow in size. Production still depended overwhelmingly on the handicraft skills of men who worked with tools
and simple machines, although some power-driven machines were invented.
These included water and windmills used particularly for grinding grain and for
pumps (important especially in drainage operations and mines). The guilds, as we
saw in Chapter 6 (page 220), stayed strong in those branches of activity which
served chiefly local markets where demand was relatively fixed. Capitalist forms of
ownership and operation developed more rapidly and vigorously in those industries
which served long-distance trade. Most common was the *putting-out system*. A
merchant entrepreneur bought raw materials which he "put out" to workers to
prepare in their own homes on machines owned by the employer. He paid them on
a piecework basis and sold the finished product. Their wages, even with wife and
children helping, usually had to be supplemented with the produce of garden
plots around their cottages. Large-scale enterprises using big machines and assembling many workers under a single roof in the fashion of a modern factory
were rare; perhaps the most notable were forges and printing plants after the
invention of printing with movable type in the mid-fifteenth century.

COMMERCE AND BANKING

After agriculture the next most important branch of economic life was commerce. It was the exchange of goods rather than the process of production which
enabled a growing number of men to amass wealth outside the traditional method
of landownership, and it was their initiative which spurred the transformation
of the economic basis of society—a process which was sometimes rapid, sometimes
slow and irregular, but ultimately never halted. Local commerce continued, very
little changed; it was still an affair of small shopkeepers, usually organized in guilds,
and often themselves the producers of the goods they sold. Trade over longer
distances took on different forms, however. More important than guilds were the
merchant companies of England and the Hanse of Germany; these were associations of merchants traveling together for safety against pirates or robbers but
trading individually. However, the great commercial centers of Flanders—Bruges
until the end of the fifteenth century and then Antwerp until the end of the next
century—did not possess their own trading fleets and depended upon foreign

shipping, Italian, English, and Dutch in particular. South Germany developed its own network of land-based trading companies, notably at Augsburg, owned by such wealthy families as the Walsers and the Fuggers.

Businesses were usually family-owned; this was true even of the most extensive, like those of some of the great merchant-banker families of north Italy. One of the most famous of these businesses was the firm of Francesco Datini (c. 1355–1410) of Prato. It engaged in banking, metal and wool manufactures, and sales. Trading between eastern and western Europe, it had branches at Florence, Genoa, Valencia, Barcelona, and Majorca, as well as correspondents in Milan, Venice, England, France, the Low Countries, eastern Europe and Africa. An alternate form of organization, the partnership, had already emerged. Seafaring partnerships often brought together some men who contributed only capital and others who had only skills and labor to give; they were always set up for single voyages after which the profits were distributed and the partnership terminated. Similar arrangements in mining companies, on the contrary, were permanent in character because of the continuing nature of the enterprise.

Economic activity was closely associated with demographic developments, that is, changes in the numbers and composition of populations. The reduction in numbers that occurred after the Black Death and the political and social disorders of the fourteenth century contributed to a general slowing down of productive activity which in turn delayed demographic recovery. By the end of the fifteenth century the population losses of the previous dozen or more decades had been barely made good. Significantly, however, the momentum of population growth had been reestablished.

3. *Society*

THE GRADUAL EMERGENCE of modern characteristics in the society of the Renaissance is evident in the increased importance of the bourgeoisie—the townsmen with the right of citizenship in their municipality who formed the *middle class,* a class of propertied commoners midway between the nobility and the poor.[1] The poor included not only the peasantry of the countryside, only a minority of whom were propertyless and without rights in the villages, but also an increasing number of working people in the towns, some of them self-employed artisans but many mere wage-earners. Nonetheless it would be a distortion of the total picture of the society of the Renaissance to see it as nothing more than an early version of modern industrial society; bourgeois businessmen and the urban working class

---

[1] The term *bourgeoisie* came to mean specifically the class of capitalist businessmen and allied professionals only in the nineteenth century.

were both numerically small segments of the population. The landholding nobility were still at the apex of the social system even in the economically most advanced countries. The one important exception to this rule was northern Italy where the wealthy and powerful patriciates in the numerous towns brought the noblemen of the neighboring countryside under their domination. Here landed aristocrats came to be mainly city-dwellers, differing little from the businessmen among whom they resided. When burghers became rich, they frequently sought to be incorporated into the nobility either by marriage or by buying a title of nobility from a reigning prince; indeed this practice, far from declining as the numbers and wealth of the bourgeoisie increased over the next centuries, became more widespread. In general, although social and economic status was fixed for the great majority, the boundaries between the social classes remained fluid and were crossed by significant numbers of men on their way up or down.

More important than belonging to a broad class such as the nobility, the bourgeoisie, or the peasantry was membership in a specific community, and, within it, in a specific occupational group. Strongest loyalties were left for the family, whose ties extended to quite broad ranges of relationship, and for the organized bodies or *corporations* which embodied economic, religious, and other ties. A man's strongest territorial identification was with his village or town, less with his province, and least of all with his country or nation (in the modern sense in which we speak of Frenchmen, Germans, or Poles, meaning those who speak French, German, or Polish and are citizens or subjects of France, Germany, or Poland). Language reflected this attitude, as the importance of dialects testifies. To be sure, national languages, such as French, Italian, Castilian, and Romanian within the Romance family and German, English, and the Scandinavian tongues within the Germanic family, had developed, but in none of these had there yet evolved a standard form, spoken and written with only minor differences by all educated persons. The use of Latin as the principal language of instruction, common to all Europe from the Atlantic to Poland and Hungary, contributed to the slow development of standard national languages. A political factor which also delayed their emergence was the continuing importance of local and regional government even in countries such as France, England, and Germany where monarchy had come to coincide more or less loosely with *nations,* that is, groups speaking a common language. The large majority of the population who stayed at or near home all their lives had no need to learn anything but their local *patois,* but the not insignificant minority who went abroad, soldiers, merchants, officials, migrants, and seekers after work, more readily adapted to other languages because learning these tongues was not made more difficult by formal grammatical rules and established standards of usage. Even among the educated minority who could read and write, there was no fixity of grammar and spelling; differences of pronunciation were reflected in spelling rather than concealed behind an official uniformity as they are today.

4. *The Changing States*

THE CONSTITUENT ELEMENTS of the modern state began to take shape during the latter Middle Ages and the Renaissance, creating a distinctive transitional form of government no longer definitely feudal nor yet clearly modern. The medieval blending of political and economic institutions in feudalism began to give way to the modern system of separating the possession of political power and the ownership of property. Feudalism as a system of distributing political power among vassals and subvassals did not disappear outright but continued to exist alongside a new and increasingly prevalent form of government in which unified power was held by a single prince over a distinct territory, with subordinate political agencies ruling on his behalf and subject to his authority and control. The sovereign territorial state was becoming predominant in Europe.

PROFESSIONAL GOVERNMENT

This consolidation of political authority and organization was made possible by the expanding commercial economy. Rulers were able to develop professional administrations and armies in which men served for wages rather than as vassals rewarded for their services by the grant of fiefs. The first branch of government to become fully professionalized was the judiciary. Courts of justice under royal jurisdiction were made a separate agency of government. They judged both crimes and claims of right according to custom as was the medieval practice, and increasingly also according to *statutes,* new laws promulgated by the kings. Judges acquired a considerable right of tenure in their offices and developed an esprit de corps which emphasized both their privileges and their duties as protectors of subjects against injustice. Yet the judges were seldom limited to salaries paid by the rulers; they were also permitted to accept from litigants fees and gifts which all too frequently became virtual bribes. The use of fees was a characteristic form of salary in many branches of government in the early modern period, with administrators receiving their authority from the sovereign but their income from payments made by those who sought the government services which they dispensed. Agencies for the collection of taxes and administration of government revenues were also becoming separate and distinct official bodies. The governmental bureaucracies which developed upon these foundations became the primary means by which the royal governments, especially in western Europe, became increasingly independent of their subjects in the collection of revenues and also became able to enforce their laws and commands, thanks to the professional armies (see below, pages 367–368) which royal taxation made possible.

Yet the finances of governments remained marked by medieval origins. Princes

10. MADONNA OF ST. FRANCIS. In this fresco in the Lower Church at Assisi, attributed to Cimabue, the Byzantine influence which dominated twelfth-century north Italian painting is still strong, yet there can also be detected, particularly in the portrait figure of St. Francis, the artist's growing interest in naturalism and human values, an interest which was to find full expression in the Renaissance.

EUROPE
About 1360

MILES 0 50 100   200   300

—— Boundary of Holy Roman Empire
‑ ‑ ‑ Boundary of France

FAEROES

ORKNEY
ISLANDS

SHETLAND
ISLANDS   Bergen

NORWAY

Oslo

Upsala

S

Calmar

North

HEBRIDES

SCOTLAND   Aberdeen
Bannockburn
Falkirk   Edinburgh
Berwick
Carlisle

DENMARK   Copenhagen

Sea

IRELAND
Dublin

Armagh

York
Lincoln
Chester

Lubeck   Stralsund
POMERANIA
Hamburg

Gnes

Wexford

WALES

Cork

ENGLAND

Norwich

Bremen

Magdeburg   BRANDENBURG

Pos

Atlantic

London

Bruges

HOLLAND

HOLY

SILESI

English Channel   Agincourt   Calais
Harfleur   Crecy

BRABANT
Ghent

Cologne

Frankfurt   Mainz

ROMAN

Prague

Ocean

Caen   Rouen
Paris
BRITTANY   Bretigny
Rennes

Reims
Compiegne
Vaucouleurs

Trier

ROMAN

BOHEMIA
Regensburg   MORAVIA

Nantes   Orleans
Loire
Chinon
Poitiers

FRANCE

Troyes
Domremy

Strassburg

Basel

Munich   Vienna
Salzburg

BAVARIA

Bay of
Biscay

Limoges

BURGUNDY

Dijon

Lyon

Besançon
SWISS
CONFED.   Constance

AUSTRIA

EMPIRE

Bordeaux

AQUITAINE

Garonne

Bayonne   Toulouse
Pau

DAUPHINY

SAVOY

LANDS
OF THE
VISCONTI

Turin   Milan

Ferrara

Trieste

Bu

PORTUGAL

Santiago
Leon

NAVARRE

Avignon
Narbonne   Marseille

PROVENCE

Po
Genoa

Bologna

Venice   REPUBLIC

OF

BOS

Salamanca

Duero

Saragossa

ARAGON

Florence

PAPAL STATES

VENICE

Adriatic

Toledo

CASTILE

Tagus
Guadiana

Lisbon

Barcelona

CORSICA
(To Genoa)

Rome   KINGDOM

OF

Rag

Sea

Seville

Cordova

Valencia

BALEARIC   ISLANDS

SARDINIA
(To Aragon)

Naples

NAPLES

Tar

Cadiz

Granada
GRANADA

Gibraltar

(To Aragon)

Mediterranean

Palermo   Messina

KINGDOM
OF
SICILY   Reggio

MOSLEM

Algiers

Tunis

STATES

MARINDS

ZIANIDS

HAFSIDS

MALTA

Copyright by Rand McNally & Company, Made in U.S.A.

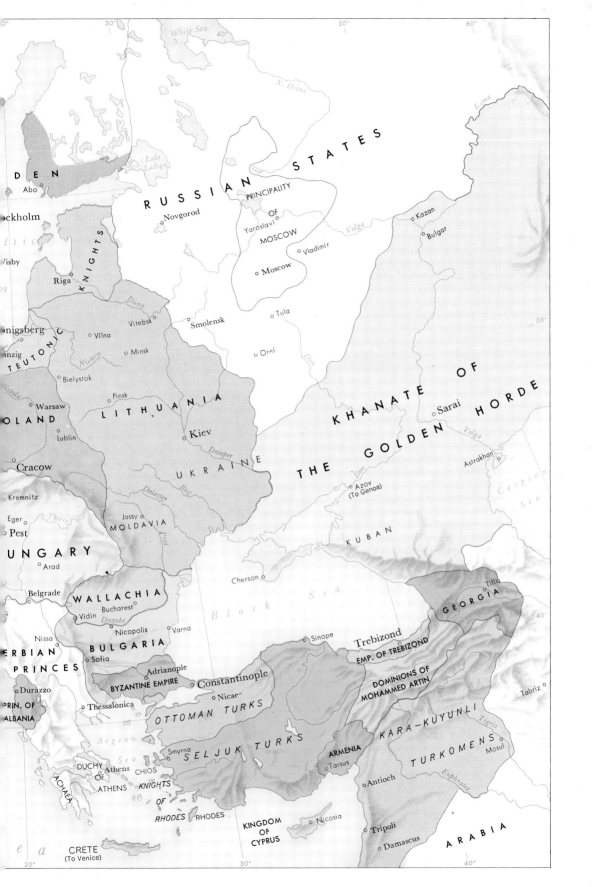

RUSSIAN STATES

White Sea

N. Dvina

Lake Ladoga

Abo

D E N

ckholm

Visby

Riga

Novgorod

PRINCIPALITY
OF
MOSCOW

Yaroslavl

Vladimir

Moscow

Volga

Kazan

Bulgar

nigsberg

anzig

TEUTONIC

KNIGHTS

Vitebsk

Smolensk

Tula

Orel

Vilna

Dūna

Minsk

Niemen

Bielystok

Pinsk

OLAND

Warsaw

LITHUANIA

Kiev

Cracow

Lublin

UKRAINE

KHANATE OF

THE GOLDEN HORDE

Sarai

Dnieper

Bug

Kremnitz

Eger

Pest

Thiess

Dniester

Prut

MOLDAVIA

Jassy

Azov
(To Genoa)

Don

Astrakhan

Volga

UNGARY

Arad

Cherson

K U B A N

Caspian
Sea

Belgrade

WALLACHIA

Bucharest

Vidin

Danube

Nicopolis

Varna

B l a c k   S e a

Sinope

Trebizond

EMP. OF TREBIZOND

GEORGIA

Tiflis

40

Nissa

ERBIAN

PRINCES

BULGARIA

Sofia

Adrianople

BYZANTINE EMPIRE

Constantinople

DOMINIONS OF
MOHAMMED ARTIN

Durazzo

PRIN. OF
ALBANIA

Thessalonica

Nicaea

OTTOMAN TURKS

Tabriz

Aegean
Sea

Smyrna

SELJUK TURKS

KARA–KUYUNLI

TURKOMENS

Mosul

ACHAEA

DUCHY
OF
ATHENS

Athens

CHIOS

KNIGHTS
OF
RHODES

ARMENIA

Tarsus

Antioch

Euphrates

Tigris

RHODES

KINGDOM
OF
CYPRUS

Nicosia

Tripoli

A R A B I A

e   a

CRETE
(To Venice)

Damascus

11. ST. FRANCIS RECEIVING THE STIGMATA. Giotto, who may well have been a student of Cimabue, here fully exploited the "new style" which he and Cimabue are traditionally credited with beginning. Although in this fresco he is depicting the most spiritual moment in the familiar episodes of the life of St. Francis, his central figure is solid and realistic, and the scene is presented with a dramatic power new in painting of this period.

12. PRIMAVERA. In this allegorical study of the coming of spring, Botticelli exhibits one of the primary interests of late fifteenth-century painting. Thus, his subject is presented through elements drawn from classical mythology and can be interpreted fully only through references to the mystical Neoplatonic thought of Ficino and his circle.

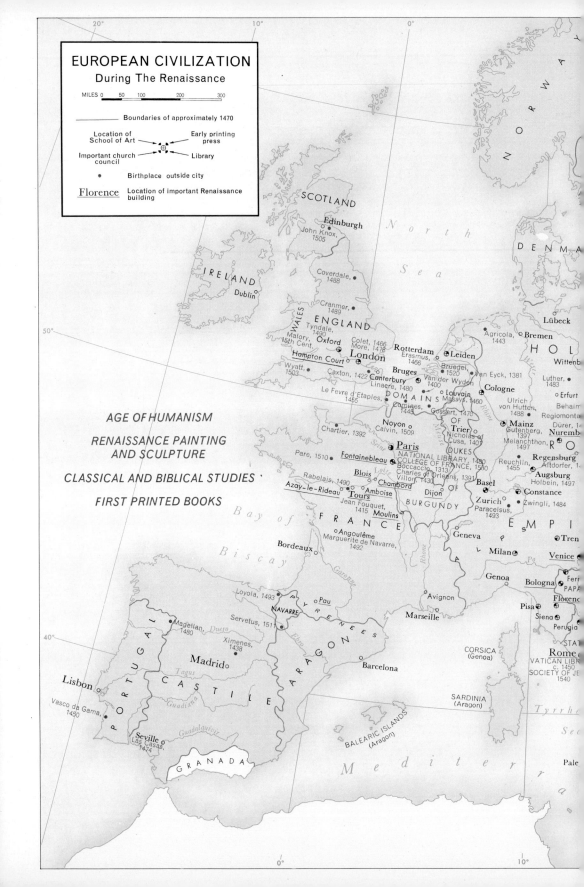

EUROPEAN CIVILIZATION
During The Renaissance

MILES 0   50   100   200   300

——————— Boundaries of approximately 1470

Location of
School of Art ————→ ⊕ ←———— Early printing
press

Important church ————→   ←———— Library
council

• Birthplace outside city

Florence   Location of important Renaissance
building

NORWAY

SCOTLAND

Edinburgh
John Knox,
1505

North

Sea

DENMA

IRELAND

Dublin

Lübeck

Coverdale,
1488

WALES
Cranmer,
1489
ENGLAND
Tyndale,
1490
Malory,   Oxford
15th Cent.
Hampton Court
London
Canterbury
Caxton, 1422
Wyatt,
1503
Bruges
Linacre, 1480
Le Fevre d'Etaples,
1455
Colet, 1466
More, 1478
Rotterdam
Erasmus,
1466
Leiden
Bruegel,
1520
Van Eyck, 1381
Van der Wyden,
1400
Louvain
Massys, 1460
Cologne

Agricola,
1443
Bremen

HOL

Wittenb

Luther,
1483

Erfurt

DOMAINS

Comines,
1449

Gossart, 1470

Ulrich
von Hutten,
1488

Behai

Regiomonta

AGE OF HUMANISM

RENAISSANCE PAINTING
AND SCULPTURE

CLASSICAL AND BIBLICAL STUDIES

FIRST PRINTED BOOKS

Chartier, 1392
Noyon
Calvin, 1509
OF
Trier
Nicholas of
Cusa, 1401

Mainz
Gutenberg,
1397
Melanchthon,
1497

Dürer, 1
Nuremb

Paris
NATIONAL LIBRARY, 1480
COLLEGE OF FRANCE, 1530
Boccaccio,
1313
Charles of Orleans,
1430
Villon, 1391

Pare, 1510
Fontainebleau

DUKES

Reuchlin,
1455

R   O

Regensburg

Aftdorfer, 1

Rabelais, 1490
Azay-le-Rideau
Blois
Chambord
Tours
Amboise
Moulins
Jean Fouquet,
1415

Dijon

OF

BURGUNDY

Basel

Zurich
Paracelsus,
1493

Augsburg
Holbein, 1497

Constance
Zwingli, 1484

E M P I

Bay of

FRANCE

Angoulême
Marguerite de Navarre,
1492

Geneva

Milan

Tren

Biscay

Bordeaux

Po

Venice

Genoa

Ferr
Bologna
PAPA
Florenc

Loyola, 1493
Pau
Servetus, 1511
NAVARRE

Avignon

Marseille

Pisa
Siena
Perugia

Magellan,
1480
Ximenes,
1438

PORTUGAL

Madrid

CASTILE

ARAGON

Barcelona

CORSICA
(Genoa)

STA
Rome
VATICAN LIBR
c. 1450
SOCIETY OF JE
1540

Lisbon

Vasco da Gama,
1450

Tagus

Guadiana

SARDINIA
(Aragon)

Tyrrhe

Se

Seville
Las Casas,
1474

Guadalquivir

GRANADA

BALEARIC ISLANDS
(Aragon)

Mediterra

Pale

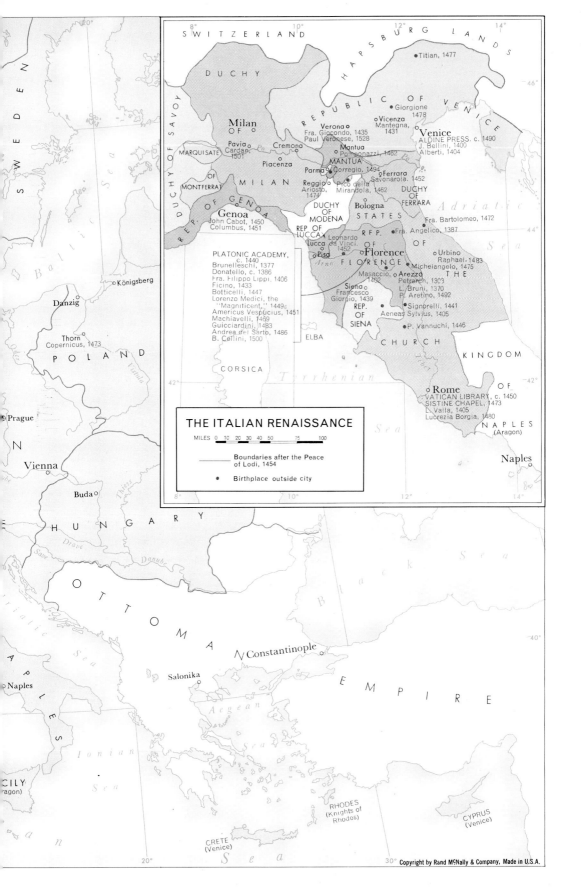

THE ITALIAN RENAISSANCE

MILES 0 10 20 30 40 50   75   100

Boundaries after the Peace
of Lodi, 1454

● Birthplace outside city

SWITZERLAND

HAPSBURG LANDS

DUCHY

●Titian, 1477

REPUBLIC OF VENICE

●Giorgione
1478

Milan
OF

○Vicenza
Mantegna,
1431

○Verona
Fra Giocondo, 1435
Paul Veronese, 1528

Venice
ALDINE PRESS, c. 1490
J. Bellini, 1400
Alberti, 1404

Pavia○
Cardan,
1501

Cremona○

○Mantua
Pomponazzi, 1462

Piacenza

MANTUA
Parma○ ○Correggio, 1494

DUCHY OF SAVOY

MARQUISATE

Po

DUCHY
OF SAVOY

OF
MONTFERRAT

REP. OF GENOA

MILAN

Reggio○
Ariosto,
1474

Ferrara
Savonarola, 1452
●Pico della
Mirandola, 1462

DUCHY
OF
FERRARA

Adriatic

DUCHY
OF
MODENA

Bologna

STATES

○

Genoa
John Cabot, 1450
Columbus, 1451

REP. OF
LUCCA

R.F.P.

Fra. Bartolomeo, 1472

Sea

Lucca○
●Leonardo
da Vinci,
1452

R.F.P. OF

●Fra. Angelico, 1387

44°

○Pisa

FLORENCE

Florence

○Urbino
Raphael, 1483

Arno

Masaccio,
1402

○Arezzo
Petrarch, 1303

●Michelangelo,
1475

THE

PLATONIC ACADEMY,
c. 1440
Brunelleschi, 1377
Donatello, c. 1386
Fra. Filippo Lippi, 1406
Ficino, 1433
Botticelli, 1447
Lorenzo Medici, the
  "Magnificent," 1449○
Americus Vespucius, 1451
Machiavelli, 1469
Guicciardini, 1483
Andrea del Sarto, 1486
B. Cellini, 1500

Siena
●Francesco
Giorgio, 1439

REP.
OF
SIENA

L. Bruni, 1370
P. Aretino, 1492

●Signorelli, 1441
○Aeneas Sylvius, 1405

●P. Vannuchi, 1446

ELBA

CHURCH

KINGDOM

CORSICA

Tyrrhenian

Tiber

○Rome
VATICAN LIBRARY, c. 1450
SISTINE CHAPEL, 1473
L. Valla, 1405
Lucrezia Borgia, 1480

OF

42°

Sea

NAPLES
(Aragon)

Naples

SWEDEN

Baltic Sea

○Königsberg

Danzig

Thorn
Copernicus, 1473

POLAND

9 Prague

Vienna○

N

Buda○

HUNGARY

Drave

Save

Danube

OTTOMAN

Adriatic Sea

○Naples

SICILY
(Aragon)

Ionian
Sea

∩Constantinople

Salonika○

EMPIRE

Black Sea

Aegean
Sea

RHODES
(Knights of
Rhodes)

CYPRUS
(Venice)

CRETE
(Venice)

Sea

13. POPE LEO X AND HIS TWO SONS. Exhibiting here his complete mastery of the classical style of the High Renaissance, Raphael portrays with extraordinary honesty and power the pontiff who confronted the Lutheran revolt and helped to establish the counter movement toward reform within the church.

were still expected to *live of their own,* that is, on the income from their own domains and estates; they might ask subjects to pay taxes only on extraordinary occasions, like wars, and with the approval of the estates (see below, pages 367–370). Government funds were considered to be the personal property of the ruler, although they were to be used for the general welfare; financial officials were his servants rather than servants of an abstract and impersonal state. No distinction of principle was drawn between expenditures for the king's household and those for the defense and welfare of the realm; yet both the accepted political doctrine and emerging political practice made subjects increasingly aware of the state as an instrumentality of power that could be of service to them as well as a burden upon them.

PROFESSIONAL ARMIES

Professionalism also extended to the military arm of the state. Feudal levies, obligated to serve only for a limited period and seldom for the duration of a campaign, could not stand up against troops who served for pay, made warfare their full-time career, and lived under a discipline tighter than that which knights performing the obligations of vassalage would accept. Captains raised companies

PORTRAIT OF A CONDOTTIERE. The visage of a man of power in the Renaissance—cold, hard, determined—appears in this portrait by Giovanni Bellini of an unidentified condottiere.

whose services they offered on contract to various rulers. These *condottieri,* as the Italians called them, were not only field commanders interested in the most effective forms of combat; they were also military businessmen who were their soldiers' employers as well as their commanders. It was to the captains rather than the kings that the soldiers gave their first loyalty. These modern troops made use of the best weapons available—lances for cavalry and pikes for infantry, handborne firearms very late in the period (cannon were so expensive that they were assembled into separate units), and generally lighter armor than was worn by feudal knights.

Discipline within these forces was strictly dependent upon their receiving their pay. When, as in the Hundred Years' War between France and England, exhausted royal treasuries were unable to pay or pay off the troops, they formed roving bands which plagued the countryside, extorting supplies and funds from helpless peasants and townsmen. In Italy bolder commanders took advantage of disorders in the states which they served and established themselves as upstart rulers; but elsewhere, for all its shortcomings, the professional soldiery was one of the pillars on which the new territorial monarchies rested. However, the enormous costs of maintaining these troops especially in time of war placed immense burdens upon governments and ultimately upon subjects called upon to pay taxes which gradually ceased to be extraordinary in anything but name. Professional armies, thus, were not only the means of creating modern territorial states, but they made the new form of rule a political necessity. The cost of maintaining the new armies was so great that the organization of the state had to be made more efficient in order to obtain the necessary resources. Furthermore, the strains which the support of these new armies placed upon rulers with inadequate resources—and in time of war resources were almost always inadequate—created some of the typical crises of early modern political life, the struggles between rulers and ruled over the taxing power.

THE ESTATES

The Renaissance state was marked in most of Europe by a combination of monarchial power with some form of participation in government by groups of influential subjects, organized more or less formally in different countries and regions as *estates* or *orders.* These estates were distinguished by their role and status in society and by their particular contribution to the work of government. The first estate was almost always the clergy or its leaders, the bishops and abbots. Its importance in government was dual. The clergy in Renaissance Europe still provided a very large proportion of the personnel of secular government but normally were not themselves subject to taxation. The local clergy were an essential instrument in informing and guiding the common folk for purposes of state. The second order was customarily the nobility. In some countries the second estate included all members of noble families; even ordinary knights—generally possessors of only one or a very few manors—were usually ranked as lesser noblemen. In England, however, only peers of the realm were allowed to sit in the House of Lords, and only the eldest son of a peer inherited his father's title and seat; the lowest ranks of knighthood, including younger sons of peers along with untitled squires, constituted a gentry eligible to sit in the House of Commons. The third estate was known as the *commons,* that is, laymen without noble title; but in practice it usually included only the towns, as in the Low Countries and Germany, or privileged townsmen, as in France, or the citizens of boroughs and less-than-noble property owners of substance in the countryside, as in England. Except in Scandinavia, where in the sixteenth century the peasantry were included as a fourth estate, the mass of the population—rural and urban poor—were not ordinarily considered as members of the third estate, although they were without question taxpayers.

The estates were called together by the rulers in provincial or national assemblies known as *parliaments* or *diets.* The nobility and prelates usually took their seats in person and the third estate was represented by elected deputies. Ordinarily the three estates met separately, but sometimes they sat in a single chamber (the Low Countries) or in two chambers (England). In France the monarchs began convening national assemblies, called *Estates General,* in 1302, and these met irregularly over the next centuries until 1789. In the Low Countries the practice of calling together delegates from the provincial assemblies to meet for common discussion and decision started in 1464; the name *States General* was also used for the new Netherlands assembly. In England there was only a single national *Parliament* from the very beginning. In Germany there were not only the *Reichstag,* or national diet, but also local diets (*Landtage*) sharing power to some extent with local rulers. The powers entrusted to deputies in the representative chambers varied widely. In some cases, as in the Low Countries, they were usually bound by imperative mandates which permitted them to vote only as instructed by the bodies for which they acted; in others, as in the English House of Commons, members were free to vote as they wished. The tasks of deputies to a parliamentary assembly could be onerous, troublesome, and expensive, and even when their expenses were paid by their constituents deputies were often reluctant to serve.

The primary task of the parliamentary assemblies was to approve the imposition of new, extraordinary taxation by the rulers, usually on the occasion of war. Some but not all of these assemblies also had the right to approve—or disapprove— new legislation. Parliaments (or a single house) might also have judicial functions as a court of appeal. The assent of the assemblies to taxation and legislation usually assured acceptance of these measures by the population, since the parliaments spoke for those in the provinces and the towns who would be called upon to carry through these measures or at the very least to permit the king's officials to do so.

Although the parliamentary assemblies originated primarily as a means by which kings and other rulers sought the support of the influential classes, these bodies often became centers of resistance to unpopular policies and agencies for the defense of local interests against the burgeoning centralization of royal rule. The parliaments became most effective when they were accepted as a normal part of government, as in England, the Low Countries, and Poland. When they remained exceptional bodies convened only in emergencies, as in France and Spain, the assemblies concentrated their action on resisting the imposition of new taxation rather than upon participating in the determination of policy. In no case, however, did parliaments during the period of the Renaissance become more than bodies providing "advice and consent" to the rulers, except when, as in some French provinces and to some extent in the Holy Roman Empire and in Poland, they developed their own agencies of administration and collection. Even then, however, they were not yet thought of as sharing in sovereignty. The only exceptions to this rule were, of course, the few true republics in Europe, like Venice and Florence, where the representative assemblies ruled as collective sovereigns.

TERRITORIAL STATES AND DYNASTIES

The question of sovereignty—independent rule—was not yet clearly posed in the Renaissance state, except insofar as secular princes fought off with increased fervor and success the old claims of overlordship by the Papacy. What was emerging more clearly was the territoriality of the state, that is, the sharp definition of frontiers. Yet enclaves held by one ruler within the territory of another continued to be common. Vassalage as the system of feudal delegation of power was in decline; fiefs became either forms of simple landownership or means of holding virtually independent states under nominal overlordship of the emperor or a king (like the duchy of Milan in north Italy, a fief of the empire; or the so-called Burgundian state, the provinces mainly in the Low Countries held either of the emperor or the king of France). Many of the larger states had for centuries more or less conformed to the major nations, although, as we have noted, feelings of national commitment and allegiance were weak as compared to local and provincial ties (see above, page 365). Yet nationalism in the shape of antipathy to the foreigner was not wholly absent, particularly when wars presented the outsider in the character of an invader.

More powerful by far than such barely visible nationalism was the dynastic character of the Renaissance monarchies. Except for Switzerland and some of the northern Italian city-states, virtually all European states were monarchies. Dynasticism—government by a king or prince inheriting the crown as head of a ruling house or dynasty—was absent in the elective monarchies, like the Papacy, the Holy Roman Empire, Poland, and Hungary (although in the latter two realms the habit of electing kings from the same family created a kind of implicit dynasticism). Most other kingdoms were outright dynastic possessions. They were passed on according to laws of succession more or less closely based on the law of inheritance of private property, although in France and the Austrian archduchies the Salic Law forbade inheritance of the crown by or through women. Dynasties often extended beyond the boundaries of a single country. The result was either a personal union in which one prince ruled in several realms or a family connection between independent states, as in the Jagiellon ties between Poland and Hungary. Dynastic rulers in such cases were naturally concerned with the power of the states over which they ruled, but they were also less committed to the language and culture of these loosely connected countries than if they reigned in a single country. Subjects were bound to their rulers both by the general duty of obedience taught by the church and enforced by the state, and by a special feeling of loyalty and affection for the *natural lord* who inherited his realm by right of birth and hence as a gift of God.

The influence of these various factors may be seen in the story of the events in the major states—which were predominantly feudal in character at the beginning of the fourteenth century and were taking on many modern political characteristics by 1500.

5. *The States at War and in Politics*

As THE TERRITORIAL SOVEREIGN STATE took hold during the Renaissance, the interplay of civil and foreign wars became characteristic of the new politics. It reflected both the complex and conflicting patterns of allegiance and the still uncertain boundaries of the states.

THE HUNDRED YEARS' WAR

Nowhere was this overlapping of internal and external politics more evident than in the long conflict that kept England and France at each other's throats between 1337 and 1453. The Hundred Years' War originated in a characteristically feudal controversy; it ended with marked consolidation of central authority and the emergence of a considerable degree of nationalism in both countries.

The great stake in the war was the rich wine-producing region of southwestern France, variously known as Guienne, Aquitaine, and Gascony. The English king, Edward III (1327–1377), held Guienne as a fief under the French crown. When French officials endeavored to bring it under the effective domination of Paris, the local inhabitants, preferring prosperity under a distant lord to the exactions of French tax collectors, spurred English resistance. The immediate occasion of the

THE VALOIS KINGS

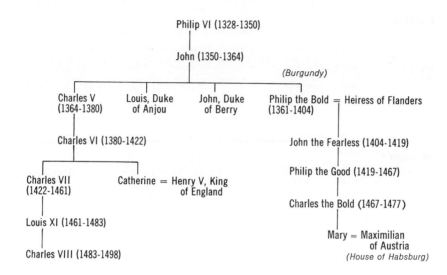

Philip VI (1328-1350)

John (1350-1364)

(Burgundy)

Charles V (1364-1380)   Louis, Duke of Anjou   John, Duke of Berry   Philip the Bold (1361-1404) = Heiress of Flanders

Charles VI (1380-1422)

John the Fearless (1404-1419)

Charles VII (1422-1461)   Catherine = Henry V, King of England

Philip the Good (1419-1467)

Louis XI (1461-1483)

Charles the Bold (1467-1477)

Charles VIII (1483-1498)

Mary = Maximilian of Austria
(House of Habsburg)

war, however, was a dynastic dispute. Whether Edward of England or Philip VI of Valois (1328–1350) was the true king of France depended upon whether the Salic Law under which the latter claimed the throne was valid. Philip was the nearest relative of the late Charles IV only in the male line, while Edward was his nephew by way of his mother. Thus the Hundred Years' War was one of the first of the great wars of succession that were to beset Europe for another five centuries.

For most of the war England, although far less rich and populous than France, held the advantage. English armies invaded France repeatedly until the banner of Saint George flew over a vast region of western France from the Pyrenees to Normandy. The commercial and industrial towns of Flanders became allies of England who supplied them with wool; their count, who supported France, had to fight hard to put down a rebellion of the Flemish towns. When the dukes of Burgundy became lords of Flanders and other provinces in the Low Countries during the latter part of the fourteenth century, however, they too became English allies as a consequence of their own endeavors first to dominate the French monarchy and then to throw off its overlordship. In France rebellion, often led by dissident members of the king's own family, became endemic. The vaunted royal power seemed doomed to vanish. France also suffered the ravages of a ravenous soldiery indifferent to the woes of either foe or friend.

Yet it was France who finally emerged triumphant from the ordeal. Thanks to the superiority of their longbowmen over French knights fighting in heavy armor, the English repeatedly destroyed French armies, notably at Crécy in 1346, Poitiers

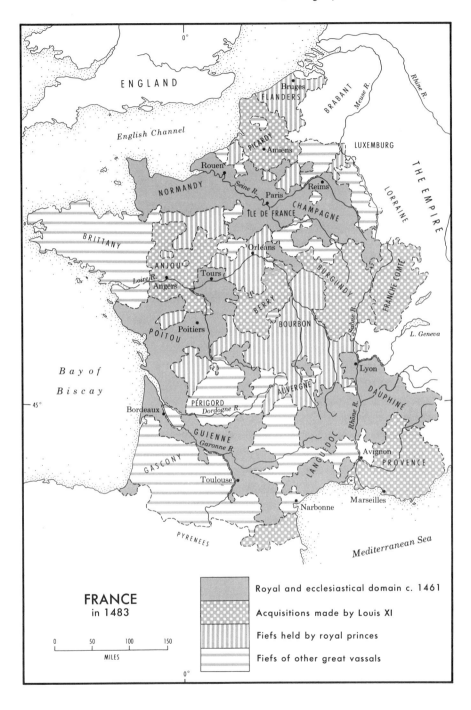

ENGLAND

English Channel

FLANDERS   Bruges

BRABANT   Meuse R.   Rhine R.

PICARDY   Amiens   LUXEMBURG

Rouen   Seine R.   Paris   Reims   LORRAINE   THE EMPIRE

NORMANDY   ÎLE DE FRANCE   CHAMPAGNE

BRITTANY   Orleans   BURGUNDY   FRANCHE COMTÉ

ANJOU   Tours   BERRY

Loire R.   Angers   BOURBON   Saône R.

POITOU   Poitiers   L. Geneva

Bay of   Lyon

Biscay   AUVERGNE   DAUPHINÉ

45°   PÉRIGORD   Rhône R.

Bordeaux   Dordogne R.

GUIENNE   LANGUEDOC   Avignon   PROVENCE

Garonne R.

GASCONY   Toulouse   Marseilles

Narbonne

PYRENEES   *Mediterranean Sea*

FRANCE
in 1483

0   50   100   150

MILES

0°

	Royal and ecclesiastical domain c. 1461
	Acquisitions made by Louis XI
	Fiefs held by royal princes
	Fiefs of other great vassals

in 1356, and Agincourt in 1415. But the English could not bring all French resistance to an end. The crisis of invasion and civil war, the pangs of misery in a land
that nature had made fair and fruitful, eventually persuaded a majority of Frenchmen to rally to the royal banner, even when the king was the weakling Charles VII
(1422–1461). The embodiment of the new spirit of patriotism and royalism that
took hold in France was Joan of Arc, a peasant girl who came out of Lorraine in
1429 to take up the king's cause. By her fervor, which merged religion and loyalism,
she spurred renewed vigor in the royal armies. Under Joan's inspiration the French
began to taste victory, and they continued to win even after she was captured by
the English in 1430 and burned as a witch. By 1453 the English armies, left bereft
of support by the inept and sometimes insane Lancastrian king, Henry VI (1422–
1461), quit all of France but Calais, a port on the Channel. The English effort
to become a first-rate continental power had failed, but the long war had sharpened
the sense of nationhood in England as it had done in France.

Nonetheless peace did not come at once to England. Civil war broke out
between the Lancastrian party supporting Henry VI and the Yorkist party led by
Richard, duke of York. Because the two parties used a red and white rose respectively as their symbols, the conflict came to be called—centuries later—the War of
the Roses. It raged fiercely from 1453 to 1485, with one interval of peace under

THE LANCASTRIAN AND YORKIST KINGS

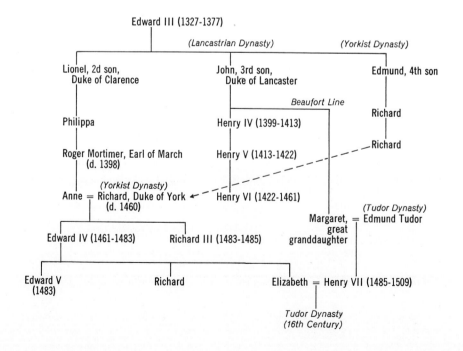

HENRY VII. The first Tudor king of England, as he appeared after twenty years of rule, is here depicted by an unknown Flemish painter.

Edward IV of York (1461–1483) after 1471. There were bloody battles, murders of kings and royal heirs, and an almost total mutual extermination of the great nobility. Finally most of the surviving Yorkist and Lancastrian leaders combined against Richard III who had become king in 1483 and was slain at Bosworth Field in 1485 by the army of Henry Tudor. The victor became king as Henry VII (1485–1509). Yet, amidst the turmoil, the ordinary work of government had gone on and the powers and duties of Parliament in making laws and granting taxes, in particular, had been strengthened and sharpened.

Meanwhile, in France the monarchy was consolidated and made more absolute by Louis XI (1461–1483). His principal task was to defeat the dukes of Burgundy, the hostile branch of his own dynasty that ruled a buffer state between France and Germany.

THE RISE AND FALL OF BURGUNDY

No wave of the future, whatever its name, assured success to the other states in western Europe which groped toward territorial and political consolidation during this age. The most dramatic story of swift rise followed by almost instantaneous failure belongs to the so-called Burgundian state. Its origins lay in the duchy and county of Burgundy, the former located in eastern France and the latter, more usually called Franche-Comté, immediately to the east within the Holy Roman Empire. Both Burgundies had been held since the fourteenth century by a younger branch of the Valois dynasty of France, but even combined under one ruler they did not provide the basis of a great state. Marriage of Duke Philip the Bold (1364–1404) of Burgundy to the heiress of the reigning count of Flanders in 1369 brought the rich Netherlands province into the dynastic possessions of the Burgundians. It furnished a more than adequate foundation for the state-building enterprise of the Burgundians. Duke Philip the Good (1419–1467) astutely concentrated his endeavors on extending his possessions in the Low Countries, although he continued to maintain the Burgundian position in France during the last phase of the Hundred Years' War. His ducal court at Brussels rivaled that of the wealthiest kings in Christendom in ostentation and luxury, symbolizing the heights to which his house now aspired. His son and successor Charles the Bold (1467–1477) made his central objective the creation of a middle kingdom extending from the North Sea to Switzerland, like that of the Carolingian Lothair (see above, page 115). Charles's instrument for attaining this great aim was a ponderous army of heavy cavalry. Although it represented the military art of medieval knighthood at its very best, it was a largely mercenary force paid out of the duke's revenues from his Netherlands

DUKE PHILIP THE GOOD OF BURGUNDY. In this miniature from the *Chronique de Hainaut* by Jean Wauquelin, Roger van der Weyden has shown the duke receiving his own copy of the manuscript.

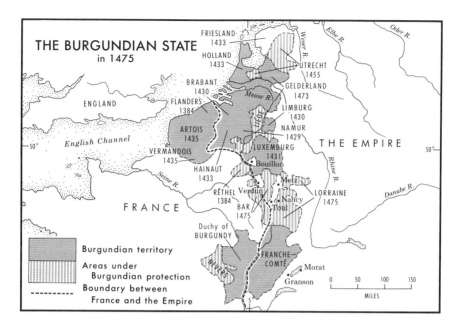

THE BURGUNDIAN STATE
in 1475

FRIESLAND 1433
HOLLAND 1433
UTRECHT 1455
BRABANT 1430
GELDERLAND 1473
ENGLAND
FLANDERS 1384
LIMBURG 1430
Meuse R.
NAMUR 1429
ARTOIS 1435
THE EMPIRE
English Channel
VERMANDOIS 1435
LUXEMBURG 1431
Bouillon
HAINAUT 1433
Seine R.
Metz
RÉTHEL 1384
Verdun
Nancy
LORRAINE 1475
Toul
Rhine R.
Danube R.
FRANCE
BAR 1475
Duchy of BURGUNDY
FRANCHE-COMTÉ
Morat
Granson

Elbe R.
Weser R.
Oder R.

Burgundian territory
Areas under Burgundian protection
Boundary between France and the Empire

0   50   100   150
MILES

provinces where trade and industry thrived. The victories achieved by this army in spreading Charles's influence over intervening lands in Lorraine between the Netherlands and Burgundy brought a new foe into the fray. The Swiss cantons, anxious to preserve the virtual political independence they had won from the Holy Roman Empire, now employed for their own defense the infantry companies they had created to serve other powers as mercenaries. The Swiss pikemen, arranged in dense squares, cut down the Burgundian cavalry at Nancy in 1477, and the duke himself was slain. His temerity and ambition had met their final retribution.

Charles's daughter Mary, who succeeded him, faced a mortal threat to the composite Burgundian state from Louis XI of France who seized the duchy of Burgundy and moved to extend his gains into the Low Countries. She warded off this peril by a marriage which brought the Netherlands an ally in the hour of greatest need. But, by taking as her husband Archduke Maximilian of Austria, son of the Habsburg emperor, she linked the Low Countries and the Habsburgs in a fateful dynastic union.

DECLINE OF THE GERMAN EMPIRE

The sudden rise of the Burgundian state only highlighted the decline of the Holy Roman Empire, now reduced to little more than Germany. The Golden Bull promulgated in 1356 confirmed the elective status of the imperial throne by limiting the electoral college to four secular rulers and three archbishops. The *electors,* as

THE LUXEMBURG AND HABSBURG DYNASTIES

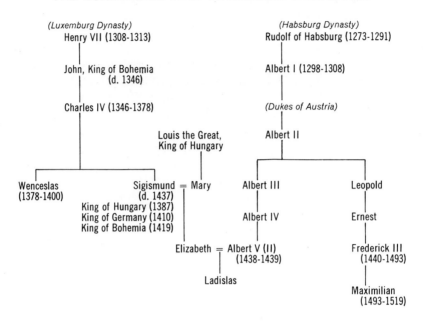

they were called, became the key figures in German politics; they enforced upon each emperor-elect a *capitulation* or treaty in which he guaranteed their privileges at the expense of his own. The electors now became a separate chamber in the Reichstag, alongside far more numerous lesser princes without electoral rights and the imperial towns. The principalities continued to expand their independence from imperial authority. The imperial crown passed from the Luxemburg House, which had held it since 1308, to the Habsburgs, who had twice held it in the late thirteenth and early fourteenth century. Albert II, who renewed the Habsburg line in 1438, reigned less than two years before he was slain by the Turks. His successor, Frederick III (1440–1493), was an incompetent whose only important political act was to arrange the marriage of his son Maximilian to Mary of Burgundy.

The Hanseatic League whose financial resources had made it the other great force in Germany also slipped into political and economic decline with the rise of Denmark. The Union of Kalmar, which put Denmark, Norway and Sweden under one king in 1397, made the associated Scandinavian powers a rival of the Hanse for control of the trade of the North, especially since Denmark dominated the straits between the Baltic and North seas. The prosperity of the Hanseatic towns suffered even greater and more permanent damage from the ascendancy of Atlantic trade routes that began during the fifteenth century and was accelerated by the overseas discoveries that came at the end of the century.

ITALY: MICROCOSM OF EUROPE

Where the emergence of the territorial state elsewhere in Europe led to the consolidation of the power of large political units, the Italian states of the fourteenth and fifteenth centuries were at best small and often tiny. Nonetheless they functioned as authentic sovereign powers. They enforced their authority over their subjects, threw off the vestiges of feudal overlordship, and engaged in complex diplomatic and military competition among themselves. Indeed, the modern system of professional diplomacy with the use of permanent ambassadors was first developed here. Italian politics was also marked by the special role of the *condottieri*, the military captains and entrepreneurs. As has been remarked, they frequently used their military power to take over political command in states which they were serving. The seizure of Milan by Francesco Sforza in 1450 was the outstanding venture of this kind. Italy became a microcosm of the developing Europe of sovereign territorial states; there we can for the first time see with clarity the pattern adopted everywhere in subsequent centuries.

There were five great powers in Italy: Milan, Florence, Venice, the Papal States, and Naples. Although small compared to states beyond the Alps, they effectively dominated Italian political life. The even smaller city-states and principalities so numerous in north-central Italy were not able to rival the power of the big five who prevented any one of their own number from becoming dominant. In Venice, a merchant republic set on islands in the marshlands of the northern Adriatic Sea, an aristocracy of tradesmen-nobility ruled with envied efficiency and lack of civil conflict. Their primary concern was to defend Venice's seagoing trade routes to the Levant which the rise of Ottoman power disturbed but did not destroy. Their secondary concern was to defend the city's trade routes in Europe, especially over the Alps, by bringing the adjacent land region of Italy under Venetian jurisdiction. The very success of this policy of acquiring a *terra firma* led, however, to Venice's deeper involvement in the controversies and perils of Italian politics from which its leaders sought to keep it apart.

The duchy of Milan, which ran from the foothills of the Alps down to below the Po River, was the leading power of northernmost Italy. Milan, thanks to its military prowess and diplomatic leadership, came very close to achieving total domination of the northern part of the peninsula in the early fifteenth century. It was thwarted, however, by the resistance of Florence, its most important neighbor just to the south. The prosperity and strength of this republican city-state rested on a combination of industry, trade, and banking. The internal politics of Florence was marked by a bitterness of civil strife unusual even at a time and in a region where domestic turbulence was commonplace. During the fifteenth century effective if unofficial leadership of Florence came into the hands of the Medici banking family.

ITALY
in the
Late Fifteenth Century

By 1492 when Lorenzo de' Medici, called *the Magnificent* for his patronage of arts and learning, died, Florence had replaced Milan as the leader in north Italy.

Central Italy was ruled by the Pope. The absence of the pontiffs during their residence at Avignon had resulted in a period of virtual anarchy in the Papal States. The return of Gregory XI in 1377, and even more the end of the Great Schism in 1418, brought the Papal States under more effective control by the Popes, who re-established their authority in Rome and sought to reduce the great vassals who had become independent in everything but name (see below, page 386).

The Kingdom of the Two Sicilies in southern Italy was split between the Angevin kings in Naples and the Aragonese kings in Sicily who also reigned in Aragon on the Iberian peninsula.

THE OTHER STATES OF EUROPE

On the Iberian peninsula political life remained highly disturbed by both civil wars and conflicts among the states into which the region west of the Pyrenees was still divided. The marriage of Ferdinand, heir of Aragon, to Isabella, heiress to Castile, resulted in a personal union of most of Spain on his accession in 1474 and

CHRISTOPHER COLUMBUS. The discoverer of America is shown at the height of his success in this posthumous portrait by the Venetian painter Sebastiano del Piombo.

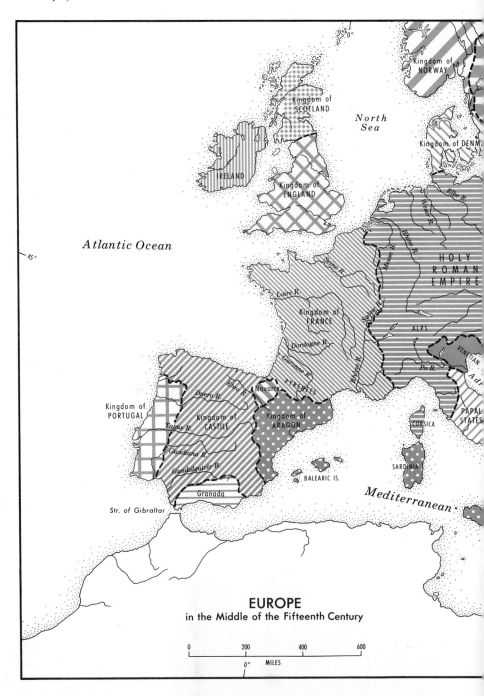

EUROPE
in the Middle of the Fifteenth Century

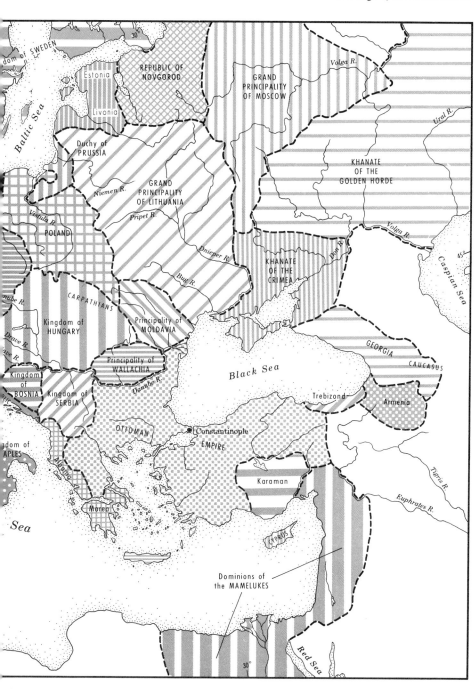

dom of SWEDEN

Baltic Sea

Estonia

Livonia

Duchy of
PRUSSIA

Niemen R.

POLAND

Vistula R.

GRAND
PRINCIPALITY
OF LITHUANIA

Pripet R.

CARPATHIANS

Kingdom of
HUNGARY

Danube R.

Principality of
MOLDAVIA

Drave R.

ve R.

Kingdom
of
BOSNIA

Kingdom of
SERBIA

Principality of
WALLACHIA

Danube R.

dom of
APLES

Albania

OTTOMAN

EMPIRE

Morea

Sea

REPUBLIC OF
NOVGOROD

GRAND
PRINCIPALITY
OF MOSCOW

Volga R.

KHANATE
OF THE
GOLDEN HORDE

Ural R.

Volga R.

Don R.

KHANATE
OF THE
CRIMEA

Bug R.

Dnieper R.

45°

Caspian Sea

Black Sea

GEORGIA

CAUCASUS

Trebizond

Armenia

Constantinople

Karaman

CYPRUS

Tigris R.

Euphrates R.

Dominions of
the MAMELUKES

30°

Red Sea

hers in 1479. Ruling jointly, although their kingdoms remained constitutionally separate, they brought to an end the interminable civil turbulence of the nobility. Earning the name of the *Catholic Kings,* they established their domination over the church within their realms, began its reform decades before the rise of Luther, and resumed the medieval *reconquista* by completing the conquest of the Moorish emirate of Granada in 1492.

The decision to sponsor Columbus's westward voyage of discovery across the Atlantic, which at the time was of far less interest than the triumph over Granada, in the end proved to be of immense consequence for Spain as well as for all Europe. Another immediate result of the Granadan victory was the decision, more Isabella's than Ferdinand's, to terminate once and for all the intimate participation of Spanish Jewry in the economic, governmental, and intellectual life of Spain which had been one of the notable characteristics of the Spanish medieval world. The command to Jews to convert to Catholicism or be expelled from the country deprived Spain of the extraordinarily valuable skills of those who departed, while most of those who accepted baptism did so without abandoning their innermost convictions. The fear and distrust of the *Marranos,* as the converted Jews were called, created an atmosphere of religious intolerance that was the very opposite of the spirit that had largely dominated the relations of Christian and Jew in Spain in earlier centuries. The investigation and punishment of the continued practice of Judaism among the Marranos became a principal task of the Spanish Inquisition.

In Central Europe the resurgence of Poland to a position of great power resulted from a personal union of the ruling house of Poland with the Jagiellon dukes of Lithuania who converted their duchy, the last stronghold of paganism in Europe, to Roman Catholicism. The Poles brought to a halt the advances of the Teutonic Knights in the Baltic region; they established their own sovereignty in West Prussia and their suzerainty over East Prussia.

In the Balkans the native Christian principalities were one by one defeated and taken over by the Ottoman Turks until the capture of long-encircled Constantinople in 1453 ended the thousand-year-old empire of Byzantium. The Turks were then able to consolidate their power in the southeastern corner of Europe, to begin their expansion across North Africa, and thereby to confront Christian Europe on both its southern and southeastern flanks.

In Russia the grand princes of Muscovy continued their gathering in of the Russian lands in the great forested plains of easternmost Europe. The overlordship of the Tartar khans of the Golden Horde, which had been the shield behind which the Muscovite power had grown after the downfall of the old Kievan state, was now thrown off. An independent Russia began to take form. The destruction of Byzantium gave the Orthodox church in Russia an independence to which it responded by proclaiming that Moscow had become the "third Rome," destined by

THE CAPTURE OF CONSTANTINOPLE. With naive explicitness this fifteenth-century manuscript illustration shows the Ottoman Turks scaling the walls of Constantinople in 1453.

God to prevail over the whole world in religion and politics. It was a claim virtually unheard in western Europe and would have seemed ludicrous there in view of the contrast between the crudeness and weakness of Muscovy and the civilization and power of western Europe.

6. *The Crisis of the Late Medieval Church*

DURING THE FOURTEENTH AND FIFTEENTH CENTURIES Latin Christendom slipped into spiritual and moral degeneration. The defeats and insults endured by Pope Boniface VIII at the hands of the French and English kings were a clear indication that the Papacy and church had lost prestige and power. When succeeding Popes took up residence at Avignon on the Rhône River and lived there under French royal tutelage during most of the fourteenth century, papal prestige fell even lower; in the eyes of western Europe the Papacy lost its independence and became a captive of the French kings. The famous Italian scholar and writer Petrarch aptly reflected European feeling against the Popes at Avignon when he compared their stay there to the captivity of the Jews in Babylon. From this time the residence of the Popes at Avignon between 1305 and 1378 has been called the *Babylonian Captivity*.

THE BEGINNING OF THE GREAT SCHISM

Finally in 1378 an aged Pope, Gregory XI, decided to resume residence at Rome but died soon after arriving. Under the pressure of Roman mobs the predominantly French college of cardinals elected an Italian as Pope Urban VI. But when the cardinals withdrew from Rome to safer quarters they elected a Frenchman as Pope Clement VII. There were now two Popes, and neither would relinquish his office. The result of this double election was the *Great Schism* that split the church until 1415. One line of Popes lived at Rome with its college of cardinals while another lived at Avignon with its cardinals. The contending pontiffs hurled excommunications at each other and their followers; western Europe was cleft in two in its religious obedience. France, Scotland, and the Spanish states supported the Avignonese Popes, while England, the Low Countries, and Germany adhered to the Popes at Rome. This division, however, reflected political interests rather than religious convictions. A host of compromises and solutions were proposed by learned and devout men to heal the schism. The University of Paris took the lead and suggested a general church council that would secure the abdication of both reigning Popes, Benedict XIII and Gregory XII, and elect in their stead a man suitable to all Europe. Both Popes stubbornly fought this and all the other proposals. Nevertheless, in 1406 they were persuaded to meet in northern Italy and to attempt a settlement. When after long journeys they came within sight of each other, the two pontiffs suddenly became stubborn and would not meet. Infuriated by this obstinacy, the cardinals supporting both Popes assembled in a council at Pisa to heal the schism. The council deposed both the nominal heads of the Roman church who had refused to appear and present their cases, and then elected another Pope, Alexander V. The new pontiff was unable to remove the other two and so the Council of Pisa resulted in three simultaneous Popes.

The Babylonian Captivity and the Great Schism shook the faith of Catholics in their church. The Popes and prelates showed themselves to be politicians as greedy for power as kings and feudal barons. Many Christians found it hard to respect a church which behaved so scandalously, and Christian morale sank almost to the depths reached prior to the revival of the church in the eleventh century. The church seemed blind to its own ideals and invited criticism; the way was open for the great religious upheaval in the sixteenth century.

THE RISE OF ANTICLERICALISM

Although there had always been men and movements critical of the church, the fourteenth century ushered in a series of protests and religious movements of great strength and bitterness. At the outset of the century the lawyer and adviser of Philip the Fair, Peter Du Bois (1255?–1321?), wrote a treatise entitled *Concerning the Recovery of the Holy Land.* Du Bois bitterly denounced the clergy; no good could be expected from them, he wrote, because they were too wealthy and corrupt. His brutal frankness and his open scorn for the church were signs of a changing mood.

Another critic of the church was William of Ockham (1285?–1349?), the foremost scholar of Europe in the fourteenth century. Denying that the Pope had any temporal authority or absolute power in matters of faith, he felt that the ultimate authority was the Scriptures as interpreted by men of learning and piety. Marsiglio of Padua (1270–1342?), a contemporary of Ockham, attacked the claims of the Papacy in a treatise on political theory called the *Defender of Peace* (*Defensor Pacis*). Blaming the Popes as the most important cause of Italian disunity, as Dante had done before him, Marsiglio turned his fiery invective against the political authority of the pontiffs. He favored government of the church by general councils consisting of delegates from the entire mass of Christians, in whom he held that sovereign authority resided, not in the Popes. The councils should elect Popes and order the affairs of the church. Clergymen without exception should be limited to purely spiritual functions and not be permitted to hold property. The conciliar ideas of Marsiglio foreshadowed the great church councils of the fifteenth century.

The concern for the spiritual decay of the church extended beyond learned scholars to men of little education or intellectual distinction. A flood of anticlerical literature came from their pens. At the outset of the fourteenth century, the French writer Jean de Meung (1250?–1305?) completed the *Romance of the Rose* begun by William of Lorris (see above, page 282). He composed his portion of the poem in the form of a savage satire against church and society. One of the principal characters—False-Seeming—who constantly attempts to lead men astray, prefers to live among churchmen who are portrayed as cowardly, avaricious, and without use to other men. Most live in luxury while pretending to be poor. The worst of the lot are the wandering friars who would rather beg for a living than earn it. When searching for a saint one must hunt among pious laymen.

The English clerk William Langland (1332?–1400?) in his poem *Piers Plowman,* written toward the end of the fourteenth century, criticized contemporary society for its sinful and materialistic preoccupations but singled out the clergy as the worst sinners and the greatest hypocrites. To discover a true Christian is most difficult; he is more likely by far to be found among husbandmen at the plow who come closest to following in Christ's footsteps than among great prelates.

Although quite content with his own lot and more satisfied with a society in which he had achieved substantial personal advancement, Geoffrey Chaucer (1344?–1400), England's greatest medieval poet who wrote a few years after Langland, also saw shortcomings in the church and poked his most telling barbs at the clergy in his *Canterbury Tales.* He painted a gregarious Benedictine monk who loved the things of this world but not St. Benedict's strict rule, and a clerk who cast loving glances at parishioners' wives. The friar, however, received his most scathing satire:

> In towns he knew the taverns, every one,
> And every good host and each barmaid too—
> Better than begging lepers, these he knew.[2]

A different kind of criticism of the church was expressed in the sermons of devout Dominicans and Franciscans who made passionate appeals to their fellow-churchmen to return to early apostolic poverty and to learn Christ's teachings again. They also spoke to laymen and helped to arouse them against the crass materialism of the church and to incite the widespread social and economic discontent of the fourteenth and fifteenth centuries.

MYSTICS AND HERETICS

More serious for the church than this criticism were numerous religious movements that called for specific reforms. Usually denounced by the Papacy, these groups were pushed into radical positions that were then branded as heretical. In almost all can be seen the germ of the religious individualism that was to mark many Protestant movements in the sixteenth century. In Italy and southern Germany during the fourteenth century arose the Spiritual Franciscans who denounced the regular Franciscans for abandoning the example of St. Francis, decried the riches and property acquired by the friars, and called for a strict interpretation of the Franciscan rule. Some of the most vehement agitators among them were excommunicated by the Pope and felt the rigors of the Inquisition.

Other groups emphasized austerity, poverty, and individual communion with God. In northern Europe, especially in Germany, two Dominican preachers, Master Eckhart (1260?–1328?) and Tauler (1300?–1361?), advocated a way of life essentially contemplative and mystical and organized an association of laymen known as the Friends of God. Another group of religious mystics called the Brothers of the Common Life was founded in the Low Countries by Gerard Groote (1340–1384) of Deventer. His adherents practiced what they called the *new piety* (*devotio moderna*), which emphasized individual use of the Bible for fathoming divine truth and required long hours of contemplation. The Brothers disregarded the ceremonies of the church which they saw as empty and formalistic in favor of simple forms of worship. The two mystical strands influenced the German Thomas à Kempis (1380?–1471) in writing his *Imitation of Christ,* the supreme literary achievement of the north European mystics. A simple Italian girl, St. Catherine of

---

[2] From *Canterbury Tales in Modern English* by J. U. Nicolson. © 1934 by Covici Friede, Inc. Used by permission of Crown Publishers, Inc.

Siena, had, however, even greater impact upon her contemporaries. Her visions and mystical experiences spurred her to work tirelessly for a return to Christ's teachings, but like the German and Dutch mystics she did not break with the church.

The two most powerful and influential religious movements of the fourteenth and fifteenth centuries, the Lollards in England and the Hussites in Bohemia, were, on the contrary, plainly heretical. The Lollards were followers of the teachings of John Wycliffe (1324?–1384), a noted professor of theology at Oxford University. Intimately familiar with the works of Ockham, Marsiglio, the Spiritual Franciscans, and the German mystics, he wrote a number of tracts that expressed views like theirs. Some of his other writing, however, was far more radical. Although damned by the Pope for his heretical and erroneous opinions, Wycliffe was not punished; he was protected by the royal court which looked with favor upon his condemnation of papal taxation, papal claims to secular authority, and papal abuses such as the sale of indulgences and the appointment of prelates in return for a share of their ecclesiastical revenue. Wycliffe's repudiation of the Popes as heads of the church, his denial of the doctrine of transubstantiation, and his arguments that men could attain salvation without the help of the clergy, were more truly revolutionary. He taught that men should go directly to the Bible for their inspiration and authority rather than to the church and translated the Bible into English to enable ordinary Englishmen to follow his precepts. Wycliffe won numerous disciples who followed a life of poverty and went among the common folk to preach to them in the vernacular. They had broad influence among the English people until the latter part of the century, when the Lancastrian kings moved against them and passed a statute providing for the burning of those found guilty of heresy.

In Bohemia religious agitation was closely bound up with the Czechs' resentment of German domination. In the early fifteenth century the University of Prague became the center of Bohemian nationalist agitation. John Hus (1369?–1415), a theologian and noted preacher, became the leader of a group of masters convinced that the evils of the church had to be eradicated. Through various Bohemians who had studied at Oxford, Hus became familiar with the teachings of Wycliffe and taught them in turn to his compatriots in sermons and tracts. Like Wycliffe he soon attracted a devoted band of followers who carried his ideas throughout Bohemia. By 1415 Hus and his followers (the Hussites) had made such gains that the question of the new movement was put upon the agenda for consideration by a general church council convened at Constance to heal the schism.

THE BOHEMIAN REVOLT

Although the Council of Constance was opposed by the three reigning Popes, it declared that it acted directly by God's authority and deposed them all. They had to abide by the sentence when the emperor, Sigismund (1411–1457), threatened to imprison any of the recalcitrant pontiffs. Before electing a new Pope, the council turned to the charges against Hus, who came to Constance under promise of safe-conduct from Sigismund. The council, much as it desired to heal the schism and initiate reform in the church, was firmly set against any deviation in fundamental doctrine. Despite Hus's courageous defense of his views, the council found them to be heretical and informed Sigismund that he was not bound to respect the safe-conduct he had given to Hus. The Bohemian was turned over to the secular authorities and burned at the stake.

The council's attempts at reform foundered in hopeless wrangles. Its hope of putting restrictions upon the Pope elected by it, Martin V (1417–1431), failed. A man of high character and sincere piety, Martin was also a skillful politician who worked tirelessly to unshackle himself from the limitations placed upon him and to reassert papal mastery over a united church. In 1418 he dissolved the council and assumed sole leadership of the church.

The Council of Constance had ended the schism, but its condemnation of Hus and the emperor's violation of his word fired a religious and national revolt in Bohemia in 1419. The Bohemians fought for national independence from the Habsburg emperor, who was also king of Bohemia, and for the theological principles advocated by the Hussites. Some Bohemians even went beyond Hus's own position which consisted essentially in abolition of the church's temporal power, freedom to preach the Gospel, and communion in both kinds (the communicant receiving wine as well as bread). These radicals, known as Taborites (from the Bohemian village named after the biblical mountain of Tabor), looked upon the Bible as the sole authority and rejected the doctrines of purgatory and indulgences, monasticism, adoration of saints, and all sacraments except baptism and the eucharist. In spite of their great theological differences, the moderates and the Taborites united in their efforts to win national freedom. For eleven years they defeated all German and papal armies sent against them.

By 1431 the Bohemian situation had become so desperate for orthodox Catholicism that the clergy of western Europe forced the Pope to convene another council at Basel to deal with the Hussites. Many feared that religious revolt would spread to other areas of Europe and that the church would be submerged. Despite papal opposition to negotiating with the Hussites, the council went over the head of the Pope and concluded a religious settlement with the moderate Hussites that met most of their demands but limited their application to Bohemia. The Taborites, however, continued fighting and were not put down until 1434. Finally in 1436 peace again reigned in Bohemia and Sigismund entered Prague.

TRIUMPH OF THE PAPACY

The Hussite wars ended, the Council of Basel seriously tackled reform of the church. It abolished oppressive papal taxes, limited papal powers of appointment, and promulgated decrees subordinating papal authority to that of the council. For a while it appeared that the council was going to establish church government on the pattern of parliamentary monarchy, with church councils developing into regularly convened assemblies in which would reside the ultimate sovereignty over the church and to which the Popes would be responsible for their actions. But the council pressed its reform proposals beyond what the more conservative delegates were ready to accept, and they went over to the Pope's cause. An acrimonious struggle broke out between the reforming majority of the council and the Papacy, and in 1439 the council made the tactical error of electing a second Pope. All Catholic Europe was unanimously opposed to another schism and hastily rallied around the Papacy. Although the council continued to sit until 1449, it lost all prestige and authority. In 1450 the Pope was once more unchallenged head of the church and celebrated his victory and church peace with a grand jubilee at Rome.

The jubilee of 1450 was an even greater farce than that of Boniface VIII in 1300. It celebrated papal headship over a demoralized and much corrupted organization. The conciliar reforms had come to nothing and the Popes, secure in their newly won power, submerged themselves in petty Italian politics until they became no better than the despots they fought in fruitless wars to expand the boundaries of the Papal States. Neither the Popes nor the great prelates seemed to understand that the religious discontent and protest of the fourteenth and fifteenth centuries were serious matters which augured ill for the church. Nor did they sense the danger to the international structure of the church in the growing national feeling of the European peoples. Instead of attempting to restore the church to health, they let the illness become more grave and criticism more severe. The Popes had forfeited the respect of western Christendom decades before the start of the Lutheran revolt in 1517, even among those who remained faithful to the church in dogma and doctrine.

7. Renaissance Arts and Letters

THE REVIVAL OF ANTIQUITY

The esthetic and intellectual life of Europe during the Renaissance is defined first and foremost by the triumph of a new outlook upon classical antiquity. On the one hand, antiquity was seen as different from the medieval world of values, tastes, and methods with which artists and writers remained fundamentally familiar; to this extent, a historical quality—difference due to time—was now recognized. On the other hand, the ideals and practices of classical antiquity were taken as a timeless standard of beauty and truth; to this extent, the Renaissance enterprise of renewing arts and letters by explicit imitation of antiquity was a denial of the reality of historical development, for it tended to reduce change to no more than the restoration of the good or the descent into the bad. Yet the Renaissance itself was an example of true historical change; it blended the *old*—actually the *recent old,* as it were, of medieval life—with the *new*—the revived arts and letters of antiquity. Out of these it created an esthetic and intellectual life which, combining elements both medieval and ancient, was neither one nor the other but rather something quite new and distinctive.

It has therefore long been the habit of historians and those taught by historians to hold that the period of the Renaissance was the time when the modern world emerged. They have asserted that the Renaissance was not just a transformation of European cultural life but that the change in the culture was itself a sign of a vaster transformation of all social and even personal experience. Except in the obvious and not very helpful sense, however, that the subject matter of Renaissance culture continued to be primarily the experience of its own day even when decked out in the garments of antiquity, the view of the wholeness and oneness of the Renaissance asserts a uniformity of historical change in all aspects of life which goes against the evidence. In politics, as we have seen, the emerging states system already visible in the fourteenth and fifteenth centuries, although it had some similarity to the complicated political world of the ancient Near East, had none whatever to the unified state structure of the Roman Empire. The early modern economic pattern of changing manorialism and incipient capitalism was distinct from the ancient system with its central reliance upon slavery.

Furthermore, the Renaissance was for almost a century and a half, until nearly the end of the fifteenth century, an overwhelmingly Italian movement. It was, at least in part, the Italian attempt to throw off the leadership which France had exercised during the Middle Ages in arts, thought, and literature. To hearken back to Rome—and the classicism of the Renaissance was always more Latin than Greek—was to affirm the superiority of the Italians, the heirs of the Romans, over the descendants of barbarians. Even when the Renaissance took hold beyond the Alps in the next century (see below, pages 435–443), it was Italy that the North learned from and imitated.

THE NEW STYLE

The persistence of the medieval forms and their partial transformation under the impact of the new concern for antiquity can be seen clearly in artistic life. Contemporaries singled out for emphasis the *new style,* those characteristics which distinguished it from the art of the age just past, notably Byzantine art in Italy and Gothic art in northern Europe. They did not take note of the continuation of Byzantine, Gothic, and other medieval practices in their own art, for familiarity had made these elements, as it were, invisible to them. The novelty of the new style lay in its combination of close and precise observation of nature with formal rules drawn mainly from classical antiquity—either by the repetition of the explicit rules or comments of ancient authors, or by strict, even mathematical, analysis of the works of ancient artists.

PAINTING

The more theoretical-minded Renaissance artists, like Leonardo da Vinci (1452–1519), put special emphasis on fixed mathematical harmonies among the various parts of a work of art, as distinct from a subjective sense of proportion. Mathematical analysis proved most successful in solving the painter's problem of transferring visual perspective from the three dimensions of real space to the two dimensions of his canvas or panel. The Renaissance artists for the first time treated perspective as a constantly receding reduction in apparent size according to distance from the observer's eye; it thus became possible for them to populate the entire space from the eye to infinity with figures whose relative size corresponded to ordinary experience, as medieval artists had not done. Once the mechanism of geometric perspective had been solved, artists employed it regularly, and some deliberately chose subjects that illustrated its workings, like scenes set within a room or hallway or, as in Mantegna's *Dead Christ,* a recumbent cadaver painted from a point just before the feet.

Of equal importance to this solution of the problem of perspective was that of lighting. Instead of the equal illumination common in medieval painting, painters began to show the light as coming from a definite source, so that shadows fell uniformly on the opposite side, with light and darkness corresponding to experience. This distinction of light and shadow also enabled painters to give the effect of three-dimensionality to objects.

Although medieval Flemish artists in particular had already shown great interest in the specific observation of nature, naturalism—the reproduction of concrete reality—became commonplace during the Renaissance. Artists increasingly made exact studies of objects, animate and inanimate, both in preparation for specific works and as part of their training.

The attitude of Renaissance painters toward the function of art continued and further developed a medieval practice which is in the sharpest contrast to the practice of modern and contemporary artists. Renaissance artists almost always composed their works within a symbolic framework derived from religion and mythology. Not only did a whole host of objects and positions stand for known equivalents, but the artists received specific instructions from their patrons on the content and organization of works of art. Paintings like Botticelli's *Primavera* which present-day viewers observe simply as pictures to be valued on the basis of composition, color, and expressiveness were originally judged equally for their iconographic message.

The gradual emergence of these Renaissance characteristics can be traced back to the mid-thirteenth century, to the work of the Italian painter Giotto (1276–1337). Primarily a painter of frescoes, murals painted on the plaster walls, for churches and abbeys, he broke with the prevailing Byzantine traditions by portraying his figures realistically, in natural poses and with three-dimensionality brought out by side lighting. However his subject matter remained strictly religious; and it is not without significance for understanding the Renaissance that the enormous majority of works of art down to the end of the fifteenth century, even works designed for private patrons, remained religious in content and usually intensely religious in feeling as well. Giotto's innovations did not have an immediate following, and Byzantine-inspired painting continued to predominate for more than a century. Architecture, too, saw the Romanesque style which had originated in Italy continue its prevalence, although the Gothic architecture which had developed in northern Europe came into use in Italy in this period, but without the characteristic Gothic feeling for upward thrust of spire and column.

In the late fourteenth and especially the fifteenth centuries, painters, architects, and sculptors, following the same inspiration that moved men of letters from Petrarch on, began to study and to follow the models of antiquity as far as they could grasp them. For painters this was more a matter of breaking with their immediate past than following antique models; but since classical letters were understood to stress order and naturalness, these were made the key elements in the new style of painting. Masaccio (1401–1429?) carried forward with great power the technique of three-dimensional modeling of his figures, and Paolo Ucello (1397–1475) solved difficult problems of perspective, particularly that of foreshortening, in battle paintings that also possess stupendous force of color and design. The Renaissance innovations were employed less melodramatically but with far more feeling of inwardness in such painters as Giovanni da Fiesole, known as Fra Angelico (1387–1455). The culmination of fifteenth century Italian Renaissance painting came with the work of the Florentine Sandro Botticelli (1444?–1510) who was closely associated with the literary and philosophical school of Florence. His work combines an elaborate mythological iconography worked out with his literary friends and the skills of composition, coloration, and expression developed by his artistic predecessors.

ARCHITECTURE AND SCULPTURE

Similar developments took place in architecture and sculpture. The Florentine Leone Battista Alberti (1404–1472) expounded the doctrines of architectural design on the pattern of antiquity and applied his own principles in a number of buildings. However, he and his successors were for the most part able to employ classical elements like columns, pilasters, and capitals only as decorative devices applied to buildings built essentially in the traditional way. Sculptors, having a large number of pieces recovered from antiquity to go by, were more successful in their neo-

DAVID. The awakening interest of Renaissance sculptors in the portrayal of the human body and their new mastery of classical forms are displayed in this bronze sculpture by Donatello of the biblical David.

classical enterprise. Although much of their work continued to be used in good medieval fashion for decorating churches and tombs, free-standing statues began to be made. The *David* of Donatello (1386?–1466) emphasized the concern for realistic portrayal of the nude or nearly nude human body that continued to be a permanent part of the sculptor's interest in the future. In the same artist's *Gatta-melata,* the figure of a *condottiere* on horseback, the interest in direct portrayal of a human being is emphasized.

NORTHERN EUROPEAN ACHIEVEMENTS

In the period of the Italian Renaissance art also flourished in northern Europe, primarily in the Netherlands, France, and western and southern Germany, but it worked primarily within its own traditions. During the later fifteenth century, however, the northern artists began to show the influence of Italy. We may take the Flemish painters, the greatest of all northerners in this period, for more detailed comparison with their Italian compeers and contemporaries. The work of the brothers Hubert (1366?–1426) and Jan (1370?–1440?) van Eyck and Roger van der Weyden (1399?–1464) is distinguished by an acute observation of specific people and things presented with punctilious precision; this detailed naturalism was aided by the use of the new medium of oil painting (as distinguished from the earlier use

ST. JEROME IN HIS STUDY. This fine engraving by Albrecht Dürer illustrates both in subject and in style the Christian humanism particularly characteristic of the northern Renaissance.

of egg tempera). As portraitists and creators of scenes of reality they were unsurpassed, but they handled the problem of perspective crudely. Not least, the content of their paintings remains overwhelmingly religious, a medievalism not yet replaced by or overlaid with humanist mythologizing. The south German Albrecht Dürer (1471–1528) who comes at the very end of this period carried on these traditions, but he combined them with an avid interest in the new Italian developments which he went to the peninsula to study personally. Yet the quality of his work—a realism of manner frequently combined, as in his woodcuts, with late medieval obsession with decay, death, and doom—is quite distinct from that of the Italians he admired.

GOOD LETTERS

The impact of the Renaissance impulse on literature and intellectual life in general was especially strong. The literary achievements of antiquity, like works of architecture and sculpture, had been preserved in considerable quantity. The quest for manuscripts of the works of ancient authors began in the mid-fourteenth century. Francesco Petrarch (1304–1374), more famed as a poet, hunted eagerly through the libraries of monasteries where the works had often remained untouched for the many centuries since they had been copied in Merovingian and Carolingian times. He was followed by many others who discovered almost all the works of the writers of Latin antiquity that are known to this day. The works of the Greeks began to be available not so much from the translations by way of Arabic that had been used in the Middle Ages as from Greek texts which had been kept by Byzantine scholars and were now brought to Italy. Greek books had to be translated into Latin, as few scholars and writers had yet acquired a mastery of Greek.

The central cultural phenomenon of the later fourteenth and the fifteenth centuries was the deliberate renewal of *bonae letterae—good letters*. This meant the vocabulary and style of Latin antiquity, primarily in the form it had taken in the intricate and highly rhetorical prose of Cicero. The style of Cicero and other Roman authors was set against the sturdy medieval Latin which, as we have seen, had served primarily as the technical language of the various branches of formal knowledge. Renaissance writers also deliberately cultivated classical literary forms, such as the epic, the eclogue or pastoral, the dialogue, and the formal letter, forms which had largely passed out of use in the medieval period.

The Renaissance in literature was confined almost exclusively to Italy until almost the very end of the fifteenth century. It too began with Petrarch who not only became the foremost practitioner of neoclassical Latin writing in his time but encouraged others to follow the same models. He and his successors put a new stress upon deliberate expression of subjective feeling, as well as upon the artist's quest for glory and fame, symbolized by the poet's laurel crown bestowed upon Petrarch in Rome. Although Petrarch idolized the ancients, he remained a devout Christian. He could compose fictitious letters in the style of the Romans and address some of the most important of these to Saint Augustine. Ultimately, however, Petrarch is also significant for the fact that his lasting achievement as a literary artist has remained his Italian poetry, based not on classical reminiscences but on late medieval practices, particularly of the Provençal poets of southern France where he had lived as a youth.

Petrarch's friend Giovanni Boccaccio (1313–1375) carried on in much the same way. His outstanding literary achievement was to give power, shape, and subtlety to Italian prose in such works as the *Decameron*. Like the contemporary *Canterbury Tales* of the Englishman Geoffrey Chaucer and other similar collections of ribald tales down into the sixteenth century, the *Decameron* was based on the popular stories and fabliaux of medieval Europe. Boccaccio too prided himself more on his propaganda for a purified Latin than on his works in Italian. He was also like Petrarch in that he went from a matter-of-fact Christianity during most of his life to a stern piety in his old age.

HUMANISM

The deliberate learning of the style and forms of classical antiquity and their application to the literature of the Renaissance writers' own day were soon embodied in educational and literary practice. Those who achieved this mastery of what Cicero had called *humanitas* or *humane letters* came to be called *humanists,* first in student slang and later in formal language. The humanists were a mixed bag of men. At their core were the men of talent and ambition who built careers as teachers, officials, and writers upon the basis of their command of neoclassical Latinity (and later Greek). But it also became customary, first in Italy and then elsewhere in Europe, for men of birth and wealth to acquire the same skills and knowledge. To be a humanist did not mean that one had adopted a new philosophy, distinct from and hostile to Christianity, as is sometimes inferred from the modern use of the term *humanism* for a non-religious philosophy or way of life. Yet by deliberately directing the attention of learned men and learners to the vast literary treasures of antiquity, which were treated as one great storehouse of both truth and beauty, the humanists opened up for thoughtful men an immense range of ideas which had been largely neglected in the Middle Ages. The great majority of humanists remained believing Christians with probably about the same range of piety among them as among other men; but they looked upon the writings of the ancients with the admiration, love, and respect that had been traditionally reserved for specifically Christian writings. Thus Renaissance humanism not only expanded the range of styles in which men wrote; it also multiplied the number of subjects on which they wrote; and, by taking man more and more as the measure of things and gradually displacing the central emphasis upon God of medieval thought, it began a momentous change in the character of thought which has continued through all modern times. These changes dominate the history of Renaissance literature and thought from their beginnings.

At the very height of the Middle Ages, we will recall, there had been savage and brilliant attacks upon the claims of the church, and of the Papacy in particular, to total supremacy. This pattern of criticism continued into the Renaissance with renewed strength and soon made use of the new materials provided it. But it was not hostile to Christianity as such, any more than it had been before, as the case of Lorenzo Valla (1406–1457) indicates. A brilliant rhetorician serving in the papal secretariat in Rome, he employed the new tools of philological and historical criticism to prove fraudulent the claim that the States of the Church had been bestowed upon the Papacy by the Roman emperor Constantine—and hence undercut the Pope's right to be their sovereign.

PHILOSOPHY AND SCIENCE

In the realm of philosophy and science the German Cardinal Nicholas (1401–1464) of Cusa (Kues) had probably the best mind of the fifteenth century. He combined mysticism and rationalism in a fashion that foreshadowed the Neoplatonism soon to flourish in Florence, and his emphasis upon the arithmetical and geometrical structure of the world anticipated the mathematical elements of the new science.

However, the entire movement of the intellectual Renaissance came to a head in Florence in the fifteenth century. There the spirit of civic humanism dominated in the earlier decades, giving a specific quality of this-worldliness to the thought of the times. The chancellor of Florence, Coluccio Salutati (1330–1406), in order to spur the resistance of the citizens of the republic in a time of peril from Milan, drew upon the ideals of the Roman Republic of antiquity to teach the virtues of active citizenship. Although Salutati in his old age, like Petrarch and Boccaccio before him, returned to the traditional piety and ascetic rejection of the world about him for the sake of the world after life, he fostered the concepts and moods of civic humanism, as the new force has been called, which took hold and became a new and increasingly important element in intellectual life.

Neoplatonism became influential in the later part of the century. Its leading exponents, Marsilio Ficino (1433–1499) and Giovanni Pico della Mirandola (1463–1494), were patronized by Lorenzo the Magnificent. Ficino and Pico picked up

LORENZO DE' MEDICI. This painted terra cotta bust of Lorenzo the Magnificent, most famous of the Medici rulers and patrons, is the work of Andrea del Verrocchio.

the thread of early Christian Neoplatonism which had reached its greatest height in Saint Augustine and applied it to the intellectual problems of the new age, emphasizing in particular the dignity of man. Deeply religious and practicing Catholics, these men nonetheless stressed the philosophical and moral qualities that underlay all religions and hence flirted with heresy in the eyes of the church, whose power was conceived to rest upon its exclusive truth.

Late medieval philosophy had both grown beyond and fallen behind the great thinkers of the twelfth and thirteenth centuries. On the one hand the technical achievements of many late scholastics in the study and development of logic were very significant contributions to philosophical thought. On the other hand they tended to divert attention from the theological and moral content of the Christian doctrines to which this logic was applied. Even to most thoughtful laymen, these *terminists*—so called because of their emphasis upon terms—were too abstract and their concerns too distant from the demands of everyday life. These later scholastics largely abandoned the effort to present all life and experience as coherent. Following the path of William of Ockham, they generally affirmed that the Christian faith was superior to and independent of reason but at the same time permitted reason and natural science to go their own way.

Scientific activity and thought, however, had not yet thrown off the connection with the work of magicians who sought to control the world of nature by means of secret formulae ("hocus-pocus"). On the one hand the understanding of nature was still very largely based on the descriptions given in the Bible and Aristotle and the explanations given by Aristotle and his successors. On the other hand the very process of debating the Aristotelian world-view led scientific thinkers of the fourteenth and fifteenth centuries not to abandon Aristotle but to attempt to redefine his science to correspond to their own observations and thinking. In this they were at once aided and hindered by the cult of antiquity in the Renaissance. The authority of the Greek philosopher was even further magnified, and both the Greek texts of his works and more accurate translations of them into Latin were made available. Furthermore, the Renaissance brought to light many other scientific and philosophic thinkers of antiquity whose work often did not coincide with that of Aristotle. By their attempts to reconcile the conflicts among the ancients, Renaissance thinkers concerned with understanding nature were increasingly driven to develop their own freer examination of and speculation upon the structure and operations of the world. In any case the Renaissance rejection of the "barbaric" (as it was called) medieval Latin of the scholastics brought in its wake a greater readiness to abandon the scholastics' conclusions as well. But this process of emancipation from scholasticism was linked with an affirmation of dependence upon antiquity. Many decades and even centuries were to pass before the moderns in science proclaimed their independence of both ancient and medieval forebears.

Further Reading

The starting point for all study of the age of the Renaissance is *J. Burckhardt, *The Civilization of the Renaissance in Italy* (orig. German ed., Basel, 1860), an attempt to capture the essential spirit of the time; it is available in translation in several modern editions. The results of modern scholarship are presented by numerous specialists in *The Cambridge Medieval History*, Volume VII, *Decline of the Papacy* (New York, 1932) and Volume VIII, *The Close of the Middle Ages* (New York, 1936); and in *The New Cambridge Modern History*, Volume I, *The Renaissance, 1493–1520* (Cambridge, 1957). *J. Huizinga, *The Waning of the Middle Ages* (New York, 1924) is a brilliant piece of reevaluation and probably the only single historical work on the Renaissance since Burckhardt's masterpiece that can be set alongside it in quality and importance. Very useful surveys are *E. P. Cheyney, *The Dawn of a New Era, 1250–1453* (New York, 1936); *M. P. Gilmore, *The World of Humanism, 1453 to 1517* (New York, 1952); and D. Hay, *Europe in the Fourteenth and Fifteenth Centuries* (London, 1966).

W. K. Ferguson, *The Renaissance in Historical Thought* (Boston, 1948) traces the development of the debate over the Renaissance. *E. Panofsky, *Renaissance and Renascences in Western Art* (New York, 1960), examines the concept of the Renaissance from the vantage point of art history. The current stage of the controversy over its character and significance may be examined in *T. Helton, ed., *The Renaissance: A Reconsideration of the Theories and Interpretations of the Age* (Madison, 1961); and *W. K. Ferguson, *et al.*, *The Renaissance: Six Essays* (New York, 1953). Suggestive individual interpretations are G. C. Sellery, *The Renaissance, Its Nature and Origins* (Madison, 1950); and *D. Hay, *The Italian Renaissance in Its Historical Background* (Cambridge, 1961).

J. W. Thompson, *Economic and Social History of Europe in the Later Middle Ages, 1300–1530* (New York, 1965) is a huge and very informative textbook. Volumes I, II, and III of *The Cambridge Economic History of Europe*, 2nd ed. (Cambridge, 1965) treat the Renaissance economy within the framework of medieval life. For agriculture, the best account of the rural economy is B. H. Slicher van Bath, *Agrarian History of Western Europe* (London, 1963). R. de Roover, *Rise and Decline of the Medici Bank, 1397–1494* (Cambridge, Mass., 1963) studies a great Renaissance business with the skills of an accountant and the understanding of a historian. The great plague of the fourteenth century is studied in *P. Zeigler, *The Black Death* (New York, 1969). *A. von Martin, *Sociology of the Renaissance* (New York, 1945) is more about the spirit of the Renaissance than a systematic study of social groups; an excellent example of the latter is G. Brucker, *Florentine Politics and Society, 1343–1378* (Princeton, 1962). Significant individuals are depicted in *E. Garin, *Portraits from the Quattrocento* (New York, 1972). Outstanding as an institutional history, with deep insight into political processes and ideas, is *G. Mattingly, *Renaissance Diplomacy* (Boston, 1955).

*E. Perroy, *The Hundred Years War* (New York, 1951) is a brilliant overview of the great conflict; it may be supplemented by *E. F. Jacob, *Henry V and the Invasion of France* (London, 1947) for England; *J. Michelet, *Joan of Arc* (Ann Arbor, 1957) is part of a classic history of France. Useful for England are V. H. H. Green, *The Later Plantagenets* (London, 1955); and *A. R. Myers, *England in the Late Middle Ages* (Baltimore, 1952). The latter period in England is covered by *P. M. Kendall, *The Yorkist Age: Daily Life during the War of the Roses* (New York, 1962); and in France by P. Champion, *Louis XI* (New York, 1929). The ruling class of the Burgundian state and its culture are studied in O. Cartellieri, *The Court of Burgundy* (New York, 1929); its politics are well portrayed in R. Vaughan, *Philip the Bold* (Cambridge, 1962) and *John the Fearless* (New York, 1966).

There are several informative studies of the Italian Renaissance city-states: for Florence see *C. M. Ady, *Lorenzo de' Medici and Renaissance Italy* (London, 1955); *F. Schevill, *The Medici* (New York, 1949); and D. Weinstein, *Savonarola and Florence: Prophecy and Patriotism in the Renaissance* (Princeton, 1970); and for Venice F. C. Lane, *Venetian Ships and Shipping of the Renaissance* (Baltimore, 1939), and *D. S. Chambers, *The Imperial Age of Venice, 1380–1580* (New York, 1970). J. K. Mariéjol, *The Spain of Ferdinand and Isabella* (orig. publ. 1904), ed. by B. Keen (New Brunswick, N.J., 1961) remains of value.

The crisis of the late medieval church is illuminated by W. Ullmann, *The Origins of the Great Schism* (Hamden, Conn., 1948); J. M. Clark, *The Great German Mystics: Eckhart, Tauler and Suso* (Oxford, 1949); A. Hyma, *The Christian Renaissance,* 2nd ed. (Hamden, Conn., 1965); and K. B. McFarlane, *John Wycliffe and the Beginnings of English Nonconformity* (London, 1952). F. G. Heymann, *George of Bohemia, King of Heretics* (Princeton, 1965) and *John Žižka and the Hussite Revolution* (Princeton, 1955) are valuable on the Bohemian revolt.

Petrarch's work as initiator of Renaissance humanism is studied in J. H. Whitfield, *Petrarch and the Renascence* (Oxford, 1943). *W. Sypher, *Four Stages of Renaissance Style: Transformations in Art and Literature, 1400–1700* (Garden City, 1955) carries system to an extreme but is highly suggestive. G. Toffanin, *History of Humanism* (New York, 1954) presents a Catholic version of Burckhardt's thesis. *H. Baron's learned and original *The Crisis of the Early Italian Renaissance,* 2 vols. (Princeton, 1955), rev. 1-vol. ed. (Princeton, 1966), links the Renaissance to contemporary politics; while *P. Kristeller, *Renaissance Thought: The Classic, Scholastic, and Humanist Strains* (New York, 1961) subjects the Burckhardtian vision of the Renaissance to fundamental criticism. The introduction of Greek into Italian humanism is illuminated in D. J. Geanakoplos, *Greek Scholars in Venice* (Cambridge, Mass., 1962). The role of science is examined in *E. Garin, *Science and Civil Life in the Italian Renaissance* (Garden City, N.Y., 1969).

Fundamental works on Renaissance art include *H. Wölfflin, *The Art of the Italian Renaissance* (New York, 1903), which stresses formal qualities of painting; B. Berenson, *The Italian Painters of the Renaissance,* rev. ed. (London, 1957), the work of a master connoisseur; and *E. Panofsky, *Studies in Iconology: Humanistic Themes in the Art of the Renaissance* (New York, 1939). Contemporaneous painting in the Low Countries is analyzed by E. Panofsky in *Early Netherlandish Painting: Its Origin and Character* (Cambridge, Mass., 1954). For Renaissance architecture see R. Wittkower, *Architectural Principles in the Age of Humanism,* 2nd ed. (London, 1952); and *G. Scott, *The Architecture of Humanism,* 2nd ed. (Garden City, 1954). Useful on literature are J. B. Fletcher, *Literature of the Italian Renaissance* (New York, 1934); E. F. Chaney, *François Villon in His Environment* (Oxford, 1946); and E. K. Chambers, *English Literature at the Close of the Middle Ages* (Oxford, 1945).

Index